Microsoft®
Training &
Certification

2154B: Implementing and Administering Microsoft® Windows® 2000 Directory Services

D1403184

Microsoft®

Course Number: 2154B
Part Number: X09-90435
Released: 03/2002

END-USER LICENSE AGREEMENT FOR MICROSOFT OFFICIAL CURRICULUM COURSEWARE –STUDENT EDITION

PLEASE READ THIS END-USER LICENSE AGREEMENT ("EULA") CAREFULLY. BY USING THE MATERIALS AND/OR USING OR INSTALLING THE SOFTWARE THAT ACCOMPANIES THIS EULA (COLLECTIVELY, THE "LICENSED CONTENT"), YOU AGREE TO THE TERMS OF THIS EULA. IF YOU DO NOT AGREE, DO NOT USE THE LICENSED CONTENT.

1.   **GENERAL.** This EULA is a legal agreement between you (either an individual or a single entity) and Microsoft Corporation ("Microsoft"). This EULA governs the Licensed Content, which includes computer software (including online and electronic documentation), training materials, and any other associated media and printed materials. This EULA applies to updates, supplements, add-on components, and Internet-based services components of the Licensed Content that Microsoft may provide or make available to you unless Microsoft provides other terms with the update, supplement, add-on component, or Internet-based services component. Microsoft reserves the right to discontinue any Internet-based services provided to you or made available to you through the use of the Licensed Content. This EULA also governs any product support services relating to the Licensed Content except as may be included in another agreement between you and Microsoft. An amendment or addendum to this EULA may accompany the Licensed Content.

2.   **GENERAL GRANT OF LICENSE.** Microsoft grants you the following rights, conditioned on your compliance with all the terms and conditions of this EULA. Microsoft grants you a limited, non-exclusive, royalty-free license to install and use the Licensed Content solely in conjunction with your participation as a student in an Authorized Training Session (as defined below). You may install and use one copy of the software on a single computer, device, workstation, terminal, or other digital electronic or analog device ("Device"). You may make a second copy of the software and install it on a portable Device for the exclusive use of the person who is the primary user of the first copy of the software. A license for the software may not be shared for use by multiple end users. An "Authorized Training Session" means a training session conducted at a Microsoft Certified Technical Education Center, an IT Academy, via a Microsoft Certified Partner, or such other entity as Microsoft may designate from time to time in writing, by a Microsoft Certified Trainer (for more information on these entities, please visit www.microsoft.com). WITHOUT LIMITING THE FOREGOING, COPYING OR REPRODUCTION OF THE LICENSED CONTENT TO ANY SERVER OR LOCATION FOR FURTHER REPRODUCTION OR REDISTRIBUTION IS EXPRESSLY PROHIBITED.

3.   **DESCRIPTION OF OTHER RIGHTS AND LICENSE LIMITATIONS**

    3.1   *Use of Documentation and Printed Training Materials.*

        3.1.1   The documents and related graphics included in the Licensed Content may include technical inaccuracies or typographical errors. Changes are periodically made to the content. Microsoft may make improvements and/or changes in any of the components of the Licensed Content at any time without notice. The names of companies, products, people, characters and/or data mentioned in the Licensed Content may be fictitious and are in no way intended to represent any real individual, company, product or event, unless otherwise noted.

        3.1.2   Microsoft grants you the right to reproduce portions of documents (such as student workbooks, white papers, press releases, datasheets and FAQs) (the "Documents") provided with the Licensed Content. You may not print any book (either electronic or print version) in its entirety. If you choose to reproduce Documents, you agree that: (a) use of such printed Documents will be solely in conjunction with your personal training use; (b) the Documents will not republished or posted on any network computer or broadcast in any media; (c) any reproduction will include either the Document's original copyright notice or a copyright notice to Microsoft's benefit substantially in the format provided below; and (d) to comply with all terms and conditions of this EULA. In addition, no modifications may made to any Document.

        Form of Notice:

        © 2000. Reprinted with permission by Microsoft Corporation. All rights reserved.

        Microsoft and Windows are either registered trademarks or trademarks of Microsoft Corporation in the US and/or other countries. Other product and company names mentioned herein may be the trademarks of their respective owners.

    3.2   *Use of Media Elements.* The Licensed Content may include certain photographs, clip art, animations, sounds, music, and video clips (together "Media Elements"). You may not modify these Media Elements.

    3.3   *Use of Sample Code.* In the event that the Licensed Content includes sample code in source or object format ("Sample Code"), Microsoft grants you a limited, non-exclusive, royalty-free license to use, copy and modify the Sample Code; if you elect to exercise the foregoing rights, you agree to comply with all other terms and conditions of this EULA, including without limitation Sections 3.4, 3.5, and 6.

    3.4   *Permitted Modifications.* In the event that you exercise any rights provided under this EULA to create modifications of the Licensed Content, you agree that any such modifications: (a) will not be used for providing training where a fee is charged in public or private classes; (b) indemnify, hold harmless, and defend Microsoft from and against any claims or lawsuits, including attorneys' fees, which arise from or result from your use of any modified version of the Licensed Content; and (c) not to transfer or assign any rights to any modified version of the Licensed Content to any third party without the express written permission of Microsoft.

3.5   *Reproduction/Redistribution Licensed Content.* Except as expressly provided in this EULA, you may not reproduce or distribute the Licensed Content or any portion thereof (including any permitted modifications) to any third parties without the express written permission of Microsoft.

4.   **RESERVATION OF RIGHTS AND OWNERSHIP.** Microsoft reserves all rights not expressly granted to you in this EULA. The Licensed Content is protected by copyright and other intellectual property laws and treaties. Microsoft or its suppliers own the title, copyright, and other intellectual property rights in the Licensed Content. You may not remove or obscure any copyright, trademark or patent notices that appear on the Licensed Content, or any components thereof, as delivered to you. **The Licensed Content is licensed, not sold.**

5.   **LIMITATIONS ON REVERSE ENGINEERING, DECOMPILATION, AND DISASSEMBLY.** You may not reverse engineer, decompile, or disassemble the Software or Media Elements, except and only to the extent that such activity is expressly permitted by applicable law notwithstanding this limitation.

6.   **LIMITATIONS ON SALE, RENTAL, ETC. AND CERTAIN ASSIGNMENTS.** You may not provide commercial hosting services with, sell, rent, lease, lend, sublicense, or assign copies of the Licensed Content, or any portion thereof (including any permitted modifications thereof) on a stand-alone basis or as part of any collection, product or service.

7.   **CONSENT TO USE OF DATA.** You agree that Microsoft and its affiliates may collect and use technical information gathered as part of the product support services provided to you, if any, related to the Licensed Content. Microsoft may use this information solely to improve our products or to provide customized services or technologies to you and will not disclose this information in a form that personally identifies you.

8.   **LINKS TO THIRD PARTY SITES.** You may link to third party sites through the use of the Licensed Content. The third party sites are not under the control of Microsoft, and Microsoft is not responsible for the contents of any third party sites, any links contained in third party sites, or any changes or updates to third party sites. Microsoft is not responsible for webcasting or any other form of transmission received from any third party sites. Microsoft is providing these links to third party sites to you only as a convenience, and the inclusion of any link does not imply an endorsement by Microsoft of the third party site.

9.   **ADDITIONAL LICENSED CONTENT/SERVICES.** This EULA applies to updates, supplements, add-on components, or Internet-based services components, of the Licensed Content that Microsoft may provide to you or make available to you after the date you obtain your initial copy of the Licensed Content, unless we provide other terms along with the update, supplement, add-on component, or Internet-based services component. Microsoft reserves the right to discontinue any Internet-based services provided to you or made available to you through the use of the Licensed Content.

10.   **U.S. GOVERNMENT LICENSE RIGHTS**. All software provided to the U.S. Government pursuant to solicitations issued on or after December 1, 1995 is provided with the commercial license rights and restrictions described elsewhere herein. All software provided to the U.S. Government pursuant to solicitations issued prior to December 1, 1995 is provided with "Restricted Rights" as provided for in FAR, 48 CFR 52.227-14 (JUNE 1987) or DFAR, 48 CFR 252.227-7013 (OCT 1988), as applicable.

11.   **EXPORT RESTRICTIONS**. You acknowledge that the Licensed Content is subject to U.S. export jurisdiction. You agree to comply with all applicable international and national laws that apply to the Licensed Content, including the U.S. Export Administration Regulations, as well as end-user, end-use, and destination restrictions issued by U.S. and other governments. For additional information see <http://www.microsoft.com/exporting/>.

12.   **TRANSFER.** The initial user of the Licensed Content may make a one-time permanent transfer of this EULA and Licensed Content to another end user, provided the initial user retains no copies of the Licensed Content. The transfer may not be an indirect transfer, such as a consignment. Prior to the transfer, the end user receiving the Licensed Content must agree to all the EULA terms.

13.   **"NOT FOR RESALE" LICENSED CONTENT.** Licensed Content identified as "Not For Resale" or "NFR," may not be sold or otherwise transferred for value, or used for any purpose other than demonstration, test or evaluation.

14.   **TERMINATION.** Without prejudice to any other rights, Microsoft may terminate this EULA if you fail to comply with the terms and conditions of this EULA. In such event, you must destroy all copies of the Licensed Content and all of its component parts.

15.   **DISCLAIMER OF WARRANTIES. TO THE MAXIMUM EXTENT PERMITTED BY APPLICABLE LAW, MICROSOFT AND ITS SUPPLIERS PROVIDE THE LICENSED CONTENT AND SUPPORT SERVICES (IF ANY) *AS IS AND WITH ALL FAULTS,* AND MICROSOFT AND ITS SUPPLIERS HEREBY DISCLAIM ALL OTHER WARRANTIES AND CONDITIONS, WHETHER EXPRESS, IMPLIED OR STATUTORY, INCLUDING, BUT NOT LIMITED TO, ANY (IF ANY) IMPLIED WARRANTIES, DUTIES OR CONDITIONS OF MERCHANTABILITY, OF FITNESS FOR A PARTICULAR PURPOSE, OF RELIABILITY OR AVAILABILITY, OF ACCURACY OR COMPLETENESS OF RESPONSES, OF RESULTS, OF WORKMANLIKE EFFORT, OF LACK OF VIRUSES, AND OF LACK OF NEGLIGENCE, ALL WITH REGARD TO THE LICENSED CONTENT, AND THE PROVISION OF OR FAILURE TO PROVIDE SUPPORT OR OTHER SERVICES, INFORMATION, SOFTWARE, AND RELATED CONTENT THROUGH THE LICENSED CONTENT, OR OTHERWISE ARISING OUT OF THE USE OF THE LICENSED CONTENT. ALSO, THERE IS NO WARRANTY OR CONDITION OF TITLE, QUIET ENJOYMENT, QUIET POSSESSION, CORRESPONDENCE TO DESCRIPTION OR NON-INFRINGEMENT WITH REGARD TO THE LICENSED CONTENT. THE ENTIRE RISK AS TO THE QUALITY, OR ARISING OUT OF THE USE OR PERFORMANCE OF THE LICENSED CONTENT, AND ANY SUPPORT SERVICES, REMAINS WITH YOU.**

16.   **EXCLUSION OF INCIDENTAL, CONSEQUENTIAL AND CERTAIN OTHER DAMAGES. TO THE MAXIMUM EXTENT PERMITTED BY APPLICABLE LAW, IN NO EVENT SHALL MICROSOFT OR ITS SUPPLIERS BE LIABLE FOR ANY SPECIAL, INCIDENTAL, PUNITIVE, INDIRECT, OR CONSEQUENTIAL DAMAGES WHATSOEVER (INCLUDING, BUT NOT**

LIMITED TO, DAMAGES FOR LOSS OF PROFITS OR CONFIDENTIAL OR OTHER INFORMATION, FOR BUSINESS INTERRUPTION, FOR PERSONAL INJURY, FOR LOSS OF PRIVACY, FOR FAILURE TO MEET ANY DUTY INCLUDING OF GOOD FAITH OR OF REASONABLE CARE, FOR NEGLIGENCE, AND FOR ANY OTHER PECUNIARY OR OTHER LOSS WHATSOEVER) ARISING OUT OF OR IN ANY WAY RELATED TO THE USE OF OR INABILITY TO USE THE LICENSED CONTENT, THE PROVISION OF OR FAILURE TO PROVIDE SUPPORT OR OTHER SERVICES, INFORMATION, SOFTWARE, AND RELATED CONTENT THROUGH THE LICENSED CONTENT, OR OTHERWISE ARISING OUT OF THE USE OF THE LICENSED CONTENT, OR OTHERWISE UNDER OR IN CONNECTION WITH ANY PROVISION OF THIS EULA, EVEN IN THE EVENT OF THE FAULT, TORT (INCLUDING NEGLIGENCE), MISREPRESENTATION, STRICT LIABILITY, BREACH OF CONTRACT OR BREACH OF WARRANTY OF MICROSOFT OR ANY SUPPLIER, AND EVEN IF MICROSOFT OR ANY SUPPLIER HAS BEEN ADVISED OF THE POSSIBILITY OF SUCH DAMAGES. BECAUSE SOME STATES/JURISDICTIONS DO NOT ALLOW THE EXCLUSION OR LIMITATION OF LIABILITY FOR CONSEQUENTIAL OR INCIDENTAL DAMAGES, THE ABOVE LIMITATION MAY NOT APPLY TO YOU.

17. **LIMITATION OF LIABILITY AND REMEDIES.** NOTWITHSTANDING ANY DAMAGES THAT YOU MIGHT INCUR FOR ANY REASON WHATSOEVER (INCLUDING, WITHOUT LIMITATION, ALL DAMAGES REFERENCED HEREIN AND ALL DIRECT OR GENERAL DAMAGES IN CONTRACT OR ANYTHING ELSE), THE ENTIRE LIABILITY OF MICROSOFT AND ANY OF ITS SUPPLIERS UNDER ANY PROVISION OF THIS EULA AND YOUR EXCLUSIVE REMEDY HEREUNDER SHALL BE LIMITED TO THE GREATER OF THE ACTUAL DAMAGES YOU INCUR IN REASONABLE RELIANCE ON THE LICENSED CONTENT UP TO THE AMOUNT ACTUALLY PAID BY YOU FOR THE LICENSED CONTENT OR US$5.00. THE FOREGOING LIMITATIONS, EXCLUSIONS AND DISCLAIMERS SHALL APPLY TO THE MAXIMUM EXTENT PERMITTED BY APPLICABLE LAW, EVEN IF ANY REMEDY FAILS ITS ESSENTIAL PURPOSE.

18. **APPLICABLE LAW.** If you acquired this Licensed Content in the United States, this EULA is governed by the laws of the State of Washington. If you acquired this Licensed Content in Canada, unless expressly prohibited by local law, this EULA is governed by the laws in force in the Province of Ontario, Canada; and, in respect of any dispute which may arise hereunder, you consent to the jurisdiction of the federal and provincial courts sitting in Toronto, Ontario. If you acquired this Licensed Content in the European Union, Iceland, Norway, or Switzerland, then local law applies. If you acquired this Licensed Content in any other country, then local law may apply.

19. **ENTIRE AGREEMENT; SEVERABILITY.** This EULA (including any addendum or amendment to this EULA which is included with the Licensed Content) are the entire agreement between you and Microsoft relating to the Licensed Content and the support services (if any) and they supersede all prior or contemporaneous oral or written communications, proposals and representations with respect to the Licensed Content or any other subject matter covered by this EULA. To the extent the terms of any Microsoft policies or programs for support services conflict with the terms of this EULA, the terms of this EULA shall control. If any provision of this EULA is held to be void, invalid, unenforceable or illegal, the other provisions shall continue in full force and effect.

Should you have any questions concerning this EULA, or if you desire to contact Microsoft for any reason, please use the address information enclosed in this Licensed Content to contact the Microsoft subsidiary serving your country or visit Microsoft on the World Wide Web at http://www.microsoft.com.

Si vous avez acquis votre Contenu Sous Licence Microsoft au CANADA :

DÉNI DE GARANTIES. Dans la mesure maximale permise par les lois applicables, le Contenu Sous Licence et les services de soutien technique (le cas échéant) sont fournis *TELS QUELS ET AVEC TOUS LES DÉFAUTS* par Microsoft et ses fournisseurs, lesquels par les présentes dénient toutes autres garanties et conditions expresses, implicites ou en vertu de la loi, notamment, mais sans limitation, (le cas échéant) les garanties, devoirs ou conditions implicites de qualité marchande, d'adaptation à une fin usage particulière, de fiabilité ou de disponibilité, d'exactitude ou d'exhaustivité des réponses, des résultats, des efforts déployés selon les règles de l'art, d'absence de virus et d'absence de négligence, le tout à l'égard du Contenu Sous Licence et de la prestation des services de soutien technique ou de l'omission de la 'une telle prestation des services de soutien technique ou à l'égard de la fourniture ou de l'omission de la fourniture de tous autres services, renseignements, Contenus Sous Licence, et contenu qui s'y rapporte grâce au Contenu Sous Licence ou provenant autrement de l'utilisation du Contenu Sous Licence. PAR AILLEURS, IL N'Y A AUCUNE GARANTIE OU CONDITION QUANT AU TITRE DE PROPRIÉTÉ, À LA JOUISSANCE OU LA POSSESSION PAISIBLE, À LA CONCORDANCE À UNE DESCRIPTION NI QUANT À UNE ABSENCE DE CONTREFAÇON CONCERNANT LE CONTENU SOUS LICENCE.

EXCLUSION DES DOMMAGES ACCESSOIRES, INDIRECTS ET DE CERTAINS AUTRES DOMMAGES. DANS LA MESURE MAXIMALE PERMISE PAR LES LOIS APPLICABLES, EN AUCUN CAS MICROSOFT OU SES FOURNISSEURS NE SERONT RESPONSABLES DES DOMMAGES SPÉCIAUX, CONSÉCUTIFS, ACCESSOIRES OU INDIRECTS DE QUELQUE NATURE QUE CE SOIT (NOTAMMENT, LES DOMMAGES À L'ÉGARD DU MANQUE À GAGNER OU DE LA DIVULGATION DE RENSEIGNEMENTS CONFIDENTIELS OU AUTRES, DE LA PERTE D'EXPLOITATION, DE BLESSURES CORPORELLES, DE LA VIOLATION DE LA VIE PRIVÉE, DE L'OMISSION DE REMPLIR TOUT DEVOIR, Y COMPRIS D'AGIR DE BONNE FOI OU D'EXERCER UN SOIN RAISONNABLE, DE LA NÉGLIGENCE ET DE TOUTE AUTRE PERTE PÉCUNIAIRE OU AUTRE PERTE

DE QUELQUE NATURE QUE CE SOIT) SE RAPPORTANT DE QUELQUE MANIÈRE QUE CE SOIT À L'UTILISATION DU CONTENU SOUS LICENCE OU À L'INCAPACITÉ DE S'EN SERVIR, À LA PRESTATION OU À L'OMISSION DE LA 'UNE TELLE PRESTATION DE SERVICES DE SOUTIEN TECHNIQUE OU À LA FOURNITURE OU À L'OMISSION DE LA FOURNITURE DE TOUS AUTRES SERVICES, RENSEIGNEMENTS, CONTENUS SOUS LICENCE, ET CONTENU QUI S'Y RAPPORTE GRÂCE AU CONTENU SOUS LICENCE OU PROVENANT AUTREMENT DE L'UTILISATION DU CONTENU SOUS LICENCE OU AUTREMENT AUX TERMES DE TOUTE DISPOSITION DE LA U PRÉSENTE CONVENTION EULA OU RELATIVEMENT À UNE TELLE DISPOSITION, MÊME EN CAS DE FAUTE, DE DÉLIT CIVIL (Y COMPRIS LA NÉGLIGENCE), DE RESPONSABILITÉ STRICTE, DE VIOLATION DE CONTRAT OU DE VIOLATION DE GARANTIE DE MICROSOFT OU DE TOUT FOURNISSEUR ET MÊME SI MICROSOFT OU TOUT FOURNISSEUR A ÉTÉ AVISÉ DE LA POSSIBILITÉ DE TELS DOMMAGES.

LIMITATION DE RESPONSABILITÉ ET RECOURS. MALGRÉ LES DOMMAGES QUE VOUS PUISSIEZ SUBIR POUR QUELQUE MOTIF QUE CE SOIT (NOTAMMENT, MAIS SANS LIMITATION, TOUS LES DOMMAGES SUSMENTIONNÉS ET TOUS LES DOMMAGES DIRECTS OU GÉNÉRAUX OU AUTRES), LA SEULE RESPONSABILITÉ 'OBLIGATION INTÉGRALE DE MICROSOFT ET DE L'UN OU L'AUTRE DE SES FOURNISSEURS AUX TERMES DE TOUTE DISPOSITION DEU LA PRÉSENTE CONVENTION EULA ET VOTRE RECOURS EXCLUSIF À L'ÉGARD DE TOUT CE QUI PRÉCÈDE SE LIMITE AU PLUS ÉLEVÉ ENTRE LES MONTANTS SUIVANTS : LE MONTANT QUE VOUS AVEZ RÉELLEMENT PAYÉ POUR LE CONTENU SOUS LICENCE OU 5,00 $US. LES LIMITES, EXCLUSIONS ET DÉNIS QUI PRÉCÈDENT (Y COMPRIS LES CLAUSES CI-DESSUS), S'APPLIQUENT DANS LA MESURE MAXIMALE PERMISE PAR LES LOIS APPLICABLES, MÊME SI TOUT RECOURS N'ATTEINT PAS SON BUT ESSENTIEL.

À moins que cela ne soit prohibé par le droit local applicable, la présente Convention est régie par les lois de la province d'Ontario, Canada. Vous consentez Chacune des parties à la présente reconnaît irrévocablement à la compétence des tribunaux fédéraux et provinciaux siégeant à Toronto, dans de la province d'Ontario et consent à instituer tout litige qui pourrait découler de la présente auprès des tribunaux situés dans le district judiciaire de York, province d'Ontario.

Au cas où vous auriez des questions concernant cette licence ou que vous désiriez vous mettre en rapport avec Microsoft pour quelque raison que ce soit, veuillez utiliser l'information contenue dans le Contenu Sous Licence pour contacter la filiale de succursale Microsoft desservant votre pays, dont l'adresse est fournie dans ce produit, ou visitez écrivez à : Microsoft sur le World Wide Web à http://www.microsoft.com

Contents

Module 8: Using Group Policy to Manage User Environments

Module 9: Using Group Policy to Manage Software

Module 10: Creating and Managing Trees and Forests

About This Course

This section provides you with a brief description of the course, audience, suggested prerequisites, and course objectives.

Description

This course provides students with the knowledge and skills necessary to install, configure, and administer Active Directory® directory service, which is the directory service for Microsoft® Windows® 2000. The course also focuses on the tasks required to implement Group Policy to centrally manage large numbers of users and computers. This course will help prepare students for the Windows 2000 MCSE Exam 70-217: *Implementing and Administering a Microsoft Windows 2000 Directory Services Infrastructure*.

Audience

This course is intended for Information Technology (IT) professionals, with little or no experience supporting previous versions of Windows, who will support a medium to large Windows 2000 network, and who will be responsible for installing, configuring, and administering Active Directory.

This course is also intended for those who are on the Microsoft Certified Systems Engineer Windows 2000 track.

Student Prerequisites

This course requires that students meet the following prerequisites:

- Completion of Course 2151, *Microsoft Windows 2000 Network and Operating System Essentials*, or equivalent skills and knowledge.

- Completion of Course 2152, *Implementing Microsoft Windows 2000 Professional and Server*, or equivalent knowledge and skills.

  This includes installing Windows 2000, using Windows 2000 administration tools, configuring hard disks and partitions, creating users, creating and using security groups to manage access to resources, creating and administering printers, and setting up and administering permissions for files and folders, implementing local security policies by using Security Templates and Security Configuration and Analysis, and implementing an Audit policy.

- Completion of Course 2153, *Implementing a Microsoft Windows 2000 Network Infrastructure*, or equivalent knowledge and skills.

  This includes installing and configuring Transmission Control Protocol/Internet Protocol (TCP/IP), Domain Name System (DNS), and Certificate services.

- A thorough understanding of DNS, including hands-on experience configuring DNS, and setting up forward and reverse lookup zones.

Course Objectives

At the end of this course, the student will be able to:

- Describe the logical and physical components of Windows 2000 Active Directory.

- Configure the Domain Name System (DNS) Server service on a computer running Windows 2000 Server to support Active Directory.

- Create a Windows 2000 domain by installing and configuring Active Directory, and implement an organizational unit (OU) structure.

- Set up and administer domain user accounts and groups to enable users to gain access to resources in a Windows 2000 network.

- Publish network resources in Active Directory to allow users to locate the resources and to allow centralized management of those resources.

- Delegate administrative control of Active Directory objects to decentralize administrative tasks in a Windows 2000 network.

- Implement Group Policy to centrally manage users and computers in a Windows 2000 network.

- Configure and manage users' desktop environments by using Group Policy.

- Deploy and manage software by using Group Policy.

- Create and manage trees and forests in a Windows 2000 network, and administer forest-wide resources.

- Manage and troubleshoot Active Directory replication within a site and between sites.

- Manage operations masters.

- Manage and restore the Active Directory database.

- Implement an Active Directory infrastructure that is based on a directory services design provided by an enterprise architect.

Student Materials Compact Disc Contents

The Student Materials compact disc contains the following files and folders:

- *Default.htm*. This file opens the Student Materials Web page. It provides students with resources pertaining to this course, including additional reading, review and lab answers, lab files, multimedia presentations, and course-related Web sites.

- *Readme.txt*. This file contains a description of the compact disc contents and setup instructions in ASCII format (non-Microsoft Word document).

- *AddRead*. This folder contains additional reading pertaining to this course. If there are no additional reading files, this folder does not appear.

- *Answers*. This folder contains answers to the module review questions and hands-on labs.

- *Appendix*. This folder contains appendix files for this course. If there are no appendix files, this folder does not appear.

- *Courses*. This folder contains the self-paced courses that are included with this course.

- *Fonts*. This folder contains fonts that are required to view the PowerPoint presentation and Web-based materials.

- *Labfiles*. This folder contains files that are used in the hands-on labs. These files may be used to prepare the student computers for the hands-on labs.

- *Media*. This folder contains files that are used in multimedia presentations for this course. If this course does not include any multimedia presentations, this folder does not appear.

- *Webfiles*. This folder contains the files that are required to view the course Web page. To open the Web page, open Windows Explorer, and in the root directory of the compact disc, double-click **Default.htm**.

- *Wordview*. This folder contains the Word Viewer that is used to view any Word document (.doc) files that are included on the compact disc. If no Word documents are included, this folder does not appear.

Document Conventions

The following conventions are used in course materials to distinguish elements of the text.

Convention	Use
◆	Indicates an introductory page. This symbol appears next to a slide title when additional information on the topic is covered on the page or pages that follow it.
bold	Represents commands, command options, and portions of syntax that must be typed exactly as shown. It also indicates commands on menus and buttons, icons, dialog box titles and options, and icon and menu names.
italic	In syntax statements, indicates placeholders for variable information. Italic is also used for introducing new terms, for book titles, and for emphasis in the text.
Title Capitals	Indicate domain names, user names, computer names, directory names, folders, and file names, except when specifically referring to case-sensitive names. Unless otherwise indicated, you can use lowercase letters when you type a directory name or file name in a dialog box or at a command prompt.
ALL CAPITALS	Indicate the names of keys, key sequences, and key combinations—for example, ALT+SPACEBAR.
`monospace`	Represents code samples, examples of screen text, or entries that you type at a command prompt or in initialization files.
[ ]	In syntax statements, enclose optional items. For example, [*filename*] in command syntax indicates that you can choose to type a file name with the command. Type only the information within the brackets, not the brackets themselves.
{ }	In syntax statements, enclose required items. Type only the information within the braces, not the braces themselves.
|	In syntax statements, separates an either/or choice.
▶	Indicates a procedure with sequential steps.
…	In syntax statements, specifies that the preceding item may be repeated.
. . .	Represents an omitted portion of a code sample.

Microsoft®
Training &
Certification

Introduction

Contents

Introduction

- ■ **Name**
- ■ **Company Affiliation**
- ■ **Title/Function**
- ■ **Job Responsibility**
- ■ **Networking Experience**
- ■ **Windows 2000 Experience**
- ■ **Expectations for the Course**

Course Materials

- Name Card
- Student Workbook
- Student Materials Compact Disc
- Course Evaluation

The following materials are included with your kit:

- *Name card.* Write your name on both sides of the name card.

- *Student workbook.* The student workbook contains the material covered in class, in addition to the hands-on lab exercises.

- *Student Materials compact disc.* The Student Materials compact disc contains the Web page that provides students with links to resources pertaining to this course, including additional readings, review and lab answers, lab files, multimedia presentations, and course-related Web sites.

The Student Materials compact disc also includes the following self-paced courses:

- Course 1080A, *Essentials of Microsoft Visual Basic Scripting Edition 3.0 for Web Site Development*, provides students who have little or no formal programming background with the knowledge and skills necessary to use the Microsoft® Visual Basic® Scripting language.

- Course 1279B, *Implementing Microsoft Windows Media Services*, provides the knowledge and skills necessary to install, configure, and maintain Microsoft Windows Media™ Services.

- Course 1400A, *Deploying and Customizing Microsoft Internet Explorer 5 Using Microsoft Internet Explorer Administration Kit*, provides the knowledge and skills necessary to customize, deploy, and administer Microsoft Internet Explorer 5.0 by using the Internet Explorer Administration Kit.

- Course 2000B, *Microsoft Windows 2000: First Look*, introduces the structure and features of the Microsoft Windows® 2000 operating systems. This course provides prospective customers with the knowledge necessary to evaluate the advantages and benefits of incorporating Windows 2000 in their business environments.

Note To open the Student Materials Web page, insert the Student Materials compact disc into the CD-ROM drive, and then in the root directory of the compact disc, double-click **Default.htm**.

- *Course evaluation.* To provide feedback on the course, training facility, and instructor, you will have the opportunity to complete an online evaluation near the end of the course.

  To provide additional comments or inquire about the Microsoft Certified Professional program, send e-mail to mcphelp@microsoft.com.

Prerequisites

- Course 2151, *Microsoft Windows 2000 Network and Operating System Essentials*, or Equivalent Skills and Knowledge

- Course 2152, *Implementing Microsoft Windows 2000 Professional and Server*, or Equivalent Skills and Knowledge

- Course 2153, *Implementing a Microsoft Windows 2000 Network Infrastructure*, or Equivalent Skills and Knowledge

- A Thorough Understanding of DNS

This course requires that you meet the following prerequisites:

- Course 2151, *Microsoft Windows 2000 Network and Operating System Essentials*, or equivalent skills and knowledge.

- Course 2152, *Implementing Microsoft Windows 2000 Professional and Server*, or equivalent knowledge and skills.

  This includes installing Windows 2000, using administrative tools in Windows 2000, configuring hard disks and partitions, creating users, creating and using security groups to manage access to resources, creating and administering printers, and setting up and administering permissions for files and folders.

- Course 2153, *Implementing a Microsoft Windows 2000 Network Infrastructure*, or equivalent knowledge and skills.

  This includes installing and configuring Transmission Control Protocol/Internet Protocol (TCP/IP), Domain Name System (DNS), and Certificate services.

- A thorough understanding of DNS, including hands-on experience configuring DNS, and setting up forward and reverse lookup zones.

Course Outline

- **Module 1: Introduction to Active Directory in Windows 2000**

- **Module 2: Implementing DNS to Support Active Directory**

- **Module 3: Creating a Windows 2000 Domain**

- **Module 4: Setting Up and Administering Users and Groups**

Module 1, "Introduction to Active Directory in Windows 2000," introduces the concept of the Active Directory® directory service, which is the directory service in Windows 2000. The module describes the logical and physical structure of Active Directory, and then describes the centralized management features of Windows 2000. At the end of this module, you will be able to identify the logical and physical components of Active Directory and describe the methods of administering a Windows 2000 network.

Module 2, "Implementing DNS to Support Active Directory," explains how to configure DNS to support an Active Directory installation for a Windows 2000 network. The module describes how Active Directory uses DNS as its location service, and describes the differences between DNS and Active Directory name resolution. The module also describes how client computers running Windows 2000 use DNS to locate domain controllers. At the end of this module, you will be able to install and configure DNS to support Active Directory.

Module 3, "Creating a Windows 2000 Domain," explains how to install Active Directory on a computer running Windows 2000 Server. The module describes the Active Directory installation process, identifies the post installation tasks that you perform after Active Directory is installed, such as changing the domain mode, configuring Active Directory integrated DNS zones, and implementing an organizational unit structure. At the end of this module, you will be able to create Windows 2000 domains by installing Active Directory.

Module 4, "Setting Up and Administering Users and Groups," explains how to set up and administer domain user accounts so that users can gain access to resources in an Active Directory network. At the end of this module, you will be able to automatically create multiple user accounts by importing the user information into Active Directory, administer domain user accounts, and implement a strategy for using security groups to manage access to domain-based resources.

Course Outline *(continued)*

- **Module 5: Publishing Resources in Active Directory**
- **Module 6: Delegating Administrative Control**
- **Module 7: Implementing Group Policy**
- **Module 8: Using Group Policy to Manage User Environments**

Module 5, "Publishing Resources in Active Directory," explains how to publish and administer resources, such as shared folders and printers, in Active Directory. At the end of this module, you will be able to set up and administer published printers in Active Directory, set up locations for published printers, and set up and administer published shared folders in Active Directory.

Module 6, "Delegating Administrative Control," explains how to decentralize administrative tasks by delegating administrative control of Active Directory objects. The module describes the security infrastructure of Active Directory, and describes how to delegate administrative control by assigning permissions to Active Directory objects. The module also describes how to create and deploy customized administrative tools for delegated administrative tasks. At the end of this module, you will be able to delegate administrative control in Active Directory.

Module 7, "Implementing Group Policy," explains how to implement Group Policy to centrally manage users and computers in a Windows 2000 network. The module describes the structure of Group Policy, and how Group Policy is applied to and inherited by organizational units (OUs), users, and computers. The module also describes the tools used to monitor and troubleshoot Group Policy. At the end of this module, you will be able to implement Group Policy to manage users and computers.

Module 8, "Using Group Policy to Manage User Environments," explains how to configure and manage the user desktop environment by using Group Policy. The module describes how to use administrative templates in Group Policy to assign registry-based Group Policy to control and configure user and computer environments. The module also describes how to use Group Policy to assign scripts that control user environments, redirect user folders to a central network location, secure the user environment, and troubleshoot managing user environments. At the end of this module, you will be able to use Group Policy to configure and manage the user desktop environment.

Course Outline *(continued)*

- **Module 9: Using Group Policy to Manage Software**
- **Module 10: Creating and Managing Trees and Forests**
- **Module 11: Managing Active Directory Replication**
- **Module 12: Managing Operations Masters**

Module 9, "Using Group Policy to Manage Software," explains how to deploy and manage software by using Group Policy. The modules introduces the Windows Installer service and describes how to use it with Group Policy to centrally deploy and manage software on user desktops. At the end of this module, you will be able to deploy, manage, upgrade, and remove software by using Group Policy.

Module 10, "Creating and Managing Trees and Forests," explains how to create and manage trees and forests. The module describes how to create child domains by installing Active Directory, and describes how trust relationships impact the sharing of resources in trees and forests. The module also describes the functions that the global catalog provides during user logons and when users search Active Directory. The module also describes strategies for using universal groups to manage access to forest-wide resources. At the end of this module, you will be able to create and manage trees and forests.

Module 11, "Managing Active Directory Replication," explains how to manage Active Directory replication, both within a site and between sites. The module describes in detail the replication process, and how to configure Windows 2000 sites to optimize and manage Active Directory replication. At the end of this module, you will be able to configure Active Directory replication, use sites to optimize and manage replication, monitor replication traffic, and troubleshoot common problems with Active Directory replication.

Module 12, "Managing Operations Masters," explains how to manage the operations masters in Active Directory. At the end of this module, you will be able to describe the five operations master roles and how they function in an Active Directory network, and transfer and seize an operations master role.

Course Outline *(continued)*

- **Module 13: Maintaining the Active Directory Database**
- **Module 14: Implementing an Active Directory Infrastructure**

Module 13, "Maintaining the Active Directory Database," explains how to manage and restore the Active Directory database. The module describes how data in Active Directory is modified, and explains the difference between an authoritative and nonauthoritative restore. At the end of this module, you will be able to move the Active Directory database to a new location, back up system state data by using the Backup utility, and restore Active Directory by restoring the system state data on a domain controller.

Module 14, "Implementing an Active Directory Infrastructure," explains how to implement an Active Directory infrastructure based on a given business scenario. At the end of this module, you will be able to implement an Active Directory structure by using an Active Directory design that is based on the functional requirements of a fictitious organization. Students will work together as a team to implement all aspects of an Active Directory infrastructure.

Microsoft Official Curriculum

- **Microsoft Windows 2000**
- **Microsoft Office 2000**
- **Microsoft BackOffice Small Business Server**
- **Microsoft SQL Server**
- **Microsoft Exchange 2000**
- **Microsoft BackOffice Server Infrastructure and Solutions**
- **Microsoft FrontPage**
- **Microsoft Systems Management Server**
- **Knowledge Management Solutions**

Microsoft® Official Curriculum (MOC) is hands-on facilitated classroom and Web-based training. Microsoft develops skills-based training courses to educate computer professionals who develop, support, and implement solutions by using Microsoft products, solutions, and technologies. MOC courses are available for the following products and solutions:

- Microsoft Windows® operating systems
- Microsoft Office
- Microsoft BackOffice® Small Business Server
- Microsoft SQL Server™
- Microsoft Exchange
- Microsoft BackOffice Server Infrastructure and Solutions
- Microsoft FrontPage®
- Microsoft Systems Management Server
- Knowledge Management Solutions

MOC provides a curriculum path for each product and solution. For more information on the curriculum paths, see the Microsoft Official Curriculum Web page at http://www.microsoft.com/traincert.

The Microsoft Official Curriculum Web page provides information about MOC courses. In addition, you can find recommended curriculum paths for individuals who are entering the Information Technology (IT) industry, who are continuing their training on Microsoft products and solutions, or who currently support non-Microsoft products.

Microsoft Certified Professional Program

The Microsoft Certified Professional program is a leading certification program that validates your experience and skills to keep you competitive in today's changing business environment. The following table describes each certification in more detail.

Certification	Description
MCSA on Microsoft Windows 2000	The Microsoft Certified Systems Administrator (MCSA) certification is designed for professionals who implement, manage, and troubleshoot existing network and system environments based on Microsoft Windows 2000 platforms, including the Windows .NET Server family. Implementation responsibilities include installing and configuring parts of the systems. Management responsibilities include administering and supporting the systems.
MCSE on Microsoft Windows 2000	The Microsoft Certified Systems Engineer (MCSE) credential is the premier certification for professionals who analyze the business requirements and design and implement the infrastructure for business solutions based on the Microsoft Windows 2000 platform and Microsoft server software, including the Windows .NET Server family. Implementation responsibilities include installing, configuring, and troubleshooting network systems.
MCSD	The Microsoft Certified Solution Developer (MCSD) credential is the premier certification for professionals who design and develop leading-edge business solutions with Microsoft development tools, technologies, platforms, and the Microsoft Windows DNA architecture. The types of applications MCSDs can develop include desktop applications and multi-user, Web-based, N-tier, and transaction-based applications. The credential covers job tasks ranging from analyzing business requirements to maintaining solutions.
MCDBA on Microsoft SQL Server 2000	The Microsoft Certified Database Administrator (MCDBA) credential is the premier certification for professionals who implement and administer Microsoft SQL Server databases. The certification is appropriate for individuals who derive physical database designs, develop logical data models, create physical databases, create data services by using Transact-SQL, manage and maintain databases, configure and manage security, monitor and optimize databases, and install and configure SQL Server.

(*continued*)

Certification	Description
MCP	The Microsoft Certified Professional (MCP) credential is for individuals who have the skills to successfully implement a Microsoft product or technology as part of a business solution in an organization. Hands-on experience with the product is necessary to successfully achieve certification.
MCT	Microsoft Certified Trainers (MCTs) demonstrate the instructional and technical skills that qualify them to deliver Microsoft Official Curriculum through Microsoft Certified Technical Education Centers (Microsoft CTECs).

Certification Requirements

The certification requirements differ for each certification category and are specific to the products and job functions addressed by the certification. To become a Microsoft Certified Professional, you must pass rigorous certification exams that provide a valid and reliable measure of technical proficiency and expertise.

For More Information See the Microsoft Training and Certification Web site at http://www.microsoft.com/traincert/.

You can also send e-mail to mcphelp@microsoft.com if you have specific certification questions.

Acquiring the Skills Tested by an MCP Exam

Microsoft Official Curriculum (MOC) and MSDN® Training Curriculum can help you develop the skills that you need to do your job. They also complement the experience that you gain while working with Microsoft products and technologies. However, no one-to-one correlation exists between MOC and MSDN Training courses and MCP exams. Microsoft does not expect or intend for the courses to be the sole preparation method for passing MCP exams. Practical product knowledge and experience is also necessary to pass the MCP exams.

To help prepare for the MCP exams, use the preparation guides that are available for each exam. Each Exam Preparation Guide contains exam-specific information, such as a list of the topics on which you will be tested. These guides are available on the Microsoft Training and Certification Web site at http://www.microsoft.com/traincert/.

Facilities

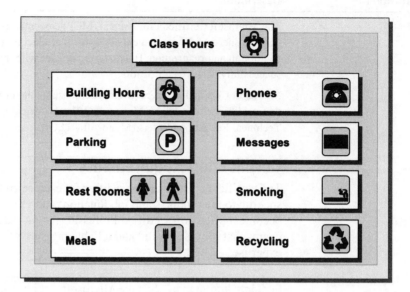

Microsoft®
Training &
Certification

Module 1: Introduction to Active Directory in Windows 2000

Contents

Overview

- **Introduction to Active Directory**
- **Active Directory Logical Structure**
- **Active Directory Physical Structure**
- **Methods for Administering a Windows 2000 Network**

In a Microsoft® Windows® 2000 network, the Active Directory® directory service provides the structure and functions for organizing, managing, and controlling network resources. To implement and administer a Windows 2000 network, you must understand the purpose and structure of Active Directory.

Active Directory also provides the capability to centrally manage your Windows 2000 network. This capability means that you can centrally store information about the enterprise and administrators can manage the network from a single location. Active Directory supports the delegation of administrative control over Active Directory objects. This delegation enables administrators to assign specific administrative permissions for objects, such as user or computer accounts, to other users and administrators.

At the end of this module, you will be able to:

- Describe the function of Active Directory.
- Describe the logical structure of Active Directory.
- Describe the physical structure of Active Directory.
- Describe the methods for administering a Windows 2000 network.

Multimedia: Concepts of Active Directory in Windows 2000

This multimedia presentation describes basic Active Directory concepts, such as organizational units (OUs), trees, forests, DNS naming conventions, and sites.

◆ Introduction to Active Directory

- **What Is Active Directory?**
- **Active Directory Objects**
- **Active Directory Schema**
- **Lightweight Directory Access Protocol (LDAP)**

Active Directory stores information about resources on the entire network and makes it easy for users to locate, manage, and use these resources. Active Directory is made up of multiple components. You should understand the components and how to use them to administer Active Directory.

What Is Active Directory?

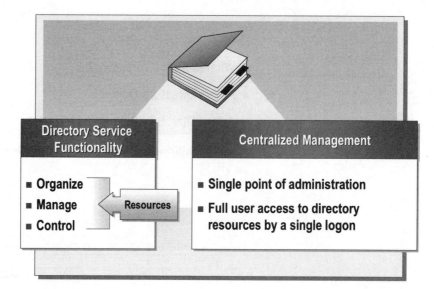

Active Directory is the directory service in a Windows 2000 network. A *directory service* is a network service that stores information about network resources and makes the resources accessible to users and applications. Directory services provide a consistent way to name, describe, locate, access, manage, and secure information about these resources.

Directory Service Functionality

Active Directory provides directory service functionality, including a means of centrally organizing, managing, and controlling access to network resources. Active Directory makes the physical network topology and protocols transparent so that a user on a network can gain access to any resource without knowing where the resource is or how it is physically connected to the network. An example of this type of resource would be a printer.

Active Directory is organized into sections that permit storage for a very large number of objects. As a result, Active Directory can expand as an organization grows, so that an organization that has a single server with a few hundred objects can grow to having thousands of servers and millions of objects.

Centralized Management

A server running Windows 2000 stores system configuration, user profiles, and application information in Active Directory. Combined with Group Policy, Active Directory enables administrators to manage distributed desktops, network services, and applications from a central location while using a consistent management interface.

Active Directory also provides centralized control of access to network resources by allowing users to log on only once to gain full access to resources throughout Active Directory.

Active Directory Objects

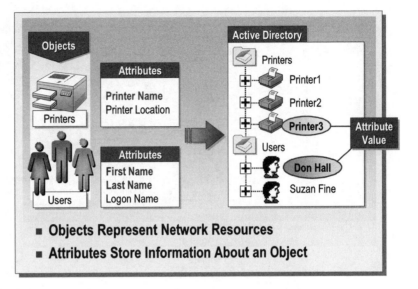

- **Objects Represent Network Resources**
- **Attributes Store Information About an Object**

Active Directory stores information about network objects. Active Directory *objects* represent network resources, such as users, groups, computers, and printers. Moreover, all servers, domains, and sites in the network are also represented as objects. Because Active Directory represents all network resources as objects in a distributed database, a single administrator can centrally manage and administer these resources.

When you create an object, the properties, or *attributes* of that object store the information that describes the object. Users can locate objects throughout Active Directory by searching for specific attributes. For example, a user can locate a printer in a specific building by searching the Location attribute of the printer object class.

Active Directory Schema

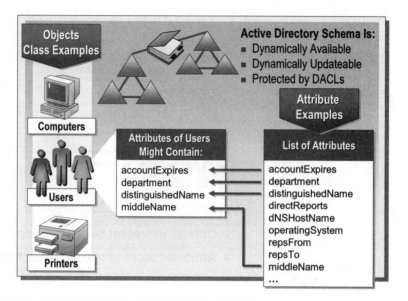

The Active Directory *schema* contains the definitions of all objects, such as computers, users, and printers that are stored in Active Directory. In Windows 2000, there is only one schema for an entire forest, so that all objects created in Active Directory conform to the same rules.

The two types of definitions in the schema are object classes and attributes. *Object classes* describe the possible directory objects that can be created. Each object class is a collection of attributes. Attributes are defined separately from object classes. Each attribute is defined only once and can be used in multiple object classes. For example, the Description attribute is used in many object classes, but is defined only once in the schema to ensure consistency.

The Active Directory database stores the schema. Storing the schema in a database means that the schema:

- Is dynamically available to user applications, which means that user applications can read the schema to discover which objects and properties are available for use.

- Is dynamically updateable, which enables an application to extend the schema with new attributes and object classes, and then use these schema extensions immediately.

- Can use discretionary access control lists (DACLs) to protect all object classes and attributes. The use of DACLs allows only authorized users to make schema changes.

Lightweight Directory Access Protocol (LDAP)

- **LDAP Provides a Way to Communicate with Active Directory by Specifying Unique Naming Paths for Each Object in the Directory**

- **LDAP Naming Paths Include:**

  - Distinguished names

  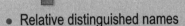
  CN=Suzan Fine,OU=Sales,DC=contoso,DC=msft

  - Relative distinguished names

Lightweight Directory Access Protocol (LDAP) is a directory service protocol that is used to query and update Active Directory. The protocol specification for LDAP specifies that an Active Directory object be represented by a series of domain components, OUs, and common names, which creates an LDAP naming path within Active Directory. LDAP naming paths are used to access Active Directory objects and include the following:

- Distinguished names
- Relative distinguished names

Distinguished Name

Every object in Active Directory has a distinguished name. The *distinguished name* identifies the domain where the object is located, and the complete path by which the object is reached. An example of a typical distinguished name is:

CN=Suzan Fine,OU=Sales,DC=contoso,DC=msft

Key	Attribute	Description
DC	Domain Component	A component of the DNS name of the domain, such as com.
OU	Organizational Unit	An organizational unit that can be used to contain other objects.
CN	Common Name	Any object other than domain components and organizational units, such as user and computer objects.

Relative Distinguished Name

The LDAP *relative distinguished name* is the portion of the LDAP distinguished name that uniquely identifies the object in its container. Its composition varies depending upon the extent of the existing search context established by the client. The search context may vary from the domain component level to the common name level. In the preceding example, the relative distinguished name of the Suzan Fine user object is Suzan Fine.

The following table provides examples of distinguished names, the search context established by the client, and relative distinguished names.

Distinguished name	Relative distinguished name
OU=Sales,DC=contoso,DC=msft	OU=Sales
CN=Suzan Fine,OU=Sales,DC=contoso, DC=msft	CN=Suzan Fine
CN=Judy Lew,OU=Shipping, DC=europe,DC=contoso,DC=msft	CN=Judy Lew

◆ Active Directory Logical Structure

- **Domains**
- **Organizational Units**
- **Trees and Forests**
- **Global Catalog**

The logical structure of Active Directory is flexible and provides a method for designing a hierarchy within Active Directory, which is comprehensible to both users and administrators. The logical components of the Active Directory structure include:

- Domains
- Organizational units
- Trees and forests
- Global catalog

You should understand the purpose and function of the logical components of the Active Directory structure so that you can complete a variety of tasks, including installing, configuring, administering, and troubleshooting Active Directory.

Domains

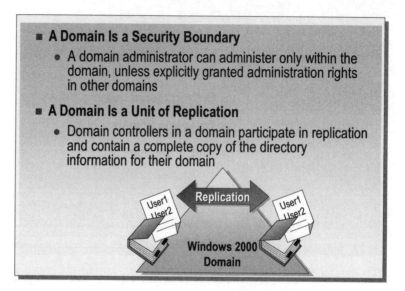

The core unit of the logical structure in Active Directory is the domain. A *domain* is a collection of computers, defined by an administrator, which share a common directory database. A domain has a unique name and provides access to the centralized user accounts and group accounts maintained by the domain administrator.

Security Boundary

In a Windows 2000 network, the domain serves as a *security boundary*. The purpose of a security boundary is to ensure that an administrator of a domain has the necessary permissions and rights to perform administration only within that domain, unless the administrator is explicitly granted these rights in another domain too. Every domain has its own security policies and security relationships with other domains.

Unit of Replication

Domains are also units of replication. In a domain, computers called *domain controllers* contain a replica of Active Directory. All of the domain controllers in a particular domain can receive changes to information in Active Directory and replicate these changes to all of the other domain controllers in the domain.

Organizational Units

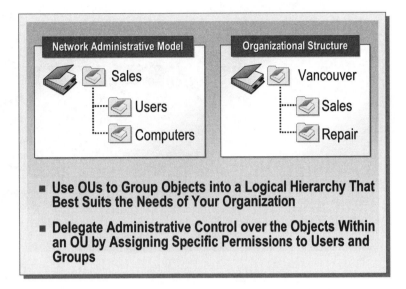

- **Use OUs to Group Objects into a Logical Hierarchy That Best Suits the Needs of Your Organization**

- **Delegate Administrative Control over the Objects Within an OU by Assigning Specific Permissions to Users and Groups**

An *organizational unit* (OU) is a container object that you use to organize objects within a domain. An OU may contain objects, such as user accounts, groups, computers, printers, and other OUs.

OU Hierarchy

You can use OUs to group objects into a logical hierarchy that best suits the needs of your organization. For example, you can create an OU hierarchy to represent the following for an organization:

- Network administrative model based on administrative responsibilities. For example, an organization might have one administrator who is responsible for all of the user accounts and another who is responsible for all of the computers. In this case, you would create one OU for users and another OU for computers.

- Organizational structure based on departmental or geographical boundaries.

The OU hierarchy within a domain is independent of the OU hierarchy structure of other domains—each domain can implement its own OU hierarchy.

Administrative Control of OUs

You can delegate administrative control over the objects within an OU. To delegate administrative control of an OU, you assign specific permissions for the OU and the objects that the OU contains to one or more users and groups.

For an OU, you can assign either complete administrative control, such as full control over all objects in the OU, or limited administrative control, such as the ability to modify e-mail information on user objects in the OU.

Trees and Forests

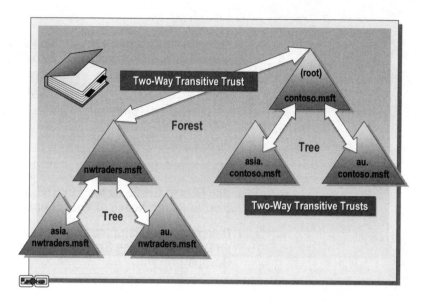

The first Windows 2000 domain that you create is called the *forest root domain*. Additional domains are added to the root domain to form the tree structure or the forest structure, depending on the domain name requirements.

Trees

A *tree* is a hierarchical arrangement of Windows 2000 domains that share a contiguous namespace.

When you add a domain to an existing tree, the new domain is a child domain of an existing parent domain. The name of the child domain is combined with the name of the parent domain to form its DNS name. Every child domain has a two-way, transitive trust relationship with its parent domain.

Two-Way, Transitive Trusts

Two-way, transitive trust relationships are the default trust relationships between Windows 2000 domains. A two-way, transitive trust is a combination of a transitive trust and a two-way trust.

A *transitive trust* means that the trust relationship extended to one domain is automatically extended to all other domains that trust that domain. For example, domain au.contoso.msft directly trusts contoso.msft. Domain asia.contoso.msft also directly trusts contoso.msft. Because both trusts are transitive, au.contoso.msft indirectly trusts asia.contoso.msft.

A *two-way trust* means that there are two trust paths going in opposite directions between two domains. For example, domain au.contoso.msft trusts contoso.msft in one direction, and contoso.msft trusts au.contoso.msft in the opposite direction.

The advantage of two-way, transitive trusts in Windows 2000 domains is that there is complete trust between all domains in an Active Directory domain hierarchy. Trees linked by trust relationships form a forest.

Forests

A *forest* is one or more trees. The trees in a forest do not share a contiguous namespace. However, the trees in a forest share a common schema and global catalog. A single tree that is related to no other trees constitutes a forest of one tree. Thus, every tree root domain has a transitive trust relationship with the forest root domain. The name of the forest root domain is used to refer to a given forest.

Each tree in a forest has its own unique namespace. For example, Contoso, Ltd. creates a separate organization called Northwind Traders. Contoso, Ltd. decides to create a new Active Directory domain name for Northwind Traders, called nwtraders.msft. Although the two organizations do not share a common namespace, adding the new Active Directory domain as a new tree in an existing forest allows the two organizations to share resources and administrative functions.

Global Catalog

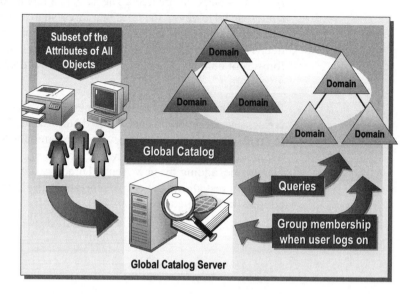

The *global catalog* is a repository of information that contains a subset of the attributes of all objects in Active Directory. By default, the attributes that are stored in the global catalog are those that are most frequently used in queries, such as a user's first name, last name, and logon name. The global catalog contains the information that is necessary to determine the location of any object in the directory.

The global catalog enables users to perform two important functions:

- Find Active Directory information in the entire forest, regardless of the location of the data.

- Use universal group membership information to log on to the network.

A *global catalog server* is a domain controller that stores a copy of queries and processes them to the global catalog. The first domain controller you create in Active Directory automatically becomes the global catalog server. You can configure additional global catalog servers to balance the traffic from logon authentication and queries.

The global catalog makes the directory structure within a forest transparent to users who perform a search. For example, if you search for all of the printers in a forest, a global catalog server processes the query in the global catalog and then returns the results. Without a global catalog server, this query would require a search of every domain in the forest.

The global catalog also contains the access permissions for each object and attribute stored in the global catalog. If you are searching for an object and you do not have the appropriate permissions to view the object, you will not see the object in the list of search results. This ensures that users can find only objects to which they have been assigned access.

◆ Active Directory Physical Structure

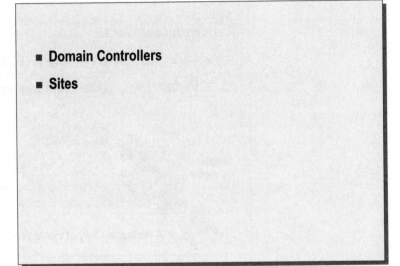

- **Domain Controllers**
- **Sites**

In Active Directory, the logical structure is separate and distinct from the physical structure. You use the logical structure to organize your network resources, and you use the physical structure to configure and manage your network traffic. Domain controllers and sites make up the physical structure of Active Directory.

The physical structure of Active Directory defines where and when replication and logon traffic occur. Understanding the physical components of Active Directory is critical to optimizing network traffic and the logon process. Also, knowing the physical structure can help in troubleshooting replication and logon problems.

Domain Controllers

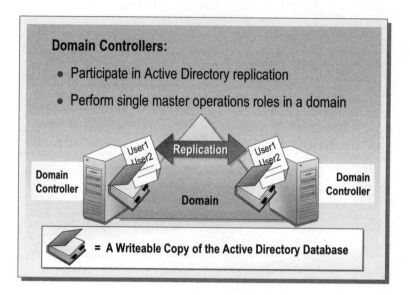

A *domain controller* is a computer running Windows 2000 Server that stores a replica of the directory. A domain controller also manages the changes to directory information and replicates these changes to other domain controllers in the same domain. Domain controllers store directory data and manage user logon processes, authentication, and directory searches.

A domain can have one or more domain controllers. A small organization that uses a single local area network (LAN) may need only one domain with two domain controllers to provide adequate availability and fault tolerance, whereas a large organization with many geographical locations needs one or more domain controllers in each location to provide adequate availability and fault tolerance.

Active Directory Replication

Domain controllers in a domain and in a forest automatically replicate any change to the Active Directory database to each other. Replication ensures that all of the information in Active Directory is available to all domain controllers and client computers across the entire network. The physical structure of Active Directory determines when and how replication occurs.

Active Directory uses a *multi-master replication model*. In a multi-master replication model, each Windows 2000 domain has one or more domain controllers. Each domain controller stores a writeable copy of the Active Directory database for its domain and manages the changes and updates to its copy of the directory. When a user or administrator performs an action that causes an update to the directory in one domain controller, that update is replicated to all domain controllers in the domain. However, domain controllers might hold different information for short periods of time until all of the domain controllers have synchronized their changes to Active Directory.

Single Master Operations

Some changes to Active Directory are impractical to perform using multi-master replication because of the potential for conflicts in essential operations. For these reasons, *single master operations* are assigned only to specific domain controllers. An operations master is a domain controller that has been assigned one or more single master operations roles in an Active Directory domain or forest. The domain controllers that are assigned these roles perform operations, such as adding or removing a domain from a forest, that are not permitted to simultaneously occur on different domain controllers in the network.

Sites

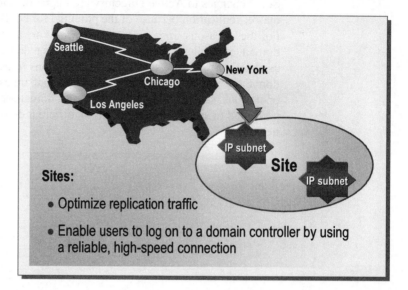

A *site* consists of one or more Internet Protocol (IP) subnets that are connected by a high-speed link. By defining sites, you can configure the access and replication topology for Active Directory so that Windows 2000 uses the most efficient links and schedules for replication and logon traffic.

You create sites for two primary reasons:

- To optimize replication traffic.

- To enable users to connect to a domain controller by using a reliable, high-speed connection.

Sites map the physical structure of your network, whereas domains map the logical structure of your organization. The logical and physical structures of Active Directory are independent of each other, which has the following consequences:

- There is no necessary correlation between the network's physical structure and its domain structure.

- Active Directory allows multiple domains in a single site, and multiple sites in a single domain.

- There is no necessary correlation between site and domain namespaces.

Note   For more information about the logical and physical structures of Active Directory, see *Active Directory Architecture* under **Additional Reading** on the Web page on the Student Materials compact disc.

◆ Methods for Administering a Windows 2000 Network

- **Using Active Directory for Centralized Management**
- **Managing the User Environment**
- **Delegating Administrative Control**

Windows 2000 and Active Directory provide administrators with the methods and utilities to centralize the management of all desktop computers in an organization and to decentralize administrative tasks. Administrators perform the following administrative tasks:

- Centralize management. Active Directory allows administrators to centrally manage large numbers of users, computers, printers, and network resources from a central location. Active Directory enables users to centrally organize network resources according to administrative requirements.

- Manage the user environment. Group Policy enables administrators to specify settings and apply management Group Policy settings to OUs in Active Directory. Moreover, Group Policy enables administrators to define a Group Policy for a user or computer once, and then use Windows 2000 to reinforce it continually.

- Delegate administrative control. Active Directory allows an administrator with the proper authority to delegate a selected set of administrative privileges to appropriate individuals or groups within an organization. This administrator can specify the privileges that these individuals have to manage different containers and objects in Active Directory. Windows 2000 also provides the tools to match administrative responsibilities and to delegate network administrative responsibilities to other administrators.

Using Active Directory for Centralized Management

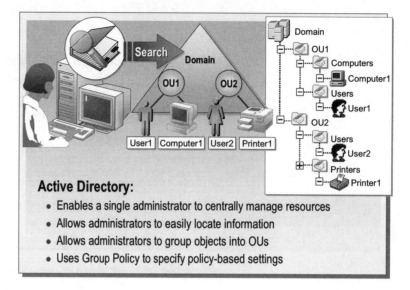

Active Directory:
- Enables a single administrator to centrally manage resources
- Allows administrators to easily locate information
- Allows administrators to group objects into OUs
- Uses Group Policy to specify policy-based settings

Active Directory provides administrators with the capability to manage resources centrally. The advantages of managing resources centrally are:

- Active Directory enables a single administrator to centrally manage and administer network resources. Active Directory contains information about all objects and their attributes. The attributes hold data that describes the resource that the directory object identifies.

- Active Directory allows administrators to easily locate information about objects. By searching for selected attributes, you can find an object located anywhere in the Active Directory tree.

- Active Directory allows you to group objects with similar administrative and security requirements into OUs. OUs provide multiple levels of administrative authority for both applying Group Policy settings and delegating administrative control. This delegation of administrative authority simplifies the task of managing these objects and allows administrators to structure Active Directory to fit their needs.

- Active Directory uses Group Policy to provide administrators with the ability to specify Group Policy settings for a site, domain, or OU. Active Directory then enforces these Group Policy settings for all of the users and computers within the container.

Managing the User Environment

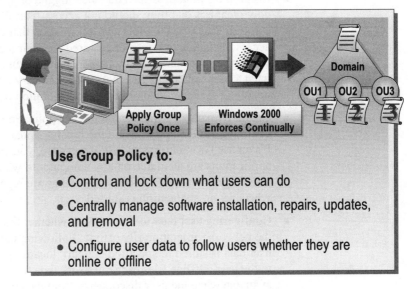

Group Policy in Windows 2000 enables policy-based centralized management of a network. Policy-based administration eases the management of even the most complex network by allowing you to apply a Group Policy to an object once, and then to rely on Windows 2000 to continually enforce the Group Policy throughout the network.

Group Policy utilizes Active Directory containers (sites, domains, and OUs) as administrative units. A Group Policy set on a container affects all users and computers that it contains. Windows 2000 applies Group Policy settings to users and computers when the computer starts or the user logs on. Group Policy provides settings for controlling computer services and users' desktop environments and capabilities. Group Policy allows you to control users' data, personal computer settings, computing environment, and software.

Group Policy settings that are associated with the user enable administrators to provide users with consistent access to all of the users' information and software, regardless of which computer they are working on.

You can use Group Policy to manage the user environment by:

- Controlling what users can do when logged on to the network, and locking down features that they should not access. This control ensures that users can gain access to the tools and information that they need but cannot gain access to anything that is not required for their jobs. You can also restrict the applications and tools that are available to users. Limiting the scope of what a user can do ensures that no unnecessary time is spent troubleshooting operating system and application configuration problems.

- Centrally managing the installation of applications, service packs, and operating system updates, and the repairs, updates, and removal of software. If you use Group Policy to install software, you can ensure that the same applications are available on any computer to which a user logs on. You can also ensure that missing files and settings are repaired automatically whenever an application is started.

- Configuring user data to *follow* users whether they are online, connected to the network, or temporarily offline. Following means that even though the user data is stored in specified network locations, it always appears as local to the user. Offline files cache network data to the local computers, so it is available when the user disconnects from the network.

Delegating Administrative Control

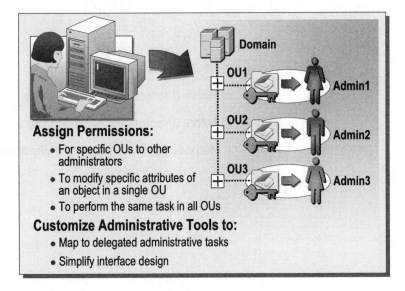

Windows 2000 enables you to delegate administrative privileges for certain objects to appropriate groups within an organization. This is possible because the structure of Active Directory allows you to assign permissions and grant user rights in very specific ways.

You can delegate the following types of administrative control:

- Assigning permissions, such as Full Control, for specific OUs to different domain local groups. Thus, three OUs could have three different domain local groups.

- Assigning the permissions to modify specific attributes of an object in a single OU. For example, assigning the permission to change name, address, and telephone number, and to reset passwords on a user account object.

- Assigning the permissions to perform the same task, such as resetting passwords, in all OUs of a domain.

Windows 2000 also provides you with the capability to customize administrative tools so that the tools match the administrative tasks that you delegate to other administrators. You can create customized administrative tools to:

- Map to the permissions that have been assigned to a user for an administrative task.

- Simplify interface design for users with limited administrative privileges.

You can also combine all of the tools needed for each administrative function into a single console.

Review

- **Introduction to Active Directory**

- **Active Directory Logical Structure**

- **Active Directory Physical Structure**

- **Methods for Administering a Windows 2000 Network**

1. What is the purpose of Active Directory in Windows 2000?

2. What are sites and domains, and how are they different from each other?

3. What are trees and forests, and how are they different from each other? What do they have in common?

Microsoft®
Training &
Certification

Module 2: Implementing DNS to Support Active Directory

Contents

Microsoft®

Overview

- **Introduction to the Role of DNS in Active Directory**
- **DNS and Active Directory**
- **DNS Name Resolution in Active Directory**
- **Active Directory Integrated Zones**
- **Installing and Configuring DNS to Support Active Directory**
- **Best Practices**

The integration of the Domain Name System (DNS) and Active Directory® directory service is a key feature of Microsoft® Windows® 2000. DNS and Active Directory use an identical hierarchical naming structure so that domains and computers are represented both as Active Directory objects and as DNS domains and resource records. The result of this integration is that computers in a Windows 2000 network use DNS to locate computers that provide specific Active Directory–related services. For example, when a user logs on from a client computer or needs to search Active Directory for a printer or shared folder, the client computer queries a DNS server to locate a domain controller. Windows 2000 also supports the integration of DNS zones in Active Directory, so that DNS primary zones can be stored in Active Directory for enhanced security and for replication to other domain controllers.

Windows 2000 requires that a DNS infrastructure is in place or is installed when you install Active Directory. Before you create Windows 2000 domains, you should understand how DNS and Active Directory are integrated, how client computers use DNS to locate domain controllers, and how to install and configure DNS to prepare for an Active Directory installation.

At the end of this module, you will be able to:

- Describe the role of DNS in an Active Directory network.
- Describe the similarities and differences between the DNS namespace and the Active Directory namespace.
- Describe how client computers locate domain controllers in Windows 2000.
- Install and configure DNS to support an installation of Active Directory.
- Apply best practices for setting up DNS to support an installation of Active Directory.

Introduction to the Role of DNS in Active Directory

- **Name Resolution**
  - DNS translates computer names to IP addresses
  - Computers use DNS to locate each other on the network
- **Naming Convention for Windows 2000 Domains**
  - Windows 2000 uses DNS naming standards for domain names
  - DNS domains and Active Directory domains share a common hierarchical naming structure
- **Locating the Physical Components of Active Directory**
  - DNS identifies domain controllers by the services they provide
  - Computers use DNS to locate domain controllers and global catalog servers

DNS provides the following primary functions in an Active Directory network:

- *Name resolution.* DNS provides name resolution by translating computer names to Internet Protocol (IP) addresses so that computers can locate each other. A computer on a Windows 2000 network sends a DNS query containing the name of the computer it wants to locate to a DNS server. The DNS server resolves the query by looking in its local database or by forwarding the query to another DNS server. DNS also performs reverse name resolution by translating IP addresses to computer names.

- *Naming convention for Windows 2000 domains.* Active Directory uses DNS naming conventions to name Windows 2000 domains. In a Windows 2000 network, the names of DNS domains and Active Directory domains share a common hierarchical naming structure. For example, asia.contoso.msft is a valid DNS domain name and could also be the name of a Windows 2000 domain.

- *Locating the physical components of Active Directory.* DNS identifies domain controllers by the specific services that they provide, such as authenticating a logon request or performing an Active Directory search. A client computer uses this service-specific information to query DNS to locate a domain controller that provides the service.

  For example, to log on to the network or to search Active Directory for published printers or folders, a computer running Windows 2000 first must locate a domain controller or global catalog server to process the logon authentication or the query. The DNS database stores information about which computers perform these roles.

◆ DNS and Active Directory

- **DNS and Active Directory Namespaces**
- **DNS Host Names and Windows 2000 Computer Names**

The integration of DNS and Active Directory is a central feature of Windows 2000 Server. DNS domains and Active Directory domains use identical domain names for different namespaces. Using identical domain names enables computers in a Windows 2000 network to use DNS to locate domain controllers and other computers that provide Active Directory–related services.

DNS and Active Directory Namespaces

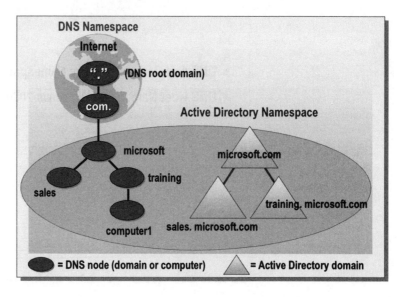

A *namespace* is a hierarchical naming structure in which the names in the namespace can be resolved to the objects that they represent. In Windows 2000, DNS domains and Active Directory domains have the same hierarchical naming structure, but they represent two different namespaces because they store different information about the same physical objects.

In the DNS namespace, zones store name information about one or more DNS domains. A DNS *zone* is a contiguous portion of the domain namespace for which a DNS server has authority to resolve DNS queries. A zone stores the resources records for the domains and computers in that zone. *Resource records* represent computers, and contain the information necessary for a DNS server to resolve DNS queries. Note that DNS zones can store information about computers that are joined to different Active Directory domains.

In the Active Directory namespace, Active Directory objects represent the same domains and computers that exist as nodes in the DNS namespace. Therefore, DNS domains and Active Directory domains share identical names.

In other words, the DNS and Active Directory namespaces use an identical naming structure so that domains and computers can be represented both as DNS nodes and Active Directory objects. For example, a Windows 2000 domain with a name training.microsoft.com also has a DNS domain name, which is training.microsoft.com. The advantage of integrating the DNS and Active Directory namespaces is that DNS can be used to locate computers that play specific roles in an Active Directory domain.

Active Directory and the Internet

The integration of DNS and Active Directory also enables the Active Directory domain structure to exist within the scope of the Internet namespace. This is possible because the global DNS namespace provides the hierarchical naming structure of the Internet. If your organization requires an Internet presence, then it must register the DNS name that will be used as the name of the root domain in the Active Directory domain structure.

When the root domain of your Active Directory domain structure has a DNS domain name that is registered, then resource records in the relevant top-level domains in the global Internet namespace point to DNS servers that are authoritative for your root domain. For example, name servers that are authoritative for the .com DNS database contain resource records for DNS name servers in the root domain of microsoft.com. These resource records enable external domains to use the Internet to find the microsoft.com domain. Similarly, the DNS name servers in your network can contain resource records for Internet name servers if you want to be able to locate other domains on the Internet.

DNS Host Names and Windows 2000 Computer Names

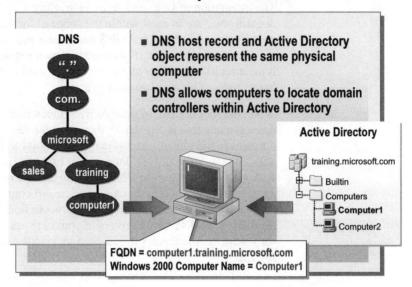

Because Windows 2000 integrates DNS and Active Directory, domains and computers are represented by resource records in the DNS namespace, and by Active Directory objects in the Active Directory namespace. Therefore, the DNS host name for a computer is the same name as that is used for the computer account that is stored in Active Directory. Note that the Windows 2000 computer name is the relative distinguished name of the Active Directory object. The DNS domain name, which is called the *primary DNS suffix*, is also the same as the name of the Active Directory domain to which the computer is joined.

In other words, a computer is represented in the DNS namespace and the Active Directory namespace by the same name. For example, a computer named Computer1 that is joined to the Active Directory domain named training.microsoft.com has the following fully qualified domain name (FQDN):

computer1.training.microsoft.com

The integration of DNS and Active Directory is essential because a client computer in a Windows 2000 network must be able to locate a domain controller to use the services provided by Active Directory. To locate a domain controller, a computer uses DNS to locate the IP address for a computer that provides the required service within Active Directory.

Note In Windows 2000, the FQDN for a computer is also called the *full computer name*.

◆ DNS Name Resolution in Active Directory

- **SRV (Service) Resource Records**

- **SRV Record Format**

- **SRV Records Registered by Domain Controllers**

- **How Computers Use DNS to Locate Domain Controllers**

In addition to being identified by an FQDN in DNS and by a Windows 2000 full computer name, domain controllers are also identified by the specific services that they provide. Windows 2000 uses DNS to locate domain controllers by resolving a domain or computer name to an IP address. This is accomplished by SRV (service) resource records, which map a particular service to the domain controller that provides that service. The format of an SRV record contains this information, as well as Transmission Control Protocol/Internet Protocol (TCP/IP) specific information.

When a domain controller starts up, the Net Logon service running on the domain controller uses the DNS dynamic update feature to register with the DNS database the SRV records for all Active Directory–related services that the domain controller provides. Therefore, a computer running Windows 2000 can query a DNS server when it needs to contact a domain controller.

Note For more information about DNS name resolution in Active Directory, see chapter 3, "Name Resolution in Active Directory" in the Distributed Systems Guide in the Microsoft Windows 2000 Server Resource Kit.

SRV (Service) Resource Records

- **SRV Records Allow Computers to Locate Domain Controllers**

- **Information in SRV Records Maps DNS Computer Names to the Service**

- **Windows 2000 Uses SRV Records to Locate:**
  - A domain controller in a specific domain or forest
  - A domain controller in the same site as a client computer
  - A domain controller configured as a global catalog server
  - A computer configured as a Kerberos KDC server

- **DNS Servers Use the Information in the SRV Record and the A Resource Record to Locate Domain Controllers**

For Active Directory to function properly, DNS servers must provide support for SRV (service) resource records. *SRV records* allow client computers to locate servers that provide specific services such as authenticating logon requests and searching for information in Active Directory. Windows 2000 uses SRV records to identify a computer as a domain controller. SRV records link the name of a service to the DNS computer name for the domain controller that offers that service.

SRV records also contain information that enables a DNS client to locate the following:

- A domain controller located in a specific Windows 2000 domain or forest.

- A domain controller located in the same site as a client computer.

- A domain controller that is configured as global catalog server.

- A computer that runs the Kerberos Key Distribution Center (KDC) service.

SRV Records and A Resource Records

When a domain controller starts up, it registers SRV records, which contain information about the services it provides, and an A resource record that contains its DNS computer name and its IP address. A DNS server then uses this combined information to resolve DNS queries and return the IP address of a domain controller so that the client computer can locate the domain controller.

Note In Windows 2000, domain controllers are also referred to Lightweight Directory Access Protocol (LDAP) servers because they run the LDAP service that responds to requests to search for or modify objects in Active Directory.

SRV Record Format

Field	Description
Service	Specifies the name for the service
Protocol	Indicates the transport protocol type
Name	Specifies the domain name referenced by the resource record
Ttl	Specifies the standard DNS resource record Time to Live value
Class	Specifies the standard DNS resource record class value
Priority	Specifies the priority of the host
Weight	Specifies the load balancing mechanism
Port	Shows the port of the service on this host
Target	Specifies the FQDN for the host supporting the service

_ldap._tcp.contoso.msft 600 IN SRV 0 100 389 london.contoso.msft.

All SRV records use a standard format, which consists of fields that contain the information used to map a specific service to the computer that provides the service. SRV records use the following format:

service.protocol.name ttl class SRV priority weight port target

The following table describes each field in an SRV record:

Field	Description
_Service	Specifies the name of the service, such as LDAP or Kerberos, provided by the server that registers this SRV record.
_Protocol	Specifies the transport protocol type, such as TCP or User Datagram Protocol (UDP).
Name	Specifies the domain name referenced by the resource record.
Ttl	Specifies the Time to Live (TTL) value (in seconds), which is a standard field in DNS resource.
Class	Specifies the standard DNS resource record class value, which is almost always "IN" for the Internet system.
Priority	Specifies the priority of the server. Clients attempt to contact the host with the lowest priority.
Weight	Denotes a load balancing mechanism that clients use when selecting a target host. When the priority field is the same for two or more records in the same domain, clients randomly choose SRV records with higher weights.
Port	Specifies the port where the server is "listening" for this service.
Target	Specifies the fully qualified domain name (FQDN), which is also called the full computer name, of the computer providing the service.

For example, the following SRV record:

_ldap._tcp.contoso.msft 600 IN SRV 0 100 389 london.contoso.msft.

would be registered by a computer that:

- Provides the LDAP service
- Provides the LDAP service by using the TCP transport protocol
- Registers the SRV record in the contoso.msft DNS domain
- Has an FQDN of london.contoso.msft

SRV Records Registered by Domain Controllers

SRV Record	Lookup Criteria
ldap._tcp._DnsDomainName._	Allows a computer to find an LDAP server in the domain
_ldap._tcp._SiteName._**_sites.dc._msdcs.**_DnsDomainName._	Allows a computer to find a domain controller in the same site
_gc._tcp._DnsForestName._	Allows a computer to find a global catalog server
_gc._tcp._SiteName._**_sites.**_DnsForestName._	Allows a computer to find a global catalog server in the same site
_kerberos._tcp._DnsDomainName._	Allows a computer to locate a KDC server in the domain
_kerberos._tcp._SiteName._**_sites.**_DnsDomainName._	Allows a computer to locate a KDC server in the same site

- **Domain Controllers Running Windows 2000 Register Additional SRV Records in the _msdcs Subdomain in the Format of:**

  _Service._Protocol.DcType.**_msdcs.**DnsDomainName

When a domain controller starts up, the Net Logon service running on the domain controller uses dynamic updates to register SRV resource records in the DNS database. These SRV records map the name of the service provided by the domain controller to the DNS computer name for that domain controller. The following table lists some of the SRV records registered by domain controllers and defines the lookup criteria that each record supports.

SRV Record	Lookup Criteria
_ldap._tcp._DnsDomainName._	Allows a computer to find an LDAP server in the domain named by _DnsDomainName._ All domain controllers register this record.
_ldap._tcp._SiteName._**_sites.dc._msdcs.**_DnsDomainName._	Allows a computer to find a domain controller in the domain named by _DnsDomainName_ and in the site named by _SiteName._ Note that _SiteName_ is the relative distinguished name of the site object that is stored in Active Directory. All domain controllers register this record.
_gc._tcp._DnsForestName._	Allows a computer to find a global catalog server in the forest named by _DnsForestName._ Note that _DnsForestName_ is the domain name of the forest root domain. Only domain controllers configured as global catalog servers register this record.

(*continued*)

SRV Record	Lookup Criteria
_gc._tcp.*SiteName.***_sites.***DnsForestName.*	Allows a computer to find a global catalog server in the forest named *DnsForestName* and in the site named by *SiteName*.
	Only domain controllers configured as global catalog servers register this record.
_kerberos._tcp.*DnsDomainName.*	Allows a computer to locate a KDC server for the domain named by *DnsDomainName*.
	All domain controllers running the Kerberos version 5 service register this record.
_kerberos._tcp.*SiteName.***_sites.***DnsDomainName.*	Allows a computer to locate a KDC server for the domain named by *DnsDomainName* and in the site named by *SiteName*.
	All domain controllers running the Kerberos V5 service register this record.

Note   In addition to Windows 2000 domain controllers, a network can contain computers that are configured as LDAP servers and global catalog servers that are not running Windows 2000. Therefore, any computer that provides appropriate services registers the SRV records listed in the previous table.

SRV Records Registered Only by Windows 2000 Domain Controllers

To enable a computer to locate domain controllers running Windows 2000, the Net Logon service registers SRV records that identify domain controllers that provide Windows 2000–specific services in the domain or forest. Therefore, in addition to the SRV records listed above, domain controllers running Windows 2000 also register SRV records in the following format:

*_Service._Protocol.DcType.***_msdcs.***DnsDomainName* or *DnsForestName*

The _msdcs component in these SRV records denotes a subdomain in the DNS namespace that is specific to Microsoft, which allows computers to locate domain controllers that have functions in the domain or forest that are specific to Windows 2000.

The possible values for the *DCType* component, which is a prefix to the _msdcs subdomain, specify the following server roles types:

- **dc** for a domain controller
- **gc** for global catalog server

The presence of the _msdcs subdomain means that domain controllers running Windows 2000 also register the following SRV records:

_ldap._tcp.dc._msdcs._DnsDomainName._

_ldap._tcp._SiteName._**_sites.dc._msdcs.**_DnsDomainName._

_ldap._tcp.gc._msdcs._DnsForestName._

_ldap._tcp._SiteName._**_sites.gc._msdcs.**_DnsForestName._

_kerberos._tcp.dc._msdcs._DnsDomainName._

_kerberos._tcp._SiteName._**_sites.dc._msdcs.**_DnsDomainName._

How Computers Use DNS to Locate Domain Controllers

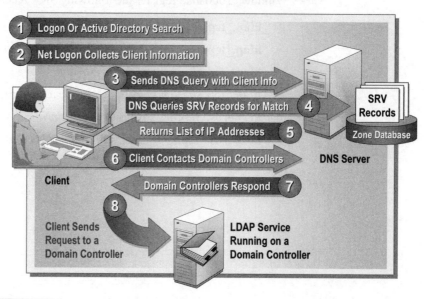

To log on to a Windows 2000 domain or to search Active Directory, a client computer must contact a domain controller. All domain controllers register both *A resource records* and *SRV records*. The A resource record contains the FQDN and IP address for the domain controller. The SRV record contains the FQDN of the domain controller and the name of the service that the domain controller. Therefore, the client computer can query DNS to locate a domain controller.

The following describes the process of how a computer locates a domain controller:

1. A user logs on to the domain, initiates an Active Directory search, or performs other tasks that require a domain controller. The Net Logon service on the client (the computer that is locating the domain controller) starts the DsGetDcName application programming interface (API).

2. Net Logon collects information about the client and the specific service required; this information will be included in the DNS query. This information is specified by the following DsGetDcName parameters:

   - *ComputerName*. The name of the client computer.

   - *DomainName*. The name of the DNS domain that will be queried.

   - *SiteName*. The name of the site in which the domain controller should be located. If the site is not specified, the domain controller that will be located is in the site that is closest to the site in which the client computer is located.

   The client also specifies that the domain controller should be an LDAP server in the domain named by *DomainName*, or a global catalog server or KDC server for the forest in which *DomainName* is located.

3. The Net Logon service sends a DNS query to a DNS server. This DNS query contains the information it collected from the client and specifies the service that is required.

4. The DNS server queries the DNS zone database for SRV records that match the service required by the client in the domain named by *DomainName*.

5. The DNS server returns a list of IP addresses of domain controllers that provide the service requested in the domain specified by the client.

6. The Net Logon service sends a datagram (an LDAP UDP message) to one or more of the located domain controllers to determine whether it is running and whether it supports the specified domain.

7. Each available domain controller responds to the datagram to indicate that it is currently operational, and then returns the information to DsGetDcName. The Net Logon service returns the information to the client from the domain controller that responds first.

8. The client computer chooses the first domain controller that responds and meets the criteria, and then sends the request to that domain controller.

The Net Logon service caches the domain controller information so that it is not necessary that the client computer repeat the discovery process for subsequent requests. Caching this information also encourages the consistent use of the same domain controller.

Active Directory Integrated Zones

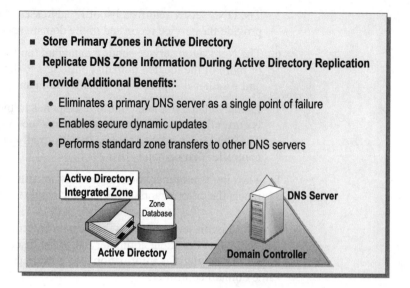

One of the benefits of integrating DNS and Active Directory is the capability to integrate DNS zones into the Active Directory database. *Active Directory integrated zones* are primary DNS zones that are stored as an object in the Active Directory database. A zone is a portion of the domain namespace that is defined by the resource records that are stored in a zone database file. A zone database file stores information that is used to resolve host names to IP addresses and IP addresses to host names. Therefore, when you configure Active Directory integrated zones, the zone database file is replicated during Active Directory replication rather than through DNS zone transfers.

An Active Directory integrated zone provides the following benefits:

- Eliminates a primary DNS server as a single point of failure. Because DNS replication is single-master, it relies on a primary DNS server to update all of the secondary servers. In contrast, Active Directory replication is multi-master, so an update can be made to any domain controller, and the change will be replicated to all other domain controllers. Therefore, if you integrate a DNS zone with Active Directory, Active Directory replication will always synchronize the DNS zone information.

- Enables secure dynamic updates. Because DNS zones are Active Directory objects in Active Directory integrated zones, you can set permissions on records within those zones to control which computers can update their records. Therefore, updates that use the dynamic update protocol can come from only authorized computers.

- Performs standard zone transfers to DNS servers that are not configured as domain controllers and performs standard zone transfers to DNS servers that are in other domains. You must use standard zone transfers to replicate the zones to DNS servers in other domains.

Important   Active Directory must first be installed before you can configure Active Directory integrated zones.

◆ Installing and Configuring DNS to Support Active Directory

- DNS Requirements for Active Directory

- Installing and Configuring DNS

- Installing DNS During the Active Directory Installation

Implementing an Active Directory infrastructure requires that a DNS infrastructure be in place or installed during Active Directory installation. To support Active Directory, your DNS implementation must support SRV records.

To implement DNS, you need to install DNS and configure the forward and reverse lookup zones. Because DNS domain names correspond to Active Directory domain names, you can configure your forward and reverse lookup zones so that they correspond to your Active Directory domains. However, DNS zones can also include data about computers in one or more Active Directory domains, so zones can also encompass more than one Active Directory domain.

DNS Requirements for Active Directory

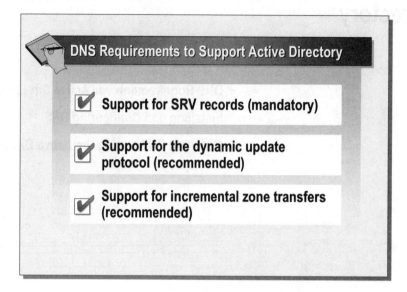

You cannot install Active Directory without having DNS on your network because Active Directory uses DNS as its location service. For DNS to function as a location service for Active Directory, you must have a DNS server that supports SRV resource records.

The version of DNS included with Windows 2000 provides the requirements necessary to support an installation of Active Directory. If you choose not to use Windows 2000 DNS, you need to determine if your DNS server provides the following support:

- *SRV records* (RFC 2052). SRV records are DNS records that map to the name of a server offering a particular service. If your existing DNS server does not support SRV records, you must switch to a DNS server that does, or delegate the domains used by Active Directory to a DNS server that supports SRV records.

- *Dynamic update protocol* (RFC 2136). The dynamic update protocol is optional but is highly recommended because it enables the servers and clients in your environment to add records to the DNS database automatically, which reduces administration costs. If you are using a DNS server that supports SRV resource records and does not support the dynamic update protocol, you must enter the SRV resource records manually. When you install Active Directory on a computer, a file containing the required SRV resource records is created as part of the installation process. This file is called Netlogon.dns and is located in the *systemroot*\System32\Config folder.

- *Incremental zone transfers* (RFC 1995). An incremental zone transfer is optional, and allows only new or modified resource records to be replicated between DNS servers, rather than to the entire zone database file.

Note   To obtain a copy of RFC 2052, RFC 2136, or RFC 1995, see the Internet Engineering Task Force Web page at http://www.ietf.org.

Installing and Configuring DNS

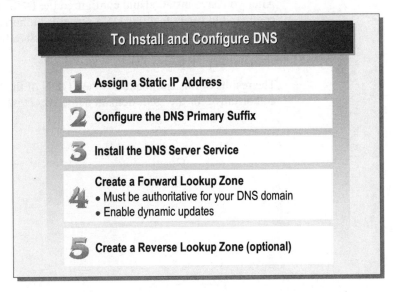

To implement a DNS infrastructure before you install Active Directory, you must install and configure the DNS Server service on a computer running Windows 2000 Server.

▶ **To install and configure DNS:**

1. Assign a static IP address. You must configure the computer with a static IP address before you install the DNS Server service.

2. Configure the DNS primary suffix. If you are creating the first DNS server in your organization, the DNS primary suffix should be the same name that you will use for the forest root of your Active Directory forest.

3. Install the DNS Server service. Use the DNS Installation wizard to install the DNS Server service.

4. Create a standard primary forward lookup zone.

   • This zone must be authoritative for the name of the first Active Directory domain that you will create.

   • Configure the forward lookup zone to enable dynamic updates.

5. Create a standard primary reverse lookup zone (optional). A reverse lookup zone is not required during the Active Directory installation, but it is a best practice to create a reverse lookup zone so that IP addresses can be resolved to computer names. If you create a reverse lookup zone, you should also configure it to enable dynamic updates.

Verifying the DNS Server is Authoritative

After you have installed and configured the DNS server, use the following command to verify that this DNS server is authoritative for the DNS domain name that you will use to name your first Active Directory domain:

nslookup -type=ns *DnsDomainName*

The results of this command list the FQDN of the DNS servers that are authoritative for the DNS domain named by *DnsDomainName*.

Installing DNS During the Active Directory Installation

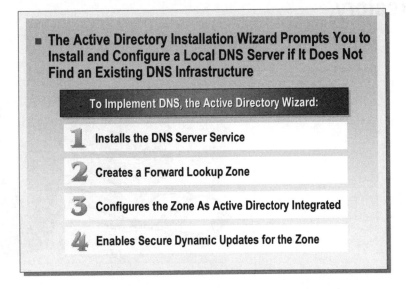

■ The Active Directory Installation Wizard Prompts You to Install and Configure a Local DNS Server if It Does Not Find an Existing DNS Infrastructure

To Implement DNS, the Active Directory Wizard:

1 Installs the DNS Server Service

2 Creates a Forward Lookup Zone

3 Configures the Zone As Active Directory Integrated

4 Enables Secure Dynamic Updates for the Zone

If you do not have a DNS infrastructure in place at the time when you create the first domain, which is the forest root domain, in your Windows 2000 forest, the Active Directory Installation wizard can install and configure the DNS Server service on the computer on which you are installing Active Directory.

The following describes how the Active Directory Installation wizard installs and configures DNS:

1. If the Active Directory Installation wizard cannot find the DNS server that is authoritative for the name of the new Active Directory domain, or if the DNS server it finds does not support dynamic updates or is not configured to accept dynamic updates, the wizard asks you whether you want the wizard to automatically install and configure a local DNS server.

2. If you answer yes, the Active Directory Installation wizard performs the following tasks to install and configure DNS:

   a. Installs the DNS Server service.

   b. Creates a forward lookup zone with the same name as the Active Directory domain you are creating.

   c. Configures the forward lookup zone as an Active Directory integrated zone.

   d. Enables secure dynamic updates on the forward lookup zone.

Note that the Active Directory Installation wizard does not create a reverse lookup zone. If you want a reverse lookup zone, you will need to create one after you complete the Active Directory installation.

Lab A: Installing and Configuring DNS to Support Active Directory

Objectives

After completing this lab, you will be able to:

- Install the DNS Server service.
- Create forward and reverse lookup zones.
- Enable dynamic update.
- Test DNS by using the **nslookup** command.

Prerequisites

Before working on this lab, you must have familiarity with DNS concepts and operations.

Lab Setup

To complete this lab, you need the following:

- A computer running Microsoft Windows 2000 Advanced Server that is configured as a standalone server.

- A static IP address and subnet mask.

- A DNS domain name, a name for the forward lookup zone, and a name for the reverse lookup zone. Refer to the table on the next page for this information.

Important The lab does not reflect the real-world environment. It is recommended that you always use complex passwords for any administrator accounts, and never create accounts without a password.

Important Outside of the classroom environment, it is strongly advised that you use the most recent software updates that are necessary. Because this is a classroom environment, we may use software that does not include the latest updates.

Forward and Reverse Lookup Zone Information

During this lab, you will be asked to enter a name for the primary DNS suffix and the forward lookup zone, and a network ID for the reverse lookup zone. Use the information from the following table to determine what to enter for these values based on the computer that you are using. Your instructor will provide the number to use in place of the x in the network ID value.

Computer Name	Network ID	DNS Domain Name	Forward Lookup Zone Name (DNS Primary Suffix)
Vancouver	192.168.x	vancouverdom	vancouverdom.nwtraders.msft
Denver	192.168.x	denverdom	denverdom.nwtraders.msft
Perth	192.168.x	perthdom	perthdom.nwtraders.msft
Brisbane	192.168.x	brisbanedom	brisbanedom.nwtraders.msft
Lisbon	192.168.x	lisbondom	lisbondom.nwtraders.msft
Bonn	192.168.x	bonndom	bonndom.nwtraders.msft
Lima	192.168.x	limadom	limadom.nwtraders.msft
Santiago	192.168.x	santiagodom	santiagodom.nwtraders.msft
Bangalore	192.168.x	bangaloredom	bangaloredom.nwtraders.msft
Singapore	192.168.x	singaporedom	singaporedom.nwtraders.msft
Casablanca	192.168.x	casablancadom	casablancadom.nwtraders.msft
Tunis	192.168.x	tunisdom	tunisdom.nwtraders.msft
Acapulco	192.168.x	acapulcodom	acapulcodom.nwtraders.msft
Miami	192.168.x	miamidom	miamidom.nwtraders.msft
Auckland	192.168.x	aucklanddom	aucklanddom.nwtraders.msft
Suva	192.168.x	suvadom	suvadom.nwtraders.msft
Stockholm	192.168.x	stockholmdom	stockholmdom.nwtraders.msft
Moscow	192.168.x	moscowdom	moscowdom.nwtraders.msft
Caracas	192.168.x	caracasdom	caracasdom.nwtraders.msft
Montevideo	192.168.x	montevideodom	montevideodom.nwtraders.msft
Manila	192.168.x	maniladom	maniladom.nwtraders.msft
Tokyo	192.168.x	tokyodom	tokyodom.nwtraders.msft
Khartoum	192.168.x	khartoumdom	khartoumdom.nwtraders.msft
Nairobi	192.168.x	nairobidom	nairobidom.nwtraders.msft

Estimated time to complete this lab: 30 minutes

Exercise 1
Installing the DNS Server Service

Scenario

You have determined that to successfully deploy Active Directory, you first need to deploy a DNS infrastructure to support Active Directory.

Goal

In this exercise, you will configure the DNS domain name of your computer and install DNS.

Tasks	Detailed Steps
1. Configure the DNS suffix for your computer. When prompted, restart the computer. • Domain Suffix: *domain*.nwtraders.msft (where *domain* is your assigned domain name)	a. Log on as Administrator with a password of **password**. b. Open the **Properties** dialog box for My Computer. c. In the **System Properties** dialog box, on the **Network Identification** tab, click **Properties**. d. In the **Identification Changes** dialog box, click **More**. e. In the **DNS Suffix and NetBIOS Computer Name** dialog box, in the **Primary DNS suffix of this computer** box, type *domain*.**nwtraders.msft** (where *domain* is your assigned domain name), and then click **OK**. f. Click **OK** to close the **Identification Changes** dialog box, and then click **OK** to close the **Network Identification** message box. g. Click **OK** to close the **System Properties** dialog box, and then click **Yes** in the **System Settings Change** message box to restart your computer.
2. Start the Windows Components wizard, and install the Domain Name System (DNS) subcomponent of Networking Services. Copy the required files from the Windows 2000 Advanced Server compact disc.	a. Log on as Administrator with a password of **password**. b. In Control Panel, double-click **Add/Remove Programs**, and then click **Add/Remove Windows Components**. c. On the **Windows Components** page, under **Components**, click **Networking Services**, and then click **Details**. d. Under **Networking Services**, verify that all check boxes are cleared, select the **Domain Name System (DNS)** check box, and then click **OK**. e. In the Windows Components wizard, click **Next**. f. If prompted, insert the compact disc labeled Windows 2000 Advanced Server, and then click **OK**. g. After the required files have been copied, click **Finish**, and then close all windows.

Exercise 2
Creating Forward and Reverse Lookup Zones

Scenario
After installing DNS, you must configure a forward lookup zone to resolve host names to IP addresses and a reverse lookup zone to resolve IP addresses to host names.

Goal
In this exercise, you will configure a forward lookup zone for your domain and a reverse lookup zone for your network ID.

Tasks	Detailed Steps
1. Add a standard primary forward lookup zone for *domain*.nwtraders.msft.	a. Click **Start**, point to **Programs**, point to **Administrative Tools**, and then click **DNS**. b. In the console tree, right-click *computer* (where *computer* is your computer name), and then click **Configure the server**. c. On the **Welcome to the Configure DNS Server Wizard** page, click **Next**. d. On the **Forward Lookup Zone** page, ensure that **Yes, create a forward lookup zone** is selected, and then click **Next**. e. On the **Zone Type** page, ensure that **Standard primary** is selected, and then click **Next**. f. On the **Zone Name** page, in the **Name** box, type *domain*.**nwtraders.msft** (where *domain* is your assigned domain name) and then click **Next**. g. On the **Zone File** page, ensure that **Create a new file with this file name** is selected, and then click **Next**.
2. Add a standard primary reverse lookup zone for your network ID.	a. On the **Reverse Lookup Zone** page, ensure that **Yes, create a reverse lookup zone** is selected, and then click **Next**. b. On the **Zone Type** page, click **Standard primary**, and then click **Next**. c. On the **Reverse Lookup Zone** page, verify that **Network ID** is selected. For the network ID, type the first three octets of the IP address of your computer, and then click **Next**. (For example, for an IP address of 192.168.1.1, type **192.168.1**) d. On the **Zone File** page, ensure that **Create a new file with this file name** is selected, and then click **Next**. e. On the **Completing the Configure DNS Server Wizard** page, click **Finish**. f. Leave DNS open.

Tasks	Detailed Steps
3. Configure the **Internet Protocol (TCP/IP)** properties of your Local Area Connection to use your computer for DNS.	a. Right-click **My Network Places**, and then click **Properties**. b. Right-click **Local Area Connection**, and then click **Properties**. c. Click **Internet Protocol (TCP/IP)**, and then click **Properties**. d. In the **Preferred DNS Server** box, type your assigned IP address, and then click **OK**. e. Click **OK** to close the **Local Area Connections Properties** box, and then close the Network and Dial-up Connections window.

Exercise 3
Configuring DNS to Support Dynamic Update

Scenario

After installing DNS and creating forward and reverse lookup zones, you must now configure DNS to support dynamic updates before you deploy Active Directory.

Goal

In this exercise, you will configure the forward and reverse lookup zones to support dynamic update.

Tasks	Detailed Steps
1. Configure the forward lookup zone for *domain*.nwtraders.msft to support dynamic update.	a. In the console tree of DNS, expand *computer* (where *computer* is your assigned computer name). b. In the console tree, expand **Forward Lookup Zone**, and then click *domain*.**nwtraders.msft**. c. Right-click *domain*.**nwtraders.msft**, and then click **Properties**. d. In the *domain*.**nwtraders.msft Properties** box, in the **Allow dynamic updates** list, click **Yes**, and then click **OK**.
2. Configure the reverse lookup zone for your subnet to support dynamic update.	a. In the console tree, expand **Reverse Lookup Zone**, and then click **192.168.*y*.x Subnet** (where *y* is your assigned classroom number). b. Right-click **192.168.*y*.x Subnet**, and then click **Properties**. c. In the **192.168.*y*.x Subnet Properties** box, in the **Allow dynamic updates** list, click **Yes**, and then click **OK**. d. Leave DNS open.
3. Use the **ipconfig** command to re-register your computer's DNS records.	a. Open a command prompt. b. At the command prompt, type **ipconfig /registerdns** and then press ENTER. c. Close the command prompt.
4. Refresh DNS to display the pointer resource record in the reverse lookup zone.	a. Switch to the DNS window. b. On the **Action** menu, click **Refresh**. *Notice that a new pointer resource record appears in the* **192.168.*y*.x Subnet** *reverse lookup zone.* c. Close all open windows.

Exercise 4
Using Nslookup to Test DNS

Scenario

After installing DNS, creating forward and reverse lookup zones, and configuring the zones to allow dynamic updates, you have decided to test DNS prior to installing Active Directory to ensure that it is functioning properly.

Goal

In this exercise, you will use the **nslookup** command to confirm that DNS is properly installed and configured.

Tasks	Detailed Steps
1. Confirm that DNS can resolve a host name to an IP address.	a. Open a command prompt. b. At the command prompt, type **nslookup** *computer.domain*.**nwtraders.msft** (where *computer* is your assigned computer name and *domain* is your assigned domain name), and then press ENTER. *The DNS server responds with its name and IP address, followed by the name and IP address of the computer name provided on the command line.* c. Leave the command prompt open.
2. Confirm that DNS can resolve an IP address to a host name.	a. At the command prompt, type **nslookup** *ip_address* (where *ip_address* is your assigned IP address), and then press ENTER. *The DNS server responds with its name and IP address, followed by the name and IP address for the IP address provided on the command line.* b. Close all open windows, and then log off.

Best Practices

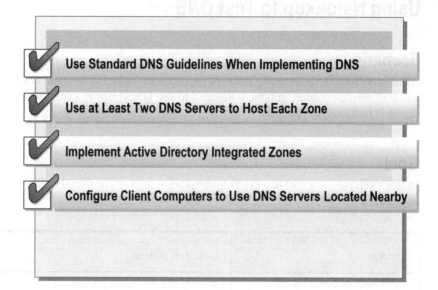

Consider the following best practices for implementing DNS to support Active Directory:

- Use standard DNS guidelines and preferred practices when planning and implementing your DNS infrastructure.

- Make sure that at least two DNS servers host each zone. They can host either primary and secondary copies of the zone, or two directory-integrated copies of each zone. This provides fault tolerance in case one of your DNS servers is not available.

- Implement Active Directory integrated zones. Active Directory integrated zones ensure that the domain controllers for each of your Active Directory domains correspond in a direct one-to-one mapping to DNS servers. When you troubleshoot DNS and Active Directory replication problems, the same server computers are used in both topologies, which simplifies planning, deployment, and troubleshooting.

  If you do not use Active Directory integrated zones, be sure to correctly configure your clients and understand that a standard primary zone becomes a single point of failure for dynamic updates and for zone replication.

- Configure client computers to use domain controllers located near the client computer as the preferred and alternate DNS servers. When you configure a list of preferred and alternate DNS servers for each client, you can specify servers corresponding to domain controllers located near each client computer.

Note For more information about planning your DNS infrastructure to support Active Directory, see Module 2, "Designing an Active Directory Naming Strategy" in Course 1561B, *Designing a Microsoft® Windows® 2000 Directory Services Infrastructure.*

Review

■ **Introduction to the Role of DNS in Active Directory**

■ **DNS and Active Directory**

■ **DNS Name Resolution in Active Directory**

■ **Active Directory Integrated Zones**

■ **Installing and Configuring DNS to Support Active Directory**

■ **Best Practices**

1. What functions does DNS provide in an Active Directory network?

2. What are the differences between the DNS namespace and the Active Directory namespace?

3. What are SRV resource records used for in an Active Directory domain?

4. What are the main benefits provided by Active Directory integrated zones?

5. What are the requirements that a DNS implementation needs to meet to support Active Directory?

Microsoft®
Training & Certification

Module 3: Creating a Windows 2000 Domain

Contents

Overview

- **Introduction to Creating a Windows 2000 Domain**
- **Installing Active Directory**
- **The Active Directory Installation Process**
- **Examining the Default Structure of Active Directory**
- **Performing Post Active Directory Installation Tasks**
- **Troubleshooting the Installation of Active Directory**
- **Removing Active Directory**
- **Best Practices**

After installing Microsoft® Windows® 2000, you can configure a computer running Windows 2000 Advanced Server to function as a domain controller in a Windows 2000 domain. By implementing a domain structure in the Windows 2000 Active Directory® directory service, you create an administrative structure for your network. To implement a domain structure, you need to create a domain, create organizational units (OUs) within the domain, and then create user, group, and resource objects within the OUs.

When you create a domain, you must identify the DNS name of the new domain, and the location for files that are created during the installation process. Windows 2000 uses the Active Directory Installation wizard to create new domain controllers.

At the end of this module, you will be able to:

- Identify the purpose of creating a Windows 2000 domain.
- Create a Windows 2000 domain by installing Active Directory.
- Describe the process for installing Active Directory.
- Examine the default structure of Active Directory.
- Perform post Active Directory installation tasks.
- Troubleshoot common problems that may occur when installing Active Directory.
- Remove Active Directory by using the Active Directory Installation wizard.
- Apply best practices for creating a Windows 2000 domain.

Introduction to Creating a Windows 2000 Domain

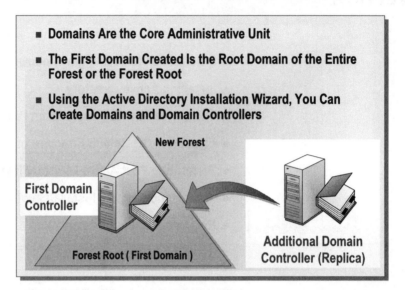

A *domain* is the core administrative unit in a Windows 2000 network. In Windows 2000, domains are used to define how information and resources are organized and stored.

The first domain created in Active Directory is the root domain of the entire forest. This domain is also called the *forest root*. When you install Active Directory for the first time in a Windows 2000 network, you create the first domain controller in a new forest, thus establishing the root domain.

The Active Directory Installation wizard guides you through the process of installing Active Directory, to build domain controllers and create Windows 2000 domains. You can promote any stand-alone or member server to a domain controller. When you promote a server to a domain controller, you can create:

- A new forest, including the root domain (first domain in the forest) and the first domain controller.

- An additional domain controller in an existing Windows 2000 domain.

Note Using the Active Directory Installation wizard, you can also create a new child domain in an existing tree, and a new tree in an existing forest. For more information about creating a child domain and creating a new tree in an existing forest, see Module 10, "Creating and Managing Trees and Forests," in Course 2154, *Implementing and Administering Microsoft Windows 2000 Directory Services*.

◆ Installing Active Directory

- Preparing to Install Active Directory

- Creating the First Domain

- Adding a Replica Domain Controller

- Using an Unattended Setup Script to Install Active Directory

When you use the Active Directory Installation wizard to install Active Directory, you must first ensure that all of the requirements necessary for installing Active Directory are met. Then you specify the placement of a domain controller within the Active Directory structure. When installing Active Directory, you also specify detailed information, such as the domain name and the location of files that are created during the installation process.

You can also run an unattended session of the Active Directory Installation wizard by using answer files. An unattended session of the Active Directory installation is helpful during disaster recovery and when installing Active Directory in branch offices where there is no technical support available.

Preparing to Install Active Directory

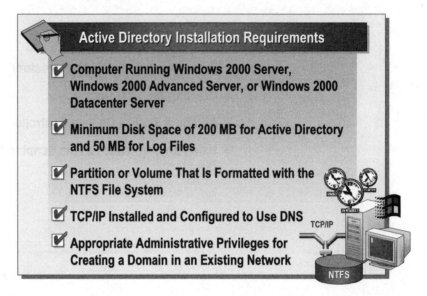

Before you install Active Directory, you must ensure that the computer that will be configured as a domain controller meets certain requirements.

The following list identifies the requirements for Active Directory installation:

- A computer running Windows 2000 Server, Windows 2000 Advanced Server, or Windows 2000 Datacenter Server.

- A minimum of 200 megabytes (MB) of disk space for the Active Directory database and an additional 50 MB for the Active Directory database transaction log files. File size requirements for the Active Directory database and log files depend on the number and type of objects in the domain. Additional disk space is also required if the domain controller is also a global catalog server.

- A partition or volume that is formatted with the NTFS file system. This is required for the SYSVOL folder.

- Transmission Control Protocol/Internet Protocol (TCP/IP) installed and configured to use Domain Name System (DNS).

- The necessary administrative privileges for creating a domain if you are creating a domain in an existing Windows 2000 network.

Note   The Active Directory Installation wizard offers the option to install the DNS Server service when you install Active Directory. A DNS server supports SRV (service) resource records and the DNS dynamic update protocol.

Creating the First Domain

- **Start the Active Directory Installation Wizard**
- **Select the Domain Controller and Domain Type**
- **Specify the Required Information**
  - Domain, DNS, and NetBIOS names
  - Database, log, and shared system volume locations
  - Select to weaken permissions
  - Specify a password to use in Directory Services Restore Mode
- **The Active Directory Installation Wizard:**
  - Installs Active Directory
  - Converts the computer to a domain controller

When you install Active Directory for the first time in a network, you create the forest root domain. The Active Directory Installation wizard directs you to specify required information for the new domain controller. The information that you must provide when you install Active Directory varies according to the options that you select.

To create the root domain, perform the following steps:

1. In the **Run** box, type **dcpromo.exe** and then press ENTER.

2. In the Active Directory Installation wizard, complete the installation by using the information in the following table.

On this wizard page	Do this
Domain Controller Type	Click **Domain controller for a new domain**.
Create Tree or Child Domain	Click **Create a new domain tree**.
Create or Join Forest	Click **Create a new forest of domain trees**.
New Domain Name	Specify the DNS name for the new domain. If your network requires a presence on the Internet, verify that you have a registered Internet domain name, and then use this domain name as the name of the forest root.
Domain NetBIOS Name	Confirm or specify the NetBIOS name for the new domain. The NetBIOS name is used to identify the domain to client computers running earlier versions of Windows and Microsoft Windows NT®.

(continued)

On this wizard page	Do this
Database and Log Locations	Specify locations for the Active Directory database and log files. The database stores the directory for the new domain, and the log file temporarily stores changes to the database. The default location for the database and log files is *systemroot*\Ntds. For best performance, place the database and log files on separate hard disks. Installing the database and log files on separate hard disks ensures that reads and writes to the database and log files are not competing for input and output resources.
Shared System Volume	Specify the location for the shared system volume. The shared system volume is a folder structure that is hosted on all Windows 2000 domain controllers. The shared system volume stores files, such as logon, logoff, startup and shutdown scripts, and Group Policy information, which are replicated among domain controllers. You must specify a partition or volume that is formatted with the NTFS file system.
Permissions	Specify whether to assign the default permissions on user and group objects that are compatible with servers running earlier versions of Windows and Windows NT, or only with servers running Windows 2000. Assigning servers running earlier versions of Windows and Windows NT permissions adds the Everyone group to the Pre-Windows 2000 Compatible Access group. This group has read-only access to user and group object attributes that existed in Windows NT 4.0.
Directory Services Restore Mode Administrator Password	Specify a password to use when starting the computer in Directory Services Restore Mode. Windows 2000 domain controllers maintain a small version of the Windows NT 4.0 account database. The only account in this database is the Administrator account and this account is required for authentication when starting the computer in Directory Services Restore mode, as the Active Directory directory service is not started in this mode.

After you finish specifying the installation information, the Active Directory Installation wizard installs Active Directory, and converts the computer to a domain controller.

Adding a Replica Domain Controller

- **Fault Tolerance Requires a Minimum of Two Domain Controllers in a Single Domain**

- **More Than One Domain Controller in a Domain Also Ensures That a Single Domain Controller Is Not Overloaded**

- **Run Dcpromo to Add a Domain Controller to an Existing Domain**

- **The Active Directory Installation Wizard:**
  - Converts the computer to a domain controller
  - Replicates Active Directory from an existing domain controller

To enable fault tolerance in the event that a domain controller goes offline unexpectedly, you must have a minimum of two domain controllers in a single domain. Because all domain controllers in a domain replicate their domain-specific data to one another, installing multiple domain controllers in the domain automatically enables fault tolerance for the data stored in Active Directory. If a domain controller fails, the remaining domain controllers will provide authentication services and access to objects in Active Directory, allowing the domain to operate as usual.

When a new domain controller is added to a domain, replication occurs to ensure consistency in Active Directory. In addition, having more than one domain controller in a domain helps to ensure that a single domain controller is not overloaded when servicing logon requests, global catalog queries, and other services provided by domain controllers.

To add a domain controller to an existing domain, perform the following steps:

1. In the **Run** box, type **dcpromo.exe** and then press ENTER.

2. In the Active Directory Installation wizard, complete the installation by using the information in the following table.

On this wizard page	Do this
Domain Controller Type	Click **Additional domain controller for an existing domain**.
Network Credentials	Specify the user name, password, and domain name of a user account that has the privileges to create domain controllers in Active Directory.
Additional Domain Controller	Specify the DNS name of the existing domain for which this computer will become an additional domain controller.

The remaining options in the Active Directory Installation wizard are identical to the options used for creating the first domain. After you finish specifying the installation information, the Active Directory Installation wizard converts the computer to a domain controller, and replicates Active Directory from an existing domain controller.

Using an Unattended Setup Script to Install Active Directory

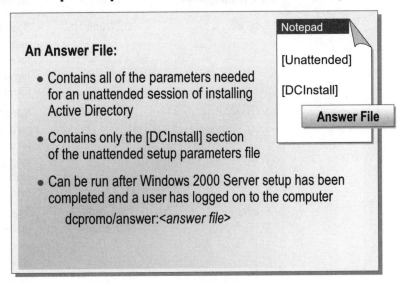

An Answer File:

- Contains all of the parameters needed for an unattended session of installing Active Directory

- Contains only the [DCInstall] section of the unattended setup parameters file

- Can be run after Windows 2000 Server setup has been completed and a user has logged on to the computer

  dcpromo/answer:*<answer file>*

Notepad

[Unattended]

[DCInstall]

Answer File

You can also install Active Directory by using an *answer file*. Administrators use answer files to specify all of the parameters for the Active Directory installation. These parameters include the domain type and the configuration of the domain being created. The answer file can then be used by anyone who does not know how to install Active Directory. The user using the answer file still needs the required administrative privileges to successfully complete the installation.

An answer file for the Active Directory Installation wizard contains only one section, [DCInstall]. Each operation in the wizard requires values for specific parameters in the [DCInstall] section of the unattend file. Default values are used if a value for a parameter is not specified. The following table describes the entries in the [DCInstall] section that enable you to automatically install Active Directory on the first domain controller in a new forest.

[DCInstall] Keys	Value	Description
RebootOnSuccess	Yes	Specifies whether the computer should be rebooted upon successful completion.
DatabasePath	C:\Winnt\Ntds	Specifies the fully qualified, non-universal naming convention (UNC) path to a folder on a fixed disk of the local computer that contains the domain database. The folder must be empty. Creates the folder if it does not exist.

(continued)

[DCInstall] Keys	Value	Description
LogPath	C:\Winnt\Ntds	Specifies the fully qualified, non-UNC path to a folder on a fixed disk of the local computer that contains the domain log files. The folder must be empty. Creates the folder if it does not exist.
SYSVOLPath	C:\Winnt\Sysvol	Specifies the fully qualified, non-UNC path to a folder on a fixed disk of the local computer. The folder must be empty. Creates the folder if it does not exist. The SYSVOL folder must be installed on an NTFS partition.
SiteName	Default-First-Site-Name	Specifies the name of an existing site to place the new domain controller. If not specified, a suitable site is selected. This option applies only when creating a new domain tree in a new forest of domains.
ReplicaOrNewDomain	Domain	Specifies that a new domain controller should be installed as the first domain controller in a new directory service domain. If you set the value to Domain, you must also specify a valid value in the TreeOrChild parameter.
TreeOrChild	Tree	Specifies that the new domain is the root of a new tree. If you set the value to Tree, you must also specify a valid value in the CreateOrJoin parameter.
CreateOrJoin	Create	Specifies the creation of a new forest of domains.
DomainNetbiosName	contoso	Assigns a NetBIOS name to the new domain. This is a required value, and the name specified must be unique in the domain.
NewDomainDNSName	contoso.msft	Specifies the required name when a new forest of domains is being installed.
DNSOnNetwork	No	Specifies that a new forest of domains is being installed and no DNS client is configured on the computer. Setting the value to No skips the DNS client configuration and creates the DNS auto-configuration for the new domain.
AutoConfigDNS	Yes	Specifies that the wizard should configure DNS for the new domain if it has detected that dynamic DNS updates are not available.

The answer file can be run after Windows 2000 Advanced Server Setup has been completed and a user has logged on to the computer. To start the unattended installation of Active Directory, open the command prompt window and type the following:

Dcpromo.exe /answer:*answer file*

Where *answer file* is name of the answer file.

Note For more information about unattended installations, see *unattend.doc* in the Deploy.cab file located in the \Support\Tools on the Windows 2000 Advanced Server compact disc.

Lab A: Creating a Windows 2000 Domain

Objectives

After completing this lab, you will be able to install Active Directory by using the Active Directory Installation wizard.

Prerequisites

Before working on this lab, you must have:

- An understanding of the logical components of Active Directory, including domains, trees, and forests.

- An understanding of the purpose and function of domain controllers.

Lab Setup

To complete this lab, you need the following:

- A computer running Windows 2000 Advanced Server that is configured as a standalone server.

- Drive C formatted with NTFS.

- A static IP address.

- A DNS server configured for your domain.

- A domain name. Your domain name is *domain*.nwtraders.msft, where *domain* is your computer name with dom appended. For example, if your computer name is Vancouver, then *domain* would be vancouverdom and your full domain name would be vancouverdom.nwtraders.msft.

- A forward lookup zone that matches your domain name. The forward lookup zone should have been created in Lab A of Module 2, "Implementing DNS to Support Active Directory," in Course 2154, *Implementing and Administering Microsoft Windows 2000 Directory Services*.

Important   The lab does not reflect the real-world environment. It is recommended that you always use complex passwords for any administrator accounts, and never create accounts without a password.

Important   Outside of the classroom environment, it is strongly advised that you use the most recent software updates that are necessary. Because this is a classroom environment, we may use software that does not include the latest updates.

Estimated time to complete this lab: 30 minutes

Exercise 1
Installing Active Directory

Scenario

Northwind Traders has decided to install Windows 2000 and use Active Directory to use all of the features and benefits that Active Directory provides. You have been assigned the task of creating the first domain on the network. You have already created a forward lookup zone in DNS. The name of the forward lookup zone is the same name that you will be using for the Active Directory domain name.

Goal

In this exercise, you will create a Windows 2000 domain by installing Active Directory.

Tasks	Detailed Steps
1. Start the Active Directory Installation wizard to create: • A new domain controller for a new domain. • A new domain tree. • A new forest of domain trees.	**a.** Log on as Administrator with a password of **password**. **b.** Click **Start**, and then click **Run**. **c.** In the **Run** box, type **dcpromo** and then click **OK**. **d.** On the **Welcome to the Active Directory Installation Wizard** page, click **Next**. **e.** On the **Domain Controller Type** page, ensure that **Domain controller for a new domain** is selected, and then click **Next**. **f.** On the **Create Tree or Child Domain** page, ensure that **Create a new domain tree** is selected, and then click **Next**. **g.** On the **Create or Join Forest** page, ensure that **Create a new forest of domain trees** is selected, and then click **Next**.
2. Complete the Active Directory installation process, providing the following information: • Full DNS name of *domain*.**nwtraders.msft** (where *domain* is your assigned domain name). • NetBIOS domain name of *DOMAIN* (where *DOMAIN* is your assigned domain name). • Default locations for the database, log files, and shared system volume.	**a.** On the **New Domain Name** page, in the **Full DNS name for new domain** text box, type *domain*.**nwtraders.msft** (where *domain* is your assigned domain name), and then click **Next**. **b.** On the **NetBIOS Domain Name** page, ensure that *DOMAIN* (where *DOMAIN* is your assigned domain name) appears, and then click **Next**. **c.** On the **Database and Log Locations** page, accept the default locations by clicking **Next**. **d.** On the **Shared System Volume** page, accept the default location by clicking **Next**. **e.** On the **Permissions** page, select **Permissions compatible only with Windows 2000 servers**, and then click **Next**. **f.** On the **Directory Services Restore Mode Administrator Password** page, in the **Password** and **Confirm password** boxes, type **password** and then click **Next**.

Tasks	Detailed Steps
2. *(continued)* • Permissions compatible with only servers running Windows 2000. • A password of **password** for the Directory Services Restore Mode Administrator password.	g. On the **Summary** page, review the options you selected, and then click **Next**. *The Active Directory installation process begins.* h. When the **Completing the Active Directory Installation Wizard** page appears, click **Finish**, and then restart your computer.

◆ The Active Directory Installation Process

- **Configuration Parameters**

- **Site Configuration**

- **Directory Service Configuration**

- **Services and Security Configuration**

- **Additional Active Directory Installation Operations**

When installing Active Directory, the Active Directory Installation wizard confirms several configuration and security parameters. Active Directory validates the parameters you specify during the installation process. The type of validation performed depends on whether the domain controller being installed is the first in the forest, or the first domain in the replica. The purpose of this verification is to validate the parameters that you specify during the Active Directory installation process.

Configuration Parameters

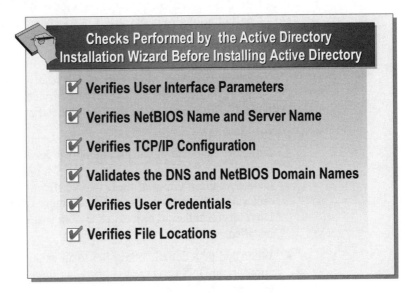

Checks Performed by the Active Directory
Installation Wizard Before Installing Active Directory

☑ **Verifies User Interface Parameters**

☑ **Verifies NetBIOS Name and Server Name**

☑ **Verifies TCP/IP Configuration**

☑ **Validates the DNS and NetBIOS Domain Names**

☑ **Verifies User Credentials**

☑ **Verifies File Locations**

The Active Directory Installation wizard performs several verifications before
the actual installation of Active Directory. These verifications are required to
ensure the integrity of the installation process.

User Interface Verification

Before the user interface is actually displayed, the Active Directory Installation
wizard verifies the following:

- The user currently logged on is a member of the local Administrators group.

- The computer is running Windows 2000 Server or Advanced Server.

- A previous installation or removal of Active Directory has not taken place
  without restarting the computer.

- An installation or removal of Active Directory is not currently in progress.

If any of these four verifications fail, an error message is displayed and you exit
the wizard. After these verifications are completed successfully, the Active
Directory Installation wizard performs the remaining verifications.

Naming Verification

Each domain controller has a server object in the Site container. When adding a
new domain controller to an existing domain, a verification is made to ensure
that the server name does not exist in the Servers container in any site or in the
Servers container in the site to which the domain controller is being added. If
the server name does exist, the wizard deletes the existing object and assumes
that a reinstallation is being performed.

TCP/IP Configuration Verification

If TCP/IP is not installed, or if it is installed and configured to use the Dynamic Host Configuration Protocol (DHCP) service and a DHCP-assigned address is not available, the installation is interrupted and you are prompted to correct the problem.

The wizard also verifies the server's DNS resolver configuration. Active Directory uses DNS to locate servers and services, so a properly configured DNS resolver is critical to the successful installation of Active Directory.

- When installing the first domain controller in a new domain, the Active Directory Installation wizard attempts to locate a DNS server that supports the dynamic update protocol and a DNS server that is authoritative for the DNS domain. If either of these two verifications fail, the user is prompted to either have the wizard install and configure DNS locally during the Active Directory installation process or to do it manually after Active Directory is installed.

- When adding a domain controller to an existing domain, the existence of an appropriate DNS server is assumed and there is no attempt to verify the DNS server.

DNS and NetBIOS Domain Names Validation

When creating a domain, you must provide a DNS name for the domain. The wizard verifies that the new domain name provided is unique in the forest. If the name is not unique, you are prompted to correct the information.

You must also provide a NetBIOS domain name. The NetBIOS domain name is generated from the DNS domain name. The NetBIOS name is formed by taking up to the first 15 characters of the leftmost label in the DNS domain name. The wizard verifies that the NetBIOS domain name is unique, and if it is not, the user is prompted to change the name.

User Credentials Verification

Because creating a new domain controller is a security-sensitive task, the wizard verifies that the user attempting to install Active Directory has the correct security permissions. If the credentials of the currently logged on user do not match these requirements, the user is prompted for an account with sufficient privileges. The following list describes the types of installations that can be performed, and the security permissions required for each installation:

- If a new forest is being created, no verification is performed, and no specific credentials are required.

- If a replica domain controller is being added to an existing domain, the supplied credentials must be sufficient to join the computer to the existing domain. Members of the Domain Admins group in the domain that you are installing the domain controller and members of the Enterprise Admins group are by default assigned the necessary permissions to create new domain controllers.

Note   The Active Directory Installation wizard requests credentials in the form of a user name, password, and domain. Therefore, a user principal name entered as *userName@domainName* is not accepted.

File Locations Verification

The locations for the Active Directory database file, log files, and the SYSVOL folder are specified during the Active Directory installation. The contents of SYSVOL are replicated to all domain controllers in the domain. Creation of SYSVOL requires a volume formatted with NTFS. If an NTFS-formatted volume cannot be found, or if there is not sufficient free disk space, the installation cannot proceed.

Note For more information about Servers container in a site, see Module 11, "Managing Active Directory Replication," in Course 2154, *Implementing and Administering Microsoft Windows 2000 Directory Services*.

Site Configuration

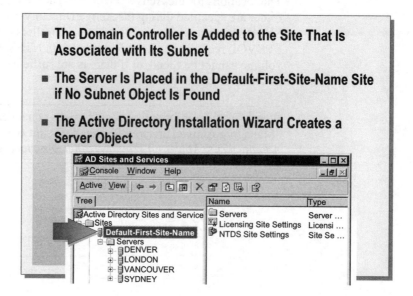

- **The Domain Controller Is Added to the Site That Is Associated with Its Subnet**

- **The Server Is Placed in the Default-First-Site-Name Site if No Subnet Object Is Found**

- **The Active Directory Installation Wizard Creates a Server Object**

The Active Directory Installation wizard queries Active Directory for site data. If the Internet Protocol (IP) address of the server being promoted to a domain controller is within the range for a given subnet defined in the Active Directory, the wizard configures the membership of the domain controller in the site associated with that subnet.

If no subnet objects are defined or if the IP address of the server is not within the range of the subnet objects present in Active Directory, the server is placed in the *Default-First-Site-Name* site. Default-First-Site-Name is the first site that is set up automatically when you create the first domain controller in a forest.

The Active Directory Installation wizard creates a *server object* for the domain controller in the appropriate site. The server object contains information required for replication. The server object contains a reference to the computer object in the Domain Controllers OU that represents the domain controller being created.

Note   If a server object for this domain controller already exists, it is deleted and then recreated, because the wizard assumes that you are performing a reinstallation of Active Directory. For more information about subnet objects and server objects, see Module 11, "Managing Active Directory Replication," in Course 2154, *Implementing and Administering Microsoft Windows 2000 Directory Services*.

Directory Service Configuration

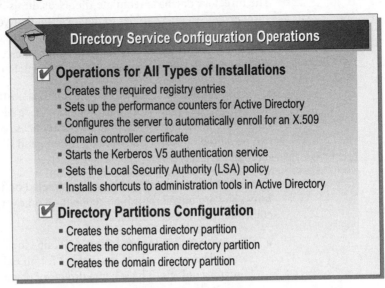

After the Active Directory Installation wizard completes all of the required verifications, a confirmation page is displayed, which lists the choices that you made in the wizard. When you accept the settings, the wizard begins the actual Active Directory installation process.

Common Active Directory Operations for All Installations

The Active Directory Installation wizard performs the following operations for all types of domain controller installations:

- Creates the required registry entries.

- Sets up the performance counters for Active Directory.

- Configures the server to automatically enroll for an X.509 domain controller certificate from the first Certificate Authority that will process the request. This certificate is required for Simple Mail Transfer Protocol (SMTP)-based replication.

- Starts the Kerberos version 5 authentication protocol.

- Sets the Local Security Authority (LSA) policy to indicate that this server is a domain controller.

- Installs shortcuts to the administration tools for Active Directory.

Directory Partitions Configuration

The directory database template file, Ntds.dit, is copied from its location in the *systemroot*\System32 folder to the location that you specify when running the Active Directory Installation wizard. The wizard configures the local server to host the directory service. This process includes creating the directory partitions and the default domain security principals, such as the Domain Admins group.

In Active Directory, a directory partition is a portion of the directory namespace. Each directory partition contains a hierarchy, or subtree of directory objects in the directory tree. Copies, or replicas, of the same directory partition can be stored on many domain controllers, and the copies are updated through directory replication.

The following directory partitions are created on the first domain controller in a forest and are updated through replication on every subsequent domain controller that is created in the forest:

- The schema directory partition. Contains the Schema container, which stores class and attribute definitions for all existing and possible Active Directory objects. The schema directory partition is replicated to all domain controllers in a forest.

- The configuration directory partition. Contains the Configuration container, which stores configuration objects for the entire forest. Configuration objects store information about sites, services, and directory partitions. The configuration directory partition is replicated to all domain controllers in a forest.

- The domain directory partition. Contains a domain container, such as the contoso.msft container, which stores users, computers, groups, and other objects for a specific Windows 2000 domain. The domain directory partition is replicated to all domain controllers within a single domain.

Services and Security Configuration

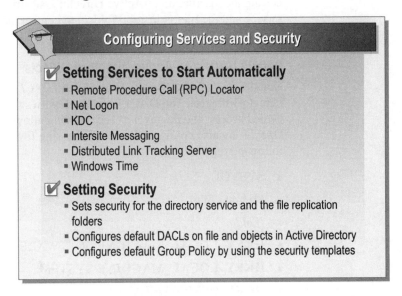

During the Active Directory installation, services are configured to start automatically, and security is enabled on the directory service.

Setting Services to Start Automatically

The following services are configured to start automatically:

- *Remote Procedure Call (RPC) Locator.* This service allows distributed applications to use the RPC name service. The RPC Locator service manages the RPC name service database.

- *Net Logon.* This service runs the Domain Controller Locator service. The Net Logon service is also responsible for creating a secure channel between client computers and domain controllers during logon, and for registering SRV resource records in DNS.

- *KDC (Key Distribution Center).* This service maintains a database with account information for all security principals in its *realm*, which is the Kerberos V5 authentication protocol equivalent of a Windows 2000 domain.

- *Intersite Messaging (ISM).* This service is used for mail-based replication between sites.

- *Distributed Link Tracking Server.* This service helps resolve shortcuts and OLE links to NTFS-resident files that have had their names changed, paths changed, or both.

- *Windows Time.* This service synchronizes clocks between client computers and servers that run Windows 2000.

Setting Security

During the installation of Active Directory, security is enabled on the directory service and the file replication folders to control the access to Active Directory objects.

Default DACLs on Active Directory Objects

Default *discretionary access control lists (DACLs)* are configured on Active Directory objects. The DACL is a list of entries that identify who is allowed or denied access, and the level of access being allowed or denied for an object. DACLs are also configured for the following file system objects and the following registry keys:

- SYSVOL
- Program Files
- *Windir*
- **HKEY_LOCAL_MACHINE**\SOFTWARE
- **HKEY_LOCAL_MACHINE**\SYSTEM
- **HKEY_USERS**\.DEFAULT

Default Group Policy Settings for Domain Controllers

For the first domain controller in a domain, default Group Policy is configured by using the security templates DCFirst.inf, DefltDC.inf, and DCUp.inf located in the *systemroot*\inf folder. When additional domain controllers are added to a domain, Group Policy is replicated from the first domain controller in a domain to all additional domain controllers.

Additional Active Directory Installation Operations

Additional Operations
• Sets the Computer DNS Root Domain Name
• Determines Whether the Server Computer Is a Member of the Domain
• Creates a Computer Account in the Domain Controllers OU
• Applies the User-Provided Password for the Administrator Account
• Creates a Cross-Reference Object in the Configuration Container
• Adds Shortcuts
• Creates the SYSVOL Folder
• Creates Schema and Configuration Containers
• Assigns the Specific Roles to the Domain Controller

Regardless of the type of domain being created, the Active Directory Installation wizard performs the following additional operations during the Active Directory installation.

- Sets the computer DNS root domain name to the name of the new domain.

- Determines whether the server computer is already a member of the domain. If the computer is a member of a domain, the wizard removes the computer account for the member server from the domain and the recreates the computer account in the Domain Controllers OU. If the computer is being promoted to a domain controller in a different domain, the user is notified that the computer account for the member server must be removed from the original domain.

- Creates a computer account in the Domain Controllers OU in the new domain. The computer account is also added to the Domain Controllers global group in the Users container. This computer account allows the computer to authenticate to other domain controllers when performing operations such as replication.

- Applies the user-provided password for the administrator account that is used to start the domain controller in Directory Services Restore Mode.

- Creates a cross-reference object in the Configuration container. This object is used by LDAP to locate resources in other domains.

- Adds two new shortcuts to Group Policy security settings.These shortcuts are Domain Security Policy and Domain Controller Security Policy.

- Creates the SYSVOL folder, which contains:
  - The SYSVOL shared folder. This shared folder contains Group Policy information.
  - The Net Logon shared folder. This shared folder is used to contain logon scripts for non-Windows 2000–based computers.
- Performs the following operations while creating the forest root domain:
  - The Schema and Configuration containers are created.
  - The Active Directory Installation wizard assigns the primary domain controller (PDC) emulator, relative identifier (RID) operations master, domain naming master, schema master, and infrastructure master roles to the domain controller.

Note For more information about the PDC emulator, RID operations master, domain naming master, schema master, and infrastructure master roles, see Module 12, "Managing Operations Masters," in Course 2154, *Implementing and Administering Microsoft Windows 2000 Directory Services*.

Examining the Default Structure of Active Directory

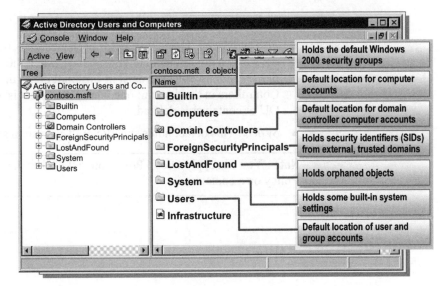

During the installation of Active Directory on the first domain controller in a new domain, several default objects are created. These objects include containers, users, computers, groups, and organizational units. You can view and manage these default objects by using the Active Directory Users and Computers administrative tool.

The following list describes the purpose of some of these default objects:

- *Builtin (container).* This object is used to hold the default built-in security groups.

- *Computers (container).* This object is the default location for computer accounts.

- *Domain Controllers (organizational unit).* This object is the default location for domain controller computer accounts.

- *ForeignSecurityPrincipals (container).* This object is used to hold security identifiers (SIDs) from external, trusted domains.

- *Users (container).* This object is the default location of user and group accounts.

You can view additional objects in Active Directory Users and Computers; to do so, on the **View** menu, click **Advanced Features**.

The following list describes the purpose of the additional objects:

- *LostAndFound*. This object holds orphaned objects. This object holds objects that are left behind, or orphaned, when their parent containers are deleted. For an object to exist in LostandFound, there must be two Domain Controllers in the domain: one where the object is added; and one where the OU or container is deleted.

- *System*. This object holds specific built-in system settings.

Note   You can apply Group Policy on an OU, but you cannot apply Group Policy on a container.

◆ Performing Post Active Directory Installation Tasks

- **Verifying the Active Directory Installation**
- **Implementing Active Directory Integrated Zones**
- **Securing Updates for Active Directory Integrated Zones**
- **Changing the Domain Mode**
- **Implementing an Organizational Unit Structure**

After you install Active Directory, it is important to verify that the necessary directory database files, SYSVOL files, and DNS SRV resource records have been created so that Active Directory works properly.

After you install Active Directory, you should also configure Active Directory integrated DNS zones so that DNS can use the functionality of Active Directory, such as replication, zone transfer, and secure dynamic updates.

If all of the domain controllers in a Windows 2000 network are running Windows 2000, you should change the domain mode from mixed mode to native mode. Only in the native mode can you add new groups within existing groups and add universal security groups.

After creating a domain, you should implement an OU structure to enhance administrative control and apply Group Policy. You can create an OU within a domain or another OU. After you create an OU, you can add objects to it.

Verifying the Active Directory Installation

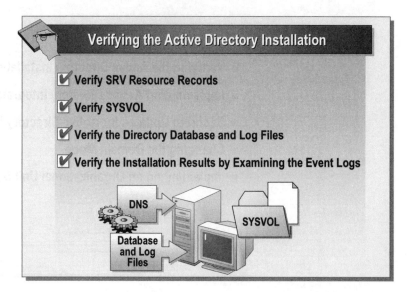

After the wizard completes the installation of Active Directory, you can verify the success of the installation by:

- Examining the DNS database to ensure that the required SRV resource records were created.

- Ensuring that SYSVOL has been properly created and shared.

- Verifying that the Active Directory database and log files were created.

- Examining the Event logs for any errors generated during the installation.

Verifying SRV Resource Records

After Active Directory is installed, the new domain controller registers its SRV resource records in the DNS database when it restarts.

You can verify the creation of these records either by using the DNS snap-in on the **Administrative Tools** menu or by using the **nslookup** command.

Using the DNS Snap-in

To verify that the SRV resource records were properly registered by using the DNS snap-in, perform the following steps:

1. Open DNS from the **Administrative Tools** menu.

2. Double-click *Server* (where *Server* is the name of your DNS server), double-click **Forward Lookup Zones**, and then double-click *domain* (where *domain* is the domain name).

   If the SRV resource records were registered, the following folders will exist in the *domain* folder:

   - _msdcs
   - _sites
   - _tcp
   - _udp

Using Nslookup

To verify that SRV resource records were properly registered by using the **nslookup** command, perform the following steps:

1. Open a command prompt window.

2. At the command prompt, type **nslookup** and then press ENTER.

3. Type **ls –t SRV** *domain* (where *domain* is the domain name), and then press ENTER.

   If the SRV resource records were properly created, they will be listed. To save the results of this list to a file, type **ls –t SRV** *domain* > *filename* (where *filename* is any name you give to the file).

Note If you do not have a reverse lookup zone configured, time-outs will be reported when you first run **nslookup**. This reporting happens because **nslookup** generates a reverse lookup to determine the host name of the DNS server based on its IP address.

Verifying SYSVOL

There are two steps involved in verifying SYSVOL. First, verify that the folder structure was created, and second, verify that the necessary shared folders were created. If the SYSVOL folder is not correctly created, data that is stored in the SYSVOL folder, such as Group Policy, and scripts, will not be replicated between domain controllers.

To verify that the folder structure was created, perform the following step:

- Click **Start**, click **Run**, type **%systemroot%\sysvol** in the **Open** box, and then click **OK**.

Windows Explorer opens and displays the contents of the SYSVOL folder, which should include the following subfolders:

- Domain
- Staging
- Staging areas
- Sysvol

To verify that the necessary shares have been created, perform the following steps:

1. Open a command prompt window.
2. At the command prompt, type **net share** and then press ENTER.

In the list of shared folders on this computer, you should see the shared folders listed in the following table.

Share name	Resource	Remark
NETLOGON	*systemroot*\SYSVOL\sysvol\domain\ SCRIPTS	Logon server share
SYSVOL	*systemroot*\SYSVOL\sysvol	Logon server share

Verifying the Directory Database and Log Files

To verify that the directory database and log files were properly created, perform the following step:

- Click **Start**, click **Run**, type **%systemroot%\ntds** in the **Open** box, and then click **OK**.

Windows Explorer opens and displays the contents of the Ntds folder, which should include the following files:

- Ntds.dit. This is the directory database file.
- Edb.*. These are the transaction logs and the checkpoint files.
- Res*.log. These are the reserved log files.

Note If you changed the location of the directory database and log files during the installation, replace **%systemroot%** with the correct location.

Verifying the Installation Results by Examining the Event Logs

After installing Active Directory, you should examine the Event logs for any errors that may have been encountered during the installation process. The following logs contain any error messages generated during the installation:

- System Log
- Directory Service
- DNS Server
- File Replication service

Implementing Active Directory Integrated Zones

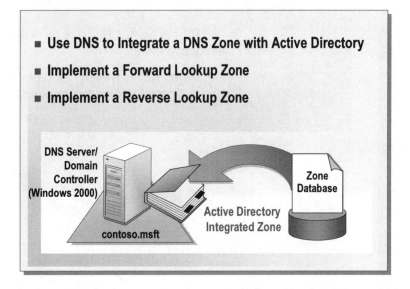

After installing Active Directory, you can integrate a DNS zone with Active Directory, so that DNS can use Active Directory to store and replicate DNS zone databases. You implement Active Directory–integrated forward and reverse lookup zones to enable client computers to perform both forward and reverse lookups.

To implement the Active Directory–integrated forward or reverse lookup zones, perform the following steps:

1. Open DNS from the **Administrative Tools** menu, and then double-click *Server* (where *Server* is your DNS server).

2. Depending on whether you are implementing a forward or a reverse lookup zone, perform one of the following steps:

   - To implement the Active Directory–integrated forward lookup zone, double-click **Forward Lookup Zones**, click *domain* (where *domain* is your domain name), right-click *domain,* and then click **Properties**.

   - To implement the Active Directory–integrated reverse lookup zone, double-click **Reverse Lookup Zones**, click *AAA.BBB.CCC*.x Subnet (where *AAA.BBB.CCC*.x is your reverse lookup zone), right-click *AAA.BBB.CCC*.x Subnet, and then click **Properties**.

3. On the **General** tab, click **Change**.

4. In the **Change Zone Type** dialog box, click **Active Directory-integrated**, and then click **OK**.

5. In the **DNS** dialog box, click **OK**, and then click **OK** again to close the *domain* **Properties** dialog box or the *AAA.BBB.CCC*.x Subnet **Properties** dialog box.

Note   The Active Directory–integrated option is not available in the **Change Zone Type** dialog box until you install Active Directory.

Securing Updates for Active Directory Integrated Zones

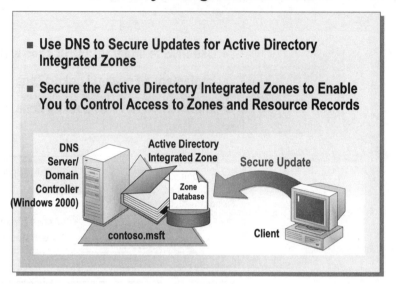

- Use DNS to Secure Updates for Active Directory Integrated Zones

- Secure the Active Directory Integrated Zones to Enable You to Control Access to Zones and Resource Records

After implementing Active Directory integrated zones, you can also configure zones for secure dynamic updates. DNS supports the DNS dynamic update protocol. The DNS dynamic update protocol allows Windows 2000–based computers to update DNS servers automatically, so that resource records can be updated without administrator intervention.

When you set the properties of an Active Directory integrated DNS zone to allow only secure updates, you can control access to zones and resource records by editing the DACL for that zone or resource record.

To allow only secure updates for a forward or a reverse lookup zone, perform the following steps:

1. Open DNS from the **Administrative Tools** menu, and then double-click *Server* (where *Server* is your DNS server).

2. Depending on whether you are securing updates for a forward or a reverse lookup zone, perform one of the following steps:

   - To allow only secure updates for a forward lookup zone, double-click **Forward Lookup Zones**, click *domain* (where *domain* is your domain name), right-click *domain*, and then click **Properties**.

   - To allow only secure updates for a reverse lookup zone, click *AAA.BBB.CCC*.x Subnet (where *AAA.BBB.CCC*.x is your reverse lookup zone), right-click *AAA.BBB.CCC*.x Subnet, and then click **Properties**.

3. On the **General** tab, in the **Allow dynamic updates** list, click **Only secure updates**, and then click **OK** to close the *domain* **Properties** dialog box or the *AAA.BBB.CCC*.x Subnet **Properties** dialog box.

Changing the Domain Mode

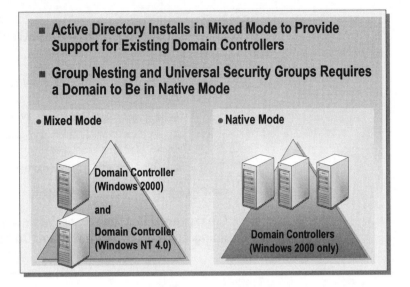

- **Active Directory Installs in Mixed Mode to Provide Support for Existing Domain Controllers**

- **Group Nesting and Universal Security Groups Requires a Domain to Be in Native Mode**

● Mixed Mode

Domain Controller
(Windows 2000)

and

Domain Controller
(Windows NT 4.0)

● Native Mode

Domain Controllers
(Windows 2000 only)

After you install Active Directory and establish a domain, the domain and Active Directory run in *mixed mode,* which is the default domain mode. A mixed mode domain supports domain controllers that are running either Windows 2000 or Microsoft Windows NT® version 4.0. Active Directory installs in mixed mode to provide support for existing domain controllers that have not been upgraded to Windows 2000. You can operate your domain in mixed mode indefinitely, which allows you to upgrade domain controllers that run Windows NT 4.0 at any time, according to the needs of your organization.

If your network does not have any domain controllers running Windows NT 4.0, or when all of your domain controllers have been upgraded to Windows 2000, you can convert the domain from mixed mode to *native mode.* In a native-mode domain, all domain controllers run Windows 2000. However, member servers and client computers do not need to be upgraded to Windows 2000 before you convert a domain to native mode. Some functions in Active Directory, such as group nesting and universal security groups, require that the domain be in native mode. Although you can no longer add domain controllers running Windows NT 4.0 to a domain in native mode, you can still have clients and member servers that run other operating systems.

To change your domain from mixed mode to native mode, perform the following steps:

1. Open either Active Directory Users and Computers, or Active Directory Domains and Trusts from the **Administrative Tools** menu.

2. Open the **Properties** dialog box for the domain.

3. On the **General** tab, click **Change Mode**.

4. Click **Yes**, and then click **OK**.

Caution   The change from mixed mode to native mode is a one-way process; you cannot change from native mode to mixed mode.

Implementing an Organizational Unit Structure

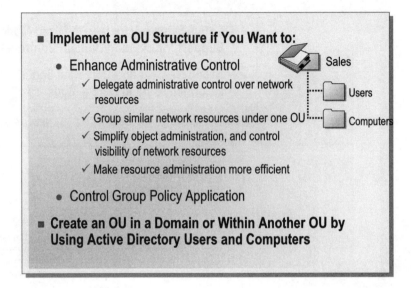

- **Implement an OU Structure if You Want to:**
  - Enhance Administrative Control
    - ✓ Delegate administrative control over network resources
    - ✓ Group similar network resources under one OU
    - ✓ Simplify object administration, and control visibility of network resources
    - ✓ Make resource administration more efficient
  - Control Group Policy Application
- **Create an OU in a Domain or Within Another OU by Using Active Directory Users and Computers**

You can use OUs for such tasks as addressing an organization's administrative requirements and centrally applying Group Policy. You should create OUs that are meaningful and will not change often. You should implement an OU structure within a domain to either enhance administrative control or control Group Policy.

- Enhancing administrative control means that you can:

  - Delegate administrative control, such as adding, deleting, and updating objects in the OU, and decide who has access to the OU. Delegate administrative control over network resources, while maintaining the ability to manage the resources. You can assign administrative permissions to users or groups of users at the OU level.

  - Group network resources with identical security requirements together under one OU to ease the task of administering these resources. For example, you could group all user accounts for temporary employees in one OU.

  - Simplify object administration, and control visibility of network resources, such as printers, users, and computers. By controlling visibility of resources, users can view only the resources to which they have access.

  - Make resource administration more efficient by assigning permissions once for an OU with many shared resources rather than multiple times for each shared resource.

- Controlling Group Policy means that you can create separate Group Policy settings to a distinct group of users, such as permanent employees or temporary contractors.

You cannot create an OU unless you have been assigned permissions to do so; moreover, these permissions can also limit where you are allowed to create an OU. By default, members of the Domain Admins and Enterprise Admins groups have permission to create OUs. Users who are not members of these groups must be explicitly assigned this permission.

Users assigned Read, List Contents, and Create Child (OU) permissions on a parent OU can create child OUs. List Contents on the parent is not required, but without it, you are not able to see the new child OU after you create it.

To create an OU, perform the following steps:

1. In Active Directory Users and Computers, right-click the domain or OU in which you want to create the new OU.

2. Point to **New**, and then click **Organizational Unit**.

3. Type the name of the OU, and then click **OK**.

Lab B: Performing Post Active Directory Installation Tasks

Objectives

After completing this lab, you will be able to:

- Verify Active Directory is correctly installed.
- Convert standard primary DNS zones to Active Directory integrated zones.
- Convert a domain from mixed mode to native mode.
- Plan an organizational unit (OU) structure.
- Create organizational units.

Prerequisite

Before working on this lab, you must have:

- An understanding of how Active Directory uses the DNS service.
- An understanding of organizational units.

Lab Setup

To complete this lab, you need a computer running Windows 2000 Advanced Server that is configured as a domain controller.

Estimated time to complete this lab: 30 minutes

Exercise 1
Verifying the Installation of Active Directory

Scenario

Having completed the installation of Active Directory, the second part of your implementation plan requires you to verify that the installation was successful.

Goal

In this exercise, you will verify that the installation of Active Directory was successful. You will do this by using DNS to verify that the required SRV resource records were created, verifying that the shared system volume (SYSVOL) was properly created and shared, and then verifying that the database file and associated log files were created.

Tasks	Detailed Steps
1. Verify that the required SRV resource records have been registered in DNS.	a. Log on as Administrator with a password of **password**. b. Open DNS from the **Administrative Tools** menu. c. In the console tree, expand *computer* (where *computer* is your assigned computer name), expand **Forward Lookup Zones**, and then expand *domain*.**nwtraders.msft** (where *domain* is your assigned domain name). *The following folders appear below your domain name: _msdcs, _sites, _tcp, and, _udp.* d. Close DNS.
Note: If the SRV resource records do not appear, open a command prompt, type **net stop netlogon** and then press ENTER, type **net start netlogon** and then press ENTER. This forces the registration of the SRV resource records.	
2. Verify that the shared system volume (SYSVOL) was created and shared.	a. In the **Run** box, type **%systemroot%\sysvol** and then click **OK**. *A window displays the contents of the SYSVOL folder. You should see the following subfolders: Domain, Staging, Staging Areas, and Sysvol.* b. Close the SYSVOL window. c. Open a command prompt window. d. At the command prompt, type **net share** and then press ENTER. *In the output of the net share command, you should see an entry for SYSVOL, indicating that it has been shared.* e. Close the command prompt window.
3. Verify that the database and associated log files were created.	a. In the **Run** box, type **%systemroot%\ntds** and then press ENTER. *A window displays the contents of the Ntds folder. You should see the following files and subfolders: Drop, Edb, Edb, Ntds.dit, Res1, Res2, and Temp.edb.* b. Close the NTDS window.

Exercise 2
Converting Standard Primary DNS Zones to Active Directory Integrated Zones

Scenario

As part of the plan to deploy Active Directory, you have decided to use Active Directory integrated zones to take advantage of the benefits provided by using Active Directory to store and replicate your DNS resource records.

Goal

In this exercise, you will convert your forward and reverse lookup zones from standard primary zones to Active Directory integrated zones.

Tasks	Detailed Steps
1. Convert the forward lookup zone for your domain from standard primary to Active Directory integrated zone.	a. Open DNS from the **Administrative Tools** menu. b. In the console tree, expand *Computer* (where *Computer* is your assigned computer name), expand **Forward Lookup Zones**, and then click *domain*.**nwtraders.msft** (where *domain* is your assigned domain name). c. Right-click *domain*.**nwtraders.msft**, and then click **Properties**. d. In the *domain*.**nwtraders.msft Properties** dialog box, on the **General** tab, click **Change**. e. In the **Change Zone Type** dialog box, click **Active Directory-integrated**, and then click **OK**. f. In the **DNS** dialog box, click **OK** to confirm the change, and then click **OK** to close the *domain*.**nwtraders.msft Properties** box.
2. Convert the reverse lookup zone for your subnet from standard primary to Active Directory integrated zone.	a. In the console tree, expand **Reverse Lookup Zones**, and then click **192.168.*y*.x Subnet** (where *y* is your assigned classroom number). b. Right-click **192.168.*y*.x Subnet**, and then click **Properties**. c. In the **192.168.*y*.x Properties** dialog box, on the **General** tab, click **Change**. d. In the **Change Zone Type** dialog box, click **Active Directory-integrated**, and then click **OK**. e. In the **DNS** dialog box, click **OK** to confirm the change, and then click **OK** to close the **192.168.*y*.x Properties** box. f. Close DNS.

Exercise 3
Converting a Domain from Mixed Mode to Native Mode

Scenario

Because you will not be using any Windows NT 4.0 domain controllers in your domain, and you want to take full advantage of all of the benefits offered by Active Directory, you have decided to convert your domain from a mixed-mode domain to a native-mode domain.

Goal

In this exercise, you will convert your domain from mixed mode to native mode.

Task	Detailed Steps
1. Convert the domain from mixed mode to native mode.	a. Open Active Directory Users and Computers from the **Administrative Tools** menu. b. In the console tree, right-click *domain*.**nwtraders.msft**, and then click **Properties**. c. In the *domain*.**nwtraders.msft Properties** box, click **Change Mode**. d. In the **Active Directory** dialog box, click **Yes** to confirm the change. e. Click **OK** to close the *domain*.**nwtraders.msft Properties** box, and then click **OK** to close the **Active Directory** dialog box. f. Close all open windows, and then log off.

Exercise 4
Planning an Organizational Unit Structure

Scenario

The headquarters of Northwind Traders is preparing to deploy Windows 2000. All computers and users in this location will belong to the same domain. Northwind Traders currently has 1,000 users at this location, working in the Sales, Administration, and Production departments. Management expects moderate growth in the next five years, with the total workforce not increasing by more than 100 percent.

Full-time network administrators centrally perform most of the Windows 2000 administration for Northwind Traders centrally. However, an administrator in each of the three departments should handle the daily administration of users and groups. These administrators will be responsible for some administrative tasks, including adding and removing user accounts and occasionally changing passwords.

Most computers at Northwind Traders are similarly configured and have the same business applications installed. However, database servers have different applications installed. Only two senior network administrators should have complete administrative control over these servers. Finally, Northwind Traders has four domain controllers.

❓ Which OUs must you add to the default Active Directory structure? Which objects will you place into these OUs? The key is to keep the structure simple, while still achieving all administrative goals.

— whichever belongs in those OU's

Exercise 5
Organizing a Windows 2000 Domain

Scenario

To achieve the administrative goals stated in exercise 1, you will create an organizational unit structure. You will implement the structure that you discussed in the previous exercise.

Goal

In this exercise, you will create a part of the organizational structure of the Northwind Traders domain.

Task	Detailed Steps
1. Create OUs within the domain domain.nwtraders.msft, with the following names: • Sales • Administration • Production • Servers	a. Log on to your domain as Administrator with a password of **password**. b. Open Active Directory Users and Computers from the **Administrative Tools** menu. c. In the console tree, expand *domain*.**nwtraders.msft** (where *domain* is your assigned domain name) if necessary, and then click *domain*.**nwtraders.msft**.

> **?** What are the default OUs and containers in your domain?
>
> *Builtin – Computers – Domain Controllers – Foreign Security Principals – Users*

Task	Detailed Steps
1. *(continued)*	d. Right-click *domain*.**nwtraders.msft**, point to **New**, and then click **Organizational Unit**. *The New Object – Organizational Unit dialog box appears. Notice that the only required information is the name of the new OU. The dialog box indicates that your domain is the location where the object will be created.* e. In the **Name** box, type **Sales** and then click **OK**. f. Repeat steps d and e to create the Administration, Production, and Servers OUs. g. Close all open windows, and then log off.

Troubleshooting the Installation of Active Directory

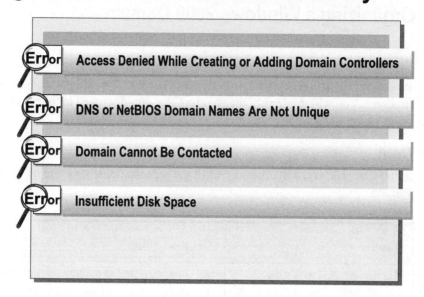

You may encounter problems when installing Active Directory. Here are some of the common problems that you may encounter and some strategies for resolving them:

- Access denied while creating or adding domain controllers. The following are the possible solutions for the access denied error message in different situations:

  - If you receive this message when creating the first domain controller in a new forest, you are not logged on to the server with an account that belongs to the Local Administrators group. Log off and then log on using an account that belongs to the Local Administrators group.

  - If you receive this message when you are adding a domain controller to an existing domain, you must supply credentials of a user account that is a member of the Domain Admins group or the Enterprise Admins group.

- DNS or NetBIOS domain names are not unique. When a domain is being created, both the DNS domain name and the NetBIOS domain names must be unique. If you receive an error message indicating that either one of the domain names is not unique, change the domain name.

- Domain cannot be contacted. When adding a replica domain controller to an existing domain, you may receive an error message indicating that the domain cannot be contacted, or that it is not an Active Directory domain. The following are the possible solutions to this problem:

  - Check DNS to ensure that the required SRV resource records exist for the domain that is being contacted.

  - If the SRV resource records are not present, you can force the registration of the SRV resource records by stopping the Net Logon service and then starting the Net Logon service on an existing domain controller.

  - If the SRV resource records are present in DNS, use **nslookup** to ensure that you can resolve DNS names from the computer on which you are trying to install Active Directory.

- Insufficient disk space. Active Directory requires a minimum disk space of 250 MB, 200 MB for the database and 50 MB for the transaction logs. If you receive an insufficient disk space error message, consider using another volume or partition to store these files.

Removing Active Directory

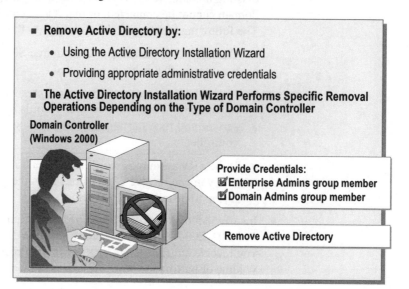

You use the Active Directory Installation wizard to remove Active Directory. When you start the wizard on a domain controller, the domain controller is identified as a server that contains Active Directory, and the wizard prompts you for the information required to remove Active Directory.

To remove Active Directory, you must provide the following administrative credentials:

- To remove Active Directory from a domain controller that is the last domain controller in the forest, you must log on to the domain as a member of the Domain Admins group or the Enterprise group.

- To remove Active Directory from a domain controller that is not the last domain controller in the domain, you do not need to provide credentials. However, you must be logged on as a member of either the Domain Admins group or the Enterprise Admins group.

Depending on whether you are removing Active Directory from the last domain controller in the domain or an additional domain controller, the same operations are common to both procedures. If any operation fails, the removal of Active Directory cannot proceed.

The following operations are common to removing Active Directory:

- Removes the shortcuts to Group Policy security settings, and restores the shortcut on the **Administrative Tools** menu to provide access to the local security settings for the member server or for the stand-alone server.

- Replicates all changes to the configuration and the schema directory partitions. For an additional domain controller, also replicates to the domain directory partition.

- Transfers to another domain controller any single-master roles that the domain controller is holding.

- Removes the system volume objects from the directory database, removes the system volume objects from the File Replication service database, and deletes the SYSVOL folder hierarchy. The File Replication service requests that Net Logon remove the share from the system volume.

- Removes the NTDS Settings object and cross-reference objects.

- Updates DNS to remove the Domain Controller Locator service records.

- Creates the local Security Accounts Manager (SAM) database in the same manner as during a fresh installation, including creating the administrator account and setting the password.

- Modifies the LSA membership policy to distinguish whether the computer is a stand-alone server or a member server.

- Stops the Net Logon service and the other services that were started during the installation of Active Directory. Services that relate only to the directory service are configured to not start automatically.

The following operations are specific to removing an additional domain controller:

- Locates and connects to a source domain controller in the same domain where the additional domain controller account exists and replicates changes to that source domain controller.

- Sets the computer account type to member server and moves the computer account for the additional server from the Domain Controllers OU to the Computers container.

The following operations are specific to removing the last domain controller in the domain:

- Verifies that no child domains exist.

- Locates and connects to a source domain controller in the parent domain and replicates changes to that source domain controller.

- Removes Active Directory objects from the forest that are specific to this domain.

- Removes trust objects on the parent server. The trusted Domain objects in the System folder are deleted.

- Places the server in a workgroup called Workgroup.

Best Practices

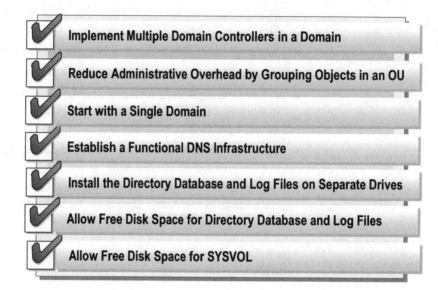

The following list provides best practices for creating a domain in Windows 2000:

- Consider implementing multiple domain controllers in each domain. Multiple domain controllers provide both fault tolerance and load balancing.

- Reduce administrative overhead by grouping objects with identical security requirements into one OU. You can then easily assign access permissions to the entire OU and all objects within it.

- Consider implementing an Active Directory structure that consists of a single domain, which lowers administrative and hardware costs, and accommodates company reorganizations more efficiently. Add additional domains only when an OU structure does not meet your needs.

- Ensure that your DNS infrastructure is in place and functioning properly before creating the first domain. Active Directory depends on DNS to function properly.

- When installing Active Directory, place the directory database and log files on separate hard drives to help improve performance.

- Verify that the volumes that hold the directory database and log files contain sufficient free disk space to allow for the growth of the Active Directory structure.

- Ensure that the volume that holds the SYSVOL folder structure contains enough free disk space to allow for future growth. Although you can move the directory database and log files by using the **ntdsutil** utility, you cannot move the SYSVOL folder structure without removing and reinstalling Active Directory.

Review

> ■ **Introduction to Creating a Windows 2000 Domain**
>
> ■ **Installing Active Directory**
>
> ■ **The Active Directory Installation Process**
>
> ■ **Examining the Default Structure of Active Directory**
>
> ■ **Performing Post Active Directory Installation Tasks**
>
> ■ **Troubleshooting the Installation of Active Directory**
>
> ■ **Removing Active Directory**
>
> ■ **Best Practices**

1. When you install Active Directory for the first time in a Windows 2000 network, what type of domain are you creating?

   Root domain

2. You want to run an unattended session of the Active Directory Installation wizard. The name of the answer file is Promote.txt. Which command do you type at the command prompt to run the answer file?

3. When you install a replica domain controller in an existing domain, does the Active Directory Installation wizard check for the existence of a functioning DNS server? Why or why not?

4. Which of the following must be located on a volume formatted with the NTFS file system:

   - Directory database

   - Log files

   - SYSVOL folder structure

5. When adding a replica domain controller to an existing domain, in which container is the computer object for the new domain controller created?

6. When attempting to install a replica domain controller, you receive a message that the Active Directory domain you are trying to join cannot be contacted. When examining the DNS database, you notice that the required SRV records have not been created. How can you force the registration of the SRV records?

7. You installed Active Directory and a default domain was created. Now you want to use the features of Active Directory, such as group nesting and universal security groups. Which domain mode is necessary to use these features in Active Directory?

8. What are the two main reasons you should plan to implement an OU structure within a domain?

Microsoft®
Training &
Certification

Module 4: Setting Up and Administering Users and Groups

Contents

Overview

- **Introduction to Users and Groups**
- **User Logon Names**
- **Creating Multiple User Accounts**
- **Administering User Accounts**
- **Using Groups in Active Directory**
- **Strategies for Using Groups in a Domain**
- **Troubleshooting Domain User Accounts and Groups**
- **Best Practices**

Active Directory® directory service is a directory service that stores and maintains data needed by network resources. A user account is an object stored in Active Directory that enables a *single sign-on* for a user account. A single sign-on means that users need to enter their names and passwords only once during a workstation logon to gain authenticated access to network resources. A domain user account provides the ability to log on to the domain to gain access to network resources, or to log on to an individual computer to gain access to resources on that computer.

A group is usually a collection of user accounts. You can use groups to efficiently manage access to domain resources, which helps simplify network maintenance and administration. You can use groups separately or you can place one group within another to further simplify administration.

At the end of this module, you will be able to:

- Identify the purpose of using user accounts and groups in Microsoft® Windows® 2000.
- Identify the different types of user logon names, and create a user principal name suffix.
- Create multiple user accounts by importing user information into Active Directory.
- Administer user accounts.
- Use groups to manage access to domain resources.
- Implement strategies for using security groups to manage access to domain resources.
- Troubleshoot common problems with administering user accounts and groups.
- Apply best practices for administering user accounts and groups.

Introduction to User Accounts and Groups

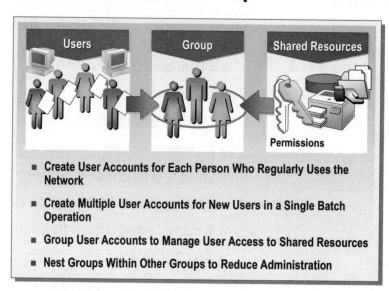

- **Create User Accounts for Each Person Who Regularly Uses the Network**
- **Create Multiple User Accounts for New Users in a Single Batch Operation**
- **Group User Accounts to Manage User Access to Shared Resources**
- **Nest Groups Within Other Groups to Reduce Administration**

An administrator must perform certain ongoing administrative tasks to ensure that the users can log on to the network and gain access to resources in a domain. Some of these administrative tasks are:

- Creating a single sign-on for a user account. In Active Directory, a single sign-on enables users to enter their names and passwords once during a workstation logon and receive authentication to gain access to network resources in a domain. An administrator can create three types of user accounts, each having a specific function:

  - A local user account enables a user to log on to a specific computer to gain access to resources on that computer.

  - A domain user account enables a user to log on to the domain to gain access to network resources.

  - A built-in user account enables a user to perform administrative tasks or gain temporary access to network resources.

- Creating multiple user accounts in Active Directory for new users in a single batch operation. For example, an administrator can create user accounts by bulk importing data into Active Directory from a file containing user data.

- Grouping user accounts to efficiently manage access to domain resources, such as network shared folders, files, directories, and printers. By using groups, an administrator needs to assign permissions for shared resources only once rather than multiple times. You can also make computers and other groups members of a group.

- Nesting groups within other groups to reduce administration when creating a model for a hierarchal structure.

◆ User Logon Names

- **Introduction to User Logon Names**
- **Creating a User Principal Name Suffix**

In Active Directory, each user account has a user logon name, and a pre-Windows 2000 user logon name, which is the security account manager (SAM) account name. The user account information is used to authenticate and authorize users anywhere in the forest, which in turn enables single sign-on. When creating user accounts, you enter the user logon name prefix and select the user principal name suffix.

When creating the user account, you also need to ensure that the user accounts follow the uniqueness rules.

Introduction to User Logon Names

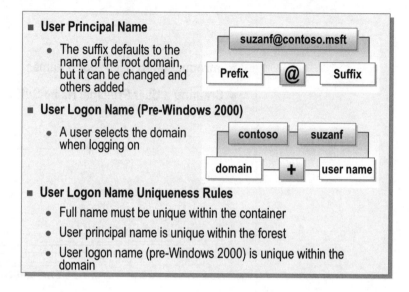

- **User Principal Name**
  - The suffix defaults to the name of the root domain, but it can be changed and others added

  suzanf@contoso.msft

  | Prefix | @ | Suffix |

- **User Logon Name (Pre-Windows 2000)**
  - A user selects the domain when logging on

  | contoso | suzanf |

  | domain | + | user name |

- **User Logon Name Uniqueness Rules**
  - Full name must be unique within the container
  - User principal name is unique within the forest
  - User logon name (pre-Windows 2000) is unique within the domain

---

In a Windows 2000 network, a user can log on with either a *user principal name* or a *user logon name* (pre-Windows 2000). Domain controllers can use either of these logon names to authenticate the logon request.

User Principal Name

The user principal name is the logon name used only for logging on to a Windows 2000 network. This name is also known as a user logon name.

There are two parts to a user principal name, and they are separated by the @ sign; for example, suzanf@contoso.msft. A user logon name has the following two components:

- The *user principal name prefix*, which in the suzanf@contoso.msft example is suzanf.

- The *user principal name suffix*, which in the suzanf@contoso.msft example is contoso.msft. By default, the suffix is the name of the root domain in the network. You can use the other domains in the network to configure additional suffixes for users. One example of when you would want to configure a suffix is when you want to create user logon names that match users' e-mail addresses.

Advantages of using the user principal names are that:

- The user principal name does not change when you move a user account to a different domain, because the name is unique within Active Directory.

- A user principal name can be the same as a user's e-mail address name, because it has the same format as a standard e-mail address.

User Logon Name (Pre-Windows 2000)

If a user logs on to the network from a client computer running a version of Windows earlier than Windows 2000, the user must log on by using the user logon name (pre-Windows 2000).

A user logon name (pre-Windows 2000) is a user account name, such as suzanf in the suzanf@contoso.msft example. When a user logs on by using a user logon name (pre-Windows 2000), the user must also provide the domain in which the user account exists, so that the authenticating domain controller can locate the user account.

If users connect to a network resource with a different user account than the one with which they logged on, the users must provide the domain and user logon name (pre-Windows 2000) for authentication, for example, contoso\suzanf.

User Logon Name Uniqueness Rules

User logon names for domain user accounts must follow *uniqueness rules* in Active Directory. When creating user logon names, consider the following uniqueness rules:

- The full name must be unique within the container in which you create the user account. The full name is used as the relative distinguished name.

- The user principal name must be unique within the forest.

- The user logon name (pre-Windows 2000) must be unique within the domain.

Creating a User Principal Name Suffix

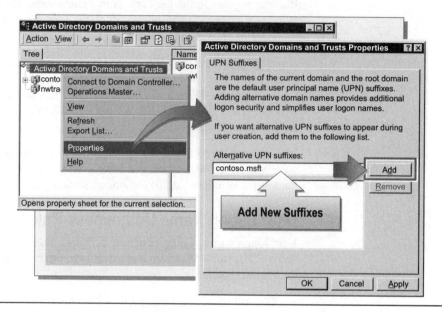

You select a user principal name suffix when creating a user account in Active Directory Users and Computers. If the suffix that you need does not exist in Active Directory User and Computers, you can add it. A user principal name suffix enables you to simplify administration and user logon processes by providing a single user principal name suffix for all users.

You must be a member of the Enterprise Admins predefined group to add suffixes in Active Directory Domains and Trusts.

To add a new suffix, perform the following steps:

1. In Active Directory Domains and Trusts, in the console tree, right-click **Active Directory Domains and Trusts**, and then click **Properties**.

2. On the **UPN Suffixes** tab, type an alternative UPN suffix for the domain, and then click **Add**.

Note   If you have created a user account by using a program other than Active Directory Users and Computers, you are not limited by the user principal name suffixes stored in Active Directory. You can define a suffix when you create the account.

◆ Creating Multiple User Accounts

- ■ The Bulk Import Process
- ■ Using CSVDE to Create Multiple User Accounts
- ■ Using LDIFDE to Create Multiple User Accounts

You can use Windows 2000 to create multiple user accounts in Active Directory by importing data from a text file to populate the attributes of user accounts. This process is known as *bulk import*. Bulk import is the importing of multiple database records into the Active Directory database. The advantage of bulk importing is that you do not need to create each user account individually. Instead, you can import an existing file that contains the user information required to create all of the user accounts.

To create user accounts in a batch operation, Windows 2000 provides administrative utilities, such as Comma Separated Value Directory Exchange (CSVDE) and Lightweight Directory Access Protocol Data Interchange Format Directory Exchange (LDIFDE). These utilities enable you to administer large numbers of user accounts, and other Active Directory objects, such as groups, computers, and printers, in one operation. These utilities are installed automatically on all computers that run Windows 2000 Server.

The Bulk Import Process

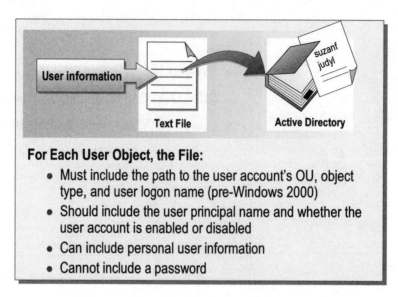

For Each User Object, the File:

- Must include the path to the user account's OU, object type, and user logon name (pre-Windows 2000)
- Should include the user principal name and whether the user account is enabled or disabled
- Can include personal user information
- Cannot include a password

The bulk import process enables you to automatically create multiple user accounts in Active Directory. This process requires using a text file that contains information about the user accounts that you want to create. The text file can be a database application that already contains information about user accounts, or can also be from other applications, such as Microsoft Excel or Microsoft Word.

Depending on the format of the text file, you use the **csvde** or the **ldifde** command to import user account data from the file to simultaneously create multiple user accounts in Active Directory. You use the **csvde** command to import the text file that uses a *comma-delimited* format, also known as a *comma-separated value* format (CSVDE format). You use the **ldifde** command to import the text file that uses a *line-separated value* format (LDIF format). Most database applications can create text files that can be imported in one of these formats.

When creating multiple user accounts, the information in the CSVDE or LDIFDE file:

- Must include the path to the user account in Active Directory, the object type, which is the user account itself, and the user logon name (Pre-Windows 2000).

- Should include the user principal name, because this is the logon name recommended for users logging on from a computer that runs Windows 2000. You should also include whether the user account is disabled or enabled. If you do not specify a value, the account is disabled.

- Can include personal information, for example, telephone numbers or home addresses. The file needs to contain the information necessary to create *attributes* for the user account. Attributes, which are also referred to as *properties*, are categories of information for Active Directory objects. The values of these attributes define the characteristics of the object. You should include as much user account information as possible to provide more items on which users can search when conducting Active Directory searches.

- Cannot include passwords. Bulk import leaves the password blank for user accounts. By default, the first time that users log on, they must change their passwords. This is not a problem if users log on immediately, but it could be a problem if users do not log on for some time. Because a blank password allows an unauthorized person to gain access to the network by knowing only the user logon name, disable the user accounts until users start logging on.

Using CSVDE to Create Multiple User Accounts

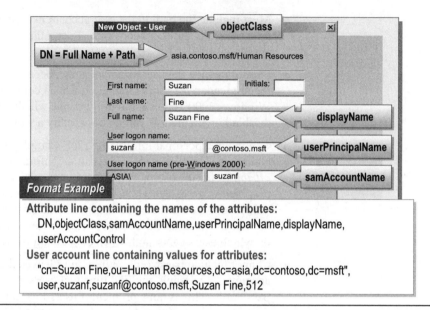

The CSVDE format can be used only to add user objects, and other types of objects, to Active Directory. You cannot use the CSVDE format for deleting or modifying objects in Active Directory. Before importing a CSVDE file, you must ensure that the file that you are importing is properly formatted, so that the import will be successful. Typically, to edit and format a text file, you use an application that has good editing capabilities, such as Excel or Word. Then, save the file as a comma-delimited text file. You can export data from Active Directory to an Excel spreadsheet or import data from a spreadsheet into Active Directory.

Preparing a CSVDE File for Importing

Format the file so that it contains the following information:

- The attribute line, which is the first line of the file. It specifies the name of each attribute that you want to define for the new user accounts. Note that you can put the attributes in any order, but you must separate the attributes with commas. The following is an example of the attribute line:

```
DN,objectClass,sAMAccountName,userPrincipalName,
displayName,userAccountControl
```

- The user account line. For each user account that you create, the import file contains a line that specifies the value for each attribute in the attribute line. The following rules apply to the values in a user account line:

  - The attribute values must follow the sequence of the attribute line.

  - If a value is missing for an attribute, leave it blank, but include all commas.

  - If a value contains commas, include the value in quotation marks.

The following is an example of a user account line:

```
"cn=Suzan Fine,ou=Human Resources,dc=asia,dc=contoso,
dc=msft",user,suzanf,suzanf@contoso.msft,Suzan Fine,512
```

The following table provides the attributes and values presented in the previous example.

Attribute	Value
DN (distinguished name)	cn=Suzan Fine,ou=Human Resources, dc=asia,dc=contoso,dc=msft (This specifies the path to the OU that contains the user account.)
objectClass	user
sAMAccountName	suzanf
userPrincipalName	suzanf@contoso.msft
displayName	Suzan Fine
userAccountControl	512 (The value 512 enables the user account, and the value 514 disables the user account.)

For more information about distinguished names, see appendix C, "LDAP Names," on the Student Materials compact disc.

Note For a list of common attributes and their display names, see appendix D, "Common User Account Attributes," on the Student Materials compact disc.

Using the csvde Command

After the file is properly formatted, you can use the **csvde** command to import the file and to create multiple user accounts in Active Directory.

To import the file, open a command prompt window, and type the following:

> **csvde –i –f** *filename*

In the previous syntax, **-i** indicates that you are importing a file into Active Directory, and **-f** indicates that the next parameter is the name of the file that you are importing.

The **csvde** command provides status information on the success or failure of the process, and it also provides the name of the file to view for detailed error information. Even if the status information indicates that the process was successful, use Active Directory Users and Computers to verify some of the user accounts that you created to ensure that they have all of the information that you provided.

Using LDIFDE to Create Multiple User Accounts

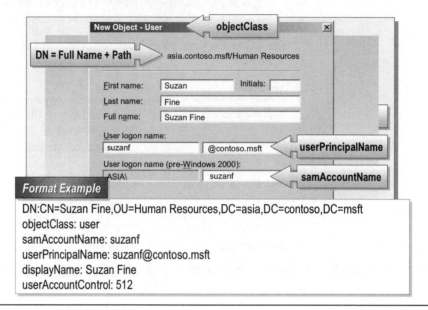

Lightweight Directory Access Protocol Interchange Format (LDIF) is another file format that is used to perform bulk import for directories that conform to LDAP standards. The LDIF file format has a command-line utility called **ldifde** that allows you to create, modify, and delete objects in Active Directory. An LDIF file consists of a series of *records* that are separated by a blank line. A *record* describes either a single directory object or a set of modifications to the attributes of an existing object and consists of one or more lines in the file.

Preparing a LDIF File for Importing

Format the LDIF file so that it contains a record that consists of a sequence of lines describing an entry for a user account in Active Directory, or a sequence of lines describing a set of changes to a user account in Active Directory. The user account entry specifies the name of each attribute that you want to define for the new user account. The Active Directory schema defines the attribute names. For each user account that you create, the file contains a line that specifies the value for each attribute in the attribute line. The following rules apply to the values for each attribute:

- Any line that begins with a pound-sign (#) is a comment line, and is ignored when you run LDIF file.

- If a value is missing for an attribute, it must be represented as *AttributeDescription* ":" FILL SEP.

    The following is an example of an entry in LDIF import file:

    ```
    # Create Suzan Fine
    DN: CN=Suzan Fine,OU=Human
    Resources,DC=asia,DC=contoso,DC=msft
    objectClass: user
    sAMAccountName: suzanf
    userPrincipalName: suzanf@contoso.msft
    displayName: Suzan Fine
    userAccountControl: 512
    ```

The following table provides the attributes and values presented in the example.

Attribute	Attribute's value
DN (distinguished name)	CN=Suzan Fine,OU=Human Resources, DC=asia,DC=contoso,DC=msft (This specifies the path to the object's container.)
objectClass	user
sAMAccountName	suzanf
userPrincipalName	suzanf@contoso.msft
displayName	Suzan Fine
userAccountControl	512 (The value 512 enables the user account, and the value 514 disables the user account.)

Using the ldifde Command

After the file is properly formatted, use the **ldifde** command to import the file and create multiple user accounts in Active Directory.

To import the file, at the command line, type:

ldifde –i –f *filename*

In the previous syntax, **-i** indicates that you are importing a file into Active Directory. If this parameter is not specified, the default mode for LDIFDE is export. The **-f** parameter indicates the name of the file that you are importing.

Note Programs use Active Directory Service Interfaces (ADSI) to gain access to Active Directory. ADSI in conjunction with the Windows Script Host enables scripting batch operations in Active Directory by using Microsoft Visual Basic®, Scripting Edition (VBScript) or Java. For more information about creating ADSI scripts, see appendix E, "Using Active Directory Service Interfaces (ADSI) Programming to Automate Administrative Tasks," on the Student Materials compact disc.

◆ Administering User Accounts

- **Performing Common Administrative Tasks**
- **Locating User Accounts**

After you have set up user accounts in Active Directory, you must perform ongoing administrative tasks to ensure that all users have the resources that they need, and that network security remains intact. Because there could be a large number of user accounts, you can use the **find** utility to help locate a particular user account.

Performing Common Administrative Tasks

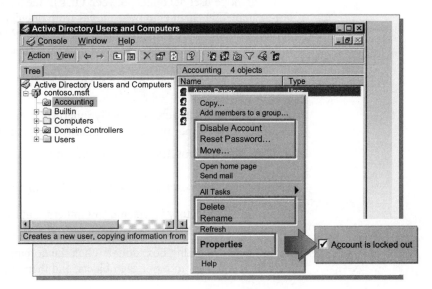

After creating user accounts, you must perform frequent administrative tasks to ensure that the network reflects the evolving needs of the organizations that it supports. These administrative tasks include disabling and enabling user accounts, resetting passwords, moving user accounts within a domain, deleting user accounts, renaming user accounts; and unlocking user accounts.

Disabling and Enabling User Accounts

Disable user accounts when users will not need their accounts for an extended period, but will need to use them at a later time. You disable a user account as a security precaution against a potential misuse of the user account. For example, if the user takes a two-month leave of absence, disable the account when the user leaves and then enable the account when the user returns.

To disable or enable user accounts, perform the following step:

- In Active Directory Users and Computers, right-click the appropriate user account, and then click **Disable Account** or **Enable Account** depending on the current status of the account.

Resetting Passwords

You reset a password when the password expires before the user changes or if the user forgets it. You do not need to know a user's password before you can reset it. You should require the users to change their passwords the next time that they log on.

To reset user account passwords, perform the following step:

- In Active Directory Users and Computers, right-click the appropriate user account, and then click **Reset Password**.

Moving User Accounts Within a Domain

You can move user accounts between OUs in the same domain when necessary. For example, when an employee moves from one department to another and another administrator will administer the employee's user account. The following conditions apply when you move user accounts between OUs:

■ Object permissions assigned directly to the user account move with the user account.

■ Permissions that were previously inherited from the parent object no longer apply. Instead, permissions are inherited from the new parent object.

■ You can move multiple user accounts at the same time.

To move a domain user account within a domain, perform the following steps:

1. In Active Directory Users and Computers, right-click the user account(s) to be moved, and then click **Move**.

2. In the **Move** dialog box, double-click the domain tree, click the OU to which you want to move the objects, and then click **OK**.

Deleting User Accounts

Delete a user account when an employee leaves the organization and you are not going to reuse the account. By deleting these accounts, you will not have unused accounts in Active Directory, that may cause a security risk if an authorized user was able log on using an obsolete account.

To delete user accounts, perform the following step:

• In Active Directory Users and Computers, right-click the appropriate user account, and then click **Delete**.

Renaming User Accounts

Rename a user account if you want to retain all rights, permissions, and group memberships that are associated with that account, and then reassign it to a different user. For example, if there is a new company accountant, rename the account by changing the first name, last name, and the user logon names to those of the new accountant. Also, you may need to change other properties for a new user, such as resetting the password, and changing the telephone number and address.

To rename user accounts, perform the following step:

• In Active Directory Users and Computers, right-click the appropriate user account, and then click **Rename**.

Unlocking User Accounts

You may be required to unlock a user account if a Group Policy setting locks that account when the user violates the Group Policy defined by the setting. For example, users are locked out if they exceed the limit that a Group Policy setting allows for failed logon attempts. When a user account is locked out, Windows 2000 displays an error message when the user attempts to log on.

To unlock a user account, perform the following step:

- In Active Directory Users and Computers, in the **Properties** dialog box for the user account, on the **Account** tab, clear the **Account is locked out** check box.

Locating User Accounts

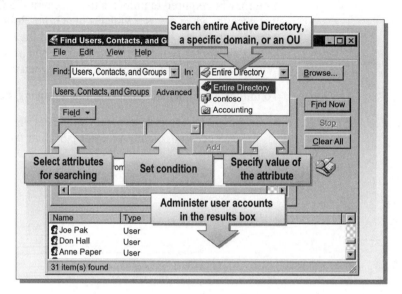

Because all user accounts reside in Active Directory, administrators can search for the user account that they need to administer. Searching Active Directory for user accounts means that you do not need to browse through hundreds or thousands of user accounts in Active Directory Users and Computers. You can also search for other Active Directory objects, such as computers, printers, and shared folders. After locating these objects, you can administer these objects from the search results box.

Performing a Basic Search Operation

To start a basic search operation, perform the following steps:

1. In Active Directory Users and Computers, on the **Action** menu, click **Find**.

2. In the **Find Users, Contacts, and Groups** dialog box, select the type of object for which you want to search.

3. Enter the search text in the search criteria boxes in the **Find Users, Contacts, and Groups** dialog box. The types of search criteria that are available vary depending on the type of object that you selected.

The following table describes the basic options in the **Find Users, Contacts, and Groups** dialog box.

Option	Description
Find	The option that you use to select the type of objects for which you can search. • Use the **Users, Contacts, and Groups** option to locate users, contacts, or groups by name or description. • Use the **Computers** option to locate computers by name, owner, or role, such as workstation, server, or domain controller. • Use the **Printers** option to locate printers by name, location, or model. • Use the **Shared Folders** option to locate shared folders by name or keywords. • Use the **Organizational Units** option to locate OUs by name. • Use the **Custom Search** option to search for a wide range of object types, such as Computer, Contact, Group, OU, and User instead of selecting one object type at a time. You can specify additional attributes to use to locate these object types. • Use the **Remote Installation Clients** option to locate remote installation client computers by GUID or RIS server.
In	The option that you use to select the location that you want to search. • Use the **Entire Directory** option to locate objects by searching the global catalog. • Use the domain name option to locate objects in a specific domain.

Performing an Advanced Search Operation

Active Directory Users and Computers provides the Advanced option in the **Find Users, Contacts, and Groups** dialog box to allow administrators to customize searches and filter data retrieved from Active Directory. The Advanced option allows you to specify search criteria that define the resources for which you are searching. By using the Advanced option, you can search for resources by using any attribute that is valid for the object type. For example, you can search Active Directory for all printers in a specific location. You can then use the search results to edit the properties of each printer object.

The following table describes the advanced options in the **Find Users, Contacts, and Groups** dialog box.

Option	Description
Field	A list of the attributes for which you can search on the resource type that you select. Different resource types have different attributes that can be used for a search operation. For example, a user would have an attribute called Home Phone, but this attribute would not apply to a computer.
Condition	The methods that are available to further define the search for an attribute.
	• Use the **Starts with** option to specify that the value of the selected attribute begins with a given character or set of characters.
	• Use the **Ends with** option to specify that the value of the selected attribute ends with a given character or set of characters.
	• Use the **Is (exactly)** option to specify that the value of the selected attribute should be the same as the given character or set of characters.
	• Use the **Is not** option to specify that the value of the selected attribute should not be the same as the given character or set of characters.
	• Use the **Present** option to specify that the selected attribute has been defined for the object, regardless of what the attribute value is.
	• Use the **Not present** option to specify that the selected attribute has not been defined for the object.
Value	The character or set of characters that you use with the condition.

Also, if users want to find objects in Active Directory, they can click **Start**, and then click **Search**. The Search options in Windows Explorer and My Network Places can also be used to locate objects in Active Directory.

Administering User Accounts in the Results Box

After a search completes successfully, the search results are displayed. You can then perform administrative functions on the objects that are listed. The functions that are available depend on the type of object you located. For example, if you searched for user accounts, you can rename and delete the user account, disable the user account, reset the password, move the user account to another OU, or modify the user account's attributes.

To administer a user account from the search results, right-click the user account, and then click **Properties**.

When you right-click the object in the results box, the same property sheet that is invoked through Active Directory Users and Computers appears. Therefore, you can manage the objects by selecting an appropriate option related to the function that you want to perform on the object. The functions that are available depend on the type of object that you located.

Lab A: Setting Up and Administering Domain User Accounts

Objectives

After completing this lab, you will be able to:

- Create and use an alternate user principal name suffix.
- Create multiple domain user accounts by using bulk import.
- Administer domain user accounts.

Lab Setup

- To complete this lab, you need to run the batch file C:\Moc\Win2154a\Labfiles\Lrights.bat to set the Log on Locally user right for the Users group, so that any user will have the right to log on locally to your computer.

Important The lab does not reflect the real-world environment. It is recommended that you always use complex passwords for any administrator accounts, and never create accounts without a password.

Important Outside of the classroom environment, it is strongly advised that you use the most recent software updates that are necessary. Because this is a classroom environment, we may use software that does not include the latest updates.

Estimated time to complete this lab: 30 minutes

Exercise 1
Creating User Accounts by Using an Alternative User Principal Name Suffix

Scenario

After acquiring a new organization, Contoso, Ltd., the parent organization Northwind Traders decides to add all Contoso, Ltd. user accounts to the Northwind Traders domain. To keep the identity of Contoso, Ltd. separate from Northwind Traders, a user principal name suffix will be created and used for the user accounts of former Contoso, Ltd. employees.

Goal

In this exercise, you will create a user principal name suffix and use this suffix to create a test user account. Then, you will verify that a user can log on by using this user principal name.

Tasks	Detailed Steps
1. Create the following user principal name suffix: • contoso.msft	a. Log on as Administrator with a password of **password**. b. Open Active Directory Domains and Trusts from the **Administrative Tools** menu. c. In the console tree, right-click **Active Directory Domains and Trusts**, and then click **Properties**. d. In the **Active Directory Domains and Trusts Properties** dialog box, in the **Alternative UPN suffixes** box, type **contoso.msft** click **Add**, and then click **OK**. e. Close Active Directory Domains and Trusts.
2. Within *domain*.nwtraders.msft (where *domain* is your assigned domain name), create the following OU: • Contoso	a. Open Active Directory Users and Computers from the **Administrative Tools** menu. b. In the console tree, right-click *domain*.**nwtraders.msft**, point to **New**, and then click **Organizational Unit**. c. In the **New Object – Organizational Unit** dialog box, in the **Name** box, type **Contoso** and then click **OK**.
3. Within the Contoso OU, create a user account with the following properties: • Full name: TestUPN • User logon name: TestUPN@contoso.msft	a. In the console tree, expand *domain*.**nwtraders.msft**, and then click **Contoso**. b. Right-click **Contoso**, point to **New**, and then click **User**. c. On the **New Object – User** page, in both the **Full name** and the **User logon name** boxes, type **TestUPN** d. Click the drop-down list next to **User logon name** to review the list of user principal name suffixes, click **@contoso.msft**, and then click **Next**. e. Click **Next**, and then click **Finish**. f. Close Active Directory Users and Computers.

Tasks	Detailed Steps
4. Log on using the user logon name of TestUPN@contoso.msft to verify that the account works, and then log off.	**a.** Log off, press CTRL+ALT+DELETE to initiate the logon process, click **Options** to display the **Log on to** box, and then in the **User name** box, delete the existing text. *Notice that the **Log on to** box is enabled.* **b.** In the **User name** box, type **TestUPN@contoso.msft** *Notice that the **Log on to** box is disabled when a user principal name is entered because the domain information is not needed.* **c.** Click **OK** to complete the logon process. **d.** After you have successfully logged on as TestUPN, log off.

Exercise 2
Creating User Accounts by Using Bulk Import

Scenario

Because Northwind Traders has acquired a new organization, it has needed to add a new Package Handling department. Therefore, you need to create new user accounts for the Package Handling department. The information about the employees in this department was provided to your organization in a file exported from a database, so you decide that the most efficient solution is to use a bulk import method to create the user accounts.

Goal

In this exercise, you will use the **csvde** utility to create the user accounts for the employees in the Package Handling department.

To speed the process of formatting the information, the PackA.txt file contains the user information already in comma-separated value format to reduce the work needed to use the **csvde** bulk import utility.

Tasks	Detailed Steps
1. Within *domain*.nwtraders.msft, create the following OU: • Package Handling	**a.** Log on as Administrator with a password of **password**. **b.** Open Active Directory Users and Computers from the **Administrative Tools** menu. **c.** In the console tree, right-click *domain*.**nwtraders.msft**, point to **New**, and then click **Organizational Unit**. **d.** In the **New Object – Organizational Unit** dialog box, in the **Name** box, type **Package Handling** and then click **OK**.
2. In the C:\Moc\Win2154a\Labfiles folder, open the file PackA.txt, view the contents, and then determine which bulk import attributes are being used.	▪ In the **Run** box, type **C:\Moc\Win2154a\Labfiles\PackA.txt** and then click **OK** to open the PackA.txt file in Notepad.

❓ Extrapolating from the data in PackA.txt, what are the seven bulk import attributes used? For a list of attributes, see Appendix D, "Common User Account Attributes," on the Student Materials compact disc.

[Handwritten answers:]

P.10   CN – OU –   department – dn – object class –
DC   SAMAccount Name – telephoneNumber –
                                     User Account Control – User PrincipalName

dn, SAMAccount Name, user PrincipalName, telephone Number, department, user Account Control, object Class

Tasks	Detailed Steps
3. Edit the distinguished name and user principal name in the PackA.txt file so you can import the user accounts into your domain by using the csvde utility.	▪ In Notepad, use the Replace feature to replace all occurrences of *domain* with your assigned domain name.
4. Add the attribute line to the PackA.txt file to match the user account bulk import data.	▪ Add the seven bulk import attributes in the correct order, separated by commas, to the first line of the file. Hint: The file C:\Moc\Win2154a\Labfiles\PackAttr.txt contains the necessary list of attributes.
5. Edit the PackA.txt file to disable all of the user accounts with no department. Save this file as Pack.txt.	a. Edit the userAccountControl column to disable all user accounts with no department. Hint: The currently used userAccountControl value, 512, indicates that the account will be enabled. b. Save the edited file as C:\Moc\Win2154a\Labfiles\Pack.txt. c. Close the Pack.txt - Notepad window.
6. Use the csvde utility to perform a bulk import of Pack.txt.	a. Open a command prompt window. b. At the command prompt, type **cd C:\Moc\Win2154a\Labfiles** and then press ENTER. c. At the command prompt, type **csvde /?** and then press ENTER. d. Review the **–i** and **–f** options in the usage statement. e. At the command prompt, type **csvde –i –f Pack.txt** and then press ENTER. *The **csvde** utility displays that 26 entries were modified successfully.* f. Close the command prompt window.

Exercise 3
Administering User Accounts

Scenario

The Help desk at Northwind Traders has received a number of administrative requests for the user accounts in the new Package Handling OU. The requests include enabling a user account, disabling a user account, resetting a password for a user account, and moving a user account.

Goal

In this exercise, you will use Active Directory Users and Computers to fulfill the administrative requests.

Tasks	Detailed Steps
1. Within the Package Handling OU, enable the following user account: • Amie Baldwin	a. In Active Directory Users and Computers, in the console tree, expand *domain*.**nwtraders.msft**, and then click **Package Handling**. b. Right-click **Package Handling**, and then click **Refresh** to display the new user accounts. c. In the details pane, right-click **Amie Baldwin**, click **Enable Account**, and then click **OK** to close the message confirming that the Amie Baldwin user account has been enabled. *Notice that the icon next to the user account Amie Baldwin reflects the enabled account status.*
2. Within the Package Handling OU, disable the following user account: • Matthew Dunn	▪ Click **Package Handling**, right-click **Matthew Dunn**, click **Disable Account**, and then click **OK** to close the message confirming that the Matthew Dunn user account has been disabled. *Notice that the icon next to the user account Matthew Dunn reflects the disabled account status.*
3. Reset the password of the following user account to Sc1234: • Scott Culp Then, ensure that Scott changes his password the next time he logs on.	a. Right-click **Scott Culp**, and then click **Reset Password**. b. In the **Reset Password** dialog box, in both the **New password** and **Confirm password** boxes, type **Sc1234** c. Select the **User must change password at next logon** check box, click **OK**, and then click **OK** again to close the message confirming that the password was changed.
4. Move the following user account to the Contoso OU: • Derek Graham Verify that the account has been moved, and then log off.	a. Right-click **Derek Graham**, and then click **Move**. b. In the **Move** dialog box, click **Contoso**, and then click **OK**. c. Click **Contoso**, and then verify that the account for Derek Graham is listed in the details pane. d. Close Active Directory Users and Computers, close all open windows, and then log off.

◆ Using Groups in Active Directory

- **Introduction to Groups in Active Directory**
- **Using Global Groups**
- **Using Domain Local Groups**
- **Using Universal Groups**

Groups simplify administration. Before you can effectively use groups, you need to understand the function of groups and the group types that you can create. Active Directory provides support for different types of groups, and also provides options to determine the group's scope, which is how the group can be used in multiple domains.

Introduction to Groups in Active Directory

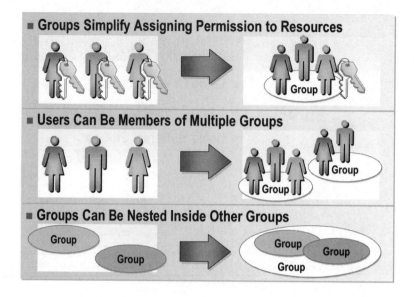

Groups in Active Directory allow you to manage domain user access to domain resources by assigning permissions once to a group rather than multiple times to individual users. There are two group types in Active Directory, security groups and distribution groups. Both of these groups support one of the three group scopes, which are domain local, global, or universal. The group type and group scope that you can choose depend on the domain mode.

Users can be members of multiple groups. You use security groups to assign permissions to groups of users and computers. Distribution groups cannot be used for security purposes. Security and distribution groups have a scope attribute. The scope of a group determines who can be a member of the group, and where you can use that group in the network.

One way to use groups effectively is through *nesting*. Nesting means that you can add a group to another group. The nested group inherits the permissions of the group of which it is a member, thus simplifying the assigning of permissions to several groups at one time and reducing the traffic caused by replication of group membership changes. In a mixed-domain mode, there can be no nesting within the same group.

Note   Groups can have up to 5,000 members. The user's primary group membership, such as Domain Users, is not stored in the group membership list.

For more information about groups, see Module 5, "Managing Access to Resources by Using Groups," in Course 2152, *Implementing Microsoft Windows 2000 Professional and Server*.

Using Global Groups

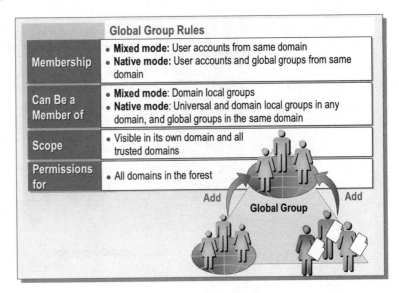

Global Group Rules	
Membership	• **Mixed mode:** User accounts from same domain • **Native mode:** User accounts and global groups from same domain
Can Be a Member of	• **Mixed mode:** Domain local groups • **Native mode:** Universal and domain local groups in any domain, and global groups in the same domain
Scope	• Visible in its own domain and all trusted domains
Permissions for	• All domains in the forest

Use a global group to organize users who share the same job tasks and need similar network access requirements.

The following summarizes the global group membership rules:

- *Membership*. Mixed mode can contain user accounts from the same domain. Native mode can contain user accounts and global groups from the same domain.

- *Can be a member of*: In mixed mode, the global group can be a member of only domain local groups. In native mode, the global group can be a member of universal and domain local groups in any domain, and global groups in the same domain.

- *Scope*. A global group is visible within its domain and all trusted domains, which include all of the domains in the forest.

- *Can be assigned permission for*: All domains in the forest.

Because global groups have a forest-wide visibility, they should not be created specifically for domain-specific resource access. Global groups are a good choice to organize users or groups of users. A different group type is more appropriate to control the access to resources within a domain.

Using Domain Local Groups

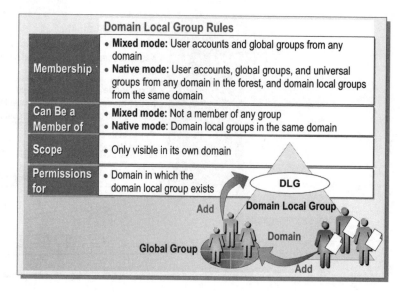

Domain Local Group Rules	
Membership	• **Mixed mode:** User accounts and global groups from any domain • **Native mode:** User accounts, global groups, and universal groups from any domain in the forest, and domain local groups from the same domain
Can Be a Member of	• **Mixed mode:** Not a member of any group • **Native mode:** Domain local groups in the same domain
Scope	• Only visible in its own domain
Permissions for	• Domain in which the domain local group exists

Use a domain local group to assign access permissions to resources that are located in the same domain in which you create the domain local group.

The following summarizes the domain local group membership rules:

- *Membership.* Mixed mode can contain user accounts and global groups from any domain. Native mode can contain user accounts, global groups, and universal groups from any domain in the forest, and domain local groups from the same domain.

- *Can be a member of:* In mixed mode, the domain local group cannot be a member of any group. In native mode, the domain local group can be a member of domain local groups in the same domain.

- *Scope.* The domain local group is visible only in its own domain.

- *Can be assigned permission for:* The domain in which the domain local group exists.

You can add all global groups that need to share the same resources into the appropriate domain local group.

Using Universal Groups

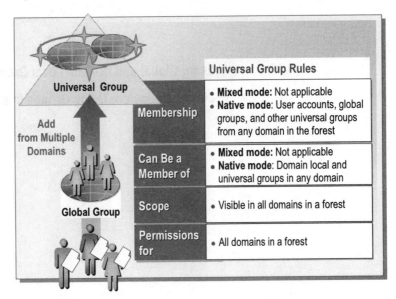

Universal Group Rules	
Membership	• **Mixed mode:** Not applicable • **Native mode:** User accounts, global groups, and other universal groups from any domain in the forest
Can Be a Member of	• **Mixed mode:** Not applicable • **Native mode:** Domain local and universal groups in any domain
Scope	• Visible in all domains in a forest
Permissions for	• All domains in a forest

Use universal groups to nest global groups so that you can assign permissions to related resources in multiple domains. A Windows 2000 domain must be in native mode to use universal groups.

The following summarizes the universal group membership rules:

- *Membership.* You cannot create universal groups in mixed mode. Native mode can contain user accounts, global groups, and other universal groups from any domain in the forest.

- *Can be a member of:* The universal group is not applicable in mixed mode. In native mode, the universal group can be a member of domain local and universal groups in any domain.

- *Scope.* Universal groups are visible in all domains in the forest.

- *Can be assigned permission for:* All domains in the forest.

◆ Strategies for Using Groups in a Domain

- **Using Global and Domain Local Groups**
- **Class Discussion: Using Groups in a Single Domain**

To use groups effectively, you need a strategy for employing different group scopes. The scope of a group identifies the extent to which the group is applied in the tree or forest. In Active Directory, there are three different types of group scopes: universal, global, and domain local.

This topic addresses the scope of groups in a single domain network. In a single domain, global groups and domain local groups are the two group scopes that are available. By using the best group strategies for global and domain local groups, users will more effectively gain access to resources in a single domain network.

Note   For more information about using groups in multiple domain networks, see Module 10, "Creating and Managing Trees and Forests," in Course 2154, *Implementing and Administering Microsoft Windows 2000 Directory Services*.

Using Global and Domain Local Groups

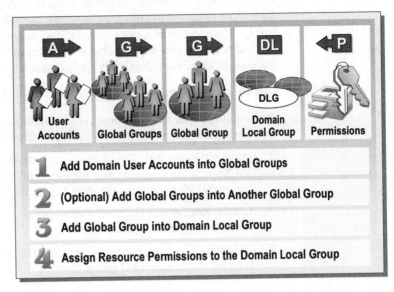

The recommended strategy for using both global and domain local groups is to add domain user accounts (A) into global groups (G), add global groups into domain local groups (DL), and then assign resource permissions (P) to the domain local groups. This strategy, *A G DL P*, provides the most flexibility while reducing the complexity of assigning access permissions to the network.

Using the A G DL P Strategy

As an example of using the A G DL P strategy, consider an organization that has users in the Accounts Payable OU and Accounts Receivable OU who need to gain access to accounting data in the Accounting database. Within the Accounts Payable OU and the Accounts Receivable OU, you create a global group for users who share the responsibility of reviewing accounting data. This global group needs to gain access to the accounting data in the accounting database. After the group is created, you add this group into a domain local group, and then the appropriate permissions on the accounting data are assigned to the domain local group.

The following example illustrates how to implement the A G DL P strategy:

1. Organize users based on administrative needs, such as their locations and job tasks, and then create a global group and add the user accounts into it. Create a global group called Accounts Payable and add all user accounts into it.

2. Create a domain local group into which you can add all global groups that need the same access to a resource. Add the Accounts Payable global group into the Accounting domain local group.

3. Assign the required permissions to the domain local group. Assign the necessary permissions to use the accounting data in the Accounting domain local group. In this way, if you add additional global groups to the Accounting domain local group, all users can gain access to the accounting data.

Using the A G G DL P Strategy

Consider another situation in which users in multiple departments need the same type of access to multiple resources. In such a situation, nesting of global groups is a good choice. For example, if all users in the Accounts Payable and Accounts Receivable departments in the Accounting division need access to the accounting data, use the existing global groups in each department.

The following example illustrates the A G G DL P strategy:

1. Create Accounts Payable and Accounts Receivable global groups, and add appropriate user accounts into each global group.

2. Create an Accounting Division global group representing all of the users in that Accounting division. Add the Accounts Payable and Accounts Receivable global groups into the Accounting Division global group.

3. Add the Accounting Division global group into the appropriate domain local groups that control access to resources.

4. Assign the necessary permissions to use the accounting data in the Accounting domain local group.

Class Discussion: Using Groups in a Single Domain

Contoso, Ltd. headquarters has a single domain that is located in Paris.
Contoso, Ltd. has managers who need to gain access to the inventory database
to perform their jobs.

- What would you do to ensure that the managers have the required access to
  the inventory database?

Contoso, Ltd. wants to react more quickly to market demands. It has been determined that the accounting data needs to be available to the entire accounting staff. Contoso, Ltd. wants to create the group structure for the entire Accounting division that includes the Accounts Payable and Accounts Receivable departments.

- What would you do to ensure that the managers have the required access and that there is a minimum of administration?

Lab B: Setting Up and Administering Groups in a Single Domain

Objectives

After completing this lab, you will be able to:

- Create and nest global groups.

- Create domain local groups and assign permissions to resources.

- Implement and test the recommended group strategy.

Prerequisites

Before working on this lab, you must:

- Know the difference between mixed mode and native domain mode.

- Understand the recommended strategy for using groups to manage access to domain resources.

Lab Setup

- To complete this lab, you need to run the batch file C:\Moc\Win2154a\Labfiles\Groups.bat to create folders and text files for the Human Resources departments so that you can assign permissions to these resources.

Estimated time to complete this lab: 30 minutes

Exercise 1
Creating the Global Group Structure

Scenario

The Human Resources division at Northwind Traders has recently grown to include the following three departments, Benefits, Payroll, and Training. The Human Resources vice president has announced a division-level initiative to make the administrative structure of all of the departments uniform. Therefore, you need to create a new global and domain local group structure for the managers in the Human Resources division. This structure must include the maintenance of groups at the department level while still maintaining a single current group for all managers at the division level. Resource access will be granted to the appropriate domain local groups for both department level data and division level data.

Goal

In this exercise, you will create the OU structure for the Human Resources division, which includes creating an OU for each of the three departments. You will then create global groups for managers in each of the departments, and then create a global group for all of the managers in the Human Resources division. You will then nest the three department global groups into the Human Resources division global group.

Tasks	Detailed Steps
❓	What domain mode should your domain be using to meet the stated goal and why?
	native
1. Within *domain*.nwtraders.msft (where *domain* is your assigned domain name), create the following OU structure: • Human Resources • Human Resources\Benefits • Human Resources\Payroll • Human Resources\Training	a. Log on as Administrator with a password of **password**. b. Open Active Directory Users and Computers from the **Administrative Tools** menu. c. In the console tree, right-click *domain*.**nwtraders.msft**, point to **New**, and then click **Organizational Unit**. d. In the New **Object – Organizational Unit** dialog box, in the **Name** box, type **Human Resources** and then click **OK**. e. Expand *domain*.**nwtraders.msft**, and then click **Human Resources**. f. Right-click **Human Resources**, point to **New**, and then click **Organizational Unit**. g. In the **New Object – Organizational Unit** dialog box, in the **Name** box, type **Benefits** and then click **OK**. h. Repeat steps f and g, changing step g as required, to create the organizational units **Payroll** and **Training** under the Human Resources OU.

Tasks	Detailed Steps
2. Within the OUs corresponding to the group names, create the following global security groups for each department: • Benefits Managers • Payroll Managers • Training Managers	a. Expand **Human Resources**, right-click **Benefits**, point to **New**, and then click **Group**. b. In the **New Object – Group** dialog box, in the **Group name** box, type **Benefits Managers** c. Ensure that **Group scope** is set to **Global** and that **Group type** is set to **Security**, and then click **OK**. d. Repeat steps a through c, changing steps a and b as required, to create **Payroll Managers** under the **Payroll** OU, and to create **Training Managers** under the Training OU.
3. Create the HR Managers global security group for the division in the Human Resources OU.	a. Right-click **Human Resources**, point to **New**, and then click **Group**. b. In the **New Object – Group** dialog box, in the **Group name** box, type **HR Managers** c. Ensure that **Group scope** is set to **Global** and **Group type** is set to **Security**, and then click **OK**.
4. Make each department managers' group a member of the HR Managers group.	a. Click **Human Resources**, in the details pane, right-click the HR Managers global group, and then click **Properties**. b. In the **HR Managers Properties** dialog box, on the **Members** tab, click **Add**. c. In the **Select Users, Contacts, Computers, or Groups** dialog box, in the **Name** box, scroll to the bottom of the list and click **Benefits Managers**, and then click **Add**. d. Repeat step c to add **Payroll Managers** and **Training Managers**, and then click **OK**. e. In the **HR Managers Properties** dialog box, on the **Members** tab, ensure that the three department global groups are listed as members of the HR Managers global group, and then click **OK**.

❓ If a user account is added to the Benefits Managers group, will you also need to update the membership of the HR Managers group?

No – it is in the Ben. Man. group, & Global but Security

Exercise 2
Creating the Domain Local Groups and Assigning Permissions to Resources

Scenario

The global group structure for the Human Resources division has been created. The domain local groups need to be created and used to assign the Human Resources managers access to resources. Permissions will be granted only to domain local groups.

Goal

In this exercise, you will create the domain local groups Benefits Data, Payroll Data, and Training Data for each department. You will assign to the domain local groups permissions to access the departmental resources. Having separate domain local groups for each department provides greater flexibility in assigning access to resources.

Tasks	Detailed Steps
1. Within the OUs corresponding to the group names, create the following domain local security groups for each department: • Benefits Data • Payroll Data • Training Data	a. In Active Directory Users and Computers, expand **Human Resources**, right-click **Benefits**, point to **New**, and then click **Group**. b. In the New **Object – Group** dialog box, in the **Group name** box, type **Benefits Data** c. Set **Group scope** to **Domain local** and ensure that **Group type** is set to **Security**, and then click **OK**. d. Repeat steps a through c, changing steps a and b as required, to create **Payroll Data** under the **Payroll** OU, and **Training Data** under the **Training** OU.
2. Within the Human Resources OU, create the following domain local security group: • HR Data.	a. Right-click **Human Resources**, point to **New**, and then click **Group**. b. In the **New Object – Group** dialog box, in the **Group name** box, type **HR Data** c. Set **Group scope** to **Domain local** and ensure that **Group type** is set to **Security**, and then click **OK**.
3. Assign the domain local group in each department full control permission to the corresponding folder under C:\Hr.	a. In the **Run** box, type **C:\Hr** and then click **OK**. b. In the C:\HR window, right-click the Benefits folder, and then click **Properties**. c. In the **Benefits Properties** dialog box, on the **Security** tab, click **Add**. d. In the **Select Users, Contacts, Computers, or Groups** dialog box, in the **Name** box, scroll toward the bottom of the list and click **Benefits Data**, click **Add**, and then click **OK**. e. In the **Benefits Properties** dialog box, in the **Permissions** box, select the check box to allow Full Control, and then click **OK**. f. Repeat steps b through e, changing steps b through e as required, to assign Full Control permissions on the Payroll folder to **Payroll Data**, and on the Training folder to **Training Data**.

Tasks	Detailed Steps
4. Remove inherited permissions and assign read permissions on the C:\Hr folder to HR Data.	**a.** In the C:\HR window, change to the C:\ folder.
	b. Right-click the HR folder and then click **Properties**.
	c. In the **HR Properties** dialog box, on the **Security** tab, click **Add**.
	d. In the **Select Users, Contacts, Computers, or Groups** dialog box, in the **Name** box, scroll toward the bottom of the list and click **HR Data**, click **Add**, and then click **OK**.
	e. Click to clear the **Allow inheritable permissions from parent to propagate to this object** check box, click **Remove** to close the dialog box asking whether to copy or remove the inherited permissions, and then click **OK** to close the **HR Properties** dialog box.
	f. Close the C:\ window.

Exercise 3
Using Global and Domain Local Groups

Scenario

Managers will have full control of file resources within their departments. Managers will also have read access to resources in the other departments. User accounts will only directly belong to the global group for their department. Connect the global and domain local groups to achieve this result. Testing will be performed to verify proper access to resources.

Goal

In this exercise, you will add the division level global group to the domain local groups to allow access to resources. You will allow managers to have full control of file resources within their departments and read access to file resources in the other departments. You will create a test user account, and verify that a manager in the Benefits department has read access to all of the human resources data and full control access to the data the manager's own department.

Tasks	Detailed Steps
1. Add each department global group as a member of the corresponding domain local group.	a. In Active Directory Users and Computers, expand the Human Resources OU.
	b. Click the **Benefits** OU, in the details pane, right-click **Benefits Data**, and then click **Properties**.
	c. In the **Benefits Data Properties** dialog box, on the **Members** tab, click **Add**.
	d. In the **Select Users, Contacts, Computers, or Groups** dialog box, in the **Name** box, scroll toward the bottom of the list and click **Benefits Managers**, click **Add**, click **OK**, and then click **OK** again to close the **Benefits Data Properties** dialog box.
	e. Repeat steps b through d, changing steps b through d as required, to add **Payroll Managers** to **Payroll Data**, and add **Training Managers** to **Training Data**.
2. Add the HR Managers global group as a member of the HR Data domain local group.	a. In the console tree, click the **Human Resources** OU, in the details pane, right-click **HR Data**, and then click **Properties**.
	b. In the **HR Data Properties** dialog box, on the **Members** tab, click **Add**.
	c. In the **Select Users, Contacts, Computers, or Groups** dialog box, in the **Name** box, scroll toward the bottom of the list and click **HR Managers**, click **Add**, click **OK**, and then click **OK** again to close the **HR Data Properties** dialog box.

Tasks	Detailed Steps
3. To test the group structure, in the Benefits OU, create a user account with the following properties: Full name: TestBenefits User logon name: TestBenefits @*domain*.nwtraders.msft Add this user account to the Benefits Managers global group.	a. Click the **Benefits** OU, right-click **Benefits**, point to **New**, and then click **User**. b. On the **New Object – User** page, in both the **Full name** and the **User logon name** boxes, type **TestBenefits** and then click **Next**. c. Click **Next**, and then click **Finish**. d. Right-click the user **TestBenefits**, and then click **Properties**. e. In the **TestBenefits Properties** dialog box, on the **Member Of** tab, click **Add**. f. In the **Select Groups** dialog box, under the **Name** column, click **Benefits Managers**, click **Add**, click **OK**, and then click **OK** again to close the **TestBenefits Properties** dialog box. g. Close Active Directory Users and Computers.
4. Log off, and then log on as TestBenefits. Verify that you can gain full control access to the resource C:\Hr\Benefits\Benefits.txt, and only read access to C:\Hr\Payroll\Payroll.txt.	a. Log off, and then log on as TestBenefits without typing a password. b. In the **Run** box, type **C:\Hr\Benefits\Benefits.txt** and then click **OK**. c. In the Benefits.txt – Notepad window, in the text box, type **Some Modifications** and then save and close the document. d. In the **Run** box, type **C:\Hr\Payroll\Payroll.txt** and then click **OK**. e. In the Payroll.txt – Notepad window, in the text box, type **Some Modifications** and then save the document. *The **Save As** dialog box appears, which indicates that you do not have the permissions to save changes to this document.* f. Click **Cancel** to close the **Save As** dialog box. g. Close the Payroll.txt – Notepad window, and then click **No** to close the dialog box indicating that your changes will be not be saved.
? Did you have full control access to C:\Hr\Benefits\Benefits.txt but only read access to C:\Hr\Payroll\Payroll.txt? _____ _____ _____	
5. Log off.	▪ Close all open windows, and then log off.

Troubleshooting Domain User Accounts and Groups

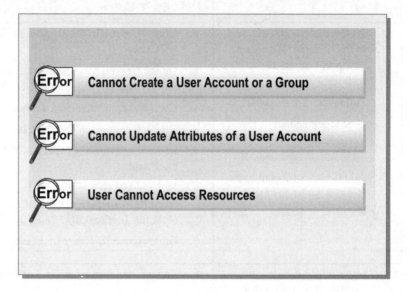

You may encounter problems when setting up and administering domain user accounts and groups. The following list describes some of these potential problems and strategies for resolving them:

- Cannot create a user account or a group. The possible cause could be a violation of uniqueness rules. Recreate the user account or the group adhering to the uniqueness rules.

- Cannot update attributes of a user account. You may not have permission to update user accounts. Check the permissions assigned to you. If you do not have the permissions, log on as an administrator and then assign the appropriate permissions. You can also ask the administrator of that OU to assign you appropriate permissions.

- Users cannot access resources. The possible cause is that the user account is a member of a nested group that has been explicitly denied access to a resource.

Best Practices

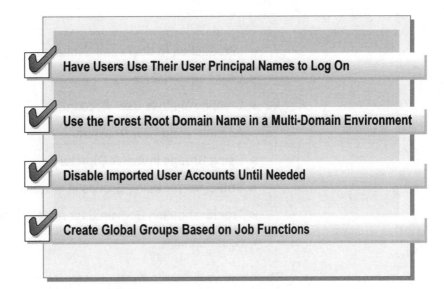

The following list provides best practices for administering user accounts and groups:

- Have users use their user principal names, for example, suzanf@contoso.msft, instead of downlevel logon names, such as user names and domain names, when logging on from a computer running Windows 2000. By using their user principal name to log on, the user account can be moved from one domain to another without impacting the user.

- Use the forest root domain name for the user principal name suffix for user accounts in a multi-domain environment so that the name can be shorter and simpler. Also consider using a user principal name suffix that matches the user's e-mail address, which may include creating an alternative user principal name suffix.

- When creating multiple user accounts by using a bulk import method, disable the accounts if users are not going to use these accounts immediately. Because the password for an imported user account is initially blank, any unauthorized person with knowledge of the user account name could log on, set a new password, and then gain access to the network.

- Create global groups that are based on job functions. When you create a global group that is based on job functions and place the global groups in domain local groups, you need only change the group membership to accommodate changes in user job functions. For example, Cornelia Kunze is a user account in the global group Accountants, which is a member of the domain local group Accountant Files. The domain local group Accountant Files has read permissions to the accountants' audit share and modify permission to the accountant's documents share. If a new user is taking over Cornelia Kunze's job function, you need only remove Cornelia Kunze from the Accountant global group and add the new user to the Accountant global group. You do not need to change any permissions, because permissions are assigned to domain local groups that contain the global groups that contain the user accounts.

Review

- Introduction to Users and Groups
- User Logon Names
- Creating Multiple User Accounts
- Administering User Accounts
- Using Groups in Active Directory
- Strategies for Using Groups in a Domain
- Troubleshooting Domain User Accounts and Groups
- Best Practices

1. Your organization has acquired a small subsidiary, and you want to use Active Directory Users and Computers to create domain user accounts for the new employees. For business reasons, the subsidiary wants to retain its former identity with its customers. How do you create user principal names for the new employees that match users' e-mail addresses without changing users' e-mail addresses?

    Add suffixes

2. Your organization has recently hired many new employees to work in its new branch office, which is opening next month. You need to set up user accounts for these employees so that they can use and share network resources. You know that the Human Resources department has data on all new employees. What is the most efficient way to bulk import the user accounts?

    Bring in as CSV file.

3. What is the purpose of adding one group into another group?

Speed up access.

Make your life easier.

4. What strategy should you apply when you use domain local and global groups?

Put users in global groups ; put them in DL groups ; assign permissions to DL.

Microsoft®
Training &
Certification

Module 5: Publishing Resources in Active Directory

Contents

Microsoft®

Overview

- **Introduction to Publishing Resources**

- **Setting Up and Administering Published Printers**

- **Implementing Printer Locations**

- **Setting Up and Administering Published Shared Folders**

- **Comparing Published Objects with Shared Resources**

- **Troubleshooting Published Resources**

- **Best Practices**

One of the key challenges of network administration is providing secure and selective publication of network resources to users. Another challenge is making it easy for employees to find information on the network. Use Microsoft® Windows® 2000 Active Directory® directory service to address these challenges by storing information about network objects, offering rapid information retrieval, and providing security mechanisms that control access to information in Active Directory.

At the end of this module, you will be able to:

- Describe the purpose of publishing resources in Active Directory.

- Set up and administer published printers in Active Directory.

- Set up printer locations for published printers.

- Set up and administer published shared folders in Active Directory.

- Differentiate between the object that is published in Active Directory and the actual shared resource.

- Troubleshoot common problems with publishing resources in Active Directory.

- Apply best practices for publishing resources in Active Directory.

Introduction to Publishing Resources

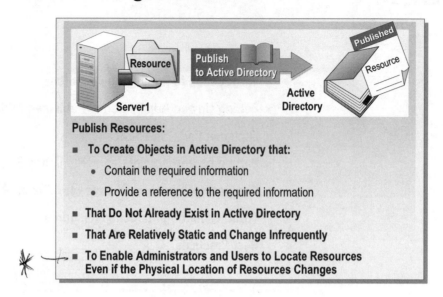

Publish Resources:

- **To Create Objects in Active Directory that:**
  - Contain the required information
  - Provide a reference to the required information
- **That Do Not Already Exist in Active Directory**
- **That Are Relatively Static and Change Infrequently**
- **To Enable Administrators and Users to Locate Resources Even if the Physical Location of Resources Changes**

Publishing means creating objects in Active Directory that either directly contain the information that you want to make available, or provide a reference to that information. For example, a user object contains useful information about a user, such as the user's telephone numbers and e-mail addresses. Alternatively, a shared folder object contains a reference to a shared folder, which resides on a computer in the network. Resources should be published in Active Directory when the information contained in them is useful to a user or when it needs to be highly accessible.

You do not need to publish resources that already exist in Active Directory, such as user accounts. However, you need to publish resources that do not exist in Active Directory. Examples of two resources that do not exist in Active Directory are printers on a computer that is not running Windows 2000 and shared folders.

The main characteristic of information published in Active Directory is that it is relatively static and changes infrequently. Not publishing highly volatile information, such as network adapter statistics, prevents extensive replication traffic across a network. Telephone numbers and e-mail addresses are examples of relatively static information that is suitable for publishing.

Publishing resources in Active Directory enables you to locate resources even if the physical location of the resources changes. For example, as long as you update the reference to the physical location, all shortcuts pointing to an Active Directory object that represents a published shared folder will continue to work after the shared folder has been moved to another computer. No user action is required to continue gaining access to the shared folder.

◆ Setting Up and Administering Published Printers

- ■ **Introduction to Printer Publishing**

- ■ **Managing Printer Publishing**

- ■ **Publishing Printers on Computers Not Running Windows 2000**

- ■ **Administering Published Printers**

Every Windows 2000–based print server that is either a member of a domain or a domain controller automatically publishes its printers in Active Directory. The integration between printer and Active Directory makes it possible to automatically publish printers, and to search across a domain for printers at different physical locations.

You can also publish printers on computers not running Windows 2000 by using Active Directory Users and Computers, or by using the Pubprn.vbs script, which is provided in the System32 folder.

Introduction to Printer Publishing

Default Behavior of Printers:

- Any Printer Shared by a Windows 2000-Based Print Server Is Published in Active Directory

- A Printer Is Automatically Removed from Active Directory When a Print Server Is Removed from the Network

- Each Print Server Is Responsible for Its Printers Being Published in Active Directory

- Windows 2000 Automatically Updates the Printer Object's Attributes in Active Directory

When you create printers in Windows 2000, the printer and Active Directory integration is configured by default and printers are automatically published in Active Directory. Publishing printers means that the print queues are being published. The object in Active Directory is called a *printQueue*. An administrator needs to administer printers only to change the default behavior. The following summarizes the default behavior of published printers:

- Any printer shared by a print server running Windows 2000 that has an account in an Active Directory domain is published in Active Directory. This means that to publish a printer in Active Directory, an administrator needs to only install and share the printer.

- If a print server is removed from the network, its published printer is automatically removed from Active Directory. This prevents users from trying to connect to a published printer that no longer exists on the network.

- Each print server is responsible for its own printers being published in Active Directory. The domain controllers do not search the network for printers to be published. When a printer is shared, the server that is hosting the shared printer contacts a domain controller to request that the printer be published in Active Directory. There is no centralized printer publishing service.

- When you configure or modify the printer's properties, Windows 2000 automatically updates the published printer object's attributes in Active Directory.

Managing Printer Publishing

- **View Printer Objects**
  - On the **View** Menu, click **Users, Groups, and Computers as containers**
- **Control the Publishing of a Printer**
  - Select or clear the **List in the Directory** check box
  - Configure the **Automatically publish new printers in Active Directory** Group Policy setting
- **Manage Orphaned Printers**
  - Active Directory removes orphaned printer objects through the orphan pruner process
  - Orphan pruner deletes printer objects for non-existent printers at frequent intervals

When you install and share a printer on a computer running Windows 2000, and that computer belongs to a domain, Windows 2000 automatically publishes the printer in Active Directory.

Viewing Printer Objects in Active Directory

When you publish a printer, the printer object is placed in the print server's computer object in Active Directory. You can view printer objects in Active Directory. To view printer objects, you enable the option in Active Directory Users and Computers to view objects as containers.

To view printer objects in Active Directory Users and Computers, perform the following step:

- On the **View** menu, click **Users, Groups, and Computers as containers**, and then in the console tree, select the computer on which you installed the printer. The published printer appears in the details pane.

Controlling Printer Publishing

Sometimes you may not want to automatically publish printers in Active Directory to prevent users from viewing or using these printers. An example of a printer that you would not want to automatically publish would be the printer that the by Payroll department uses to print paychecks. You can control the automatic publishing of a printer by using the **List in the directory** check box on the printer's **Sharing** tab. The **List in the Directory** check box is selected by default; therefore, the printers that are added using the Add Printer wizard are automatically published.

You can use Group Policy to control the default behavior of published printers. You configure the Automatically publish new printers in Active Directory Group Policy setting under Computer Configuration\Administrative Templates\Printers in Group Policy to disable or enable automatic publishing of printers.

If you do not want a shared printer to be published, you must clear the **List in the Directory** check box after installing the printer; that is, if you chose to share the printer while you were installing it. If the **List in the directory** check box for an already published printer is cleared, the printer will be unpublished.

Managing Orphaned Printers

When you delete a printer from a print server, the corresponding Active Directory object is removed. However, there are situations in which the printer is not deleted but is no longer available, such as when the print server is rebuilt or turned off. In these situations, Active Directory needs to remove these orphaned printer objects. Active Directory removes these orphaned printer objects through a process called the *orphan pruner,* which runs on each domain controller.

At frequent intervals, the orphan pruner verifies all of the printer objects in Active Directory to see if the corresponding printer still exists on the specified print server. If the orphan pruner cannot locate a printer (the orphan pruner checks three times in a row, each time at an eight hour interval), it assumes that the printer is no longer valid and deletes the printer object.

Note For more information about Group Policy, see Module 7, "Implementing Group Policy," in Course 2154, *Implementing and Administering Microsoft Windows 2000 Directory Services*.

Publishing Printers on Computers Not Running Windows 2000

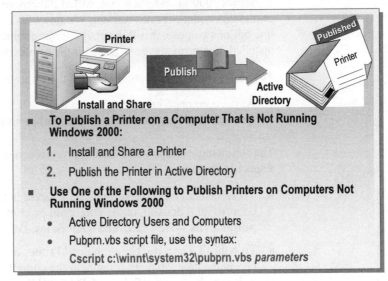

- **To Publish a Printer on a Computer That Is Not Running Windows 2000:**
  1. Install and Share a Printer
  2. Publish the Printer in Active Directory
- **Use One of the Following to Publish Printers on Computers Not Running Windows 2000**
  - Active Directory Users and Computers
  - Pubprn.vbs script file, use the syntax:

    Cscript c:\winnt\system32\pubprn.vbs *parameters*

Printers that are added to Windows 2000 and shared are automatically published in Active Directory. If you install and share a printer on a computer that is not running Windows 2000, the printer is not automatically published in Active Directory. However, after creating and sharing these printers, you can publish these shared printers in Active Directory by using either Active Directory Users and Computers or the Pubprn.vbs script. You can publish any printer that is accessible through a universal naming convention (UNC) path name.

Using Active Directory Users and Computers to Publish Printers

To publish a printer by using Active Directory Users and Computers, perform the following steps:

1. In Active Directory Users and Computers, right-click the OU where you want to publish the printer.

2. Point to **New**, and then click **Printer**.

3. Type the UNC name of the printer that you want to publish in Active Directory.

   The UNC path is the complete Windows 2000 name of a network resource that conforms to the \\servername\sharename syntax.

Using the Pubprn.vbs Script File to Publish Printers

Windows 2000 includes a script, called Pubprn.vbs that you can use to publish printers on computers not running Windows 2000. Depending on the command-line options you use, this Pubprn.vbs script publishes either all of the printers installed on a print server or just a single printer that you specify.

To run the Pubprn.vbs script, perform the following step:

- At the command prompt, type
  Cscript %systemroot%\system32\pubprn.vbs *<parameters>*

The following examples use the Pubprn.vbs script file to publish all printers or a specific printer:

- To publish all installed printers on a server in the Sales OU in the contoso.msft domain, at the command prompt, type
  pubprn.vbs *server* **"LDAP://OU=Sales, DC=contoso,DC=msft"**

- To publish a specific printer named Printer on a server in the Accounting OU in the contoso.msft domain, at the command prompt, type
  pubprn.vbs *server***Printer LDAP://OU=Accounting, DC=contoso,DC=msft"**

In the above examples, *server* is a server running earlier versions of Windows and Microsoft Windows NT®, and LDAP://OU=..,DC=..." is the path in Active Directory of the target container that will hold the published printer.

Note For more information about adding and sharing printers in Windows 2000, see Module 10, "Configuring Printing," in Course 2152, *Implementing Microsoft Windows 2000 Professional and Server*.

Administering Published Printers

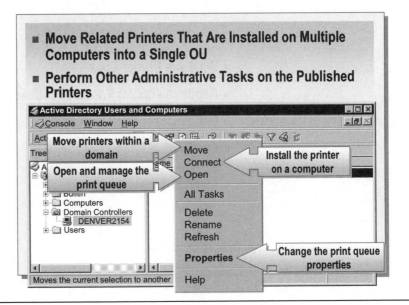

Administering printers includes some common tasks such as moving printers, connecting to printers on the network, and modifying properties of the print queue objects. After you publish printers in Active Directory, user and organization printing needs may change. This change may require you to configure printer settings so that your printing resources better fit these needs.

To organize published printers, you can move related published printers that are installed on multiple computers into a single OU. By moving printers into a single OU, you can perform similar administrative functions on all of the printers in the OU.

To move printers within a domain, perform the following steps:

1. In Active Directory Users and Computers, select the published printers to be moved.

2. Right-click the printers that you selected, and then click **Move**.

3. In the **Move** dialog box, expand the domain tree, click the OU to which you want to move the selected printers, and then click **OK**.

The following lists the other administrative tasks that you can perform on the published printers in Active Directory Users and Computers:

- To install the printer, right-click the printer object, and then click **Connect**.

- To open the print queue and perform tasks, such as canceling print jobs, reordering printers in the queue, and changing printer properties, right-click the printer object, and then click **Open**.

- To change the print queue properties, right-click printer object, and then click **Properties**. The information on the **General** tab is published with the print queue object and helps users find printers.

◆ Implementing Printer Locations

- ■ **What Are Printer Locations?**
- ■ **Requirements for Printer Locations**
- ■ **Defining Location Names**
- ■ **Configuring Printer Locations**

In a Windows 2000 network, printer locations allow users to locate and connect to print devices that are physically located near the user. When you implement printer locations, the results of an Active Directory search return a list of printers that are located in the same physical location (for example, in the same building or on the same floor) as the client computer that a person is using when searching for printers. Additionally, printer locations make it easy to find printers in any location in which a user is currently located.

What Are Printer Locations?

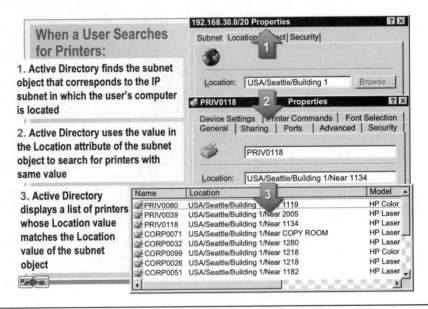

Printer locations allow users to locate and connect to print devices that are in close physical proximity to the user. When you implement printer locations, the results of an Active Directory search return a list of printers that are located in the same physical location (for example, in the same building or on the same floor) as the client computer that a person is using when searching for published printers.

This "find the nearest printer to me" capability is based on the assumption that print devices that are physically located near a user reside on the same Internet Protocol (IP) subnet as the user's client computer. In Active Directory, an IP subnet is represented by a subnet object, which contains a Location attribute that is used during a search for printers. Active Directory uses the value of this attribute as the text string in a search for printers that also have a Location attribute.

Therefore, when a user searches for a printer when printer locations is implemented, Active Directory:

1. Finds the subnet object that corresponds to the subnet on which the user's computer is located.

2. Uses the value in the Location attribute for the subnet object as the text string for a search for all published printers that have the same Location attribute value.

3. Returns to the user a list of printers whose Location attribute value matches the one that is defined for the subnet object. The user can then connect to the nearest printer.

Additionally, users can also search for printers in any location, which is useful if they need to find and connect to a printer in a physical location different from the one in which they normally work.

Requirements for Printer Locations

- **An Active Directory Network with Two or More IP Subnets**

- **An IP Addressing Scheme That Corresponds to the Physical Topology of the Network**

- **A Subnet Object for Each Site**

  - Represents an IP subnet in Active Directory

  - Contains a location attribute that Active Directory uses to find printers in the same physical location as a client computer

- **Client Computers That Can Search Active Directory**

Before you can implement printer locations, your Windows 2000 network must meet the following requirements:

- An Active Directory network configured with at least one site and two or more IP subnets. Because IP subnets are used to identify the physical location of a printer, a network with only one network ID address or one IP subnet would assume that all printers reside in one physical location and therefore would be in close proximity to users.

- An IP addressing scheme that corresponds to the geographical and physical layout of your network. Therefore, computers and printers that reside on the same IP subnet must also reside in approximately the same physical location. If this is not the case with your network, you cannot implement printer locations.

- A subnet object for each site. The subnet object, which represents an IP subnet in Active Directory, contains a Location attribute that is used during a search for printers. The value of this Location attribute is used during a search of Active Directory to locate printers that reside near the physical location of the user's client computer.

- Client computers that can search Active Directory. Users with client computers running Windows 2000 Professional or running previous versions of Windows that are configured with an Active Directory client can take advantage of printer locations when searching for printers.

Note   You use Active Directory Sites and Services to create a subnet object. For more information about Windows 2000 sites and subnet objects, see Module 11, "Managing Active Directory Replication," in Course 2154, *Implementing and Administering Microsoft Windows 2000 Directory Services.*

Defining Location Names

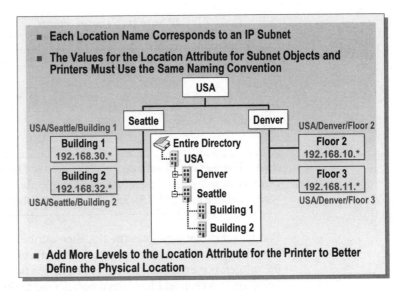

The key to implementing printer locations is to develop a naming convention for printer locations that corresponds to the physical topology of your network. These printer location names must correspond to an IP subnet. You use this naming convention to determine the values for the Location attributes for both the subnet object and the printer object.

Names for printer locations must use the following format:

> *Name/name/name/*...

The maximum length for each name is 32 characters; the maximum length for a full location name is 260 characters.

To illustrate how to define a naming convention for printer location names, assume that there is an international organization with offices in Seattle and Denver (which can correspond to sites in Windows 2000), and offices in other countries. The IP addressing scheme for the organization closely corresponds to the geographical distribution of the offices, and to characteristics such as buildings and floors. In the Seattle site, each building has its own subnet, whereas each floor in the Denver site has its own subnet. Each of these subnets corresponds to a specific subnet object in Active Directory.

Therefore, the following naming convention could be used for this example:

- The top-level node is the country.

- The next level is the city name.

The levels following the city name provide more structure as needed and vary in depth depending on the complexity of the organization and the amount of detail available in the IP network.

The following table illustrates the location names and corresponding IP subnets for the example shown in the graphic above.

Site	IP Subnet (Name of Subnet Object in Active Directory)	Location Name
Seattle	192.168.30.0/24	USA/Seattle/Building 1
Seattle	192.168.32.0/24	USA/Seattle/Building 2
Denver	192.168.10.0/24	USA/Denver/Floor 2
Denver	192.168.11.0/24	USA/Denver/Floor 3

Note The naming of subnet objects in Active Directory uses the format of *IPaddress/ActiveBits*. Therefore, in example above, for subnet 192.168.10.0 with a net mask of 255.255.255.0, the subnet object name is 192.168.10.0/24.

For the value that populates the Location attribute of the printer, you can add more levels to the location name to help further identify the physical location of the printer. For example, for the Seattle office (where the subnets correspond to buildings) you can add levels that correspond to the floor and office near where the printer is located:

- USA/Seattle/Building 1/Floor 3/Office 3334
- USA/Seattle/Building 1/Floor 4/Office 4404
- USA/Seattle/Building 1/Floor 5/Office 5517

Therefore, when a user in Building 1 in the Seattle site searches for a printer, the detailed location names appear in the results box of a search and help the user locate the closest printer.

Note For more information about developing a naming convention for printer locations, see the topic "Establishing a naming convention for printer locations" in the Windows 2000 Server Help.

Configuring Printer Locations

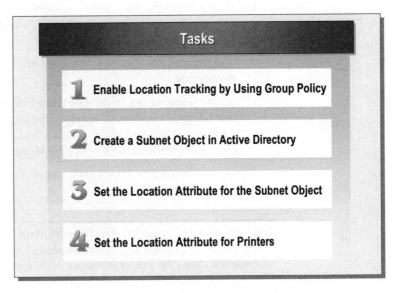

After you have met the requirements for implementing printer locations, and have devised a naming convention, perform the following tasks to configure printer locations:

1. Enable printer location tracking by using Group Policy. Printer location tracking pre-populates the location search field when a user searches Active Directory for a printer. The value used to pre-populate the search field is the *same* value that is specified in the Location attribute of the subnet object that corresponds to the IP subnet in which the user's computer is located.

    To enable printer location tracking by using Group Policy, enable the Pre-populate printer search location policy setting, which is located in Computer Configuration\Administrative Templates\Printers.

    If you do not enable printer location tracking, users must select the printer location to search.

2. Create a subnet object in Active Directory. If a subnet object does not already exist, use Active Directory Sites and Services to create a subnet object. The format of the subnet name is *IPaddress/ActiveBits*.

3. Set the Location attribute for the subnet object. Use the naming convention that you develop for printer location names as the value of this attribute. To set the Location attribute for the subnet object, perform the following steps:

    a. In Active Directory Sites and Services, right-click the subnet object, and then click **Properties**.

    b. Click the **Location** tab, type the location name that corresponds to the subnet object, and then click **OK**.

        If you have enabled printer location tracking as the first step, you can also browse for locations rather than typing the entire location string.

4. Set the Location attribute for printers. For each printer located in the physical location that corresponds to the IP subnet, you must add the Location attribute to the printer's properties. Use the same printer location name that you set for the subnet object. To set the Location attribute for printers, perform the following steps:

   a. In the Printers folder, right-click the printer object, and then click **Properties**.

   b. On the **General** tab, in the **Location** box, type the printer location name (including any additional levels in the location name to better describe the physical location of the printer), and then click **OK**. You can also browse for the location by clicking **Browse**.

   When installing a new printer, you can specify the Location attribute with the Add Printer wizard.

Note   For more information about using Group Policy, see Module 8, "Using Group Policy to Manage User Environments," in Course 2154, *Implementing and Administering Microsoft Windows 2000 Directory Services*.

Setting Up and Administering Published Shared Folders

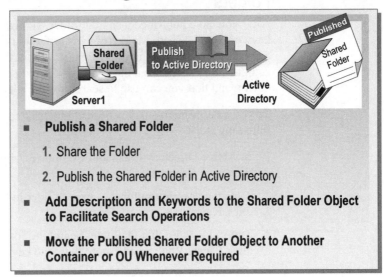

- **Publish a Shared Folder**

  1. Share the Folder

  2. Publish the Shared Folder in Active Directory

- **Add Description and Keywords to the Shared Folder Object to Facilitate Search Operations**

- **Move the Published Shared Folder Object to Another Container or OU Whenever Required**

In Active Directory, you can publish any shared folder that can be accessed by using a UNC name. A computer running Windows 2000 can use Active Directory to locate the object that represents the shared folder, and then connect to the shared folder. After publishing shared folders, you can define keywords and a description for the shared folders, and if required, move shared folders to related OUs.

Publishing Shared Folders.

You can publish shared folders in Active Directory by using Active Directory Users and Computers. To make a shared folder accessible, you first share the folder, and then publish the shared folder in Active Directory.

To publish a shared folder, perform the following steps:

1. In Active Directory Users and Computers, right-click the OU where you want to publish the shared folder, click **New**, and then click **Shared Folder**.

   - In the **Shared Folder Name** box, type the name of the folder.

2. In the **UNC Path** box, type the UNC that you want to publish in Active Directory.

   The UNC path is the complete Windows 2000 name of a network resource that conforms to the \\servername\sharename syntax.

Configuring Search Options for Published Shared Folders

After you have published a shared folder, you can add a description and keywords to the shared folder objects to facilitate searching for it. Descriptions can be used to provide more information about the shared folder, such as its contents. Keywords are a list of words that you can define for the shared folder object, and that you can use to search for the shared folder.

To add a description and keywords to the shared folder objects, perform the following steps:

1. In Active Directory Users and Computers, right-click the shared folder, and then click **Properties**.

2. Type the description for the shared folder in the **Description** box, and then click **Keywords**.

3. Type a keyword that facilitates searching for this folder, click **Add**, and then click **Close**. You can add more than one keyword for a shared folder.

Moving Published Shared Folders

After a shared folder has been published, you can move the published folder to another container or OU. When you perform the move operation, you move the shared folder object (which contains information or references the shared folder) in Active Directory. The physical location of the shared folder does not change.

To move a shared folder, perform the following steps:

1. In Active Directory Users and Computers, right-click the shared folder, and then click **Move**.

2. Select the destination container or OU, and then click **OK**.

Comparing Published Objects with Shared Resources

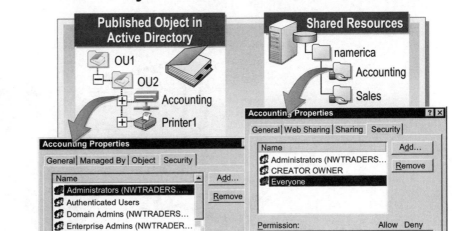

When implementing published folders and published printers, it is important to understand the difference between the object that is published in Active Directory and the actual shared resource, such as a printer or folder. Understanding this difference assists you when troubleshooting problems that users may have when accessing published resources.

The object that is published in the directory is completely separate from the shared resource that it represents. In other words, when you publish a printer or shared folder in Active Directory, two distinct objects exist, the shared printer or folder and the published object. The published object contains a reference to the location of the shared resource. When a user accesses the published object, Windows 2000 redirects the user to the shared resource.

DACLS for Shared Resources and Published Objects

Because a shared resource and the published object that refers to the shared resource are two different objects, each of these objects has its own discretionary access control list (DACL). Use the DACL on the shared resource to control access to that shared resource. For example, with a shared printer, use the DACL to control who is allowed to print to the printer, and who is allowed to manage print jobs. Use the DACL on the corresponding printQueue object published in Active Directory to control who can view or change the properties of the published object.

A user requires Read permission on the DACL of a published object to view the published object, or to have the object appear in the results list when searching for a published resource. A user may be able to view a published object, which is controlled by the DACL on the published object, but may not be able to access the shared resource, depending on the DACL on the shared resource.

Lab A: Publishing Resources in Active Directory

Objectives

After completing this lab, you will be able to:

- Publish shared folders in Active Directory.
- Publish shared printers in Active Directory.

Prerequisites

Before working on this lab, you must have:

- The knowledge and skills to create shared folders.
- The knowledge and skills to install and configure printers.

Lab Setup

To complete this lab, you need the following:

- A computer running Windows 2000 Advanced Server configured as a domain controller.

Important   The lab does not reflect the real-world environment. It is recommended that you always use complex passwords for any administrator accounts, and never create accounts without a password.

Important   Outside of the classroom environment, it is strongly advised that you use the most recent software updates that are necessary. Because this is a classroom environment, we may use software that does not include the latest updates.

Estimated time to complete this lab: 15 minutes

Exercise 1
Publishing Printers

Scenario

To take full advantage of the benefits provided by Active Directory, you have decided to publish shared printers in Active Directory. This will allow your users to easily locate and access the shared printers.

Goal

In this exercise, you will install and share a new printer. You will then modify the properties of the printer to make it easier for users to search the network for it.

Tasks	Detailed Steps
1. Install and share a new printer by using the following information: • Local printer • Do not automatically detect • Use LPT1 • HP Color LaserJet 4500 • Default printer name • Default share name • No location or comment • Do not print a test page	a. Log on as Administrator with a password of **password**. b. Open the Printers folder from the **Start/Settings** menu. c. In the Printers folder, double-click **Add Printer**. d. On the **Welcome to the Add Printer Wizard** page, click **Next**. e. On the **Local or Network Printer** page, ensure that **Local printer** is selected, clear the **Automatically detect and install my Plug and Play printer** check box, and then click **Next**. f. On the **Select the Printer Port** page, ensure that **LPT1:** is selected, and then click **Next**. g. On the **Add Printer Wizard** page, in the list of **Manufacturers**, click **HP**, in the list of **Printers**, click **HP Color LaserJet 4500**, and then click **Next**. h. On the **Name Your Printer** page, click **Next** to accept the default name. i. On the **Printer Sharing** page, click **Next** to accept the default name. j. On the **Location and Comment** page, click **Next**. k. On the **Print Test Page**, click **No**, and then click **Next**. l. On the **Completing the Add Printer Wizard** page, click **Finish**. *Windows 2000 installs the required printer drivers and then adds an icon for your printer to the Printers folder.* m. Close the Printers folder.
? Is this printer now published in Active Directory? _No – must share it._ _Yes._	

Tasks	Detailed Steps
2. Attempt to locate the printer in Active Directory Users and Computers.	**a.** Open Active Directory Users and Computers from the **Administrative Tools** menu.
❓ Can you see the published printer in Active Directory Users and Computer? Why or why not? *No — it's not shared yet.* *~~Yes~~ No. — not w/out changing *view* as containers — then can see.*	
2. *(continued)*	**b.** On the **View** menu, click **Users, Groups, and Computers as containers**. **c.** Expand **Domain Controllers**, and then click *computer* (where *computer* is your assigned computer name).
❓ What appears in the details pane? *Printer icon, representing a published printer.*	
2. *(continued)*	**d.** Leave Active Directory Users and Computers open.
3. Modify the Location property of the published printer to make it easier to search for. Set the location to Classroom.	**a.** In the details pane, double-click the published printer. **b.** In the *computer*-**HP Color LaserJet 4500 Properties** dialog box, in the **Location** box, type **Classroom** and then click **OK**. **c.** On the **View** menu, click **Users, Groups, and Computers as containers**. **d.** Close Active Directory Users and Computers.
4. Attempt to locate the published printer by searching for printers in the Classroom.	**a.** Open **For Printers** from the **Search** menu. **b.** In the **Find Printers** dialog box, on the **Printers** tab, in the **Location** box, type **Classroom** and then click **Find Now**. 🖥️ *Notice that when the search is complete, the published printer appears in the dialog box.* **c.** Close all open windows, and then log off.

Exercise 2
Publishing Shared Folders

Scenario
To take full advantage of the benefits provided by Active Directory, you have decided to publish shared folders in Active Directory. This will allow your users to easily locate and access the shared folders.

Goal
In this exercise, you will create a shared folder and then attempt to locate the shared folder on the network. You will then publish that shared folder in Active Directory, and then attempt to locate the shared folder on the network.

Tasks	Detailed Steps
1. Create and share a folder at the root of Drive C. Name the folder Accounting and use the same name for the share name.	a. Log on as Administrator with a password or **password**. b. At the root of Drive C, create a folder named **Accounting**. c. Share the Accounting folder by using the default values.
2. Attempt to locate the shared folder by browsing the network.	a. On the desktop, double-click **My Network Places**, double-click **Entire Network**, click **entire contents**, double-click **Microsoft Windows Network**, double-click *domain* (where *domain* is your assigned domain name), and then double-click *computer* (where *computer* is your assigned computer name).

❓ Does the Accounting folder appear in the window displaying the shared resources available on your computer?

Yes.

❓ Why is this not an efficient way to locate network resources?

Slow.
Too many clicks.
must know name of computer & domain shared in.

Tasks	Detailed Steps
2. *(continued)*	b. Close all open windows.
3. Publish the Accounting folder in the Domain Controllers OU by using Active Directory Users and Computers.	a. Open Active Directory Users and Computers from the **Administrative Tools** menu.
	b. Expand your domain, if necessary, and then in the console tree, click **Domain Controllers**.
	c. Right-click **Domain Controllers**, point to **New**, and then click **Shared Folder**.
	d. In the **New Object – Shared Folder** dialog box, in the **Name** box, type **Accounting**
	e. In the **Network Path (\\server\share)** box, type *computer***accounting** (where *computer* is your assigned computer name), and then click **OK**.
	Notice that Accounting now appears in the Domain Controllers OU.
	f. Leave Active Directory Users and Computers open.
4. Modify the following properties of the Accounting object to make it easier to locate: • Description: Accounts Payable. • Keywords: FY00, AP Reports.	a. In the details pane, double-click **Accounting**.
	b. In the **Accounting Properties** dialog box, in the **Description** box, type **Accounts Payable** and then click **Keywords**.
	c. In the **Keywords** dialog box, type **FY00**
	d. Click **Add**, type **AP Reports** click **Add**, and then click **OK**.
	e. Click **OK** to close the **Accounting Properties** dialog box, and then close Active Directory Users and Computers.
5. Attempt to locate the Accounting folder by searching your domain for a shared folder by using the keyword FY00.	a. On the desktop, double-click **My Network Places**, double-click **Entire Network**, click **entire contents**, and then double-click **Directory**.
	b. Right-click your domain, and then click **Find**.
	c. In the **Find Users, Contacts and Groups** dialog box, in the **Find** list, click **Shared Folders**.
	d. On the **Shared Folders** tab, in the **Keywords** box, type **FY00** and then click **Find Now**.
	Notice that when the search is complete, the Accounting folder appears in the dialog box.
	e. Double-click **Accounting**.
❓ What happens?	

Accounting ~~icon~~ object appears — shared

Opens empty dialog box

Tasks	Detailed Steps
5. *(continued)*	f. Close all open windows and dialog boxes.
6. Run the Rmpub.vbs script located in the C:\Moc\Win2154A\Labfiles folder. This script removes all of the objects created in this lab.	a. Open the C:\Moc\Win2154A\Labfiles folder. b. Double-click **Rmpub.vbs**. This batch file removes all of the objects created in this lab. c. Log off.

Troubleshooting Published Resources

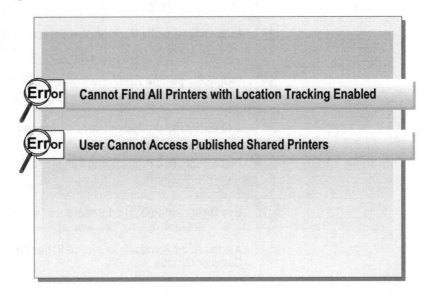

You may encounter problems when publishing resources in Active Directory. Here are some of the common problems that you may encounter and some strategies for resolving them:

- You cannot find all printers with location tracking enabled. If the location string for a printer does not match the naming convention used for the location string on the subnet objects, that printer will not be found when searching for printers based on location. To correct this problem, ensure that the location string on all printers matches the naming convention used for the subnet objects and update the location string for any printers that do not follow the naming convention.

- Users cannot access published shared printers. When a user tries to connect to a published printer, an error message appears indicating that the printer cannot be located. This error message is generated when a published printer becomes orphaned, that is, if the shared printer is no longer available but the orphan pruner process has not yet removed the published printer object from the directory. To resolve this problem, either ensure that the printer is shared and available or manually delete the published printer object from Active Directory.

Best Practices

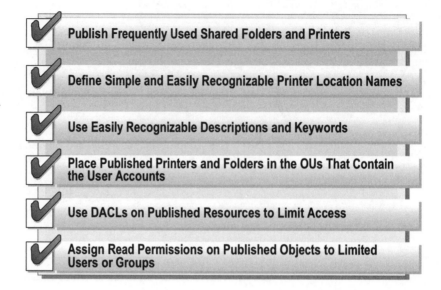

Publish Frequently Used Shared Folders and Printers

Define Simple and Easily Recognizable Printer Location Names

Use Easily Recognizable Descriptions and Keywords

Place Published Printers and Folders in the OUs That Contain the User Accounts

Use DACLs on Published Resources to Limit Access

Assign Read Permissions on Published Objects to Limited Users or Groups

The following list provides best practices for publishing resources in Active Directory:

- Publish the frequently used shared folders and printers in Active Directory. Publishing these resources makes it easier to find these resources and to keep track of the folders and printers, even if someone changes the physical location.

- The printer location names are intended to be read by users. Therefore, the names should be simple and correspond to names that users readily recognize. For example, using the postal codes known only to the facilities management group would not be helpful. In addition, avoid using special characters in printer location names. Special characters make printer location names difficult to read.

- When publishing folders, ensure that you use easily recognizable descriptions and keywords. This makes it easier for users to locate published folders when performing a search.

- Place published printers and folders in the OUs that contain the user accounts that will be accessing the published resources on a regular basis. Place published printers and folders in separate OUs eases the management burden.

- Make use of the DACLs on published resources to limit which users or groups can see the published resources. If a user or group does not have at least Read permission on a published resource, that resource will not appear when the user searches for published resources. This makes it easier for users to locate published folders and printers that they should be using.

- Assign Read permissions on the published objects to *only* those users or groups that have been assigned the necessary permissions to access the corresponding shared resource. This helps reduce support calls generated by access denied messages when users attempt to access shared folders and printers that are published in Active Directory.

Review

Introduction to Publishing Resources

Setting Up and Administering Published Printers

Implementing Printer Locations

Setting Up and Administering Published Shared Folders

Comparing Published Objects with Shared Resources

Troubleshooting Published Resources

Best Practices

1. You can control the publishing of a printer. Which option allows you to enable and disable the publishing of printers in Active Directory?

   ~~Add printer.~~ Check box in properties of printer.

2. What are the main steps involved in activating the location option in printers?

   Group Policy - "
   Sites & Services -
   Properties of Printer - fill in location.

3. You enabled the location tracking feature for all of the printers in your building so that users know where each printer is located. But when location tracking was enabled, the users could find only those printers with a Location attribute that matched the naming convention. They could not find the printers that had locations set to a different naming convention. How will you enable the viewing of all printers?

   Update location properties for all printers.

4. How do you ensure that all shortcuts pointing to a published shared folder will continue to work after the shared folder has been moved to another computer?

   Update shard folder in Act. Dir.

5. You have published a large number of printers and shared folders and your users are complaining that the list of objects returned when they perform a search is too large. Additionally, they are complaining that they are receiving access denied error messages when trying to access a number of the shared resources. How would you solve these problems?

Microsoft®
**Training &
Certification**

Module 6: Delegating Administrative Control

Contents

Overview

- **Object Security in Active Directory**
- **Controlling Access to Active Directory Objects**
- **Delegating Administrative Control of Active Directory Objects**
- **Customizing MMC Consoles**
- **Setting Up Taskpads**
- **Best Practices**

The Microsoft® Windows® 2000 Active Directory® directory service provides administrators with a high degree of control over who has access to information in Active Directory. By managing the permissions on directory objects and properties, administrators can precisely specify which accounts can gain access to Active Directory and the level of access that these accounts can have. This precision allows administrators to delegate specific authority over portions of Active Directory to groups of users, without making the information in Active Directory vulnerable to unauthorized access. The ability to delegate relieves the burden of centralized administration.

Controlling access and delegating administrative authority to Active Directory objects is important, especially when developing a decentralized administrative model.

At the end of this module, you will be able to:

- Manage object security in Active Directory.
- Control access to Active Directory objects.
- Delegate administrative control of Active Directory objects.
- Create and deploy customized consoles.
- Create and deploy customized taskpads.
- Apply best practices for delegating administrative control.

◆ Object Security in Active Directory

- ■ **Active Directory Security Components**
- ■ **Discretionary and System Access Control Lists**
- ■ **Access Control Entries**
- ■ **Inheritance**
- ■ **The Logon Process**
- ■ **Access Tokens**
- ■ **How Windows 2000 Grants Access to Resources**

Windows 2000 implements an object-based security model and access control for all objects in Active Directory. *Access control* is the process of authorizing users, groups, and computers to access objects on the network. Several security components in Active Directory make up access control and allow access control information to be passed down through inheritance. Inheritance enables the access control information defined at higher-level containers in Active Directory to flow down to sub-containers and their objects.

Windows 2000 requires users to log on, and then after Windows 2000 and Active Directory authenticate the user's unique identity, Windows 2000 grants or denies access to resources.

Active Directory Security Components

- **Security Principals**
  - User, security group, service, and computer
  - Identified by a unique ID

- **Security Identifiers (SIDs)**
  - Uniquely identify security principals
  - Are never reused

- **Security Descriptors**
  - Security information associated with an object
  - Contains DACLs and SACLs

Each object in Active Directory is associated with a unique *security descriptor* that defines the access permissions that are required to read or update the object properties. Permissions are assigned at the property level. Security principals, security identifiers, and security descriptors are the basic components of the access control model.

Security Principals

A *security principal* is an account holder to which you can assign permissions. Examples of security principals are user, security group, and computer accounts. Each security principal within a Windows 2000 domain is identified by a unique security identifier.

Security Identifiers (SIDs)   *— uniquely identify user in Active Dir.*

A *security identifier (SID)* is a value that uniquely identifies a user, group, service, or computer account within an organization. Every account is issued a SID when it is created. Access control mechanisms in Windows 2000 identify security principals by SID rather than by name. After a SID is issued to an account, it is never reused on another account.

Security Descriptors

A security descriptor is a data structure containing the security information associated with a securable object. A security descriptor identifies an object's owner by SID. If permissions are configured for the object, its security descriptor contains a discretionary access control list (DACL) with SIDs for the users and groups who are allowed or denied access. If auditing is configured for the object, its security descriptor also contains a system access control list (SACL) that controls how the security subsystem audits attempt to access the object.

Discretionary and System Access Control Lists

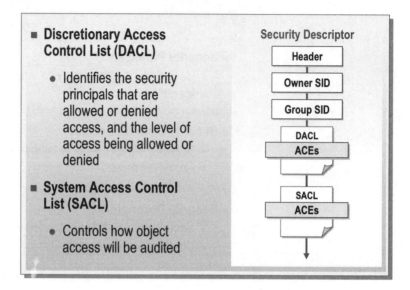

Discretionary Access Control List (DACL)

- Identifies the security principals that are allowed or denied access, and the level of access being allowed or denied

System Access Control List (SACL)

- Controls how object access will be audited

Security Descriptor

Header

Owner SID

Group SID

DACL
ACEs

SACL
ACEs

A security descriptor is a binary data structure of variable length that contains an access control list (ACL). An ACL is an ordered list of access control entries (ACEs) that define the security protections applicable to an object, a set of the object's properties, or an individual property of an object. The data structure of a security descriptor has the following parts:

- *Header.* The header field contains a revision number and a set of control flags that describe characteristics of the security descriptor, such as the memory layout, which elements are present, and how particular elements were added or modified.

- *Owner.* The Owner field contains the SID for the object's owner. The owner of an object can modify permissions and grant other users the right to take ownership.

- *Primary Group.* The Primary Group field contains the SID for the owner's primary group. This information is used for services with Macintosh and by the POSIX subsystem but is ignored by the rest of Windows 2000.

- *Discretionary access control list (DACL).* The DACL is a list of zero or more ACEs identifying who is allowed or denied access, and the level of access being allowed or denied.

- *System access control list (SACL).* The SACL is similar to the DACL except that it is used to control how Windows 2000 audits access to objects. When an audited action occurs, the operating system records the event in the security log.

Access Control Entries

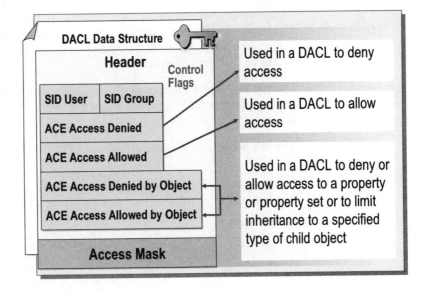

An access control entry (ACE) is used to determine which operations a security principal is allowed to perform on an object, or in the case of ACEs in a SACL, which operations are audited.

ACEs in a DACL

Each ACE in a DACL consists of:

- A SID is a value that uniquely identifies a user, group, service, or computer account within an organization.

- A header that specifies whether the ACE allows or denies access.

- An access mask that lists the operations allowed or denied.

- A set of bit flags that determine whether child objects can inherit the ACE. The header for an ACE contains a set of inheritance flags that control how the ACE is inherited and how the ACE affects a child object that inherits it.

- A flag that indicates the type of ACE.

ACE Types

There are six different types of ACEs in Windows 2000. These six types of ACEs are divided into two groups, generic ACEs, which can be applied to all objects to which security can be applied, including file system objects and Active Directory objects, and object-specific ACEs, which can be applied only to Active Directory objects.

Generic and object-specific ACEs are fundamentally alike. The difference between them is the granularity of control they offer over inheritance and object access.

The following table lists the different ACE types:

Type	Description
Access denied	Used in a DACL to deny access.
Access allowed	Used in a DACL to allow access.
System audit	Used in a SACL to log access attempts.
Access denied, object specific	Used in a DACL to deny access to a property or property set, or to limit inheritance to a specified type of child object.
Access allowed, object specific	Used in a DACL to allow access to a property or property set, or to limit inheritance to a specified type of child object.
System audit, object specific	Used in a SACL to log attempts to access a property or property set, or to limit inheritance to a specified type of child object.

Inheritance

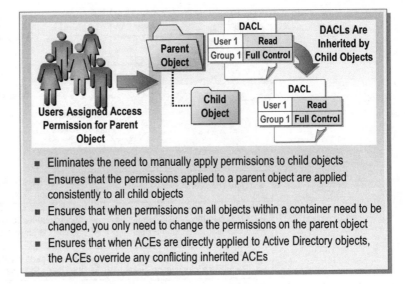

- Eliminates the need to manually apply permissions to child objects
- Ensures that the permissions applied to a parent object are applied consistently to all child objects
- Ensures that when permissions on all objects within a container need to be changed, you only need to change the permissions on the parent object
- Ensures that when ACEs are directly applied to Active Directory objects, the ACEs override any conflicting inherited ACEs

Inheritance is the process that passes ACEs in a parent object's security descriptor to a child object's security descriptor. Inheritance means that access control information that is defined at higher-level containers in Active Directory flows down to sub-containers and their objects. In Windows 2000, inheritable ACEs are propagated from a parent object to a child object when one of the following three events takes place:

- A child object is created.

- The DACL on the parent object is modified.

- The SACL on the parent object is modified.

Any object can be the child of another object. Only container objects can be parents. The DACL and SACL for a container object can carry ACEs that are not needed on the container but are present only for the purpose of inheritance, so that the ACEs are passed down to subsequent generations of objects until they reach a non-container child object, where they become effective ACEs.

Permission inheritance in Windows 2000 simplifies the task of managing permissions by:

- Eliminating the need to apply permissions manually to child objects as they are created.

- Ensuring that the permissions applied to a parent object are applied consistently to all child objects.

- Ensuring that when you need to modify permissions on all objects within a container, you only need to change the permissions on the parent object, and the child objects automatically inherit those changes.

- Ensuring that when ACEs are directly applied to Active Directory objects, they are applied before any conflicting previously inherited ACEs.

The Logon Process

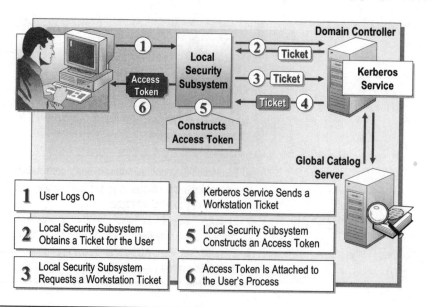

1 User Logs On	**4** Kerberos Service Sends a Workstation Ticket
2 Local Security Subsystem Obtains a Ticket for the User	**5** Local Security Subsystem Constructs an Access Token
3 Local Security Subsystem Requests a Workstation Ticket	**6** Access Token Is Attached to the User's Process

Windows 2000 controls access to resources by requiring a user to first log on to a computer. To log on to a computer, Windows 2000 requires each user to provide a unique user name and password. The logon process that occurs for a Windows 2000 computer includes the following steps:

1. A user logs on, providing the required security credentials, including user name, password, and domain name. These credentials are passed to the security subsystem on the local computer.

2. The local security subsystem uses DNS to locate a domain controller in the user's domain. The security subsystem then contacts the Kerberos service, called the Key Distribution Center, running on the domain controller, and requests a session ticket for the user to communicate with the Kerberos service. A *ticket* is a record that allows a client computer to authenticate itself to a server. The Kerberos service queries Active Directory to authenticate the user and contacts a global catalog server to obtain the user's universal group memberships. The Kerberos service then returns a session ticket to the client computer that contains the user's SID and the user's universal, global, and domain local group memberships, which are used for future transactions with the Kerberos service.

Note Every domain controller in the domain runs the Kerberos service and is capable of granting session tickets for users and computers. If a domain controller is not available, domain authentication fails and the user is logged on by cached logon credentials at the client computer. The client computer periodically attempts to locate the Kerberos service during the user's session, and will complete the domain authentication process if one is found.

3. The local security subsystem again contacts the Kerberos service on the domain controller and requests another session ticket authorizing the user to gain access to the Workstation service on the client computer to complete the user logon process. This request includes a copy of the user's session ticket that the Kerberos service uses to identify the user.

4. The Kerberos service authenticates the user's ticket by querying Active Directory and the global catalog server to verify the information contained in the user's session ticket. The Kerberos service then constructs a Workstation session ticket for the user that contains the validated security credentials copied from the user's original ticket, and returns the session ticket to the client computer.

5. The local security subsystem on the client computer extracts the user's SID and universal, global, and domain local group memberships from the Workstation session ticket. The subsystem then constructs the user's access token by adding the SIDs for local groups to which the user belongs and a list of the local user rights assigned to the user.

6. The local computer creates a process with an access token attached. The access token is used to authenticate the user and serves as an identity card whenever the user attempts to use system resources.

The Network Logon Process

A *network logon* occurs when a user establishes a network connection to a remote computer running Windows 2000, for example, when connecting to a shared folder. The authentication process is very similar to that of an interactive logon process.

The client computer obtains a server session ticket from the Kerberos service running on a domain controller in the user's domain. The client computer then sends the server session ticket to the local security subsystem on the server, which extracts the user's security credentials and constructs an access token for the remote user. This access token is used to authenticate the user whenever a resource on the server is accessed.

The Secondary Logon Process

Secondary logon provides the ability to start and run an application by using the security credentials of another user without ending a session already in progress. For example, you can run administrative tools while logged on with a standard user account.

Important For more detailed information about the steps in the Kerberos V5 authentication process, see *Windows 2000 Kerberos Authentication* under **Additional Reading** on the Web page on the Student Materials compact disc.

Access Tokens

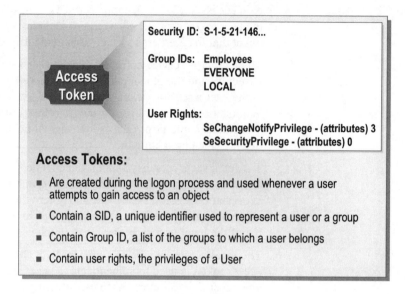

Access Tokens:

- Are created during the logon process and used whenever a user attempts to gain access to an object

- Contain a SID, a unique identifier used to represent a user or a group

- Contain Group ID, a list of the groups to which a user belongs

- Contain user rights, the privileges of a User

To gain access to any resource on the network, a user must have an access token. An *access token* is created for the user during the logon process and contains attributes that establish the security credentials for that user on the local computer. The access token is used whenever a user attempts to gain access to an object. When the user runs an application, a new process is started that inherits the user's access token. The access token is permanently attached to each of the user's processes and serves as an identity card whenever the user attempts to use system resources. When a user's process attempts to gain access to any object, Windows 2000 verifies the user's SID and the list of Group IDs in the access token against the object's DACL. This verification determines whether the user is granted access to the object.

Security Identifier (SID)

The SID is the security identifier for the user who is logged on. A SID allows the operating system to uniquely identify each user and group account, even if that account is renamed or has the same name as another account. In this way, permissions assigned to an object can be used only by that object, regardless of what the user or group is named.

Group ID

The *Group ID* is a list of the groups to which the user belongs. For a domain logon process, the domain controller compiles a list of the SIDs for the global and domain local groups of which the user is a member. The domain controller contacts a global catalog server to obtain the SIDs of any universal groups of which the user is a member. This list is returned to the client computer, which then adds any local groups of which the user is a member.

User Rights

User rights are the privileges of the user. The local computer adds the list of user rights to the access token. User rights determine which administrative actions the user can perform on the local computer, such as shutting down the computer, logging on interactively, and taking ownership of objects.

How Windows 2000 Grants Access to Resources

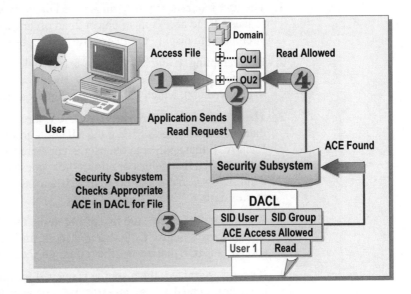

Users gain access to resources when Windows 2000 checks the DACL list of allowed permissions against the user's requested access. This process is known as *authorization*. Windows 2000 controls access to resources in two ways:

- By requiring users to log on using a set of verifiable security credentials. These credentials are then compared against a set of permissions assigned to Active Directory objects and network resources, such as shared folders and NTFS file system files.

- By granting access to only those resources that the user has permission to use. After the user's unique identity has been authenticated by Windows 2000 and then by Active Directory, the user can receive access to specific resources on the network from any computer in any domain of the organization.

The user gains access to a resource through the following process:

1. The user requests access to an Active Directory object. For example, a user requests Read access to an object in an organizational unit (OU) by attempting to display the **Properties** dialog box for a user account.

2. By attempting to display the **Properties** dialog box, the user causes Active Directory Users and Computers to generate an input/output (I/O) request to Windows 2000, which validates the request through the security subsystem.

3. The security subsystem reads the DACL for an object, searching for ACEs that contain the user's SID or the SID of a group to which the user belongs. Each ACE that applies to the user is compared against the requested access until an ACE that denies or allows the requested access is located. If a denial is encountered, or no ACE exists for the requested access, the user's request fails.

   ACEs that deny access are listed first in the DACL. The security subsystem first processes the ACEs that deny access, and grants access to the object as soon as an ACE that allows the requested access is encountered.

4. If access is granted, the resource is opened for only the requested access. If the user is denied access, an error message appears.

   A DACL is checked only when the resource is initially opened. If a user's permissions for an object are changed while the user is accessing the object, the user retains the current access to the object. The permission assignment is updated the next time the user gains access to the object.

◆ Controlling Access to Active Directory Objects

- Active Directory Permissions
- Controlling Inheritance of Permissions
- Setting Active Directory Permissions
- Object Ownership
- Changing Object Ownership

When you want to control which users have access to specific objects in Active Directory, consider the following:

- The permissions that you are allowed to attach to the object provide security for resources by allowing you to control which users can gain access to individual objects or object attributes, and the users' level of access. You can use permissions to grant administrative privileges for a single object, or to a specific user or group.

- Every object in Active Directory has an owner. The owner controls how permissions are set on an object and to whom permissions are assigned.

Active Directory Permissions

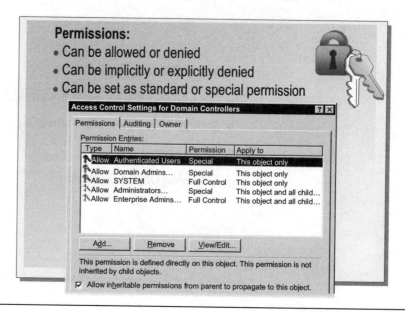

Permission is an authorization assigned by an owner so that users can perform an operation on a specific object, such as a user account. If you own an object, you can assign user or security group permission to perform some or all of the tasks that you are authorized to do. You can also assign permission to take ownership.

Every permission that an object's owner assigns to a particular user or group is stored as an ACE in a DACL that is part of the object's security descriptor. Users can view ACEs under **Permission Entries** in the **Access Control Settings** dialog box.

Allowing and Denying Permissions

You can allow or deny permissions. Denied permissions take precedence over any permissions that you otherwise allow for user accounts and groups. For example, if you deny permission for a user to gain access to an object, the user will not have that permission, even if you allow the permission for a group of which the user is a member. Deny permissions only when it is necessary to remove a permission that a user may have been assigned through a group membership.

Implicit or Explicit Permissions

You can implicitly or explicitly deny permissions as follows:

- When permission to perform an operation is not explicitly assigned, it is *implicitly denied.*

  For example, if the Marketing group is allowed Read permission on a user object, and no other security principal is listed on the DACL for that object, users who are not members of the Marketing group are implicitly denied access. The operating system does not allow users who are not members of the Marketing group to read the properties of the user object.

- Permissions can also be *explicitly denied.*

  For example, it may be necessary to prevent a user named Don from being able to view the properties of a user object, even though he is a member of the Marketing group that has permissions view the properties of the user object. You can prevent Don from accessing the user object properties by explicitly denying him Read permission. This example ideally illustrates the use of explicit denials, which is to exclude a subset, such as Don, within a larger group, such as Marketing, from performing a task that the larger group has permissions to perform.

Standard and Special Permissions

You can set *standard* and *special* permissions on objects. Standard permissions are the most frequently assigned permissions. Special permissions provide you with a finer degree of control for assigning access to objects.

The following table lists standard object permissions that are available for most objects, and the type of access that each permission allows the user to have.

Object permission	Allows the user to
Full Control	Change permissions and take ownership, plus perform the tasks that are allowed by all other standard permissions.
Read	View objects and object attributes, the object owner, and the Active Directory permissions.
Write	Change object attributes.
Create All Child Objects	Add any type of child object to an OU.
Delete All Child Objects	Remove any type of child object from an OU.

Controlling Inheritance of Permissions

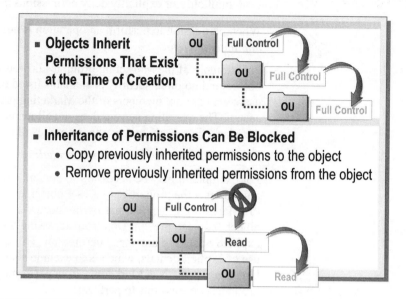

Permission inheritance in Active Directory automatically causes objects within a container to inherit the permissions of that container. For example, the files within a folder, when created, inherit the permissions of the folder. This inheritance minimizes the number of times that you need to assign permissions for objects. When an object is created within a container, the Active Directory schema defines a default DACL for the object.

Applying Permissions to Child Objects

When you assign permissions, you can have the permission apply to the object's child objects. For example, if you want a user to administer all objects in an OU, assign Full Control permissions to the user, and all child objects then inherit this permission. To indicate that permissions have been inherited, the check boxes in the **Permissions** dialog box for child objects are dimmed.

Preventing Child Objects from Inheriting Permissions

You can prevent permission inheritance so that a child object does not inherit permissions from its parent object. You prevent inheritance when you want to set more restrictive permissions on child objects than on a parent object. When you prevent inheritance, only the permissions that you explicitly assign to the object apply.

When you prevent permission inheritance, Windows 2000 allows you to:

- Copy previously inherited permissions to the object. Then, according to your needs, you can make any necessary changes to the permissions.

- Remove previously inherited permissions from the object. Then, according to your needs, you can assign new permissions for the object.

Setting Active Directory Permissions

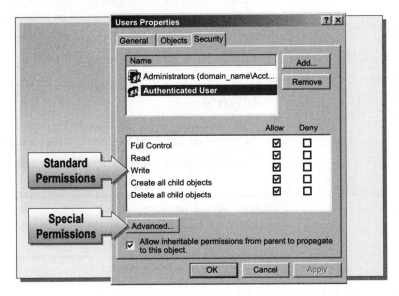

Windows 2000 determines a user's authorization to use an object by checking the DACL for permissions assigned to the user on that object. These permissions are visible in Active Directory by viewing an object's **Properties** dialog box.

Standard Permissions

To add or change permissions for an object, perform the following steps:

1. In Active Directory Users and Computers, on the **View** menu, click **Advanced Features**.

2. Right-click the object, click **Properties**, and then in the **Properties** dialog box, click the **Security** tab.

3. Perform either or both of the following steps:

   - To add a new permission, click **Add**, click the user account or group to which you want to assign permissions, click **Add**, and then click **OK**.

   - To remove a permission, select the user account or group that you want to remove, click **Remove**, and then click **OK**.

4. In the **Permissions** box, select the **Allow** or **Deny** check box for each permission that you want to add or change.

Special Permissions

Standard permissions are sufficient for most administrative tasks. However, you may need to view the special permissions available within a standard permission to further refine the access permissions.

To view special permissions, perform the following steps:

1. On the **Security** tab in the **Properties** dialog box for the object, click **Advanced**.

2. In the **Access Control Settings** dialog box, on the **Permissions** tab, click the entry that you want to view, and then click **View/Edit**.

3. To view the permissions for specific attributes, click the **Properties** tab.

Caution Avoid assigning permissions for specific attributes of objects. Errors can result, such as objects in Active Directory not being visible, preventing users from completing tasks.

Object Ownership

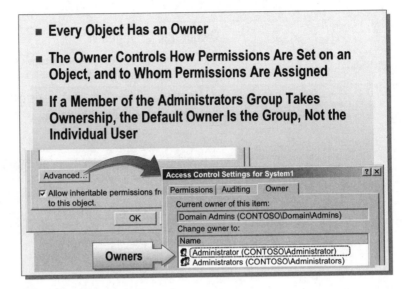

Every object in Active Directory has an owner. The person who creates the object automatically becomes the owner and, by default, has full control over the object. The owner controls how permissions are set on an object, and to whom permissions are granted, even if the owner is not listed in the DACL.

The default owner of an object is normally an individual user who is currently logged on. The only exceptions occur when the user is a member of either the Administrators group or the Domain Admins group. If a member of the Administrators group takes ownership, the default owner is the group, not the individual user. In both cases, the Owner field in the user's access token contains the SID for the group, not the SID for the individual user account.

To determine who owns which objects, perform the following steps:

1. Right-click the object, and then click **Properties**.

2. In the **Properties** dialog box, click the **Security** tab, and then click **Advanced**.

3. In the **Access Control Settings** dialog box, click the **Owner** tab.

4. The name of the object's owner is shown after **Current owner of this item** box.

Note   For more information about object ownership, see chapter 12, "Distributed Security" in the Distributed Systems Guide in the Microsoft Windows 2000 Server Resource Kit.

Changing Object Ownership

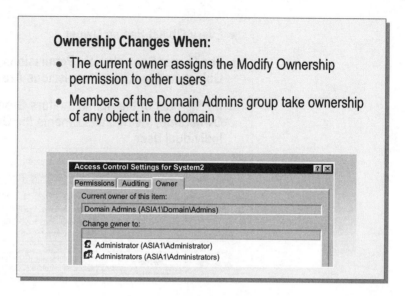

As an administrator, you can take ownership of any object, and then change the permissions for the object.

You can change ownership in the following ways:

- The current owner, any user with Full Control permission, or any user with Change Permission assigns the Modify Owner permission to another user who takes ownership of the object.

  For example, if an employee who owns an object leaves the company, you can let another user take ownership of that object, thereby reassigning responsibility for the object.

- A member of the Administrators group takes ownership of any object.

Note   Although members of the Administrators group can take ownership of an object, members of the Administrators group cannot transfer ownership.

To change ownership of an object, perform the following steps:

1. In the **Properties** dialog box for an object, on the **Security** tab, click **Advanced**.

2. Click the **Owner** tab, and then click your user account. If you are a member of the Administrators group, you can also click **Administrators**. This makes the Administrators group the owner.

3. Click **OK**, and then click **OK** again to take ownership.

◆ Delegating Administrative Control of Active Directory Objects

- **Overview of Delegating Administrative Control**
- **Using the Delegation of Control Wizard**
- **Guidelines for Delegating Administrative Control**

Delegation is the ability to assign responsibility of the management of Active Directory objects to another user, group, or organization.

You delegate by using the Delegation of Control wizard to set specific permissions on Active Directory objects. The Delegation of Control wizard allows you to select the user or group to which you want to delegate control, the organizational units and objects you want to grant those users the right to control, and the permissions to access and modify objects.

By delegating administrative control, you can eliminate the need for multiple administrative accounts that have broad authority, such as for an entire domain. Although you will most likely use the predefined Domain Admins group for administration of the entire domain, you can delegate the accounts that are members of the Domain Admins group to highly trusted administrative users.

Important It is recommended that you delegate administrative control to domain local groups when assigning permissions to objects in a domain. It is recommended that you delegate administrative control to global or universal groups when assigning permissions to objects in the configuration naming context. It is recommended that you delegate administrative control to global or universal groups for attributes that are published to the global catalog for Read permission. For more information on delegating control see The Windows 2000 Deployment Planning Guide at http://wwd/windows2000/library/resources/reskit/dpg/default.asp and the Active Directory Service Interfaces Overview at http://www.microsoft.com/windows2000/techinfo/howitworks/activedirectory/adsilinks.asp.

Overview of Delegating Administrative Control

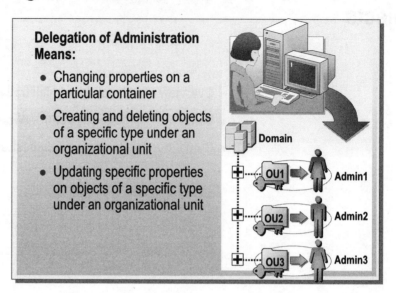

You delegate administrative control by creating organizational units within a domain and delegating administrative control for specific organizational units.

Windows 2000 contains specific permissions and user rights that you can use to delegate administrative control. By using a combination of organizational units, groups and permissions, you can designate administrative rights to a particular user such that the user has an appropriate level of administration over an entire domain, all organizational units within a domain, or even a single organizational unit.

There are three ways to define the delegation of administration responsibilities:

- Change properties on a particular container.

- Create and delete objects of a specific type under an organizational unit, such as users, groups, or printers.

- Update specific properties on objects of a specific type under an organizational unit. For example, you can delegate the right to set a password on a User object.

Using the Delegation of Control Wizard

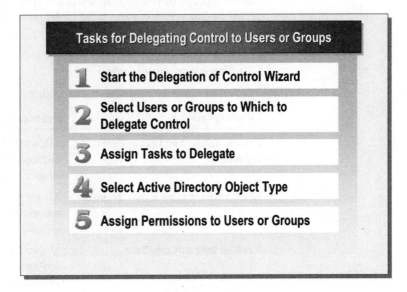

To assign permissions at the OU level, use the Delegation of Control wizard. You can assign permissions for managing objects, or you can assign permissions for specific attributes of those objects. Using the Delegation of Control wizard is the preferred method for delegating control because it reduces the possibility of unwanted effects from permission assignments.

To delegate administrative control to users or groups, perform the following tasks:

1. Start the Delegation of Control wizard.

   a. In Active Directory Users and Computers, click the OU for which you want to delegate control; for example, *AUAdmins*.

   b. On the **Action** menu, click **Delegate control** to open the wizard.

2. Select users or groups to which you want to delegate control.

   After you have opened the Delegation of Control wizard, perform the following step to select users or groups:

   • Click **Next** to open the **Users and Groups** page, select a user or group to which you want to assign permissions, and then click **Next** to assign tasks to delegate.

3. Assign tasks to delegate.

The Delegation of Control wizard allows you to either select common tasks to delegate or create custom tasks to delegate, by performing the following steps:

a. To delegate an existing task from a list of tasks, click **Delegate the following common tasks**.

The following table describes the available tasks:

Common task	Description
Create, delete, and manage user accounts	Allows the user or group to create, delete, and modify user accounts and attributes of all user accounts in the selected OU.
Reset passwords on a user account	Allows the user or group to change the passwords of all user accounts in the selected OU.
Read all user information	Allows the user or group to view all attributes of the objects in the selected OU. The user or group cannot modify any information.
Create, delete, and manage groups	Allows the user or group to create, delete, and modify group accounts and attributes of all group accounts in the selected OU.
Modify the membership of a group	Allows the user or group to change the members of groups in the selected OU.
Manage Group Policy links	Allows the user or group to add, delete, or modify the Group Policy links of the selected OU.

b. After you delegate a common task, end the wizard by clicking **Next** to display the **Completing the Delegation of Control Wizard** page.

Note   You can delegate a custom task to users or groups by selecting **Create a custom task to delegate** and continuing forward to the next pages in the Delegation of Control wizard.

---

4. Select an Active Directory object type.

The Delegation of Control wizard allows you to select to delegate control of one of the following:

- A specific OU. The control of a specific OU gives you authority over all existing objects in the OU, and authority to create new objects in that OU.

- Specific objects within an OU. The wizard displays a list of object types that you can select to delegate control; for example, computer objects, group objects, and printer objects.

After you select an object type to control, click **Next** to continue.

5. Assign permissions to users or groups to which you want to delegate control.

    The Delegation of Control wizard allows you to select the types of permissions you want to assign for the OU or its objects, by using the following filter options:

    - *General*. Displays the most commonly used permissions available for the selected OU or the objects in the OU.

    - *Property specific*. Displays all attribute permissions applicable to the type of object.

    - *Creation/deletion of specific child object*. Displays permissions that are needed to create new objects in the OU.

    After you select the permissions you want to assign, click **Next** to go to the **Completing the Delegation of Control** wizard page, and then click **Finish** to close the wizard.

Important   It is recommended that you delegate control to groups rather than to users.

Guidelines for Delegating Administrative Control

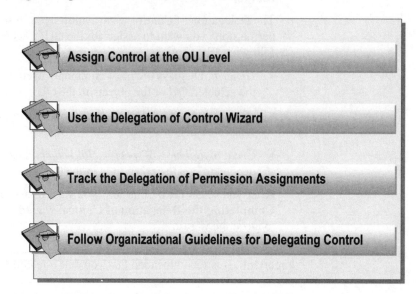

When you delegate administrative control of objects, you should follow these guidelines:

- Assign control at the OU level whenever possible to more easily track permission assignments. Tracking permission assignments becomes more complex when you assign permissions to specific objects and object attributes.

- Use the Delegation of Control wizard. The wizard simplifies the process of assigning object permissions by stepping you through the process.

- Track the delegation of permission assignments so that you can maintain records when you need to review security settings.

- Follow any guidelines that your organization uses for delegating control.

Lab A: Delegating Administrative Control

Objectives

After completing this lab, you will be able to:

- View permissions on Active Directory objects.
- Delegate control of an organizational unit.

Prerequisites

Before working on this lab, you must have:

- An understanding of Active Directory permissions.
- Knowledge of how to create users.

Lab Setup

To complete this lab, you need the following:

- A computer running Microsoft Windows 2000 Server that is configured as a domain controller.

- The Log On Locally user right granted to all users. To grant this right, run the Lrights.bat batch file from C:\Moc\Win2154A\Labfiles folder.

Important The lab does not reflect the real-world environment. It is recommended that you always use complex passwords for any administrator accounts, and never create accounts without a password.

Important Outside of the classroom environment, it is strongly advised that you use the most recent software updates that are necessary. Because this is a classroom environment, we may use software that does not include the latest updates.

Estimated time to complete this lab: 30 minutes

Exercise 1
Reviewing Active Directory Permissions

Scenario

Northwind Traders is expanding, so you are preparing to modify security in Active Directory. Before you make any changes to security, you want to verify default security in Windows 2000, so that you do not make unnecessary changes.

Goal

In this exercise, you will review the default security settings on components in Active Directory.

Tasks	Detailed Steps

1. Create the following objects in Active Directory:
 	
• OU: Security
 	
• Users:
First Name: Assistant
Last Name: User
User logon name:
assistant@*domain*.nwtraders.msft
Password: password
 	
First Name: Secretary
Last Name: User
User logon name:
secretary@*domain*.nwtraders.msft
Password: password
 	
First Name: Password
Last Name: Reset
User logon name:
passreset@*domain*.nwtraders.msft
Password: password
	a. Open Active Directory Users and Computers from the **Administrative Tools** menu.
	
	b. Expand *domain*.**nwtraders.msft** (where *domain* is your assigned domain name), if necessary.
	
	c. Right-click *domain*.**nwtraders.msft**, point to **New**, and then click **Organizational Unit**.
	
	d. In the **Name** box, type **Security** and then click **OK**.
	
	e. Create a user account in the Security OU by using the following information:
	  • First name: Assistant
	  • Last name: User
	  • User logon name: assistant@*domain*.nwtraders.msft
	  • Password: password
	
	f. Create a second user account in the Security OU by using the following information:
	  • First name: Secretary
	  • Last name: User
	  • User logon name: secretary@*domain*.nwtraders.msft
	  • Password: password
	
	g. Create a third user account in the Security OU by using the following information:
	  • First name: Password
	  • Last name: Reset
	  • User logon name: passreset@*domain*.nwtraders.msft
	  • Password: password

Tasks	Detailed Steps
2. View default permissions for the OU you created in task 1. Note the results.	a. On the **View** menu, click **Advanced Features**. b. In the console tree, right-click **Security**, and then click **Properties**. c. Click the **Security** tab. d. In the following table, list the groups that have permissions for the Security OU, and list the permissions that each group has been assigned. If an account has special permissions, just record Special Permissions in the table. You will need to refer to these permissions in the next exercise.

Group	Permission
Admin.s	R-W-C
Auth. Users	Read
Dom. Admin.s	Full Control
Ent. "	"
System	Full

❓ Why are all permission check boxes for some groups cleared?

Explicitly denied

Tasks	Detailed Steps
❓ Are any of the default permissions inherited from the domain, which is the parent object? How can you tell? _Yes. Box is checked._	
3. View special permissions for the Account Operators group for the Security OU. Note the results.	a. In the **Security Properties** dialog box, on the **Security** tab, click **Advanced**. b. In the **Access Control Settings for Security** dialog box, in the **Permission Entries** box, click each entry for the Account Operators group, and then click **View/Edit**.
❓ Which object permissions are granted to Account Operators? What can Account Operators do in this OU? _Create - Delete computer objects_ _" user objects_ _" group objects_	
❓ Do any objects within this OU inherit the permissions that are granted to the Account Operators group? Why or why not? _No — box is greyed out._	
3. _(continued)_	c. Close all open dialog boxes, and then log off.

Exercise 2
Delegating Control

Scenario

You are the Information Technology (IT) Manager of Northwind Traders. The company is becoming larger, and it is becoming more challenging for you to perform the daily tasks of adding users and managing the OUs. You need to transfer some of the administrative tasks by delegating control of an OU to a user. You also need to delegate the ability to reset passwords for the entire domain to a user who works on the Help Desk.

Goal

In this exercise, you will delegate control over objects in an OU. Refer to the table that you completed in the previous exercise to answer the following questions.

Tasks	Detailed Steps
1. Log on as Assistant and attempt to view the contents of the Security OU.	a. Log on as Assistant with a password of **password**. b. Open Active Directory Users and Computers from the **Administrative Tools** menu. c. In the console tree, expand your domain if necessary, and then click **Security**.
❓ Which user objects appear in the Security OU? *Assist. User* *Password Reset* *Secretary User*	
❓ Which permissions allow you to see these objects? (Hint: refer to your answers in the preceding exercise.) *Read* *Full control*	
2. Attempt to change the logon hours for the Secretary user account.	a. In the details pane, double-click **Secretary User**. b. In the **Secretary User Properties** dialog box, on the **Account** tab, attempt to change the allowed logon hours.

Tasks	Detailed Steps
? Were you successful? Why or why not? *No — don't have permission*	
2. *(continued)*	c. Close Active Directory Users and Computers, and then log off.
3. Log on as Passreset and attempt to change the password for the TsInternetUser in the Users container.	a. Log on as Passreset with a password of **password**. b. Open Active Directory Users and Computers from the **Administrative Tools** menu. c. In the console tree, expand your domain if necessary. d. In the Users container, right-click **TsInternetUser**, and then click **Reset Password**.
? Were you successful? Why or why not?	
3. *(continued)*	e. Close Active Directory Users and Computers, and then log off.
4. Use the Delegation of Control wizard to grant Active Directory permissions for creating, deleting and managing user accounts in the Security OU to the Assistant user account.	a. Log on as Administrator with a password of **password**. b. Open Active Directory Users and Computers from the **Administrative Tools** menu. c. In the console tree, expand your domain if necessary. d. Right-click **Security**, and then click **Delegate Control**. e. In the Delegation of Control wizard, click **Next**. f. On the **Users or Groups** page, click **Add**. g. In the **Select Users, Computers, or Groups** dialog box, click **Assistant User**, click **Add**, click **OK**, and then click **Next**. h. On the **Tasks to Delegate** page, click **Create, delete and manage user accounts**, and then click **Next**. i. On the **Completing the Delegation of Control Wizard** page, click **Finish**. j. Leave Active Directory Users and Computers open.

Tasks	Detailed Steps
5. Use the Delegation of Control wizard to grant Active Directory permissions for resetting passwords in the domain to the Password Reset user account.	a. In the console tree, right-click *domain*.**nwtraders.msft**, and then click **Delegate Control**. b. In the Delegation of Control wizard, click **Next**. c. On the **Users or Groups** page, click **Add**. d. In the **Select Users, Computers, or Groups** dialog box, click **Password Reset**, click **Add**, click **OK**, and then click **Next**. e. On the **Tasks to Delegate** page, click **Create a custom task to delegate**, and then click **Next**. f. On the **Active Directory Object Type** page, click **Only the following objects in the folder**, click **User objects**, and then click **Next**. g. On the **Permissions** page, click **Reset Password**, and then click **Next**. h. On the **Completing the Delegation of Control Wizard** page, click **Finish**. i. Close all open windows, and log off.
6. Log on as Assistant and attempt to change the log on hours for the Secretary User account.	a. Log on as Assistant with a password of **password**. b. Open Active Directory Users and Computers from the **Administrative Tools** menu. c. In the console tree, expand your domain if necessary, and then click **Security**. d. Attempt to change the logon hours for the **Secretary User** account in the Security OU.

? Were you successful? Why or why not?

Yes. had permission.

6. *(continued)*	e. Attempt to change the logon hours for a user in the Users container.

? Were you successful? Why or why not?

No.

Tasks	Detailed Steps
7. Log on as Passreset and attempt to reset the password for the TsInternetUser account in the Users container.	a. Log on as Passreset with a password of **password**. b. Open Active Directory Users and Computers from the **Administrative Tools** menu. c. In the console tree, expand your domain if necessary, and then click **Users**. d. Attempt to reset the password for the **TsInternetUser** account in the Users container.
❓ Were you successful? Why or why not? _____ _____ _____ _____	
8. Attempt to change the logon hours for the Secretary User account in the Security OU.	a. In the console tree, click **Security**. b. Attempt to change the logon hours for the **Secretary User** account.
❓ Were you successful? Why or why not? _____ _____ _____ _____	
8. *(continued)*	c. Close Active Directory Users and Computers, and then log off.

◆ Customizing MMC Consoles

- Creating Customized MMC Consoles

- Distributing Customized MMC Consoles

- Installing Windows 2000 Snap-ins

Windows 2000 provides customized tools to administer Active Directory. You can create customized administrative tools to:

- Map to the permissions that have been assigned to a user for an administrative task.

- Simplify the user desktop for users with limited administrative privileges.

You can create customized MMC consoles that fit your administrative responsibilities or the responsibilities of other administrators. These customized consoles allow you to control the options available to groups to whom you have delegated administrative responsibilities by restricting access to specific operations within that customized console.

In addition to creating customized consoles, you may need to install the Windows 2000 Administration Tools, which contain the snap-ins needed to run the customized consoles you create.

Creating Customized MMC Consoles

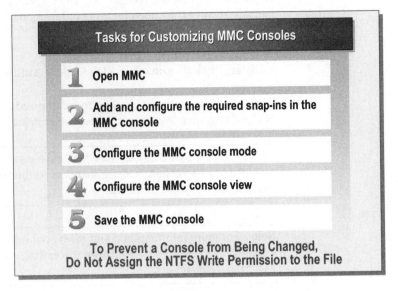

Tasks for Customizing MMC Consoles

1 Open MMC

2 Add and configure the required snap-ins in the MMC console

3 Configure the MMC console mode

4 Configure the MMC console view

5 Save the MMC console

To Prevent a Console from Being Changed, Do Not Assign the NTFS Write Permission to the File

Customizing an MMC console allows you create consoles that fit the responsibilities of administrators. Therefore, after you delegate administrative control, you can ensure that administrators have only the administrative tools that they require to perform their jobs. You can also customize a console to fit your own administrative needs. For example, you can create a console that contains all of the snap-ins that you typically use to perform one task or a set of related tasks, such as tasks for administering an OU.

Tasks for Customizing MMC Consoles

To customize an MMC console, perform the following tasks:

1. Open MMC by typing **mmc** in the **Run** box, and then clicking **OK**.

2. Add snap-ins and extensions that you require by using the **Add/Remove Snap-ins** dialog box.

3. Open the **Option** dialog box and click the **Console** tab. Select one of the following modes:

   • *Author mode.* Use this mode if you want other administrators to be able to easily modify the console as their administrative responsibilities change.

   • *User mode.* Use this mode when you want to limit the ability of other administrators to modify the console. You can determine the amount of the console tree to which the user can gain access and, therefore, the tasks that the user can perform.

   To prevent MMC from prompting users to save the console after each use, open the **Option** dialog box, and then click **Do not save changes to this console** on the **Console** tab.

4. Configure the MMC console view. You can control the parts of the console to which the user can gain access by removing the console tree and toolbars. You can configure these on the **View** menu of the console.

5. Save the MMC console.

Modifying the Customized Console

Regardless of whether you save an MMC console in Author or User mode, you can still modify it by opening it in Author mode.

▶ **To open a console in Author mode:**

- Right-click the console, and then click **Author**.

The only way to prevent changes to customized consoles is to *not* assign the NTFS file system Write permission to the .msc file.

Tip   If you configure a customized MMC console in User mode, ensure that you also have a version that you saved in Author mode so that you can easily make modifications if required.

Note   For more information about MMC consoles, see *Microsoft Management Console: Overview* under **Additional Reading** on the Web page on the Student Materials compact disc.

Distributing Customized MMC Consoles

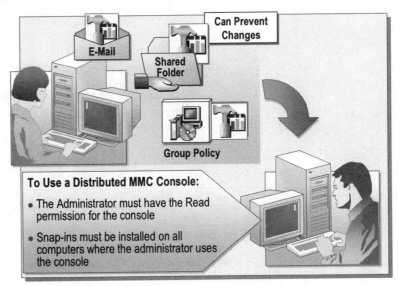

You can use the following methods to centrally distribute customized MMC consoles:

- Send the console file through e-mail as you would send any file. This is the quickest way to distribute a console file. However, you cannot prevent the administrator from changing the console file upon receiving it.

- Place the console file in a shared folder on a network server. The advantage of this method is that the console file is accessible from any computer in the network. Also, you can use NTFS file system permissions to prevent administrators from changing the console file.

- Package the console file for distribution so that you can distribute it by using Group Policy. This method guarantees that an administrator always has access to the customized console, but it does not prevent the administrator from changing the file upon receiving it.

For an administrator to successfully use an MMC console that you have distributed, the following conditions must be met:

- The administrator must have at least the Read permission for the console file.

- All snap-ins that the console references must be installed on the computers on which the administrator uses the console.

Note For more information about distributing software by using Group Policy, see Module 9, "Using Group Policy to Manage Software," in Course 2154, *Implementing and Administering Microsoft Windows 2000 Directory Services.*

Installing Windows 2000 Snap-ins

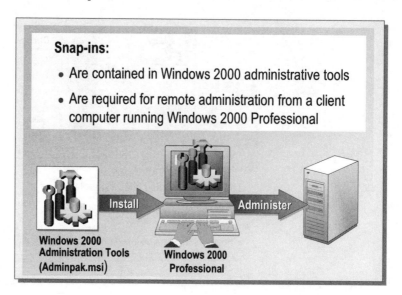

Snap-ins:

- Are contained in Windows 2000 administrative tools
- Are required for remote administration from a client computer running Windows 2000 Professional

Windows 2000 Administration Tools (Adminpak.msi)   Windows 2000 Professional

Windows 2000 Administration Tools are a complete set of all of the Windows 2000 snap-ins, which is a part of Windows 2000 Advanced Server. You must install these snap-ins to perform network administration remotely from a client computer running Windows 2000 Professional. Windows 2000 Professional has only the snap-ins required to perform routine administrative tasks on the client computer.

Even if an administrator has an MMC console to use on a client computer, the console is useless without the required snap-ins installed on this computer. To install Windows 2000 Administration Tools, use the Windows 2000 Administration Tools Setup wizard as follows:

1. In Control Panel, click **Add/Remove Programs**, and then click **Add**.

   The Windows 2000 Administration Tools Setup wizard guides you through the process of selecting the installation mode.

2. You must provide the location of the Adminpak.msi file. You can get this file:

   - From a computer running Windows 2000 Advanced Server in *systemroot*\System32.

   - From the Windows 2000 Advanced Server compact disc.

◆ Setting Up Taskpads

- ■ What Is a Taskpad?
- ■ Creating and Configuring a Taskpad
- ■ Adding Tasks in a Taskpad

A *taskpad* is an administrative tool that you set up for subadministrators and users whose primary job responsibilities do not include network administration. After you delegate administrative tasks, set up a taskpad that provides a subadministrator or user the ability to perform the specific tasks for which they are responsible.

To set up taskpads, you must create a customized MMC console, create a taskpad within the console, and then define the specific tasks that the user can perform.

What Is a Taskpad?

A Taskpad:

- **Is a Customized Administrative Tool**

- **Contains Tasks That Are Shortcuts to Specific Commands in an MMC Console**

- **Provides Advantages:**

  - Makes it easier for novice users to perform their jobs

  - Makes complex tasks easier

A taskpad is a further customization of an MMC console. A *taskpad* is created to add shortcuts to functions that exist both inside and outside a given console. Each task created in a taskpad is a shortcut to a specific administrative task or command in an MMC snap-in. You can use these shortcuts to run tasks such as starting wizards, opening property pages, performing menu commands, running command lines, and opening Web pages. You can configure a taskpad view so that it contains all of the tasks a given user might need. Also, you can create multiple taskpad views in a console, so that you can group tasks by function or user.

The advantages of creating a taskpad are:

- A taskpad makes it easier for novice users to perform their jobs. For example, you can add applicable tasks to a taskpad view and then hide the console tree, so that users can begin using tools before they are familiar with the location of particular items in the console tree or operating system.

- A taskpad makes complex tasks easier by hiding the complexity of MMC. For example, if a user must frequently perform a task that involves multiple snap-ins, in a single location, you can present tasks that open or run the necessary dialog boxes, property pages, command lines, and scripts.

The taskpad can contain several elements that make it easy to use:

- At least one button for each shortcut to a task.

- A list of items that appear in the details pane of the MMC console from which the taskpad was created. Users perform the task on these items.

- The **Change** button. This button allows the user to select different items in the console tree to administer.

Important   To use a taskpad successfully, a user must have the appropriate permissions to perform the task for which the taskpad is designed.

Creating and Configuring a Taskpad

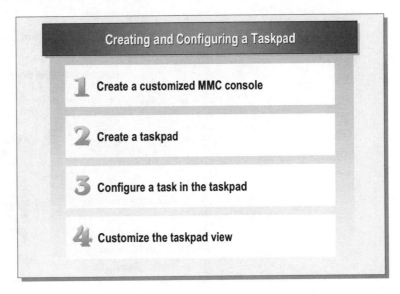

You create a taskpad by using the Taskpad Creation wizard and then customize tasks by using the Task Creation wizard. To create a taskpad, perform the following steps:

1. Create an MMC console and add the required snap-in.

2. Create a taskpad by using the Taskpad Creation wizard. To open the Taskpad Creation wizard, right-click the item in the console tree to which the task applies, and then click **New Taskpad**.

    The wizard guides you through the process of defining a taskpad's appearance, name, description, and the item in the console tree to which it applies.

3. Configure a task by using the Task Creation wizard. The Task Creation wizard is discussed in the Adding Tasks in a Taskpad topic.

4. Customize the taskpad by removing the console tree and changing the console to User mode. To remove the console tree, on the **View** menu, click **Customize**, and then clear the **Console Tree** check box.

Adding Tasks in a Taskpad

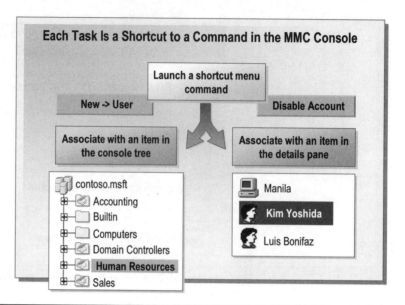

You can create tasks in taskpads for users who have limited administrative responsibilities. In this way, users do not have to use the MMC console interface to complete their administrative tasks. Each task in a taskpad is a shortcut to a command in the MMC console. These are the same commands that are available when you right-click an item in the console tree or the details pane.

To set up a task that corresponds to a shortcut menu command, you use the Task Creation wizard to start and select either of the following options:

- *Console tree.* This option allows you to select an item in the console tree and a command that a user can perform on that item.

  For example, you can select an OU in the console tree and then select a command available for OUs, such as creating new user accounts. The user of the taskpad can then create user accounts only in that OU.

- *List in details pane.* This option allows you to select an item that appears in the details pane, and then select a command that the user can perform on the item.

  For example, you can select a user account in an OU and then select a command available for that object type, such as resetting passwords. The users of the taskpad can then reset passwords for any user account that they select in the details pane for that OU.

  This option is not available if you selected the stand-alone option in the Taskpad Creation wizard when creating the taskpad.

Note   You can also set up a task that runs an application from the command prompt; for example, batch files and scripts. A user can then run an application by clicking a task icon rather than typing a command at the command line. You must provide the command and any arguments that are required.

Lab B: Creating Custom Administrative Tools

Objectives

After completing this lab, you will be able to:

- Create custom administrative tools by using the Microsoft Management Console (MMC).

- Create custom taskpads.

Prerequisites

Before working on this lab, you must have:

- Knowledge of how to use the snap-ins included with Windows 2000.

- Knowledge of MMC.

- Knowledge of how to use Active Directory and Computers to modify user account properties.

Lab Setup

To complete this lab, you need a computer running Windows 2000 Server configured as a domain controller.

Estimated time to complete this lab: 30 minutes

Exercise 1
Creating Custom Administrative Tools

Scenario

Now that you have delegated administrative control of the Security OU to the Assistant User, you need to create custom administrative tools that will allow this user to perform the delegated job functions.

Goal

In this exercise, you will create a custom administrative tool for the Assistant User that will allow the user to manage user accounts in the Security OU.

Tasks	Detailed Steps
1. Create a custom MMC console for the Assistant User account that contains the Active Directory Users and Computers snap-in.	a. Log on as Administrator with a password of **password**. b. In the **Run** box, type **mmc.exe** and then click **OK**. c. On the **Console** menu, click **Add/Remove Snap-in**. d. In the **Add/Remove Snap-in** dialog box, click **Add**. e. In the **Add Standalone Snap-in** dialog box, click **Active Directory Users and Computers**, click **Add**, click **Close**, and then click **OK**.
2. Create a new window in the console that displays only the contents of the Security OU and close the original Console Root window.	a. In the console tree, expand **Active Directory Users and Computers**, expand your domain, right-click **Security**, and then click **New Window from Here**. b. On the **Window** menu, click **1 Console Root**, and then close the Console Root window.
3. Create a new taskpad with the following properties: • Style for the details pane: Horizontal list. • Style for task descriptions: InfoTip. • List size: Small. • Apply this Taskpad view to: Selected tree item. • Name: Security OU User Management. • Description: Tool for Managing User Accounts.	a. In the console tree, right-click **Security** and then click **New Taskpad View**. b. On the **Welcome to the New Taskpad View Wizard** page, click **Next**. c. On the **Taskpad Display** page, in the **List size** list, click **Small**, and then click **Next**. d. On the **Taskpad Target** page, click **Selected tree item**, and then click **Next**. e. On the **Name and Description** page, in the **Name** box, type **Security OU User Management** f. In the **Description** box, type **Tool for Managing User Accounts** and then click **Next**. g. On the **Completing the New Taskpad View Wizard** page, ensure that **Start the New Task** wizard is selected, and then click **Finish**.

Tasks	Detailed Steps
4. Add the following menu commands to the new taskpad: • Disable Account • Reset password • Delete • Properties	a. On the Welcome to the New Task Wizard page, click Next. b. On the **Command Type** page, ensure that **Menu command** is selected, and then click **Next**. c. On the **Shortcut Menu Command** page, in the **Command source** list, ensure that **List in details pane** is selected, under **Available commands**, click **Disable Account**, and then click **Next**. d. On the **Name and Description** page, accept the default Task name and Description by clicking **Next**. e. On the **Task Icon** page, select an icon, and then click **Next**. f. On the **Completing the New Task Wizard** page, click **Run this wizard again**, and then click **Finish**. g. Repeat steps a through f, changing step c as required to add the following tasks to the taskpad: • Reset password • Delete • Properties h. After adding the Properties task, on the **Completing the New Task Wizard** page, ensure that **Run this wizard again** is not selected, and then click **Finish**.
5. Add a task to the taskpad that allows the creation of new user accounts.	a. In the console tree, right-click **Security**, and then click **Edit Taskpad View**. b. In the **Security OU User Management Properties** dialog box, on the **Tasks** tab, click **New**. c. On the **Welcome to the New Task Wizard** page, click **Next**. d. On the **Command Type** page, ensure that **Menu command** is selected, and then click **Next**. e. On the **Shortcut Menu Command** page, in the **Command source** list, click **Tree item task**. f. Under **Available commands**, click **New->User**, and then click **Next**. g. On the **Name and Description** page, accept the default Task name and Description by clicking **Next**. h. On the **Task Icon** page, select an icon, and then click **Next**. i. On the **Completing the New Task Wizard** page, click **Finish**. j. Click **OK** to close the **Security OU User Management Properties** box.

Tasks	Detailed Steps
6. Modify the following properties of the console: • Hide the console tree. • Remove the standard menus. • Remove the standard toolbar. • Remove the Status bar. • Remove the Taskpad navigation tabs. • Remove the snap-in menus. • Remove the snap-in toolbars. • Console name: Security OU User Management. • Console mode: User mode – limited access, single window. • Disable context menus on taskpads. • Do not allow changes to this console. • Do not allow users to customize views. • Save the console in the All Users Administrative Tools folder as Security OU User Management.	a. On the **View** menu, click **Customize**. b. In the **Customize View** dialog box, clear all of the check boxes, and then click **OK**. c. On the **Console** menu, click **Options**. d. Change the name of the console to **Security OU User Management**. e. In the **Console mode** list, click **User mode – limited access, single window**. f. Clear the **Enable context menus on taskpads in this console** and **Allow the user to customize views** check boxes. g. Select **Do not save changes to this console**, and then click **OK**. h. Save the console in the C:\Documents and Settings\All Users\Start Menu\Programs\Administrative Tools folder as **Security OU User Management**. i. Close the console, and then log off.

Exercise 2
Using a Custom Administrative Console

Scenario

The network administrator has created a custom administrative tool for the Assistant User to help that user perform user account management tasks in the Security OU.

Goal

In this exercise, you will log on as the Assistant User and use the custom administrative tool to manage user accounts in the Security OU.

Tasks	Detailed Steps
1. Log on as Assistant and perform the following user management tasks by using the Security OU User Management tool: • Create a new user. • Disable the Password Reset account. • Reset the password for the Secretary User account. • Enter an address for the Secretary user account. • Delete the new user account.	a. Log on as Assistant with a password of **password**. b. Open Security OU User Management from the **Administrative Tools** menu. c. Using the Security OU User Management tool, perform the following user management tasks: • Create a new user. • Disable the Password Reset account. • Reset the password for the Secretary User account. • Enter an address for the Secretary User account. • Delete the new user account.
2. Attempt to access the shortcut menu for one of the user accounts.	a. Right-click one of the user accounts and attempt to display the shortcut menu.
❓ Where you able to access the shortcut menu for the user account? Why or why not? _____ _____ _____ _____	
2. *(continued)*	b. Close the Security OU User Management tool, and then log off.

Best Practices

good all over

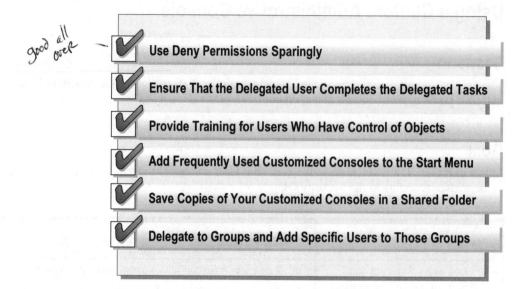

- **Use Deny Permissions Sparingly**
- **Ensure That the Delegated User Completes the Delegated Tasks**
- **Provide Training for Users Who Have Control of Objects**
- **Add Frequently Used Customized Consoles to the Start Menu**
- **Save Copies of Your Customized Consoles in a Shared Folder**
- **Delegate to Groups and Add Specific Users to Those Groups**

The following list provides best practices for delegating administrative control:

- Use Deny permissions sparingly. If you assign permissions correctly, you do not need to deny permissions. In most cases, denied permissions indicate mistakes that were made in assigning group membership. Denying permissions can also make it more difficult to track permissions.

- Ensure that delegated users take responsibility and that the tasks are completed. As an administrator, you are ultimately responsible for whether or not the delegated tasks are completed.

- Provide training for users who have delegated control of objects. Training ensures that the users to whom you delegate responsibility understand their responsibilities and know how to perform the administrative tasks.

- Add customized MMC consoles that you frequently use to the **Start** menu of the computer that you typically use for administration, so that you can quickly gain access to the consoles when you need to use them.

- If you perform administrative tasks from multiple computers, or administer remotely, save a copy of each of your customized MMC consoles in a shared folder. In this way, you can easily gain access to your consoles from any computer that has the necessary snap-ins installed.

- It is recommended to delegate to groups instead of to specific users. You can then add specific users to the groups with the required permissions.

Review

> ■ **Object Security in Active Directory**
>
> ■ **Controlling Access to Active Directory Objects**
>
> ■ **Delegating Administrative Control of Active Directory Objects**
>
> ■ **Customizing MMC Consoles**
>
> ■ **Setting Up Taskpads**
>
> ■ **Best Practices**

1. How does Windows 2000 determine who has permission to gain access to Active Directory objects and the type of access that is allowed?

   Access Control list
   "   "   entries w/ exact permissions.

2. You want to assign an administrative assistant the permissions required to reset passwords for all user accounts in a single OU. What is the best way to do this?

   ~~Custom taskpad.~~
   Delegate control

3. When delegating administrative control of objects, why should an administrator assign control at the OU level whenever possible?

   Easier; less risky.

4. You customize an MMC console and give it to administrators to use on their client computers running Windows 2000 Professional. What must they do before they can successfully use the console?

   Must give them admin. pack.

5. An assistant in Marketing has only one administrative responsibility, which is resetting passwords for users. You do not want the assistant to use Active Directory User and Computers for this one task. What do you do?

   Set it up on task pad on MMC.

Microsoft®
Training &
Certification

Module 7: Implementing Group Policy

Contents

Overview

- **Introduction to Group Policy**
- **Group Policy Structure**
- **Working with Group Policy Objects**
- **How Group Policy Settings Are Applied in Active Directory**
- **Modifying Group Policy Inheritance**
- **Delegating Administrative Control of Group Policy**
- **Monitoring and Troubleshooting Group Policy**
- **Best Practices**

Group Policy in Microsoft® Windows® 2000 provides you with greater administrative control over users and computers in your network. By using Group Policy, you can define the state of a user's work environment once, and then rely on Windows 2000 to continually enforce the Group Policy settings that you defined. You can apply Group Policy settings across a network or you can apply Group Policy that pertains only to specific groups of users and computers.

Lost productivity is frequently attributed to user error. By using Group Policy to reduce the complexity of user environments and remove the possibility of users incorrectly configuring these environments, productivity increases, and the network requires less technical support. Consequently, you lower your total cost of ownership (TCO).

At the end of this module, you will be able to:

- Identify how Group Policy simplifies administering a Windows 2000 network.
- Identify the structure of Group Policy in a Windows 2000 network.
- Identify the options provided by Windows 2000 for creating Group Policy objects and managing them.
- Describe how Group Policy is applied in Active Directory® directory service.
- Modify Group Policy inheritance.
- Delegate administrative control of Group Policy objects.
- Monitor and troubleshoot Group Policy.
- Apply best practices for implementing Group Policy.

Introduction to Group Policy

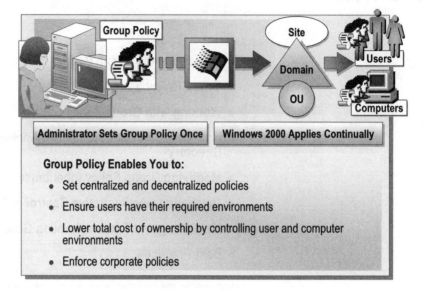

Group Policy is the technology that allows you to define user desktop environments once, with user and computer settings, and then rely on Windows 2000 to continually enforce throughout the network the Group Policy that you defined. You can associate Group Policy settings with the following Active Directory containers, sites, domains, and organizational units (OUs). Group Policy then affects all users and computers in those containers.

By using Group Policy, you can:

- Centralize policies by setting Group Policy for an entire organization at the site or domain level, or decentralize Group Policy settings by setting Group Policy for each department at an OU level.

- Ensure that users have the user environments that they need to perform their jobs. You can make sure users have Group Policy settings that control the application and system configuration settings in the registry, scripts to modify the computer and user environments, automated software installations, and security settings for local computers, domains, and networks. You can also control where users' data folders are stored.

- Lower the total cost of ownership by controlling user and computer environments, thereby reducing the level of technical support that users require and the lost user productivity due to user error. For example, by using Group Policy, you can prevent users from making changes to system configurations that can make a computer inoperable, or you can prevent them from installing applications that they do not require.

- Enforce a corporation's policies, including business rules, goals, and security needs. For example, you can ensure that security requirements for all users match the security required by the corporation, or that all users have a particular set of applications installed.

Note   Group Policy applies only to Windows 2000 and not earlier versions of the Windows operating system family.

◆ Group Policy Structure

- **Types of Group Policy Settings**
- **Group Policy Objects**
- **Group Policy Settings for Computers and Users**
- **Group Policy Objects and Active Directory Containers**

The structure of Group Policy provides flexibility in managing users and computers. The detailed settings contained in a Group Policy object (GPO) allow you to control specific user and computer configurations. You can associate GPOs with specific Active Directory containers—sites, domains, or OUs.

Types of Group Policy Settings

Types of Group Policy Settings	
Administrative Templates	Registry-based Group Policy settings
Security	Settings for local, domain, and network security
Software Installation	Settings for central management of software installation
Scripts	Startup, shutdown, logon, and logoff scripts
Remote Installation Services	Settings that control the options available to users when running the Client Installation wizard used by RIS
Internet Explorer Maintenance	Settings to administer and customize Microsoft Internet Explorer on Windows 2000–based computers
Folder Redirection	Settings for storing of users' folders on a network server

You can configure Group Policy settings to define the policies that affect users and computers. The types of settings that you can configure are:

- *Administrative templates*. Registry-based settings for configuring application settings and user desktop environments. These settings include the operating system components and applications to which users can gain access, the degree of access to Control Panel options, and control of users' offline files.

- *Security*. Settings for configuring local computer, domain, and network security settings. These settings include controlling user access to the network, setting up account and audit policies, and controlling user rights. For example, you can set the maximum number of failed logon attempts that a user account can have before it is locked out.

- *Software installation*. Settings for centralizing the management of software installations, updates, and removals. You can cause applications to automatically install on client computers, to be automatically upgraded, or to be automatically removed. You can also publish applications so that they appear in Add/Remove Programs in Control Panel, which provides users with a central location to obtain applications for installation.

- *Scripts*. Settings for specifying when Windows 2000 runs specific scripts. You can specify scripts to run when a computer starts and shuts down, and when a user logs on and logs off. You can specify scripts to perform batch operations, control multiple scripts, and determine the order in which they run.

- *Remote installation services.* Settings that control the options available to users when running the Client Installation wizard used by Remote Installation Services (RIS).

- *Internet Explorer maintenance.* Settings to administer and customize Microsoft Internet Explorer on Windows 2000–based computers.

- *Folder redirection.* Settings for storing specific user profile folders on a network server. The settings create a link in the profile to the network shared folder, but the folders appear locally. The user can gain access to the folder on any computer on the network. For example, you can redirect a user's My Documents folder to a network shared folder.

Group Policy Objects

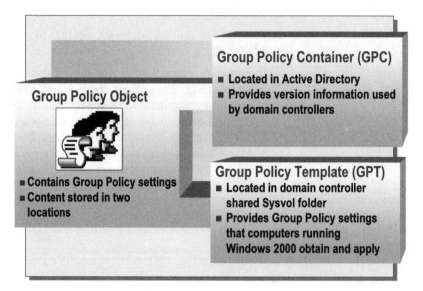

You can implement Group Policy by using the Group Policy object (GPO). Windows 2000 applies the Group Policy settings contained in the GPO to the user and computer objects in the site, domain, or OU with which the GPO is associated.

The content of a GPO is stored in two different locations. Those locations are:

- *The Group Policy container (GPC)*. The GPC is an Active Directory object that contains GPO attributes and version information. Because the GPC is in Active Directory, computers can access it to locate Group Policy templates, and domain controllers can access it to obtain version information.

  A domain controller uses the version information to verify that it has the most recent version of the GPO. If the domain controller does not have the most recent version, replication occurs with the domain controller that has the latest version of the GPO.

Note To view the GPC in Active Directory, enable Advanced Features in Active Directory Users and Computers, expand the domain, expand the System container, and then expand the Policies container.

- *The Group Policy template (GPT)*. The GPT is a folder hierarchy in the shared sysvol folder on domain controllers. When you create a GPO, Windows 2000 creates the corresponding GPT folder hierarchy. The GPT contains all Group Policy settings and information, including administrative templates, security, software installation, scripts, and folder redirection settings. Computers connect to the SYSVOL folder to obtain the settings.

  The name of the GPT folder is the globally unique identifier (GUID) of the GPO that you created. It is identical to the GUID used to identify the GPO in the GPC. The path to the GPT on a domain controller is *systemroot*\SYSVOL\sysvol.

Group Policy Settings for Computers and Users

- **Group Policy Settings for Computers:**

  - Specify operating system behavior, desktop behavior, security settings, computer startup and shutdown scripts, computer-assigned application options, and application settings

  - Apply when the operating system initializes and during the periodic refresh cycle

Computers

- **Group Policy Settings for Users:**

  - Specify operating system behavior, desktop settings, security settings, assigned and published application options, application settings, folder redirection options, and user logon and logoff scripts

  - Apply when users log on to the computer and during the periodic refresh cycle

Users

You can enforce Group Policy settings for computers and users on the network by using the Computer Configuration and User Configuration nodes in Group Policy, respectively.

Group Policy Settings for Computers

Group Policy settings for computers specify operating system behavior, desktop behavior, security settings, computer startup and shutdown scripts, computer-assigned application options, and application settings. Computer-related Group Policy is applied when the operating system initializes and during the periodic refresh cycle. In general, computer Group Policy takes precedence over conflicting user Group Policy.

Group Policy Settings for Users

Group Policy settings for users specify operating system behavior, desktop settings, security settings, assigned and published application options, application settings, folder redirection options, and user logon and logoff scripts. User-related Group Policy is applied when users log on to the computer and during the periodic refresh cycle.

Note For more information about Group Policy settings for computers and users, see *Introduction to Windows 2000 Group Policy* under **Additional Reading** on the Web page on the Student Materials compact disc.

Group Policy Objects and Active Directory Containers

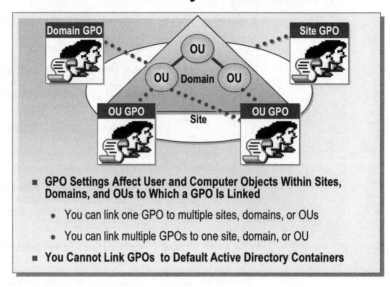

- **GPO Settings Affect User and Computer Objects Within Sites, Domains, and OUs to Which a GPO Is Linked**
  - You can link one GPO to multiple sites, domains, or OUs
  - You can link multiple GPOs to one site, domain, or OU
- **You Cannot Link GPOs to Default Active Directory Containers**

GPOs are associated with, or linked to, sites, domains, and OUs to allow you to set centralized policies that affect the entire organization and decentralized policies that are localized by department. The linking of a GPO to a site, domain, or OU causes the Group Policy settings to affect user and computer objects in that site, domain, or OU. The information that describes which GPOs are linked to an Active Directory container is stored in two attributes of that container—gPLink and gPOptions. The gPLink attribute contains the prioritized list of GPOs linked to a container and the gPOptions attribute contains the container setting that prevents the inheritance of any GPO.

The ability to link existing GPOs provides flexibility when implementing Group Policy settings. You can link GPOs in the following ways:

- Link one GPO to multiple sites, domains, or OUs in your network. This provides you with the ability to configure Group Policy settings that apply to users and computers in different sites, domains, or OUs. For example, you can create a GPO that runs a logon script and then link it to OUs that have users for whom you want the script to run.

- Link multiple GPOs to one site, domain, or OU. Rather than have all of the types of Group Policy settings for a site, domain, or OU in one GPO, you can create several GPOs for different types of Group Policy settings and then link them to the appropriate sites, domains, or OUs. For example, you can link a GPO that contains network security settings, and another GPO that contains software installation, to the same OU. These multiple GPOs can also be linked to other OUs.

Important You cannot link GPOs to the default Active Directory containers—Users, Computers, and Builtin. Although these containers exist within Active Directory, they are not OUs.

◆ Working with Group Policy Objects

- ■ Creating Linked Group Policy Objects

- ■ Creating Unlinked Group Policy Objects

- ■ Linking an Existing Group Policy Object

- ■ Specifying a Domain Controller for Managing Group Policy Objects

Windows 2000 provides you with various options to create a new Group Policy object (GPO) if any of the existing GPOs do not have the settings that you want. When creating a GPO, you can either create a linked GPO or an unlinked GPO. However, if the Group Policy settings that you want to apply to computers and users in an OU are in an existing GPO, you can link the GPO to the container.

When you create a new GPO, or open Group Policy to edit an existing GPO, the default behavior is to manage GPOs on the domain controller that holds the PDC emulator role.

Creating Linked Group Policy Objects

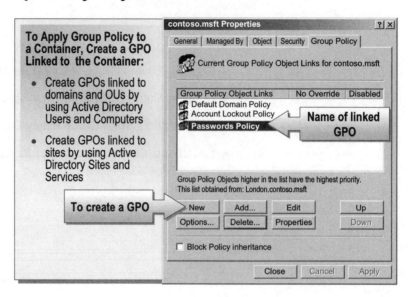

When you create a GPO, it is linked to the container for which you create it. However, there is no Group Policy setting defined in a new GPO.

Creating GPOs Linked to Domains and OUs

You create a GPO for domains and OUs by using Active Directory Users and Computers. To create a new GPO for a domain or OU, perform the following steps:

1. Open Active Directory Users and Computers.

2. Right-click the domain or OU for which you want to create a GPO, and then click **Properties**.

3. On the **Group Policy** tab, click **New**, type a name for the new GPO, and then press ENTER. The GPO that you create appears in the list of GPOs associated with the OU or domain on the **Group Policy** tab for the OU or domain.

Creating GPOs Linked to Sites

Creating a GPO for a site is different from creating a GPO for a domain or OU because you use Active Directory Sites and Services to administer sites. To create a new GPO for a site, perform the following steps:

1. Open Active Directory Sites and Services.

2. Right-click the site for which you want to create a GPO, and then click **Properties**.

3. On the **Group Policy** tab, click **New**, type a name for the new GPO, and then press ENTER. The GPO that you create appears in the list of GPOs associated with the site on the **Group Policy** tab for the site.

Note   You must be a member of the Enterprise Admins group to create GPOs linked to sites.

Creating Unlinked Group Policy Objects

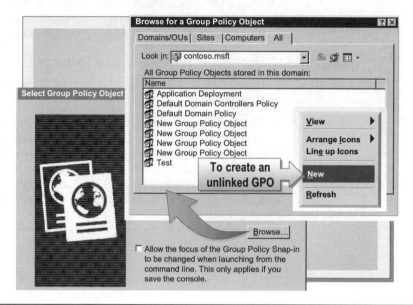

When you create a GPO linked to a site, domain, or OU, you actually perform two separate operations: creating a new GPO, and then linking it to the site, domain, or OU. To link a GPO to a site, domain, or OU, you must have read and write permissions on the gPLink and gPOptions attributes of the container to which the GPO is being linked. By default, only members of the Domain Admins and Enterprise Admins groups have the necessary permissions to link GPOs to domains and OUs, whereas only members of the Enterprise Admins group have the permissions to link GPOs to sites. Members of the Group Policy Creator Owners group can create GPOs, but cannot link them. You can create an unlinked GPO by adding a Group Policy snap-in to the MMC console.

To create an unlinked GPO, perform the following steps:

1. Run Mmc.exe and add the Group Policy snap-in.

2. In the **Select Group Policy Object** dialog box, click **Browse**.

3. In the **Browse for a Group Policy Object** dialog box, on the **All** tab, right-click anywhere in the **All Group Policy Objects stored in this domain** list, and then click **New**.

4. Type a name for the new GPO, and then click **OK** to close the **Browse for a Group Policy Object** dialog box.

5. If you want to edit the new GPO, in the **Select Group Policy Object** dialog box, click **Finish**, otherwise click **Cancel**.

Unlinked GPOs may be created in big organizations where one group is responsible for creating GPOs while another group links the GPOs to the required site, domain, or OU.

Linking an Existing Group Policy Object

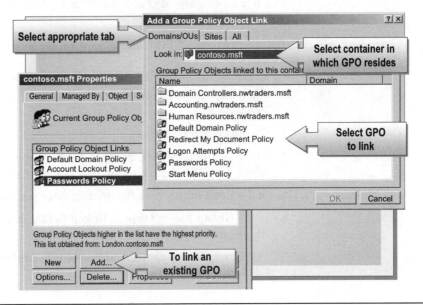

You can apply existing Group Policy settings to additional Active Directory containers by linking the GPO that contains the required settings to those containers. To link a GPO to a site, domain or OU, you must have read and write permissions on the gPLink and gPOptions attributes of that site, domain, or OU.

Linking an Existing GPO to Domains and OUs

You link an existing GPO to domains and OUs by using Active Directory Users and Computers.

To link a GPO to a domain or OU, perform the following steps:

1. Open Active Directory Users and Computers.

2. Right-click the domain or OU that you want to link to an existing GPO, and then click **Properties**.

3. On the **Group Policy** tab, click **Add**.

4. Click the **Domain/OUs**, **Sites**, or **All** tab, depending on the location to which the GPO that you want to link is presently linked.

5. In the **Look in** list, click the domain that contains the GPO that you want.

6. In the **Group Policy Objects linked to this container** list, click the GPO to which you want to link, and then click **OK**.

   The **Group Policy Objects linked to this container** list contains all of the GPOs that exist in the domain.

Linking an Existing GPO to a Site

You link an existing GPO to a site by using Active Directory Sites and Services.

To link an existing GPO to a site, perform the following steps:

1. Open Active Directory Sites and Services.

2. Right-click the site that you want to link to an existing GPO, and then click **Properties**.

3. On the **Group Policy** tab, click **Add**.

4. Click the **Domain/OUs**, **Sites**, or **All** tab, depending on the location to which the GPOs that you want to link are presently linked.

5. In the **Look in** list, click the domain that contains the GPO that you want.

6. In the **Group Policy Objects linked to this container** list, click the GPO to which you want to link, and then click **OK**.

   The **Group Policy Objects linked to this container** list contains all of the GPOs that exist in the site.

Caution Although you have the ability to link existing GPOs to sites, you need to think carefully about using this ability. If you link a GPO to a site, anyone who has read and write permissions to that GPO can make changes to it, and because the GPO is linked to the site, those changes are processed throughout the entire site. Consider always creating new GPOs for sites, rather than linking existing ones.

Note By default, the GPO for a site is created in the root domain of the forest. This could affect network traffic patterns with cross-domain traffic.

Specifying a Domain Controller for Managing Group Policy Objects

- **When You Create a New GPO or Edit an Existing GPO, by Default, the Domain Controller That Holds the PDC Emulator Role Performs the Operation**

- **The Options Available to Specify a Domain Controller for Managing GPOs Include:**

  - The one with the Operations Master token for the PDC emulator

  - The one used by the Active Directory snap-ins

  - Use any available domain controller

- **To Specify a Domain Controller for Managing Group Policy Objects:**

  - Use the DC Options command on the View menu in the Group Policy snap-in

  - Enable a Group Policy setting that specifies which domain controller should be used

When you create a new GPO or open Group Policy to edit an existing GPO, by default, the operation is performed on the domain controller that holds one of the operations master roles, specifically the primary domain controller (PDC) emulator role. Understanding which domain controller is used while creating or editing GPOs helps you resolve problems associated with creating or editing GPOs.

This default behavior forces the Group Policy snap-in to use the same domain controller regardless of the computer from which it is being run. Data loss could occur if two administrators work on changes to the same GPO on different domain controllers within the same replication cycle. In Windows 2000, Group Policy writes data to the GPO for each change. If two administrators edit a GPO on different domain controllers, it increases the possibility of changes being overwritten by replication. It is strongly recommended that the number of administrators be limited, that Group Policy use the PDC Emulator role, and that the administrator be aware of other administrators that may be editing the same GPO.

Options for Selecting a Domain Controller

You can specify a domain controller for managing GPOs by selecting any of the following three options:

- *The one with the Operations Master token for the PDC emulator.* This is the default and preferred option. Using this option helps ensure that no data loss occurs.

- *The one used by the Active Directory Snap-ins.* Uses the domain controller that the Active Directory management snap-in tools are currently using. Each of these snap-ins includes an option for changing which domain controller is the focus of its current operation. When this option is selected, the Group Policy snap-in uses the same domain controller.

- *Use any available domain controller.* The third, and least desirable option in most cases, allows the Group Policy snap-in to choose any available domain controller. When this option is used, it is likely that a domain controller in the local site will be selected.

Methods for Specifying a Domain Controller

To specify a domain controller for managing GPOs:

- Use the **DC Options** command on the Group Policy snap-in **View** menu. Clicking this command displays a dialog box with the three options for selecting a domain controller.

- Enable a Group Policy setting that specifies which domain controller option should be used. If that option is not available, an error message will be displayed. In such cases, the **DC Options** command will be disabled because a Group Policy is in place that overrides any setting that the user picks. The DC options Group Policy setting is located in the Administrative Templates node for User Configuration in the System\Group Policy sub-container. The available DC options are the same as the preference settings listed in the Options for Selecting a Domain Controller section. This functionality is useful in some corporate scenarios. For example, if you are an administrator in Japan and the PDC Emulator is in New York, you can implement a Group Policy to ensure that all changes are made locally.

◆ How Group Policy Settings Are Applied in Active Directory

- Group Policy Inheritance
- How Group Policy Settings Are Processed
- Controlling the Processing of Group Policy
- Group Policy and Slow Network Connections (Links)
- Resolving Conflicts Between Group Policy Settings
- Class Discussion: How Group Policy Is Applied

How Group Policy is applied in Active Directory determines the resultant Group Policy settings that are applied. *Resultant Group Policy settings* are the settings that take effect when there are multiple GPOs and multiple settings that could affect computer and user objects. To obtain the results that you want, you need to be aware of how resultant Group Policy settings are determined; otherwise you may configure settings that are never applied.

Group Policy Inheritance

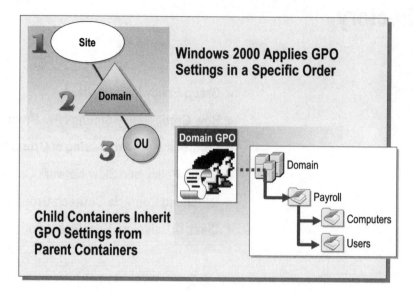

Group Policy inheritance is the order in which Windows 2000 applies GPOs. The order in which Group Policy is applied and how Group Policy settings are inherited ultimately determines which settings affect users and computers.

Order of Application

The order in which Windows 2000 applies GPOs is based on the Active Directory container to which the GPOs are linked. The GPOs are applied first to the site, which is the furthest away from the computer or user, and then applied to domains, and then to OUs. Thus, the Group Policy settings of the OU of which a user or computer is a member are the final Group Policy settings that are applied.

Flow of Inheritance

By default, GPOs are inherited. Inheritance flows down the Active Directory tree from site, to domain, and then to OU. The child container inherits the GPO from the parent container. This means that the child container could have a multitude of Group Policy settings applied to its users and computers without having a GPO linked to it.

If a child container does have GPOs linked to it, the Group Policy settings from parent containers higher in the Active Directory tree are applied to its users and computers first. Then the child container's own Group Policy settings are applied.

Note   There is no hierarchy of domains as there is for OUs, such as parent OU, child OU, and so on.

GPOs Linked to Sites

Because sites represent the physical network, and domains and OUs represent the logical network, it is important to understand how GPOs linked to sites are applied. Any given site may contain computers from one or more domains. If a site contains computers from more than one domain, the Group Policy settings defined in the GPO linked to that site will apply to all computers in that site and all users who log on to computers in that site, regardless of the domain in which the computer or user accounts exist.

How Group Policy Settings Are Processed

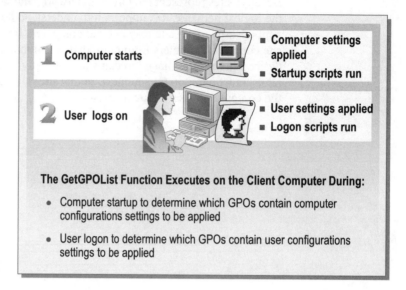

Windows 2000 processes the Group Policy settings in a specific order and at established intervals. By understanding the order in which Windows 2000 processes Group Policy settings, you can avoid overriding Group Policy settings. When a computer is started and a user logs on, Windows 2000 processes computer settings first and then user settings. When Windows 2000 processes computer settings, the startup scripts run. Similarly, the logon scripts run when Windows 2000 processes user settings.

Determining Which GPOs to Process

The list of GPOs that need to be processed is determined by a Win32® function, GetGPOList. This function is executed on the client computer during computer start up to determine which GPOs contain computer configuration settings that should be applied, and it is executed again during the user log on process to determine which GPOs contain user configuration settings that should be applied.

Processing Group Policy

The processing of Group Policy occurs at the client side. Group Policy is actually processed by a number of different dynamic-link libraries (DLLs) that are known as client-side extensions. Each client-side extension is responsible for processing a different type of Group Policy setting. The following table lists the client-side extensions and the type of Group Policy setting for which each is responsible:

Client-side Extension	Group Policy Settings
Userenv.dll	Registry-based settings (Administrative Templates)
Dskquota.dll	Disk Quota settings (Administrative Templates)
Fdeploy.dll	Folder Redirection settings
Gptext.dll	Script and IP Sec settings
Appmgmts.dll	Software Installation
Scecli.dll	Security and Encrypting File System Recovery Settings
Iedkcs32.dll	Internet Explorer Maintenance settings

After the list of GPOs that need to be processed is determined by the GetGPOList function, the client computer loops through the client-side extensions and determines whether each client-side extension has any data to process in the GPOs. If the client-side extension has data to be processed in the GPOs, it is executed and processes the data in the applicable GPOs. If there is no data for a particular client-side extension, it is not executed.

Controlling the Processing of Group Policy

- **Synchronous and Asynchronous Processing**
  - By default, the processing of Group Policy is synchronous
  - You can change the processing of Group Policy to asynchronous by using a Group Policy setting for both computers and users

- **Refreshing Group Policy at Established Intervals of:**
  - 90 minutes for computers running Windows 2000 Professional and for member servers running Windows 2000 Server
  - 5 minutes for domain controllers

- **Processing Unchanged Group Policy Settings**
  - You can configure each client-side extension to process all applicable Group Policy settings

[handwritten margin note: can force in 2000 use secedit in 200? GP update]

You can control the processing of Group Policy, which can be synchronous or asynchronous. Asynchronous refers to processes that do not depend on each other's outcome, and can therefore occur on different threads simultaneously. The opposite is synchronous. Synchronous processes wait for the previous one to complete before beginning the next. For those Group Policy settings for which both types of processing are available as options, you can choose between the faster asynchronous or the safer, more predictable synchronous processing.

Synchronous and Asynchronous Processing

By default, the processing of Group Policy is synchronous. The Group Policy setting for computers is completed before the Welcome to Windows message is presented, and the Group Policy setting for users is completed before the command interpreter that is used to pass commands to the operating system is active and available for the user to interact with it.

You can change this default behavior by using a Group Policy setting for each so that processing is asynchronous. This is not recommended unless there are compelling performance reasons. To provide the most reliable operation, leave the processing as synchronous.

Refreshing Group Policy at Established Intervals

Computers running Windows 2000 refresh, or reapply, Group Policy settings at established intervals. The refresh ensures that Group Policy settings are applied to computers and users even if users never restart their computers or log off.

The following list provides the default refresh intervals:

- Computers running Windows 2000 Professional and not configured as domain controllers, and member servers running Windows 2000 Server, refresh every 90 minutes with a randomized time offset of 30 minutes. The time offset ensures that multiple computers do not contact a domain controller at the same time.

- Domain controllers refresh every five minutes. This means that critical new Group Policy settings, such as security settings, are applied after no more than five minutes.

You can change the default refresh values by modifying the administrative template settings for the user or computer configuration. Group Policy refreshing can not be scheduled to occur at a specific time.

Note The processing of software installation and folder redirection settings in a GPO occurs *only* when a computer starts or when the user logs on, rather than on a periodic basis.

Processing Unchanged Group Policy Settings

By default, each client-side extension, with the exception of the Remote Installation Service client-side extension, only processes Group Policy settings that have changed since the last time Group Policy was processed by the client-side extension. Although this default behavior provides the best performance, it may not produce the desired results. For example, if a user changes a setting that is controlled by a Group Policy setting during a session and the Group Policy setting has not been changed in the GPO, the user's change will not be reversed when Group Policy is applied again. Each client-side extension can be configured to process all applicable Group Policy settings regardless of whether they have been changed. This configuration can be accomplished with an administrative template setting.

Group Policy and Slow Network Connections (Links)

- Group Policy Can Detect a Slow Link

- Group Policy Uses an Algorithm to Determine Whether a Link Should Be Considered Slow

- Group Policy Sets a Flag to Indicate a Slow Link to the Client-side Extensions

Group Policy has the ability to detect a slow link, and, if a slow link is detected, it sets a flag to indicate that fact to the client-side extensions. If this flag is set, the individual client-side extensions can determine whether to process applicable Group Policy settings. The connection speed of the link is compared with 500 kilobits per second (Kbps), or with an alternative threshold of your choice if you change from the default Group Policy setting of 500 Kbps. Group Policy uses an algorithm to determine whether a link should be considered slow. If the connection speed is less than 500 Kbps, the connection is considered slow.

The following table indicates the default settings for slow link processing:

Client-side Extension	Slow Link Processing
Registry-based settings (Administrative Templates)	On (cannot be turned off)
Internet Explorer Maintenance settings	Off
Software Installation settings	Off
Folder Redirection settings	Off
Scripts settings	Off
Security settings	On (cannot be turned off)
IP Security settings	Off
EFS Recovery settings	On
Disk Quota settings	Off

The behavior of the client-side extensions over a slow link can be modified with an administrative template setting, except for Registry-based settings and Security settings, which are always processed.

Note For more information about how Group Policy detects slow links, see Appendix B, "Determining Slow Network Connections," on the Student Materials compact disc.

Resolving Conflicts Between Group Policy Settings

- **All Group Policy Settings Apply Unless There Are Conflicts**

- **The Last Setting Processed Applies**
  - When settings from different GPOs in the Active Directory hierarchy conflict, the child container GPO settings apply
  - When settings from GPOs linked to the same container conflict, the settings for the GPO highest in the GPO list apply

- **A Computer Setting Applies When It Conflicts with a User Setting**

But

Group Policy is cumulative, that is, all Group Policy settings in all of the GPOs that affect a user or computer account (as determined by the GetGPOList function) are applied, unless two or more settings conflict.

The rules for determining which Group Policy settings apply when they conflict are as follows:

- Settings from a parent container GPO conflict with settings from a child container GPO. When this happens, the settings in the child container are applied last and take effect.

- Settings from different GPOs linked to the same container conflict. When this happens, the settings in the GPO at the top of the list of GPOs on the **Group Policy** tab of the **Properties** dialog box for the container are applied last and take effect. To change the order in which multiple GPOs assigned to the same container are processed, click a GPO in the list on the **Group Policy** tab, and then click **Up** or **Down** to change its position.

The one exception to the application of the most recent setting processed is when computer and user settings conflict. When this occurs, in almost all instances the computer setting overrides the user settings and applies, even though the user setting was processed last. You can verify whether the computer or user setting applies by using the **Explain** tab of the **Properties** dialog box for a setting. This is not enforced by the Group Policy infrastructure, but is rather a convention that is followed by the operating system and by applications that take advantage of Group Policy. This convention is followed unless there are specific reasons that the convention is not appropriate for a given Group Policy setting.

The exceptions to the cumulative processing of Group Policy are IP Security settings and User Rights settings. When processing IP Security or User Rights settings, the last GPO processed overwrites any previous GPOs.

Class Discussion: How Group Policy Is Applied

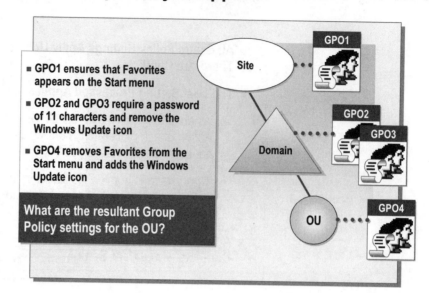

- GPO1 ensures that Favorites appears on the Start menu

- GPO2 and GPO3 require a password of 11 characters and remove the Windows Update icon

- GPO4 removes Favorites from the Start menu and adds the Windows Update icon

What are the resultant Group Policy settings for the OU?

On your network, you have the following GPOs linked to Active Directory containers:

GPO	Contains
GPO1	An account Group Policy setting that ensures **Favorites** appears on the **Start** menu
GPO2	An account Group Policy setting that requires a minimum of 11 characters in a password
GPO3	A **Start** menu setting that removes the **Windows Update** icon from the **Start** menu
GPO4	**Start** menu settings that ensure the **Windows Update** icon is on the **Start** menu and that remove **Favorites** from the **Start** menu

What are the resultant Group Policy settings for user objects in the OU, and why?

GPO2 & GPO4
  would be

GPO result –
Can run on
comd line – it will
show you the result of these.

◆ Modifying Group Policy Inheritance

- Enabling Block Inheritance
- Enabling No Override
- Filtering Group Policy Settings
- Class Discussion: Changing Group Policy Inheritance

Windows 2000 provides you with the ability to modify Group Policy inheritance and control how Group Policy settings are applied to specific computers and users. Modifying inheritance enables you to block, force, or filter the inheritance of Group Policy settings for your network, computers, and users.

Enabling Block Inheritance

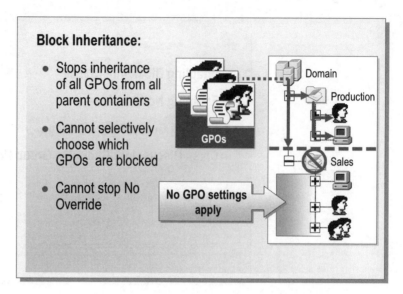

Block Inheritance:

- Stops inheritance of all GPOs from all parent containers

- Cannot selectively choose which GPOs are blocked

- Cannot stop No Override

No GPO settings apply

Domain
Production
GPOs
Sales

You can prevent a child container from inheriting any GPOs from parent containers by enabling Block Inheritance on the child container. Enabling Block Inheritance on a child container prevents the container from inheriting all Group Policy settings and not individual settings. This is useful when an Active Directory container requires unique Group Policy settings and you want to ensure that settings are not inherited. For example, you can use Block Inheritance when it is necessary that the administrator of an OU control all GPOs for that container.

To block inheritance of a GPO for a child container, perform the following steps:

1. Open the **Properties** dialog box for the domain or OU at which you want to block inheritance.

2. On the **Group Policy** tab, click **Block Policy Inheritance**.

The two limitations to blocking inheritance are as follows:

- You cannot selectively choose which GPOs are blocked. Block Inheritance affects all GPOs from all parent containers, except when the GPO is configured with the No Override option.

- Block Inheritance cannot stop the inheritance of a GPO linked to a parent container if the link is configured with the No Override option.

Enabling No Override

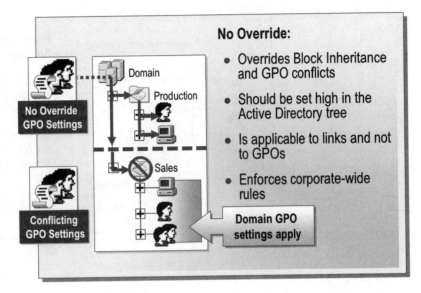

No Override:

- Overrides Block Inheritance and GPO conflicts
- Should be set high in the Active Directory tree
- Is applicable to links and not to GPOs
- Enforces corporate-wide rules

Enabling No Override means that all Group Policy settings contained in the GPO whose link is configured with No Override apply, even if they conflict with settings processed after them, or if blocking occurs lower in the Active Directory tree. You should set to No Override only the links to GPOs that represent critical corporate-wide rules. Link the GPO high in the Active Directory tree so that it affects multiple OUs. For example, link a GPO with network security settings to a domain or site.

Note that the No Override option is actually being set on the link and not on the actual GPO. This means that if you have a GPO that is linked to multiple containers, you can configure the No Override option on each container, independently of the others.

When more than one link is set to No Override, and the linked GPOs all apply to a common container, and they contain conflicting settings, the GPO that is highest in the Active Directory hierarchy takes precedence.

To set the No Override option, perform the following steps:

1. Open the **Properties** dialog box for the container to which the GPO is linked.

2. On the **Group Policy** tab, click **Options**.

3. In the **Options** dialog box for the GPO, click **No Override**, and then click **OK**.

Note Include only critical settings in linked GPOs that are marked as No Override, because they take effect regardless of how other GPOs are set up. You want to be sure that you are not overriding important GPOs.

Filtering Group Policy Settings

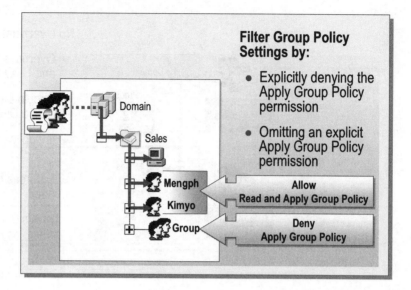

By default, for any given container, the Group Policy settings contained within all of the GPOs that affect the container are applied to all users and computers within that container. This may not produce the results that you desire. For example, if you have delegated administrative control of a child OU to one or more users whose accounts are in that OU, you may not want Group Policy to apply to those user accounts. You can control or filter the application of Group Policy by using security groups and the discretionary access control list (DACL) of one or more GPOs.

For Group Policy to apply to a user or computer account, the account needs to have an access control entry (ACE) in the DACL for a GPO that allows the Read permission and an ACE that allows the Apply Group Policy permission. The default DACL for a new GPO has the following ACEs:

- Authenticated Users – Allow Read and Allow Apply Group Policy.
- Domain Admins, Enterprise Admins and SYSTEM – Allow Read, Allow Write, Allow Create All Child Objects, Allow Delete All Child Objects.

Note Authenticated Users, CREATOR OWNER, Domain Admins, Enterprise Admins, and SYSTEM also have special permissions on GPOs. These special permissions are not listed in the previous paragraph because they do not affect the application of Group Policy.

To filter Group Policy so that Group Policy settings that would normally apply to all accounts in the OU do not affect the OU administrators in the example, you can use one of the following two methods:

Method 1

The first method is to explicitly deny the Apply Group Policy permission for the security group that contains the OU administrators. To filter Group Policy by explicitly denying the Apply Group Policy permission, perform the following steps:

1. Create a domain local security group and add the OU administrators to this group.

2. In the **Properties** dialog box, on the **Security** tab, add the security group for the GPO that you do not want to apply to the OU administrators.

3. Deny the Apply Group Policy permission for this security group.

Method 2

The second method is to remove Authenticated Users. By omitting the OU administrators from the security group, they have no explicit permissions on the GPO. To filter Group Policy by omitting an explicit Apply Group Policy permission, perform the following steps:

1. Remove the Authenticated Users groups from the DACL.

2. Create a domain local security group and add all computer and user accounts except the OU administrator accounts to this group.

3. In the **Properties** dialog box, on the **Security** tab, add the security group for the GPO that you do not want to apply to the OU administrators.

4. Allow the security group Read and Apply Group Policy permissions.

Class Discussion: Changing Group Policy Inheritance

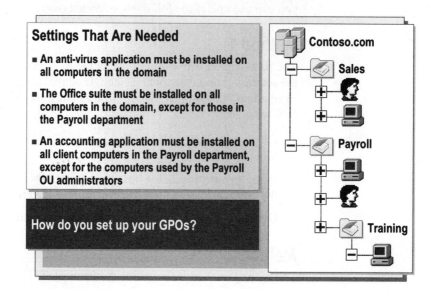

Settings That Are Needed

- An anti-virus application must be installed on all computers in the domain

- The Office suite must be installed on all computers in the domain, except for those in the Payroll department

- An accounting application must be installed on all client computers in the Payroll department, except for the computers used by the Payroll OU administrators

How do you set up your GPOs?

Contoso.com
  — Sales
  — Payroll
  — Training

You have determined that the following conditions must exist in your network:

- An anti-virus application must be installed on all computers in the domain.

- The Microsoft Office suite must be installed on computers in the domain, except for users in the Payroll department.

- A line-of-business accounting application must be installed on all computers in the Payroll department, except those that are used by the Payroll OU administrators.

How should you set up GPOs so that the above conditions are met?

Lab A: Implementing Group Policy

Objectives

After completing this lab, you will be able to:

- Link a Group Policy object (GPO) to an organizational unit (OU).
- Identify the effects of inheritance when multiple GPOs are assigned.
- Block Group Policy inheritance.
- Force a Group Policy to be applied to child OUs.
- Filter a Group Policy to be applied to selected users and groups within an OU.

Prerequisite

Before working on this lab, you must have experience using Active Directory Users and Computers.

Lab Setup

To complete this lab, you need the following:

- A computer running Windows 2000 Advanced Server configured as a domain controller.

- An OU structure. To create the required OUs and users, run the 2154A.cmd batch file from C:\Moc\Win2154A\Labfiles.

Important The lab does not reflect the real-world environment. It is recommended that you always use complex passwords for any administrator accounts, and never create accounts without a password.

Important Outside of the classroom environment, it is strongly advised that you use the most recent software updates that are necessary. Because this is a classroom environment, we may use software that does not include the latest updates.

Estimated time to complete this lab: 45 minutes

Exercise 1
Creating and Linking Group Policy Objects

Scenario

You need to assign a number of standard Group Policy settings to OUs in your domain. You also need to create GPOs for each OU so that you can delegate some of the Group Policy administration tasks to junior administrators in your organization. Users in the Accounting OU require only moderate restrictions. For these users, you will apply the Corporate Standard Desktop GPO. Users in the Accounts Payable and Accounts Receivable OUs are task workers and require a more restricted desktop environment. For these users, you will apply the Restricted Desktop GPO to add additional restrictions to the Corporate Standard Desktop Group Policy settings inherited from the parent OU.

Goal

You will link the Corporate Standard Desktop GPO in the nwtraders.msft domain to the Accounting OU. You will then link the Restricted Desktop GPO to the Accounts Payable OU and to the Accounts Receivable OU. For each OU, you will create a GPO that you will later use to delegate Group Policy administration for the Accounting OUs.

Tasks	Detailed Steps

1. Link the Corporate Standard Desktop GPO to the Accounting OU.	a. Log on as Administrator with a password of **password**.
	
	b. Open Active Directory Users and Computers from the **Administrative Tools** menu.
	
	c. In the console tree, expand your domain, right-click **Accounting**, and then click **Properties**.
	
	d. In the **Accounting Properties** dialog box, click the **Group Policy** tab.
	
	    Notice that no Group Policy objects are currently linked to this OU.
	
	e. On the **Group Policy** tab, click **Add**.
	
	f. In the **Add a Group Policy Object Link** dialog box, on the **All** tab, under **All Group Policy Objects stored in this domain**, click **Corporate Standard Desktop**, and then click **OK**.
	
	    Corporate Standard Desktop appears in the list of Group Policy Object Links. The Corporate Standard Desktop GPO is now linked to the Accounting OU.
	
	g. Leave the **Accounting Properties** dialog box open.

2. Create a new GPO for the Accounting OU. Name the new GPO Accounting Policy.	a. In the **Accounting Properties** dialog box, click **New**. b. Type **Accounting Policy** and then press ENTER. c. Click **Close** to close the **Accounting Properties** dialog box. d. Leave Active Directory Users and Computers open.

Tasks	Detailed Steps
3. Link the Restricted Desktop GPO to the Accounts Payable OU.	a. In the console tree, expand **Accounting**, right-click **Accounts Payable**, and then click **Properties**.
	b. In the **Accounts Payable Properties** dialog box, on the **Group Policy** tab, click **Add**.
	c. In the **Add a Group Policy Object Link** dialog box, on the **All** tab, under **All Group Policy Objects stored in this domain**, click **Restricted Desktop**, and then click **OK**.
	d. Leave the **Accounts Payable Properties** dialog box open.
4. Create a new GPO for the Accounts Payable OU. Name the new GPO Accounts Payable Policy.	a. In the **Accounts Payable Properties** dialog box, click **New**.
	b. Type **Accounts Payable Policy** and then press ENTER.
	c. Click **Close** to close the **Accounts Payable Properties** dialog box.
	d. Leave Active Directory Users and Computers open.
5. Link the Restricted Desktop GPO to the Accounts Receivable OU.	a. In the console tree, right-click **Accounts Receivable**, and then click **Properties**.
	b. In the **Accounts Receivable Properties** dialog box, on the **Group Policy** tab, click **Add**.
	c. In the **Add a Group Policy Object Link** dialog box, on the **All** tab, under **All Group Policy Objects stored in this domain**, click **Restricted Desktop**, and then click **OK**.
	d. Leave the **Accounts Receivable Properties** dialog box open.
6. Create a new GPO for the Accounts Receivable OU. Name the new GPO Accounts Receivable Policy.	a. In the **Accounts Receivable Properties** dialog box, click **New**.
	b. Type **Accounts Receivable Policy** and then press ENTER.
	c. Click **Close** to close the **Accounts Receivable Properties** dialog box.
	d. Close Active Directory Users and Computers, and then log off.

Exercise 2
Verifying Group Policy Settings

Scenario

The Corporate Standard Desktop GPO contains settings that make the following changes to users' desktop environments:

- The Administrative Tools folder does not appear on the Start menu.
- The Windows Update icon does not appear on the Start menu.
- The list of recent documents should not be kept.

The Restricted Desktop GPO contains settings that make the following changes to users' desktop environments:

- Taskbar and Start Menu settings cannot be changed.
- Users cannot browse the network.

You need to log on as a user from the Accounting and Accounts Receivable OUs to verify that the correct settings are being applied.

Goal

You will log on by using user accounts in the Accounting and Accounts Receivable OUs and record which Group Policy settings are enforced.

Tasks	Detailed Steps
1. Log on as Acctguser and verify the Group Policy settings for a user in the Accounting OU.	a. Log on as Acctguser with a password of **password**.

 Are the following settings, contained in the Corporate Standard Desktop GPO, enforced?

- The **Administrative Tools** menu does not appear on the **Start** menu.
- The **Windows Update** icon does not appear on the **Start** menu.
- The **Documents** icon does not appear on the **Start** menu.

Yes, all are enforced.

Tasks	Detailed Steps
1. *(continued)*	**b.** Log off.
2. Log on as Aruser and verify the Group Policy settings for a user in the Accounts Receivable OU.	**a.** Log on as Aruser with a password of **password**.

❓ Are the following Group Policy settings, contained in the Corporate Standard Desktop GPO, enforced?

- The **Administrative Tools** menu does not appear on the **Start** menu.
- The **Windows Update** icon does not appear on the **Start** menu.
- The **Documents** icon does not appear on the **Start** menu.

_____Yes._____

_____

_____

_____

❓ Are the following settings, contained in the Restricted Desktop GPO, enforced?

- Taskbar and Start Menu settings cannot be changed.
- Users cannot browse the network.

_____Yes._____

_____

_____

_____

❓ Why did the restrictions in the Corporate Standard Desktop GPO apply to the user in the Accounts Receivable OU?

_____Forced._____

_____

_____

_____

2. *(continued)*	**b.** Log off.

Exercise 3
Blocking Group Policy Inheritance

Scenario

Group Policy settings assigned anywhere else in Active Directory should not affect the Accounts Receivable department.

Goal

You will configure the Accounts Receivable OU so that policies that exist higher in the hierarchy are not applied by blocking Group Policy inheritance. You will then verify the new settings for Accounts Receivable and Account Payable users.

Tasks	Detailed Steps
1. Block Group Policy inheritance for the Accounts Receivable OU.	a. Log on as Administrator with a password of **password**. b. Open Active Directory Users and Computers from the **Administrative Tools** menu. c. In the console tree, expand your domain, expand **Accounting**, right-click **Accounts Receivable**, and then click **Properties**. d. On the **Group Policy** tab, click **Block Policy inheritance**, and then click **OK**. e. Log off.
2. Log on as Aruser and verify that Group Policy inheritance is blocked for the Accounts Receivable OU.	a. Log on as Aruser with a password of **password**.
❓	Are the following settings, contained in the Corporate Standard Desktop GPO, enforced? Why or why not? ▪ The **Administrative Tools** menu does not appear on the **Start** menu. ▪ The **Windows Update** icon does not appear on the **Start** menu. ▪ The **Documents** icon does not appear on the **Start** menu. _No – blocked Not forced_

Tasks	Detailed Steps
❷	Are the following settings, contained in the Restricted Desktop GPO, enforced? Why or why not? ■ Taskbar and Start Menu settings cannot be changed. ■ Users cannot browse the network. _Yes._
2. *(continued)*	b. Log off.
3. Log on as Appuser and verify that Group Policy inheritance is not blocked for the Accounts Payable OU.	a. Log on as Appuser with a password of **password**.
❷	Are the following settings, contained in the Corporate Standard Desktop GPO, enforced? Why or why not? ■ The **Administrative Tools** menu does not appear on the **Start** menu. ■ The **Windows Update** icon does not appear on the **Start** menu. ■ The **Documents** icon does not appear on the **Start** menu. _Yes._
3. *(continued)*	b. Log off.

Exercise 4
Forcing Group Policy Inheritance

Scenario

A new GPO has been created that specifies that all users should be prevented from changing the location of My Documents. You have to ensure that even OUs configured to block Group Policy inheritance receive the new settings.

Goal

You will link the Restricted My Documents GPO to the Accounting OU, and verify the users to which the settings apply. You will then configure the Restricted My Documents GPO with the No Override option so that it will always be applied to all child containers.

Tasks	Detailed Steps
1. Link the Restricted My Documents GPO to the Accounting OU and enable the No Override option for the GPO.	a. Log on as Administrator with a password of **password**. b. Open Active Directory Users and Computers from the **Administrative Tools** menu. c. In the console tree, expand your domain, right-click **Accounting**, and then click **Properties**. d. In the **Accounting Properties** dialog box, on the **Group Policy** tab, click **Add**. e. In the **Add a Group Policy Object Link** dialog box, on the **All** tab, under **All Group Policy Objects stored in this domain**, click **Restricted My Documents**, and then click **OK**. f. In the **Group Policy Object Links** list, right-click **Restricted My Documents**, and then click **No Override**. *Notice that a check mark now appears in the No Override column to the right of the Restricted My Documents GPO.* g. Click **OK**, close Active Directory Users and Computers, and then log off.
2. Log on as Aruser and verify that the Restricted My Documents GPO is applied.	a. Log on as Aruser with a password of **password**. b. On the desktop, right-click **My Documents**, and then click **Properties**.
❓	Can you change the target folder location? Why or why not? No — it has been linked to that GP.
2. *(continued)*	c. Log off.

Exercise 5
Filtering Group Policy

Scenario

A line of business applications used by the Accounting department requires a domain user account in the Accounting OU. Because of compatibility problems, the Corporate Standard Desktop GPO cannot apply to the user. You need to configure the GPO to filter the application user account from having the Group Policy applied.

Goal

You will configure permissions for the Corporate Standard Desktop GPO so that it will not be applied to the Application User account in the Accounting OU. You will then verify that the GPO settings no longer apply to the Application User.

Tasks	Detailed Steps
1. Configure the Corporate Standard Desktop GPO so that it will not be applied to the Application User account.	a. Log on as Administrator with a password of **password**.
	b. Open Active Directory Users and Computers from the **Administrative Tools** menu.
	c. In the console tree, expand your domain, right-click **Accounting**, and then click **Properties**.
	d. In the **Accounting Properties** dialog box, on the **Group Policy** tab, right-click **Corporate Standard Desktop**, and then click **Properties**.
	e. On the **Security** tab, click **Add**.
	f. Under **Name**, double-click **Application User**, and then click **OK**.
	g. With **Application User** selected, select the **Deny** check box next to **Apply Group Policy**, and then click **OK**.
	h. In the **Security** dialog box, click **Yes** to continue.
	i. Click **OK** to close the **Accounting Properties** dialog box, close Active Directory Users and Computers, and then log off.
2. Verify that the settings in the Corporate Standard Desktop GPO do not apply to the Application User account.	a. Log on as Appuser with a password of **password**.

Tasks	Detailed Steps
❓	Are the following settings, contained in the Corporate Standard Desktop GPO, enforced? Why or why not? ▪ The **Administrative Tools** menu does not appear on the **Start** menu. *NO* ▪ The **Windows Update** icon does not appear on the **Start** menu. *No* ▪ The **Documents** icon does not appear on the **Start** menu. *No* *Denied then — filtered then*
2. *(continued)*	b. Log off.

Delegating Administrative Control of Group Policy

- **Enable a User to Manage Group Policy Links for a Site, Domain, or OU by:**
  - Assigning the user read and write permissions to the gPLink and gPOptions attributes of the site, domain, or OU
  - Using the Delegation of Control wizard
- **Enable a User or Group to Create GPOs by:**
  - Adding the user or group to the Group Policy Creator Owners group
- **Enable a User to Edit GPOs by:**
  - Assigning the user read and write permissions to the GPO
  - Making the user a member of either Domain Admins, Enterprise Admins, or GPO Creator Owners groups
  - Granting the user access to the GPO by using the Security tab in the GPO Properties dialog box

---

Active Directory enables an administrator to delegate control of Group Policy objects (GPOs). This section explains how Group Policy fits in with the delegation of sites, domains, and organizational units.

The delegation of Group Policy consists of the following three aspects, which can be used together or separately, as a particular situation requires:

- Managing Group Policy links for a site, domain, or OU
- Creating GPOs
- Editing GPOs

Managing Group Policy Links for a Site, Domain, or OU

The **Group Policy** tab in the **Properties** dialog box of a site, domain, or OU allows the administrator to specify which GPOs are linked to that site, domain, or OU. This information is stored in the gPLink and gPOptions attributes of the container to which the GPO is linked.

Active Directory supports security settings on a per-property basis. This means that a non-administrator can be given read and write access to specific properties. In this case, if non-administrators have read and write access to the gPLink and gPOptions attributes, they can manage the list of GPOs linked to that site, domain, or OU.

To give a group read and write access to these attributes, use the Delegation of Control wizard and select the Manage Group Policy links predefined task.

Creating GPOs

In Windows 2000, by default, only the System account and members of the Domain Admins, Enterprise Admins, and Group Policy Creator Owners groups can create GPOs. If you want a non-administrator or group to be able to create GPOs, you can add that user or group to the Group Policy Creator Owners security group.

When a non-administrator who is a member of the Group Policy Creator Owners group creates a GPO, that user becomes the creator and owner of the GPO; therefore, the user can edit the GPO. Being a member of the Group Policy Creator Owners group gives the non-administrator full control of only those GPOs that the user creates or those explicitly delegated to that user; it does not give the non-administrator full control of all of the GPOs for the domain.

If you add a user or group to the Group Policy Creator Owners group, but do not also use the Delegation of Control wizard to allow the user or group read and write access to the gPLink and gPOptions attributes of a site, domain, or OU, the user or group will be able to create GPOs, but will not be able to link the new GPOs.

Note　When an administrator creates a GPO, the Domain Administrators group becomes the Creator Owner of the GPO.

Editing GPOs

To edit a GPO, the user must have both read and write access to the GPO. To edit a GPO, the user must be one of the following:

- A member of Domain Admins or Enterprise Admins.
- A Creator Owner.
- A user with access to the GPO. That is, an administrator or a user to whom the Creator Owner has granted access to the GPO.

By default, GPOs give members of Domain Admins, Enterprise Admins, the Group Policy Creator Owners groups, and the System account full control without the Apply Group Policy attribute. This means that they can edit the GPO, but the policies contained in that GPO do not apply to them.

Authenticated Users have read access to the GPO with the Apply Group Policy attribute set to Allow.

Administrators are also authenticated users, which means that they have the Apply Group Policy attribute set. If this is not desired, administrators have two choices:

- Remove authenticated users from the list and add their own security group with the Apply Group Policy attribute set to Allow. This new group should contain all of the users whom this Group Policy is intended to affect.

- Set the Apply Group Policy attribute to Deny for the Domain and Enterprise Administrators, and possibly the Creator Owner groups. This setting prevents the GPO from being applied to members of those groups. Remember that an ACE set to Deny always takes precedence over an ACE set to Allow. Therefore, if a given user is a member of another group that is set to explicitly Allow the Apply Group Policy attribute for this GPO, it will still be denied.

Note   For more information about delegating administrative control of Group Policy, see *Using Group Policy Scenarios* under **Additional Reading** on the Web page on the Student Materials compact disc.

Lab B: Delegating Group Policy Administration

Objectives

After completing this lab, you will be able to:

- Delegate control of Group Policy to allow a user to manage Group Policy links.

- Delegate control of Group Policy to allow a user to create Group Policy objects.

- Delegate control of Group Policy to allow a user to edit Group Policy objects.

Prerequisite

Before working on this lab, you must have experience using Active Directory Users and Computers and configuring permissions for objects.

Lab Setup

To complete this lab, you need the following:

- A computer running Windows 2000 Advanced Server configured as a domain controller.

Estimated time to complete this lab: 30 minutes

Exercise 1
Delegating Group Policy Administration

Scenario

You have decided to delegate Group Policy administration for the Accounting, Accounts Payable, and Accounts Receivable organizational units (OUs) to a junior administrator. The junior administrator will be responsible for linking and unlinking Group Policy objects (GPOs), creating new GPOs, and modifying the existing GPOs. Additionally, the junior administrator must be able to manage any other objects in the OUs.

Goal

In this exercise, you will modify the discretionary access control lists (DACLs) for the existing GPOs to allow the junior administrator to modify them, add the junior administrator's account to the Group Policy Creator Owners group to allow the junior administrator to create new GPOs, and then delegate the ability to manage Group Policy links to the junior administrator.

Tasks	Detailed Steps
1. Verify whether the acctadmin user can currently accomplish the following tasks: • Link and unlink GPOs in the Accounting OU. • Create new GPOs in the Accounting OU. • Modify the current GPOs linked to the Accounting OU.	a. Log on as Acctadmin with a password of **password**. b. Open Active Directory Users and Computers by typing **dsa.msc** in the **Run** box. c. In the console tree, expand your domain, right-click **Accounting**, and then click **Properties**. d. In the **Accounting Properties** dialog box, click the **Group Policy** tab.

❓ Can the acctadmin user accomplish any of the following tasks?

 ▪ Link and unlink GPOs?

 ▪ Create new GPOs?

 ▪ Edit existing GPOs? ~~No~~

_____No._____

_____

_____

_____

| 1. (continued) | e. Click **Cancel**, close Active Directory Users and Computers, and then log off. |

Tasks	Detailed Steps
2. Modify the DACL on the GPOs currently linked to the Accounting OU to allow the acctadmin account to modify them.	**a.** Log on as Administrator with a password of **password**. **b.** Open Active Directory Users and Computers from the **Administrative Tools** menu. **c.** In the console tree, expand your domain, right-click **Accounting**, and then click **Properties**. **d.** On the **Group Policy** tab, in the **Group Policy Object Links** list, right-click **Corporate Standard Desktop**, and then click **Properties**. **e.** On the **Security** tab, click **Add**, type **acctadmin** and then click **OK**. **f.** On the **Security** tab, with the **Accounting Admin** account selected, select the **Allow** check box beside **Write**, and then click **OK**. **g.** Repeat steps d, e, and f for the Accounting Policy and the Restricted My Documents GPOs. **h.** Click **OK** to close the **Accounting Properties** dialog box, close Active Directory Users and Computers, and then log off.
3. Verify whether the acctadmin user can currently accomplish the following tasks: • Link and unlink GPOs in the Accounting OU. • Create new GPOs in the Accounting OU. • Modify the current GPOs linked to the Accounting OU.	**a.** Log on as Acctadmin with a password of **password**. **b.** Open Active Directory Users and Computers by clicking **Start**, clicking **Run**, typing **dsa.msc** and then clicking **OK**. **c.** In the console tree, expand your domain, right-click **Accounting**, and then click **Properties**. **d.** In the **Accounting Properties** dialog box, click the **Group Policy** tab.

❓ Can the acctadmin user accomplish any of the following tasks?

- Link and unlink GPOs? — *No*
- Create new GPOs? — *No*
- Edit existing GPOs? — *Yes*

Yes, No.

| 3. *(continued)* | **e.** Click **Cancel**, close Active Directory Users and Computers, and then log off. |

Tasks	Detailed Steps
4. Use the Delegation of Control wizard to delegate the Manage Group Policy Links task to the acctadmin user account.	a. Log on as Administrator with a password of **password**. b. Open Active Directory Users and Computers from the **Administrative Tools** menu. c. In the console tree, expand your domain, right-click **Accounting**, and then click **Delegate Control**. d. On the **Welcome to the Delegation of Control Wizard** page, click **Next**. e. On the **Users or Groups** page, click **Add**, type **acctadmin** click **OK**, and then click **Next**. f. On the **Task to Delegate** page, click **Manage Group Policy links**, and then click **Next**. g. On the **Completing the Delegation of Control Wizard** page, review the settings, and then click **Finish**. h. Close Active Directory Users and Computers, and then log off.
5. Verify whether the acctadmin user can currently accomplish the following tasks: • Link and unlink GPOs in the Accounting OU. • Create new GPOs in the Accounting OU. • Modify the current GPOs linked to the Accounting OU.	a. Log on as Acctadmin with a password of **password**. b. Open Active Directory Users and Computers by clicking **Start**, clicking **Run**, typing **dsa.msc** and then clicking **OK**. c. In the console tree, expand your domain, right-click **Accounting**, and then click **Properties**. d. In the **Accounting Properties** dialog box, click the **Group Policy** tab.
❓ Can the acctadmin user accomplish any of the following tasks? ▪ Link and unlink GPOs? — Yes. ▪ Create new GPOs? — No ▪ Edit existing GPOs? — Yes. _Yes._ _____ _____ _____ _____	
5. *(continued)*	e. Click **Cancel** to close the **Accounting Properties** dialog box, close Active Directory Users and Computers, and then log off.

Tasks	Detailed Steps
6. Allow the acctadmin user account to create new GPOs by making it a member of the Group Policy Creator Owners group.	a. Log on as Administrator with a password of **password**. b. Open Active Directory Users and Computers from the **Administrative Tools** menu. c. In the console tree, expand your domain, and then click **Users**. d. In the details pane, double-click **Group Policy Creator Owners**. e. On the **Members** tab, click **Add**, type **acctadmin** and then click **OK**. f. Click **OK** to close the **Group Policy Creator Owners Properties** dialog box, close Active Directory Users and Computers, and then log off.
7. Verify whether the acctadmin user can currently accomplish the following tasks: • Link and unlink GPOs in the Accounting OU. • Create new GPOs in the Accounting OU. • Modify the current GPOs linked to the Accounting OU.	a. Log on as Acctadmin with a password of **password**. b. Open Active Directory Users and Computers by typing **dsa.msc** in the **Run** box. c. In the console tree, expand your domain, right-click **Accounting**, and then click **Properties**. d. In the **Accounting Properties** dialog box, click the **Group Policy** tab.

Can the acctadmin user accomplish any of the following tasks?

- Link and unlink GPOs?
- Create new GPOs?
- Edit existing GPOs?

Yes.

7. *(continued)*	e. Click **Cancel** to close the **Accounting Properties** dialog box, close Active Directory Users and Computers, and then log off.

◆ Monitoring and Troubleshooting Group Policy

- **Monitoring Group Policy**
- **Group Policy Troubleshooting Tools**
- **Troubleshooting Group Policy**

There are various methods of monitoring Group Policy for implementation problems. If you encounter any problem in the implementation of Group Policy, you can use one of the many tools provided by Windows 2000 to troubleshoot such problems. To successfully resolve any problem in the implementation of Group Policy, you must know the common implementation problems and understand their possible causes.

Monitoring Group Policy

You Can Monitor Group Policy by:

- **Enabling Diagnostic Logging to the Event Log**
  - Causes Group Policy to generate detailed events in the Event Log
- **Enabling Verbose Logging**
  - Tracks all changes and settings applied to the local computer and the users who log on to the computer
  - Involves the addition of the registry keys for verbose logging

There are various methods of monitoring Group Policy. You can monitor Group Policy by enabling diagnostic logging and verbose logging.

Enabling Diagnostic Logging to the Event Log

Enabling diagnostic logging for Group Policy causes Group Policy to generate detailed events in the Event Log. These detailed events can help assist in diagnosing problems associated with Group Policy processing by backtracking the events and providing additional information about them.

▶ **To enable diagnostic logging:**

1. Log on as the local administrator.

2. Click **Start**, and then click **Run**.

3. In the **Open** text box, type **regedit** and then click **OK**.

4. Open the **HKEY_LOCAL_MACHINE\Software\Microsoft\WindowsNT\CurrentVersion** key.

5. On the **Edit** menu, point to **New**, click **Key**, type **Diagnostics** and then press ENTER.

6. With the **Diagnostics** key selected, on the **Edit** menu, point to **New**, click **DWORD Value**, type **RunDiagnosticLoggingGlobal** and then press ENTER.

7. Double-click **RunDiagnosticLoggingGlobal**, type **1** and then click **OK**.

   Events generated by Group Policy are recorded in the Application log.

in registry,
value of
0 or 1
to enable or
disable

Note Enabling diagnostic logging for Group Policy generates a large number of events during computer startup and when a user logs on. You should increase the size of the Application log prior to enabling diagnostic logging so that the Application log does not fill up. Also, enable diagnostic logging only when troubleshooting Group Policy and disable it when you are finished.

Enabling Verbose Logging

Verbose logging tracks all changes and settings applied to the local computer and to users who log on to the computer by Group Policy. The log file is located in the *systemroot*\Debug\UserMode folder and is named Userenv.log. Enabling verbose logging involves adding the registry key for verbose logging.

To enable verbose logging, add a DWORD value named **UserEnvDebugLevel** with a value of 30002 to the **HKEY_LOCAL_MACHINE\Software\ Microsoft\Windows NT\CurrentVersion\Winlogon** key in the registry.

Note A value of 30002 enables verbose logging, 30001 enables logging of errors and warnings only, and 30000 logs nothing.

To disable verbose logging, delete the UserenvDebugLevel value from the registry.

Group Policy Troubleshooting Tools

- **Windows 2000 Support Tools for Group Policy Troubleshooting:**
  - Netdiag.exe
  - Replmon.exe
- **Windows 2000 Resource Kit Tools for Group Policy Troubleshooting:**
  - Gpotool.exe
  - Gpresult.exe

replication monitor

Windows 2000 provides a number of different tools that you can use to help troubleshoot and resolve problems associated with Group Policy. Some of these tools are included on the Windows 2000 Server CD-ROM in the Windows 2000 Support Tools\Tools folder, whereas others are included in the Windows 2000 Resource Kit.

Windows 2000 Support Tools for Group Policy Troubleshooting

You can resolve Group Policy issues by using the following tools that are included in the Windows 2000 Support Tools package on the Windows 2000 Server CD-ROM:

Allows see where problems in communication are on network.

- *Netdiag.exe.* This command-line diagnostic tool helps isolate networking and connectivity problems by performing a series of tests to determine the state of your network client and whether it is functional. These tests and the key network status information they expose give network administrators and support personnel a more direct means of identifying and isolating network problems. This tool can help you diagnose and resolve Group Policy problems that are related to network connectivity.

- *Replmon.exe.* This tool can help you diagnose and resolve Group Policy problems that are related to incomplete replication of the GPC and the GPT. This tool enables administrators to view the low-level status of Active Directory replication, force synchronization between domain controllers, view the topology in a graphical format, and monitor the status and performance of domain controller replication through a graphical interface.

Windows 2000 Resource Kit Tools for Group Policy Troubleshooting

You can resolve Group Policy issues by using the following tools that are included in the Windows 2000 Resource Kit:

- *Gpotool.exe*. This command-line tool allows you to check the health of the Group Policy objects on domain controllers.

- *Gpresult.exe*. This command-line tool displays information about the result Group Policy has had on the current computer and logged-on user.

Note   For details and usage of these tools, refer to the Windows 2000 Resource Kit.

Troubleshooting Group Policy

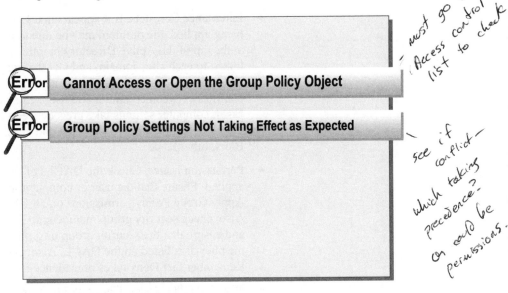

[Handwritten margin notes: "must go into Access control list to check" and "see if conflict — which taking precedence — or could be permissions."]

You may encounter problems when implementing Group Policy. Here are some of the more common problems that you may encounter, along with suggested strategies for resolving them.

- You attempt to either open or edit a Group Policy object, and receive an error indicating that the Group Policy object cannot be accessed or opened. Possible causes and their solutions are:

  - You do not have permissions to access the GPO. Check the DACL for the GPO that you are trying to open or edit. You must have both Read and Write permissions to open or edit a GPO.

  - The domain controller that Group Policy is trying to reach is offline or cannot be resolved with Domain Name System (DNS). Confirm that the domain controller is online, if it is, confirm that you can resolve the name of the domain controller with DNS.

- Group Policy settings are not applied as expected. Possible causes and their solutions are:

  - Inheritance Conflicts. If it appears that Group Policy settings are not being applied, the problem may be due to inheritance conflicts. Starting at the top of the Active Directory hierarchy, check the order of the GPOs linked to each site, domain, and OU that may affect the user or computer that is not receiving Group Policy settings. Next, see if there are conflicts between computer and user settings. Remember that in most cases, computer settings take precedence over conflicting user settings. Check GPO links for No Override and check domains and OUs for Block Inheritance.

  - Permission Issues. Check the DACLs of the GPOs that you expect to be applied. Ensure that the user or computer account has both Read and Apply Group Policy permissions on all GPOs that should be applied. Also, check security group membership for the computer or user account and ensure that the security group or groups that the account is a member of is listed on the DACL. Also, check for Deny ACEs. Remember that Deny takes precedence over all Allow permissions.

  - Disabled GPO Nodes. Check all GPOs to see if either the Computer Configuration or User Configuration nodes have been disabled.

  - Replication Issues. Ensure that both Active Directory replication and Sysvol replication are complete. Remember that if the GPC and GPT portions of a GPO are not both replicated, Group Policy will not be applied.

  - Inter-Domain GPO Link Issues. If a site, domain, or OU is linked to a GPO in another domain, the GPO is accessed through a trust relationship. If the trust fails for any reason, access to the linked GPO fails and so does Group Policy processing. You can prevent this type of problem by ensuring that you have multiple domain controllers per domain, or by creating explicit trusts between domains.

  - Computer or User Object Moved. Client computers cache the Active Directory location for thirty minutes. If the computer or user account is moved from one OU to another, the client computer may not have the correct location for the object. If Group Policy refreshes before the cached location does, the new Group Policy settings will not be processed. However, the new Group Policy settings will be processed the next time Group Policy is refreshed.

Best Practices

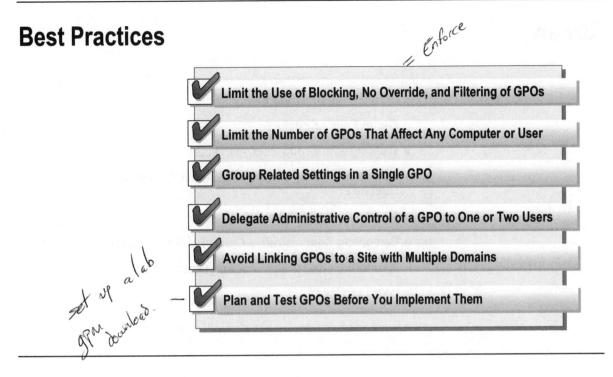

The following list provides best practices for implementing Group Policy. Review this checklist before you implement Group Policy:

- Limit the use of Block Inheritance, No Override, and filtering of GPOs, especially across domains. Each one of these introduces a further level of complexity. When you must use one of these methods, try to use only one at a time.

- Limit the number of GPOs that affect any given computer or user. If there is a problem with the settings that apply to a computer or user, it will be easier to troubleshoot if there are fewer GPOs.

- Group related settings in a single GPO. For example, a GPO that you use to publish Microsoft Office 2000 should also contain any registry-based Group Policy settings for Office 2000, which makes it easier to manage related settings.

- Limit the number of administrators to whom you delegate control of a GPO to one or two. This limits the possibility of multiple administrators making changes to Group Policy settings at the same time.

- Avoid linking a GPO to a site that contains multiple domains. A GPO linked to a site affects all computers in that site, requiring all computers to contact a domain controller in the domain in which the GPO resides. This can increase network traffic. Instead, link the GPO to all domains in the site.

- Plan a model of how you want to implement Group Policy in your network before you start adding GPOs. Create two or more models and compare them to determine what best meets your needs. Planning ensures that your Group Policy settings match your corporate and network needs, are easy to manage, and that you have the flexibility to make future changes.

Review

- Introduction to Group Policy
- Group Policy Structure
- Working with Group Policy Objects
- How Group Policy Settings Are Applied in Active Directory
- Modifying Group Policy Inheritance
- Delegating Administrative Control of Group Policy
- Monitoring and Troubleshooting Group Policy
- Best Practices

1. You want to set corporate-wide Group Policy settings and at the same time set policies that affect only certain departments. How do Active Directory and Group Policy facilitate this?

   Allow overrides. — set policies at domain-level or
   Inheritance.   Ou level.

2. Users in three OUs (Sales, Production, and Training) need the same applications. Each OU has a different parent OU. What is the simplest way to use Group Policy to ensure that the users in the three OUs have the applications that they need?

   Set it at the Domain level & let it be inherited.

3. Your network has one domain. All user accounts in your network reside in either the Sales OU or the Production OU. You need to ensure that all users have a specific application on their desktops. How do you set up the Group Policy?

   IBid

4. All domain user accounts are in the Employees OU. You want to prevent users from accessing the Internet, except for a few users who do research. What can you do to make sure that these users can gain access to the Internet, but not other users?

   Make a child OU. Put all who don't need it into that OU

   OU Filter.

5. You have linked a GPO to the domain that prevents users from installing a particular application on their client computers. Yet you notice that several users in the Developers OU have the application installed. Why might this have happened? How do you ensure that the application is not installed?

   No override at domain level.

6. Your company has a software administrator who is responsible for installing the correct applications on the computers for all users in the Human Resources OU by using Group Policy. The software administrator should not be able to make changes to users or computers. What do you do to ensure that the software administrator can install the necessary software by using Group Policy?

   Create GPO linked to ---
   then delegate control.

   OU - give them read-write.

Microsoft®
Training & Certification

Module 8: Using Group Policy to Manage User Environments

Contents

Microsoft®

Overview

- **Introduction to Managing User Environments**
- **Introduction to Administrative Templates**
- **Using Administrative Templates in Group Policy**
- **Assigning Scripts with Group Policy**
- **Using Group Policy to Redirect Folders**
- **Using Group Policy to Secure the User Environment**
- **Troubleshooting User Environment Management**
- **Best Practices**

Group Policy in Microsoft® Windows® 2000 allows an organization to reduce total cost of ownership (TCO) by allowing administrators to enhance and control users' desktops. Administrators can enhance and control users' desktops by creating a managed desktop environment that is tailored to the user's job responsibilities and experience level. TCO is the cost that is involved in administering distributed personal computer networks.

Microsoft Windows 2000 Advanced Server includes many Group Policy settings that provide administrators with greater control over computer configurations. Group Policy allows administrators to specify Group Policy settings to manage desktop configurations for groups of computers and users. Group Policy is flexible and includes settings for registry-based Group Policy, security, software installation, scripts, computer startup and shutdown, user logon and logoff, and folder redirection.

At the end of this module, you will be able to:

- Identify how Group Policy simplifies user environment management.
- Identify the purpose and the process of applying Administrative Templates.
- Use Administrative Templates in Group Policy to assign registry-based policies to control and configure user and computer environments.
- Assign scripts, such as startup, shutdown, logon, and logoff, with Group Policy to control user environments.
- Use Group Policy to redirect folders to a central network location.
- Use Group Policy to apply security policies to secure the user environment.
- Troubleshoot managing user environments by using Group Policy.
- Apply best practices for using Group Policy to manage user environments.

Introduction to Managing User Environments

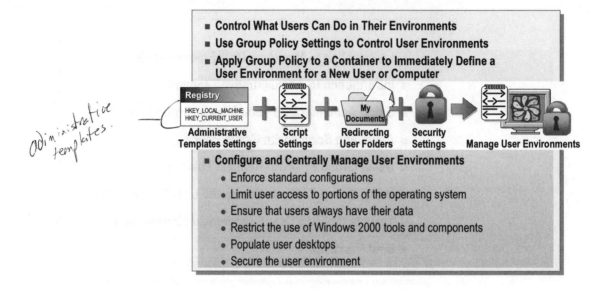

- Control What Users Can Do in Their Environments
- Use Group Policy Settings to Control User Environments
- Apply Group Policy to a Container to Immediately Define a User Environment for a New User or Computer

Registry
HKEY_LOCAL_MACHINE
HKEY_CURRENT_USER

Administrative Templates Settings + Script Settings + Redirecting User Folders + Security Settings → Manage User Environments

administrative templates.

- Configure and Centrally Manage User Environments
  - Enforce standard configurations
  - Limit user access to portions of the operating system
  - Ensure that users always have their data
  - Restrict the use of Windows 2000 tools and components
  - Populate user desktops
  - Secure the user environment

Managing user environments means controlling what users can do when logged on to the network. You do this by controlling their desktops, network connections, and user interfaces. You control user environments to ensure that users have what they need to perform their jobs, but do not have the ability to corrupt or incorrectly configure their environments.

The types of Group Policy settings that you typically use to manage user environments are administrative template settings, script settings, folder redirection, and security settings. You configure these settings in Group Policy in the Administrative Templates and Script extensions.

If you have used Group Policy to set up user environments for an Active Directory® directory service container, such as an organizational unit (OU), any computer or user who you add to that OU has the Group Policy settings applied automatically.

To centrally configure and manage user environments, you can perform the following tasks:

- Enforce standard configurations. Group Policy settings provide an efficient way to enforce standards, such as logon scripts and password settings. For example, you can prevent users from making changes to their desktops that could make their user environments more complex than necessary.

- Limit user access to selected portions of the operating system. You can prevent users from opening Control Panel and shutting down their computers. By preventing users from accessing critical operating system components and configuration options, you reduce the possibility of users corrupting their systems, and therefore, the number of technical support calls required.

- Ensure that users always have their desktops and personal data. By managing user desktop settings with registry-based policies, you ensure that users have the same computing environments even if they log on from different computers. You can control how Windows 2000 manages user profiles, which includes how users' personal data is made available. By redirecting user folders from users' local hard disks to a central location on a server, you can ensure that users' data is available to them regardless of the computers to which they log on.

- Restrict the use of tools and components in Windows 2000. These tools and components include Microsoft Internet Explorer, Windows Explorer, and the Microsoft Management Console (MMC). You can ensure that users never see these tools unless they have a genuine need for them.

- Populate user desktops. You can ensure that users have their required files, shortcuts, and network connections.

- Secure the user environment. Through the use of Group Policy in Active Directory, administrators can centrally apply the security settings required to protect the user environment. In Windows 2000, you can use the Security Settings extension in Group Policy to define the security settings for local and domain security policies.

◆ Introduction to Administrative Templates

- **What Are Administrative Templates?**
- **How Computers Apply Administrative Template Settings**

To effectively configure and manage user environments, ensure that users can gain access to only the resources that they require do to their jobs. You can use Administrative Templates to simplify user environments and prevent users from corrupting their environments or spending time on unnecessary applications, software, or files.

By using the Administrative Templates extensions in Group Policy, you can set up the environments for multiple users and computers once, and then rely on Windows 2000 to continually implement and apply those settings.

What Are Administrative Templates?

- **Administrative Template Settings Modify Registry Settings That Control User Environments**

- **Settings Modify Registry Settings in the Registry Subtrees**
  - **HKEY_LOCAL_MACHINE** for computer settings
  - **HKEY_CURRENT_USER** for user settings

- **If a GPO No Longer Applies, Policy Settings Are Removed**

- **Windows 2000 Applies Both Group Policy and Local Default-Registry Settings Unless There Is a Conflict**

Administrative Templates are a collection of Group Policy settings that modify registry settings. You use Administrative Templates in Group Policy to configure user and computer registry-based settings that control the user's working environment. This includes controlling users' desktops, interface options, operating system components, and the default values for application settings.

Administrative template settings modify the values located in the following registry locations:

- **HKEY_LOCAL_MACHINE (HKLM)**. When a computer starts, the Group Policy settings contained within the Computer Configuration portion of the Group Policy objects (GPOs) that apply to the computer are written to either the SOFTWARE\Policies key or to the \SOFTWARE\Microsoft\Windows\CurrentVersion\Policies key below HKLM.

- **HKEY_CURRENT_USER (HKCU)**. When a user logs on to a computer, Group Policy settings contained within the User Configuration portion of the GPOs that apply to the user are written to either the SOFTWARE\Policies key or to the \SOFTWARE\Microsoft\Windows\CurrentVersion\Policies key below HKCU.

Windows 2000 applies both the Group Policy settings and any default registry settings to users and computers. If there are conflicts, the Group Policy settings prevail. If the GPO containing the settings that affect the user or computer account no longer applies (for example if it is removed or if the account is moved to a location that is not affected by the GPO) the settings are removed from the registry the next time that Group Policy is refreshed, and the local default registry settings apply.

How Computers Apply Administrative Template Settings

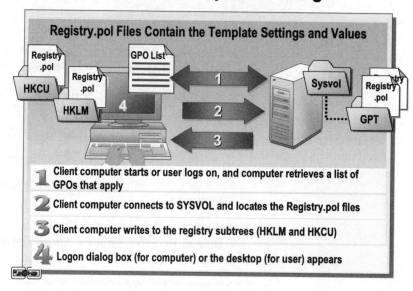

The administrative template settings and the values for the settings that Windows 2000 applies are stored in a Registry.pol file in the Group Policy template (GPT) on domain controllers. There are two files: one for computer settings, and one for user settings.

Note   The path for the Registry.pol file is *systemroot*\SYSVOL\Sysvol*domain_name*\\ Policies*GPO_GUID_identifier*\Machine or \User.

The process that a computer running Windows 2000 uses to apply administrative template settings during the start up process is as follows:

1. When the client computer starts, it retrieves the list of GPOs that contain computer configuration settings and determines the order in which to apply them.

2. The client computer connects to the SYSVOL folder on the authenticating domain controller, and then locates the Registry.pol files in the Machine folder in the GPT for each GPO that contains administrative template settings that apply to the computer.

3. The client computer writes the registry settings and their values in the Registry.pol file to the appropriate registry subtree. The computer continues initializing the operating system and enforces the registry settings.

4. When the registry settings have been enforced, the logon dialog box appears.

The following process is repeated during the user logon process:

1. After the user has initiated the logon process, the client computer retrieves the list of GPOs that contain user configuration settings, and determines the order in which to apply them.

2. The client computer connects to the SYSVOL folder on the authenticating domain controller, and then locates the Registry.pol files in the User folder in the GPT for each GPO that contains administrative template settings that apply to the user.

3. The client computer writes the registry settings and their values in the Registry.pol file to the appropriate registry subtree. The computer continues the logon process and enforces the registry settings.

4. When the registry settings have been enforced, the desktop is displayed.

The settings in the Group Policy section of the registry apply even when there is a conflict with settings in the local default registry settings.

◆ Using Administrative Templates in Group Policy

- **Types of Administrative Template Settings**

- **Settings for Locking Down the Desktop**

- **Settings for Locking Down User Access to Network Resources**

- **Settings for Locking Down User Access to Administrative Tools and Applications**

- **The Loopback Processing Mode Setting in Group Policy**

- **Implementing Administrative Templates**

Administrative template settings are registry-based Group Policy settings that you can use to mandate registry settings that control the behavior and appearance of the desktop, including the operating system components and applications. There are administrative template settings available for both computers and user accounts.

You can control the user environment by configuring specific administrative settings to lock down user environments. You should only lock down the desktops of users who perform defined and specific tasks, for example, users who perform telemarketing, data entry, or training.

Types of Administrative Template Settings

Setting types	Controls	Available for
Windows Components	The parts of Windows 2000 and its tools and components to which users can gain access, including MMC	🖥️ 👤
System	Logon and logoff, Group Policy, disk quotas, and loopback policy	🖥️ 👤
Network	The properties of network connections and dial-in connections	🖥️ 👤
Printers	Printer settings that can force printers to be published in Active Directory and disable Web-based printing	🖥️
Start Menu & Taskbar	What users can gain access to from the **Start** menu and what makes the **Start** menu read-only	👤
Desktop	The Active Desktop, including what appears on desktops, and what users can do with the My Documents folder	👤
Control Panel	The use of Add/Remove Programs, Printers, and Display in Control Panel	👤

Administrative template settings are organized into seven types, for which there are both user and computer settings. The computer settings focus more on the management of Windows 2000, whereas user settings focus more on controlling how users can affect their desktop environments.

The following table provides the types of settings in the Administrative Templates extension.

Setting type	Controls	Available for
Windows Components	The parts of Windows 2000 and its tools and components to which users can gain access. This includes controlling user access to MMC.	Computers and users
System	Logon and logoff procedures. With System settings, you can manage Group Policy and refresh intervals, enable disk quotas, and implement loopback processing.	Computers and users
Network	The properties of network connections and dial-in connections, which include shared network access.	Computers and users
Printers	Printer settings that can force printers to be automatically published in Active Directory and can disable Web-based printing.	Computers

(continued)

Setting type	Controls	Available for
Start Menu & Taskbar	Which features users can access from the **Start** menu. For example, by removing the **Run** command, users are prevented from running applications for which there is no icon or shortcut. You can also make the **Start** menu read-only and disable the user's ability to make changes.	Users
Desktop	The Active Desktop. You can control users' ability to gain access to the network and the Internet by hiding the appropriate desktop icons and controlling what they can do with their My Documents folder.	Users
Control Panel	Several applications in Control Panel. This includes restricting the use of Add/Remove Programs, Display, and Printers.	Users

Note   Windows 2000 provides you with the ability to add additional templates to Administrative Templates in Group Policy if the preconfigured templates do not provide you with the settings that you require.

Settings for Locking Down the Desktop

```
┌─────────────────────────────────────────────────────────────┐
│         Group Policy Settings to Lock Down the Desktop        │
├─────────────────────────────────────────────────────────────┤
│                                                               │
│   • Hide all icons on desktop                                 │
│                                                               │
│   • Don't save settings at exit                               │
│                                                               │
│   • Hide these specified drives in My Computer                │
│                                                               │
│   • Remove Run menu from Start menu                           │
│                                                               │
│   • Prohibit user from running Display control panel          │
│                                                               │
│   • Disable and remove links to Windows Update                │
│                                                               │
│   • Disable changes to Taskbar and Start Menu settings        │
│                                                               │
│   • Disable/Remove the Shut Down command                      │
│                                                               │
└─────────────────────────────────────────────────────────────┘
```

There are several Group Policy settings that you can use to customize a user's desktop environment. Securing the desktop involves setting up a computer so that it can perform only a limited number of functions that users cannot modify. For example, a computer in a public information kiosk can be configured to run only a Web browser.

The following table describes common Group Policy settings to configure when locking down user desktops, and examples of the possible effect of these configurations.

Group Policy setting and location	Action
Hide all icons on desktop (User Configuration\ Administrative Templates\Desktop)	Hides all desktop items, including menus, folders, and shortcuts. This provides users with a simpler user interface.
Don't save settings at exit (User Configuration\ Administrative Templates\Desktop)	Disables the ability to save any configuration changes made during the logon session. The original settings are restored each time users log off and then log back on.
Hide these specified drives in My Computer (User Configuration\ Administrative Templates\ Windows Components\ Windows Explorer)	Removes icons representing the selected drives from My Computer, Windows Explorer, and My Network Places. Drive letters will not appear in the **Open** dialog box of any application. By hiding drives, you help limit users to running only the applications that are on the **Start** menu.

(*continued*)

Group Policy setting and location	Action
Remove Run menu from Start menu (User Configuration\ Administrative Templates\ Start Menu & Taskbar)	Removes the **Run** command from the **Start** menu. However, users can still access this command through Task Manager.
Prohibit user from running Display in Control Panel (User Configuration\ Administrative Templates\ Control Panel\Display)	Prevents users from changing display settings such as the wallpaper, screen saver, or color schemes. This setting also reduces problems that can arise when users change their desktop settings.
Disable and remove links to Windows Update (User Configuration\ Administrative Templates\ Start Menu & Taskbar)	Removes the **Windows Update** command from the **Settings** menu. However, this command will still be available in Internet Explorer. Removing this command helps prevent users from applying unauthorized updates or changes to their operating systems.
Disable changes to Taskbar and Start Menu settings (User Configuration\ Administrative Templates\ Start Menu & Taskbar)	Removes the **Taskbar & Start Menu** command from the **Settings** menu. This helps prevent users from overriding any changes that you make to the **Start** menu.
Disable/Remove the Shut Down command (User Configuration\ Administrative Templates\Desktop)	Prevents users from shutting down and restarting Windows 2000. This is useful on computers that need to run continually, such as a computer in a public library.

Settings for Locking Down User Access to Network Resources

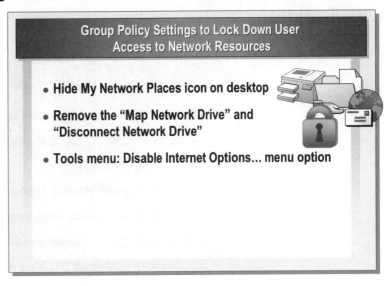

You can restrict the network resources to which users can gain access. The following table provides types of Group Policy that contain settings to configure when locking down user access to network resources, and examples of the possible effect of these configurations.

Group Policy setting and location	Action
Hide My Network Places icon on desktop (User Configuration\ Administrative Templates\Desktop)	Removes **My Network Places** from the desktop and disables support for universal naming convention (UNC) file names. By using logon scripts to map network drives, you can control the network resources to which users have access.
Remove the "Map Network Drive" and "Disconnect Network Drive" (User Configuration\ Administrative Templates\ Windows Components\ Windows Explorer)	Removes the Map Network Drive and Disconnect Network Drive options from Windows Explorer. This setting also removes the Add Network Places wizard from My Network Places. However, users can still connect to computers by using the **Run** command on the **Start** menu.
Tools menu: Disable Internet Options… menu option (User Configuration\ Administrative Templates\ Windows Components\ Internet Explorer\Browser Menus)	Removes the **Internet Options** command from Internet Explorer. This prevents users from modifying their Internet Explorer configurations. You can also disable individual pages by using Group Policy settings located under User Configuration\ Administrative Templates\ Windows Components\Internet Explorer\ Internet Control Panel.

Settings for Locking Down User Access to Administrative Tools and Applications

> **Group Policy Settings to Lock Down User Access to Administrative Tools and Applications**
>
> • **Remove Search menu from Start menu**
>
> • **Remove Run menu from Start menu**
>
> • **Disable Task Manager**
>
> • **Run only allowed Windows applications**
>
> • **Remove the Documents menu from the Start menu**
>
> • **Disable changes to Taskbar and Start Menu settings**
>
> • **Hide common program groups in Start menu**

The following table provides the setting types that contain settings to configure when locking down user access to administrative tools and applications, and examples of the possible effect of these configurations.

Group Policy setting and location	Action
Remove Search menu from Start menu (User Configuration\ Administrative Templates\ Start Menu & Taskbar)	Removes the **Search** menu from the **Start** menu. However, the **Search** menu will still appear in Windows Explorer and Internet Explorer. Removing the **Search** command helps prevent users from conducting bandwidth-intensive searches across the network.
Remove Run menu from Start menu (User Configuration\ Administrative Templates\ Start Menu & Taskbar)	Removes the **Run** command from the **Start** menu. This makes it more difficult for users to run unauthorized applications.
Disable Task Manager (User Configuration\ Administrative Templates\System\ Logon/Logoff)	Prevents the user from starting applications by using Task Manager.

(continued)

Group Policy setting and location	Action
Run only allowed Windows applications (User Configuration\ Administrative Templates\System)	Prevents users from running applications other than those you specify in this Group Policy setting. This restriction applies only to applications that are started through Windows Explorer.
Remove the Documents menu from the Start menu (User Configuration\ Administrative Templates\ Start Menu & Taskbar)	Removes the **Documents** command from the **Start** menu.
Disable changes to Taskbar and Start Menu settings (User Configuration\ Administrative Templates\ Start Menu & Taskbar)	Removes the **Taskbar & Start Menu** command from the **Settings** menu. This helps prevent users from overriding any changes that you make to the **Start** menu.
Hide common program groups in Start menu (User Configuration\ Administrative Templates\ Start Menu & Taskbar)	Removes common program groups from the **Start** menu. This means that users receive only the **Start** menu items specified in their user profiles.

The Loopback Processing Mode Setting in Group Policy

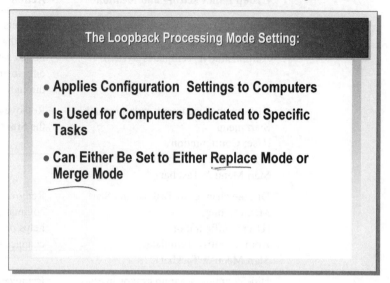

Loopback processing mode is a Group Policy setting that enforces the User Configuration settings in the GPOs that apply to the computer, rather than enforcing the User Configuration settings in the GPOs that apply to the user object.

Group Policy is normally applied to a user or computer based on where the user object or the computer object is located in Active Directory. For example, the user whose user object is located in the Sales OU logs on to a computer. The computer object is located in the Servers OU. The Group Policy settings that are applied to the user are based on any GPOs that are linked to the Sales OU, and GPOs linked to any parent containers. The settings that are applied to the computer are based on any GPOs that are linked to the Servers OU, and GPOs linked to any parent containers. However, this default behavior may not be appropriate for certain computers, such as servers or computers that are dedicated to a certain task. For example, applications that are assigned to a user should not be automatically available on a server.

There are two possible modes for loopback processing:

- *Replace mode.* Processes only the GPOs that apply to the computer.

- *Merge mode.* First processes the GPOs that apply to the user object, and then the GPOs that apply to the computer object. If settings conflict, the computer object settings in the GPO are enforced, because those GPO settings are applied last.

To enable the loopback processing mode, perform the following steps:

1. Open Group Policy, expand **Computer Configuration**, expand **Administrative Templates**, expand **System**, and then click **Group Policy**.

2. Double-click **User Group Policy loopback processing mode**.

3. Click **Enabled** if it is not already selected, and then in the **Mode** list, click either **Replace** or **Merge**.

Implementing Administrative Templates

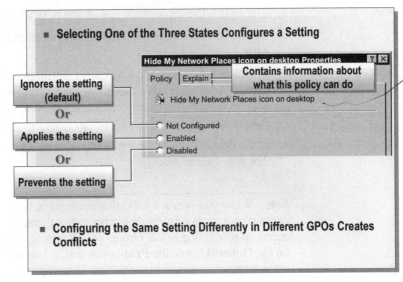

Implement administrative template settings by configuring the settings in the Administrative Templates extension in Group Policy. In most instances, you configure a setting by selecting one of three states for the setting. You select the state on the **Policy** tab of the **Properties** dialog box for the Group Policy setting.

The following list provides descriptions of the three states:

- *Not configured.* Windows 2000 ignores the setting and makes no changes to the computer. This state does not specify a value change in the registry.

- *Enabled.* Windows 2000 applies the setting and adds the change to the appropriate Registry.pol file.

- *Disabled.* Windows 2000 prevents the setting from being applied and adds the change to the appropriate Registry.pol file.

Besides selecting a state for a setting, you may need to provide additional information, such as the mode for Loopback processing, or the size for a disk quota.

The enabled and disabled states can create conflicting GPOs. This occurs, for example, when a setting is enabled in one GPO and the same setting is disabled in another GPO—but both GPOs apply to the same users or computers. Unless Group Policy inheritance is modified, the last setting applied prevails.

To gain access to the **Policy** tab for an administrative template setting, perform the following steps:

1. Right-click the appropriate site, domain, or OU, and then click **Properties**.

2. On the **Group Policy** tab, create or select an existing GPO, and then click **Edit**.

3. In Group Policy, expand **Computer Settings** or **User Settings**, and then expand **Administrative Templates** until you locate the setting that you want to modify, for example, User Configuration\
   Administrative Templates\Desktop.

4. In the details pane of Group Policy, double-click the Group Policy setting that you want to modify.

Note When you create a GPO that contains only settings for users or computers, you can disable the other type of settings (user or computer) to speed up processing of the Group Policy settings. You can disable the settings on the **General** tab of the **Properties** dialog box for the GPO.

Lab A: Using Administrative Templates to Assign Registry-Based Group Policy

Objectives

After completing this lab, you will be able to configure, apply, and test registry-based Group Policy by using Administrative Templates.

Prerequisites

Before working on this lab, you must have experience:

- Working with Active Directory Users and Computers.
- Managing disk quotas and scheduled tasks.

Lab Setup

To complete this lab, you need the following:

- A computer running Windows 2000 Advanced Server configured as a domain controller.
- An OU structure. To create the required OUs and users, run the Sales.vbs script file from C:\Moc\Win2154A\Labfiles.

Important   The lab does not reflect the real-world environment. It is recommended that you always use complex passwords for any administrator accounts, and never create accounts without a password.

Important   Outside of the classroom environment, it is strongly advised that you use the most recent software updates that are necessary. Because this is a classroom environment, we may use software that does not include the latest updates.

Estimated time to complete this lab: 30 minutes

Exercise 1
Implementing an Administrative Templates Policy for Computers

Scenario

You need to assign additional Group Policy settings for a domain controller in your domain. The Group Policy settings that you need to apply to enhance the settings in the default domain controller Group Policy need to satisfy the following management requirements:

- Disk quotas must be enabled for all volumes so that disk space usage can be easily tracked.

- Disk quota limits should not be enforced. No limits will be enforced until you can determine the average disk utilization for the server and install additional disk capacity, if required.

- Users must not be able to run the New Task wizard so that server performance is not impacted.

Goal

Create a Group Policy object (GPO) linked to the Domain Controllers OU, and configure the GPO with Group Policy settings that satisfy the scenario requirements. After the GPO is configured, restart your computer to ensure that the Group Policy settings have been applied.

Tasks	Detailed Steps
1. Create a new GPO linked to the Domain Controllers OU. Name the new GPO Admin Template Policy.	a. Log on as Administrator with a password of **password**. b. Open Active Directory Users and Computers from the **Administrative Tools** menu. c. In the console tree, expand your domain, right-click **Domain Controllers**, and then click **Properties**. d. On the **Group Policy** tab, click **New**, type **Admin Template Policy** and then press ENTER.

2. Edit the administrative template settings for the new GPO to:
 	
  • Enable disk quotas.
 	
  • Prevent disk quota limits from being enforced.
 	
  • Prevent users from running the New Task wizard.
	a. Select the new Group Policy, and then click **Edit**.
	
	b. In the Group Policy console tree, under **Computer Configuration**, expand **Administrative Templates**.
	
	c. In the console tree, expand **System**, click **Disk Quotas**, and then in the details pane, double-click **Enable disk quotas**.
	
	d. In the **Enable disk quotas Properties** dialog box, on the **Policy** tab, click **Enabled**, and then click **OK**.
	
	e. In the details pane, double-click **Enforce disk quota limit**.
	
	f. In the **Enforce disk quota limit Properties** box, click **Disabled**, and then click **OK**.
	
	g. In the console tree, expand **Windows Components**, click **Task Scheduler**, and then in the details pane, double-click **Disable New Task Creation**.
	
	h. In the **Disable New Task Creation Properties** dialog box, on the **Policy** tab, click **Enabled**, and then click **OK**.
	
	i. Close Group Policy, and then click **Close** to close the **Domain Controllers Properties** dialog box.
	
	j. Leave Active Directory Users and Computers open.

Exercise 2
Implementing an Administrative Templates Policy for Users

Scenario

Telemarketing users are typically temporary workers who accept orders by telephone and enter the customer's data into a database by using in-house software installed on preconfigured computers. You need to implement Group Policy settings that enforce the following restrictions for telemarketing users:

- Prevent users from mapping network drives.

- Prevent users from using My Network Places to browse the corporate network.

- Prevent users from making changes to Taskbar & Start Menu settings.

- Prevent users from accessing the Windows Update icon. The Information Services department should install all software updates for corporate computers.

- Enable users to run the New Task wizard to schedule an in-house tool to perform maintenance tasks on the order database.

Goal

Create a GPO linked to the Telemarketing OU, and configure the GPO with Group Policy settings that satisfy the restrictions described in the scenario.

Tasks	Detailed Steps
1. Create a GPO for the Telemarketing OU. Name this new GPO Telemarketing Policy.	a. In the console tree, expand your domain, expand **Sales**, right-click **Telemarketing**, and then click **Properties**. b. On the **Group Policy** tab, click **New**, type **Telemarketing Policy** and then press ENTER.
2. Edit the administrative template settings for the Telemarketing Policy GPO to prevent users from mapping network drives.	a. With **Telemarketing Policy** selected, click **Edit**. b. In the console tree, under **User Configuration**, expand **Administrative Templates**. c. In the console tree, expand **Windows Components**, click **Windows Explorer**, and then in the details pane, double-click **Remove the "Map Network Drive" and "Disconnect Network Drive."** d. In the **Remove "Map Network Drive" and "Disconnect Network Drive" Properties** dialog box, on the **Policy** tab, click **Enabled**, and then click **OK**.

Tasks	Detailed Steps
3. Edit the remaining administrative template settings for the Telemarketing GPO to: • Prevent users from using My Network Places to browse the corporate network. • Prevent users from making changes to Taskbar & Start Menu settings. • Prevent users from accessing Windows Update. • Enable users to run the New Task wizard.	a. Using the following information, configure the remaining required restrictions: • Enable the Hide My Network Places icon on Desktop policy, which is located in the Desktop folder. • Enable the Disable changes to Taskbar and Start Menu Settings policy, which is located in the Start Menu & Taskbar folder. • Enable the Disable and Remove links to Windows Update policy, which is located in the Start Menu & Taskbar folder. • Disable the Disable New Task Creation policy, which is located in the Windows Components\Task Scheduler folder. b. Close all open windows, and then restart your computer.

Exercise 3
Verifying Administrative Templates Policies

Scenario

Now that the required GPOs are in place and configured, you need to confirm that the Group Policy settings are being applied as expected.

Goal

Log on as Administrator to verify which computer Group Policy settings are in effect. Then log on as a Telemarketing user to verify which user Group Policy settings are in effect for members of the Telemarketing OU.

Tasks	Detailed Steps
1. Verify that the Group Policy settings contained in the Admin Template GPO are being properly applied.	a. Log on as Administrator with a password of **password**. b. On the desktop, double-click **My Computer**, right-click the icon for drive C, and then click **Properties**. c. Click the **Quota** tab.
❓ Are disk quotas enabled? Why or why not? _No._	
❓ Are disk quota limits enforced? Why or why not? _No._	
1. *(continued)*	d. Click **Cancel** to close the **Local Disk (C:) Properties** dialog box. e. In the My Computer window, double-click **Control Panel**. f. In Control Panel, double-click **Scheduled Tasks**.

Tasks	Detailed Steps
❓ Are you able to run the Add Task wizard? _No._	
❓ Were all of the Group Policy settings in the Admin Template Policy GPO applied?	
1. *(continued)*	g. Close all open windows, and then log off.
2. Log on as TMUser and verify that the Group Policy settings contained in the Telemarketing GPO are being properly applied.	a. Log on as TMUser with a password of **password**.
❓ Are the following settings contained in the Telemarketing Policy GPO enforced? Why or why not? ■ The **My Network Places** icon does not appear on the desktop. — enforced ■ Unable to map a network drive. — no ■ Unable to modify Taskbar & Start Menu settings. — enforced ■ The **Windows Update** icon does not appear on the **Start** menu. — ■ Able to schedule a new task using the Add a New Task wizard.	
2. *(continued)*	b. Close all open windows, and then log off.

◆ Assigning Scripts with Group Policy

- **What Are Group Policy Script Settings?**
- **The Process of Applying Script Settings with Group Policy**
- **Assigning Group Policy Script Settings**

You can use Group Policy script settings to automate the running of scripts. There are script settings under both Computer Configuration and User Configuration in Group Policy. You can use Group Policy to run scripts when a computer starts and shuts down, and when a user logs on and logs off. As with all Group Policy settings, you configure a setting once, and Windows 2000 continually implements and enforces it throughout your network.

What Are Group Policy Script Settings?

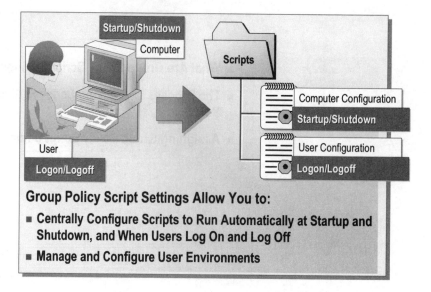

Group Policy Script Settings Allow You to:
- **Centrally Configure Scripts to Run Automatically at Startup and Shutdown, and When Users Log On and Log Off**
- **Manage and Configure User Environments**

Group Policy script settings allow you to centrally configure scripts to run automatically at startup and shutdown, and when users log on and log off. You can specify any script that runs in Windows 2000, including batch files, executable programs, and Windows Script Host supported scripts. For more information about Windows Script Host, see the Windows Script Technologies Web site at: http://msdn.microsoft.com/scripting/.

To help you manage and configure user environments, you can:

- Run scripts that perform tasks that you cannot configure through other Group Policy settings. For example, you can populate user environments with network connections, printer connections, shortcuts to applications, and corporate documents.

  You can also use scripts to clean up desktops when users log off and shut down computers. You can remove connections that you added with logon or startup scripts so that the computer is left in the same state as when the user started the computer.

- Run pre-existing scripts already set up to manage user environments until you have set up other Group Policy settings to replace the tasks that these scripts perform.

Note You can assign logon scripts individually to user accounts in the **Properties** dialog box for each user account. However, Group Policy is the preferred method of running scripts because you can manage these scripts centrally, along with startup, shutdown, and logoff scripts.

The Process of Applying Script Settings with Group Policy

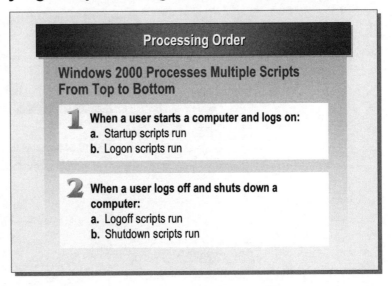

Windows 2000 executes multiple scripts from top to bottom as listed on the **Script** tab of the **Script Properties** dialog box. If there is a conflict between different scripts, the script processed last prevails. Windows 2000 processes and runs Group Policy assigned scripts in the following order:

1. When a user starts a computer and logs on, the following occurs:

   a. Startup scripts are hidden and run synchronously by default.

   When scripts run synchronously, each script must complete or timeout before the next one starts.

   b. Logon scripts are hidden and run asynchronously by default.

   When scripts run asynchronously, a script can start running, even while a previous script is running. Multiple scripts can run at the same time.

   Non-Group Policy logon scripts associated with a specific user account run after the Group Policy logon scripts run for the user account.

2. When a user logs off and shuts down a computer, the following occurs:

   a. Logoff scripts run.

   b. Shutdown scripts run.

Note The default timeout value for processing scripts is 10 minutes. If a script requires more than 10 minutes to process, you must adjust the timeout value by configuring the wait time in Computer Configuration\
Administrative Templates\System\Logon\Maximum wait time for Group Policy scripts. This setting affects all scripts that run, not just logon scripts.

Assigning Group Policy Script Settings

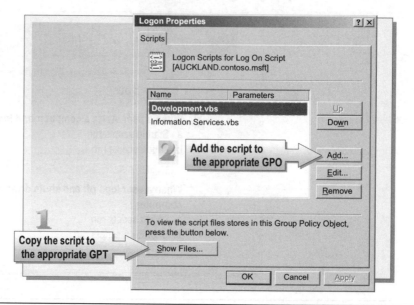

Implementing a script means using Group Policy to add that script to the appropriate setting in the GPT. This designates that the script runs during startup, shutdown, logon, or logoff.

1. To copy a script into the appropriate GPT, perform the following steps:

    a. Locate the script on your hard disk by using Windows Explorer.

    b. Open the appropriate GPO in Group Policy, expand either **Computer Configuration** (for startup and shutdown scripts) or **User Configuration** (for logon and logoff scripts), expand **Windows Settings**, and then click **Scripts**.

    c. Double-click the appropriate script type (**Startup**, **Shutdown**, **Logon**, or **Logoff**), and then click **Show Files**.

    d. Copy the script file from Windows Explorer to the window that appears, and then close the window.

2. To add a script to a GPO, perform the following steps:

    a. In the **Properties** dialog box for the script type, click **Add**, click **Browse**, select a script, and then click **Open**.

    b. Add any necessary script parameters, and then click **OK**.

For more information about creating a script in the Microsoft Visual Basic®, Scripting Edition (VBScript) language, see Course 1080, *Essentials of Microsoft® Visual Basic® Scripting Edition 3.0* under the Student Materials Web page on the Student Materials compact disc.

Lab B: Using Group Policy to Assign Scripts to Users and Computers

Objectives

After completing this lab, you will be able to assign scripts to users and computers by using Group Policy.

Prerequisites

Before working on this lab, you must have a working knowledge of Active Directory Users and Computers.

Lab Setup

To complete this lab, you need the following:

- A computer running Windows 2000 Advanced Server configured as a domain controller.

Estimated time to complete this lab: 15 minutes

Exercise 1
Using Group Policy to Assign Scripts

Scenario

All Sales users in your organization need to run scripts to configure their desktop environments at logon and perform cleanup tasks at logoff. Retail users must run additional scripts to configure their computers to use proprietary software. You need to assign the following script Group Policy for users in the Sales organizational unit (OU) and its child OUs:

- All users in the Sales OU and the child OUs must run the Sales Logon.vbs script at logon.

- All users in the Sales OU and the child OUs must run the Sales Logoff.vbs script at logoff.

- All users in the Retail OU must run the Retail Logon.vbs script and the Retail Config.vbs script at logon.

Goal

In this exercise, you will create a GPO for the Sales OU and a second GPO for the Retail OU. You will configure the settings in the two GPOs to run the required scripts.

Tasks	Detailed Steps
1. Create a GPO linked to the Sales OU. Name this GPO Sales Script Policy.	a. Log on as Administrator with a password of **password**. b. Open Active Directory Users and Computers from the **Administrative Tools** menu. c. In the console tree, expand your domain, right-click **Sales**, and then click **Properties**. d. On the **Group Policy** tab, click **New**, type **Sales Script Policy** and then press ENTER.
2. Copy the Sales Logon script from C:\MOC\Win2154A\ Labfiles\Scripts to the Logon folder in the Sales Script Policy GPT folder.	a. With **Sales Script Policy** selected, click **Edit**. b. In the console tree, under **User Configuration**, expand **Windows Settings**, and then click **Scripts (Logon/Logoff)**. c. In the details pane, double-click **Logon**, and then in the **Logon Properties** box, click **Show Files**. *A window appears showing the contents of the Logon folder in the Group Policy Template (GPT) for this GPO. Before you can assign a script with this GPO, you must copy the script file to this folder.* d. Open the C:\MOC\Win2154A\Labfiles\Scripts folder. e. Copy the Sales Logon script file from the Scripts folder to the Logon folder. f. Minimize the Scripts folder, and then close the Logon folder. g. Leave the **Logon Properties** dialog box open.

Tasks	Detailed Steps
3. Add the Sales Logon script to the list of Logon scripts for the Sales Script Policy GPO.	a. In the **Logon Properties** dialog box, click **Add**. b. In the **Add a Script** dialog box, click **Browse**, click the **Sales Logon** script, click **Open**, and then click **OK**. c. Click **OK** to close the **Logon Properties** dialog box. d. Leave Group Policy open.
4. Copy the Sales Logoff script from C:\MOC\Win2154A\Labfiles\Scripts to the Logoff folder in the Sales Script Policy GPT folder.	a. In the details pane, double-click **Logoff**, and then in the **Logoff Properties** dialog box, click **Show Files**. b. Restore the Scripts window and copy the Sales Logoff script to the Logoff folder. c. Minimize the Scripts window, and then close the Logoff window. d. Leave the **Logoff Properties** dialog box open.
5. Add the Sales Logoff script to the list of Logoff scripts for the Sales Script Policy GPO.	a. In the **Logoff Properties** dialog box, click **Add**. b. In the **Add a Script** dialog box, click **Browse**, click the **Sales Logoff** script, click **Open**, and then click **OK**. c. Click **OK** to close the **Logoff Properties** dialog box, and then close **Group Policy**. d. Click **Close** to close the **Sales Properties** dialog box. e. Leave Active Directory Users and Computers open.
6. Create a GPO linked to the Retail OU. Name this GPO Retail Script Policy.	a. In the details pane, expand **Sales**, right-click **Retail**, and then click **Properties**. b. On the **Group Policy** tab, click **New**, type **Retail Script Policy** and then press ENTER.
7. Copy the Retail Logon and Retail Config scripts from C:\MOC\Win2154A\Labfiles\Scripts to the Logon folder in the Retail Script Policy GPT folder.	a. With Retail Script Policy selected, click **Edit**. b. In the console tree, under **User Configuration**, expand **Windows Settings**, and then click **Scripts (Logon/Logoff)**. c. In the details pane, double-click **Logon**, and then in the **Logon Properties** dialog box, click **Show Files**. d. Restore the Scripts window and copy the Retail Logon and Retail Config scripts from the Scripts folder to the Logon folder. e. Close the Scripts window and the Logon window.
8. Add the Retail Logon and the Retail Config scripts to the list of Logon Scripts for the Retail Script Policy GPO.	a. In the **Logon Properties** dialog box, click **Add**. b. In the **Add a Script** dialog box, click **Browse**, click the **Retail Logon** script, click **Open**, and then click **OK**. c. In the **Logon Properties** dialog box, click **Add**. d. In the **Add a Script** dialog box, click **Browse**, click the **Retail Config** script, click **Open**, and then click **OK**. e. Click **OK** to close the **Logon Properties** dialog box, and then close Group Policy. f. Close the **Retail Properties** dialog box, close Active Directory Users and Computers, and then log off.

Exercise 2
Verifying Script Assignment

Scenario

Now that the required GPOs are setup and configured, you need to confirm that the Group Policy settings are being applied as expected.

Goal

Log on using a user account in the Sales OU to verify that the proper scripts are executed. Log on as a user in the Retail OU to verify that the proper scripts are executed.

Tasks	Detailed Steps
1. Log on as salesuser to verify that the Sales Logon script executes.	▪ Log on as Salesuser with a password of **password**.
❓ Did the Sales Logon script execute? Why or why not? *Yes - it was set up.*	
2. Log off to verify that the Sales Logoff script executes.	▪ Log off.
❓ Did the Sales Logoff script execute? *Yes.*	

Tasks	Detailed Steps
3. Log on as retailuser to verify that the Sales Logon, Retail Logon and Retail Config scripts execute.	■ Log on as Retailuser with a password of **password**.

❓ Which logon scripts executed and why?

Retail logon
    config
  Sales logon

| 4. Log off to verify that the Sales Logoff script executes. | ■ Log off. |

❓ Did the Sales Logoff script execute?

Yes.

◆ Using Group Policy to Redirect Folders

- **What Is Folder Redirection?**
- **Selecting the Folders to Redirect**
- **Redirecting Folders to a Server Location**

Windows 2000 allows you to redirect folders, which are part of the user profile, from users' local hard disks to a central location on a server. By redirecting these folders, you can ensure that users' data is located at a central location, and that users' data is available to them regardless of the computers to which they log on. It is easier to manage and back up centralized data. The folders that you can redirect are My Documents, Application Data, Desktop, and Start Menu. Windows 2000 automatically creates these folders and makes them part of the user profile for each user account.

What Is Folder Redirection?

Redirected Personal Folders

My Documents

My Documents

Documents Are Stored on the Server but Appear to Be Stored Locally

Advantages of Folder Redirection:

- Data Is Always Available to Users Regardless of the Computer Logged on to

- Data Is Centrally Stored for Ease of Management and Backup

- Network Traffic Is Generated Only When Users Gain Access to Files

- Files Are Not Saved on the Client Computer

When you redirect folders, you change the storage location of folders from the local hard disk on the user's computer to a shared folder on a network file server. After you redirect a folder to a file server, it still appears to the user as if it were stored on the local hard disk. You can redirect four folders that are part of the user profile: My Documents, Application Data, Desktop, and Start Menu.

The following list describes the advantages of redirecting folders:

- The data in the folders is available to the user regardless of the client computer to which the user logs on.

- The data in the folders is centrally stored, so the files that they contain are easier to manage and back up.

- Network traffic is reduced. When users have roaming user profiles and folders are not redirected, changes to the data in the folders are copied between the local computer and the server each time that the user logs on and logs off. Network traffic is generated only when a user accesses a file.

- Files in redirected folders, unlike files that are part of a roaming user profile, are not copied and saved on the computers where the user logs on. This means that when a user logs on to a client computer, no storage space is used to store these files, and data that might be confidential does not remain on a client computer.

Selecting the Folders to Redirect

Folder	Contains	Redirect to a server so that
My Documents	A user's personal data	Users can access their data from any computer, and this data can be backed up and managed centrally
Start Menu	Folders and shortcuts on the **Start** menu	Users' **Start** menus are standardized
Desktop	All files and folders that a user places on the desktop	Users have the same desktop regardless of the computer to which they log on
Application Data	User-specific data stored by applications	Applications use the same user-specific data for a user regardless of the computer to which the user logs on

Depending on the needs of users and your network, you may redirect all or some of the folders that can be redirected. The following table describes what each folder contains and provides specific reasons for redirecting the folder.

Folder	Contains	Redirect to a server so that
My Documents	The default location where users store their personal work data. It is the default location for the **Open** and **Save As** commands on the **File** menu. Windows 2000 places a **My Documents** shortcut icon on the desktop. It also includes the My Pictures folder, where users can save their graphics.	User can access data from any computer, and this data can be backed up and managed centrally, and the amount of data saved in the user profile is reduced. Always redirect the My Documents folder, because it is important that users are always able to gain access to their data.
Start Menu	Folders and shortcuts on the **Start** menu.	Users' **Start** menus are standardized. Redirect multiple users' Start Menu folders to the same network location and then assign only the NTFS file system Read permission so that users cannot change their **Start** menu content.
Desktop	The folder that contains all files, folders, and shortcuts that a user places on his or her desktop.	Users' desktops are standardized. Use the same strategy that you use for the **Start** menu.
Application Data	User-specific data stored by applications, such as configuration files and personal dictionaries for spell checking.	Applications use the same user-specific data for a user, regardless of the computer to which the user logs on.

Redirecting Folders to a Server Location

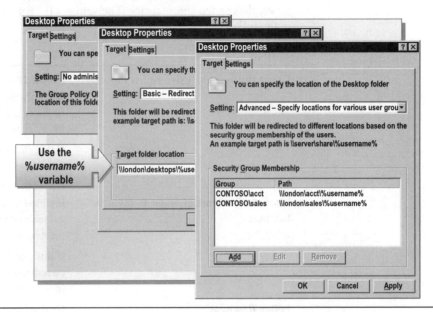

Use the %username% variable

To store the My Documents, Application Data, Desktop, and Start Menu folders on a server, use the Folder Redirection extension in Group Policy.

To redirect a folder, perform the following steps:

1. Create a new GPO or select an existing GPO, and then click **Edit**.

2. Expand **User Configuration**, expand **Windows Settings**, and then expand **Folder Redirection**.

3. Right-click the name of the folder that you want to redirect, click **Properties**, and then provide the target location and path to the location.

The options on the **Target** tab are described in the following table.

Options	Description
Setting	**No administrative policy specified**. Selected by default.
	Basic. Redirects all folders to the same location.
	Advanced. Specifies locations for various security groups. This option allows you to redirect the folders of users to whom this GPO applies and to specify different locations, depending on group membership.
Target folder location	This option appears when you select **Basic**. This option redirects all folders to the same location and allows you to specify a universal naming convention (UNC) path name to the new location. You can use the following syntax to create target folders named after a user's logon name: *\\server_name\share_name\%username%*
Security Group Membership	This option appears when you select **Advanced**. This option specifies locations for various security groups. The security groups and the path to the redirected folders appear here. As with the previous option, you can use *\\server_name\share_name\%username%* to create folders named after a user's logon name.

The options on the **Setting** tab control the behavior of folder redirection. You should be aware of the defaults for these settings, as they have implications for server disk space and security. The settings for folder redirection are explained in the following table:

Setting	Effect
Grant the user exclusive rights to *folder*.	Enabled by default, this setting ensures that only the user and the system have rights to the folder. Administrators do not have access to the folder.
	If this check box is cleared, the new folder location will retain the rights of the previous location.
Move the contents of *folder* **to the new location.**	Enabled by default, this setting moves the contents of the folder to the new location the next time Group Policy is applied.
	If this check box is cleared, the folder will be redirected, but the contents will remain in the previous location.
Policy Removal.	By default, when a folder redirection Group Policy is removed, the folder remains in the redirected location.
	You can also choose to return redirected folders to the local user profile location when Group Policy is removed.

Lab C: Implementing Folder Redirection Policy

Objective

After completing this lab, you will be able to implement folder redirection by using Group Policy.

Prerequisites

Before working on this lab, you must have an understanding of Group Policy.

Lab Setup

To complete this lab, you need the following:

- A computer running Windows 2000 Advanced Server that is configured as a domain controller.

Estimated time to complete this lab: 15 minutes

Exercise 1
Implementing Folder Redirection Policy

Scenario

Northwind Traders has a policy that only data on the servers will be backed up. To address fault tolerance concerns, you do not want the contents of the My Documents folder to be stored locally. You want to redirect the folder to the user's home directory on the server because the servers get backed up every evening.

Goal

In this exercise, you will redirect the My Documents folder to a new location on the network by using Group Policy.

Tasks	Detailed Steps
1. Confirm the current location of My Documents for the salesuser account and create a text file in the My Documents folder.	a. Log on as Salesuser with a password of **password**. b. Open the **Properties** dialog box for My Documents.
❓ What is the current location of My Documents? C:\Documents and Settings\salesuser	
❓ Can the user change this location? No.	
1. *(continued)*	c. Close the **My Documents Properties** dialog box, and then open the My Documents folder. d. Create a text file in the My Documents folder. e. Close My Documents, and then log off.

Tasks	Detailed Steps
2. Redirect the My Documents folder for a user in the Sales OU. Use the following settings for the redirected folder: • Setting: Basic – Redirect everyone's folder to the same location. • Target: *computer*\redirect\ %username% (where *computer* is your computer name). • Policy Removal: Redirect the folder back to the local user profile location when Group Policy is removed.	a. Log on as Administrator with a password of **password**. b. At the root of drive C, create a folder named Redirect, and then share it with the default permissions. c. Open Active Directory Users and Computers from the **Administrative Tools** menu. d. In the console tree, expand your domain, right-click **Sales**, and then click **Properties**. e. On the **Group Policy** tab, create a new GPO named **Folder Redirect Policy**, and then click **Edit**. f. Under **User Configuration**, expand **Windows Settings**, expand **Folder Redirection**, right-click **My Documents**, and then click **Properties**. g. In the **Setting** list, click **Basic – Redirect everyone's folder to the same location**. h. Under **Target folder location**, type *computer***redirect\%username%** (where *computer* is your computer name), and then click the **Settings** tab.
❓ Record the default settings for folder redirection in the following space. _Grant user exclusive rights_ _Move contents of My Documents_ _Leave folder in new location_	
2. *(continued)*	i. Click **Redirect the folder back to the local user profile location when policy is removed**, and then click **OK**. j. Close all open windows, and then log off.
3. Verify that the Folder Redirection Group Policy is being applied properly.	a. Log on as Salesuser with a password of password. b. Open the Properties dialog box for My Documents.

Tasks	Detailed Steps
❓	**What is the current location of My Documents?** \\ denver \ redirect
❓	**Can the user change the location of My Documents? Why or why not?** No.
❓	**What permissions are set on My Documents? Why?**
3. *(continued)*	c. Close the **My Documents Properties** dialog box, and then open My Documents.
❓	**Does the My Documents folder contain the text file that you created earlier? Why or why not?** Yes.
3. *(continued)*	d. Close My Documents, and then log off.

Tasks	Detailed Steps
4. Remove the Folder Redirection Policy GPO.	a. Log on as Administrator with a password of **password**.
	b. Open Active Directory Users and Computers from the **Administrative Tools** menu.
	c. In the console tree, expand your domain, right-click **Sales**, and then click **Properties**.
	d. On the **Group Policy** tab, select the **Folder Redirect Policy** GPO, and then click **Delete**.
	e. In the **Delete** dialog box, click **Remove the link and delete the Group Policy Object permanently**, and then click **OK**.
	f. In the **Delete Group Policy Object** dialog box, click **Yes**, and then click **Close** to close the **Sales Properties** box.
	g. Close all open windows, and then log off.
5. Test the results of deleting the Folder Redirect Policy GPO.	a. Log on as Salesuser with a password of **password**.
	b. Right-click **My Documents**, and then click **Properties**.
❓ What is the current location of My Documents? Is this the default behavior when folder redirection Group Policy is removed?	
	C:\Documents & Settings\Salesuser
5. *(continued)*	c. Close all open windows, and then log off.

Using Group Policy to Secure the User Environment

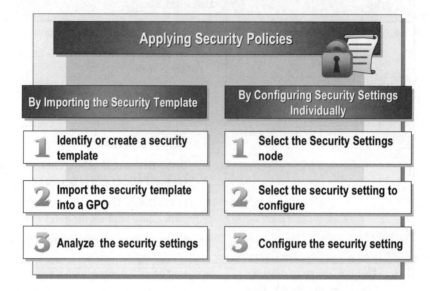

Group Policy also includes security settings to ensure that the user environment is secured against unauthorized access and define an organization's prevention and response to security infractions. Group Policy allows you to standardize security settings by applying the same security template to multiple computers in one step. Security templates are groups of security settings that can be imported into GPOs or used for analysis.

Setting Account Policies

When you set account policies in Active Directory, keep in mind that Windows 2000 allows only one domain account policy for each domain. The domain account policy becomes the default account policy of any Windows 2000–based workstation or server that is a member of the domain. The only exception to this rule is when another account policy is defined for an organizational unit. The account policy settings for the organizational unit affect the local policy on any computers contained in the organizational unit. This means that the account policies set at the domain level always apply when logging on using an account that exists in the domain. The local policy settings apply only when logging on using an account that is local to the computer to which you are logging on.

Applying Security Policies

To apply security policies for a local computer or an Active Directory container, you import one or more security templates, which contain security settings for all security areas, into Security Settings in Group Policy. Importing a security template into Group Policy ensures that all members of the container automatically receive the security template when Group Policy propagates. When you apply a template to existing security settings, the settings in the template are merged into the computer's security settings database.

To import a security template into a GPO, perform the following tasks:

1. Identify an existing Windows 2000 security template that contains the required security configuration, or create a new security template.

2. Import the security template into the GPO:

   a. Expand **Computer Configuration**, expand **Windows Settings**, and then expand **Security Settings**.

   b. Right-click **Security Settings**, and then click **Import Policy**.

   c. Select the security template that you want to import, and then click **OK**.

3. Analyze the security settings for each computer to determine if the current security settings should be modified to meet your organization's security requirements.

Note Before deploying a security template to large groups of computers, it is important to analyze the results of applying a configuration to ensure there are no adverse effects on applications, connectivity, or security. A thorough analysis can also help you identify security breaches and deviations from standard configurations. The Security Configuration and Analysis snap-in allows you to create and review hypothetical scenarios and make adjustments to a configuration.

An alternative method of applying security policies is to individually configure the security settings for each computer. You can edit the security settings in a Group Policy object (GPO) for any site, domain, or OU.

To configure a security setting, perform the following tasks:

1. Expand **Computer Configuration**, expand **Windows Settings**, and then expand **Security Settings**.

2. In the Policy details pane, double-click the security setting that you want to configure.

3. On the Policy tab, configure the security setting by selecting one of three states, Enabled, Disabled, or Not Configured, for the setting.

For more information about the different types of security policies, and the utilities used to configure and analyze security settings, see Course 2152, *Implementing Microsoft Windows 2000 Professional and Server*.

Note Security settings, unlike other Group Policy settings, are persistent. That is, security settings remain in the registry even when the GPO that contains the security settings has been removed.

Lab D: Implementing Security Settings by Using Group Policy

Objectives

After completing this lab, you will be able to implement security settings by using Group Policy.

Prerequisites

Before working on this lab, you must have an understanding of Group Policy.

Lab Setup

To complete this lab, you need the following:

- A computer running Windows 2000 Advanced Server configured as a domain controller.

Estimated time to complete this lab: 15 minutes

Exercise 1
Implementing Security Policy

Scenario

You are a domain administrator for a domain in the Northwind Traders organization, and are required to implement the following security settings on your domain controllers:

- Passwords must be at least six characters.

- A dialog box should appear during the logon process, informing users that unauthorized access is not allowed.

- Domain Admins should have only the Administrator account as a member.

- Telnet, which is set to start manually, should be disabled.

Goal

In this exercise, you will create a new GPO, which is linked to the Domain Controllers OU and named Additional Security Settings Policy, to implement the required security settings.

Tasks	Detailed Steps
1. Create a new GPO linked to the Domain Controllers OU. Name this new GPO Additional Security Settings Policy.	a. Log on as Administrator with a password of **password**. b. Open Active Directory Users and Computers from the **Administrative Tools** menu. c. In the console tree, expand your domain, right-click **Domain Controllers**, and then click **Properties**. d. On the **Group Policy** tab, click **New**, type **Additional Security Settings Policy** and then press ENTER.
2. Modify the Additional Security Settings Policy GPO to implement the following security setting: • Passwords must be at least six characters.	a. With the Additional Security Settings Policy GPO selected, click **Edit**. b. Under **Computer Configuration**, expand **Windows Settings**, expand **Security Settings**, expand **Account Policies**, and then click **Password Policy**. c. In the details pane, double-click **Minimum password length**. d. In the **Security Policy Setting** dialog box, click **Define this policy setting**, change the value for the minimum password length to **6**, and then click **OK**.
3. Modify the Additional Security Settings Policy GPO to implement the following security setting: • Display a dialog box at logon that warns users that unauthorized access is not allowed.	a. In the console tree, expand **Local Policies**, and then click **Security Options**. b. In the details pane, double-click **Message text for users attempting to logon**. c. In the **Security Policy Setting** dialog box, click **Define this policy setting**, type **Authorized access only** and then click **OK**. d. In the details pane, double-click **Message title for users attempting to logon**. e. In the **Security Policy Setting** dialog box, click **Define this policy setting**, type **Warning** and then click **OK**.

Tasks	Detailed Steps
4. Modify the Additional Security Settings Policy GPO to implement the following security setting: • Domain Admins should have only the Administrator account as a member.	a. In the console tree, click **Restricted Groups**. b. Right-click **Restricted Groups**, and then click **Add Group**. c. In the **Add Group** dialog box, click **Browse**, type **Domain Admins** click **OK**, and then click **OK** again to close the **Add Group** dialog box. d. In the details pane, double-click *Domain***Domain Admins**. e. In the **Configure Membership for** *Domain***Domain Admins** dialog box, click **Add** to the right of **Members of this group**. f. In the **Add Member** dialog box, click **Browse**, type **Administrator** click **OK**, and then click **OK** again to close the **Add Member** dialog box. g. Click **OK** to close the **Configure Membership for** *Domain***Domain Admins** dialog box.
5. Modify the Additional Security Settings Policy GPO to implement the following security setting: • The Telnet service should be disabled.	a. In the console tree, click **System Services**. b. In the details pane, double-click **Telnet**. c. In the **Security Policy Setting** dialog box, click **Define this policy setting**. *Notice that the **Security for Telnet** security editor appears. System services need to be properly secured, so this dialog box appears for any service in the list.* d. Select **Everyone**, and then click **Remove**. e. Click **Add**, type **Domain Admins** and then click **OK**. f. Select the **Allow** check box beside **Full Control**, and then click **OK**. g. In the **Security Policy Setting** dialog box, ensure that **Disabled** is selected, and then click **OK**. h. Close all open windows, and then restart the computer.
6. Verify that the modifications to the Additional Security Settings Policy GPO are being applied correctly.	a. Log on as Administrator with a password of **password**.

❓ Did the warning message appear when you tried to log on?

No.

Tasks	Detailed Steps
6. *(continued)*	b. Change your password from **password** to **123**.
❓ Did the minimum password length Group Policy setting of six characters prevent you from changing your password to one that contained only three characters? Why or why not? _No._	
6. *(continued)*	c. If necessary, change your password back to password. d. Add the Guest user account to the Domain Admins group. e. Force a refresh of Group Policy by opening a command prompt, typing **secedit /refreshpolicy machine_policy /enforce** and then pressing ENTER.
❓ Is the Guest user account still listed as a member of the Domain Admins group? Why or why not? _No._	
6. *(continued)*	f. Open Services from the Administrative Tools menu.
❓ What is the value in the **Startup Type** column for the Telnet service? _Disabled._	
6. *(continued)*	g. Close all open windows.
7. Run the Delpol.cmd batch file in the C:\Moc\Win2154A\Labfiles folder. This batch file removes all GPOs created in the labs in this module.	a. Open the C:\Moc\Win2154A\Labfiles folder. b. Double-click **Delpol.cmd** to remove all of the GPOs created during the labs in this module. c. Restart your computer.

Troubleshooting User Environment Management

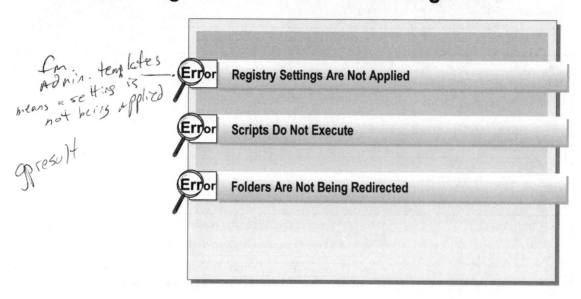

fm. Admin. templates means a setting is not being applied

gpresult

You may encounter problems when using Group Policy to manage user environments. Here are some of the more common problems that you may encounter, along with suggested strategies for resolving them:

- Registry settings using Administrative Templates are not applied. The possible problem could be that the administrative template settings are not applied to the user or computer affected by Group Policy. Another possible problem could be that Active Directory replication had not yet completed on the Domain Controller. Run Gpresult.exe in verbose mode on the client computer to confirm that Administrative Templates Group Policy settings are not applied.

  - If the text "The user (or computer) received "Registry" settings from these GPOs." does not appear in the output, no administrative template settings were applied. If this text does not appear, verify to make sure that the user or computer account has at least Read and Apply Group Policy permissions on all GPOs that should be processed.

  - Also, verify the relevant GPOs to see if either the User Configuration or Computer Configuration nodes are disabled.

  - Finally, verify to see if the *Loopback processing* mode is enabled.

- Scripts do not execute.

  - Confirm that the Group Policy Scripts client-side extension is executing. Run Gpresult.exe in verbose mode, and examine the output under the User received Scripts settings from these GPOs heading. If the text is missing from the output, verify permissions on the relevant GPOs and check for inheritance issues.

  - If the text appears in the output, but certain scripts are not executing, verify to insure that SYSVOL is being properly replicated to all domain controllers.

- Folders are not being redirected.
  - If you are using redirected folders and they are not being redirected, verify the discretionary access control list (DACL) on the network share where the folders are being redirected. Ensure that the user has sufficient permissions.
  - If the volume that contains the redirected folders has disk quotas enabled, verify that the user has not exceeded his or her quota limit.
  - If the folder on the network share existed before you implemented redirection, ensure that the DACL for the folder allows the user Full Control.

Note For additional strategies for troubleshooting Group Policy to manage user environments, see Module 7, "Implementing Group Policy," in Course 2154, *Implementing and Administering Microsoft Windows 2000 Directory Services*.

Best Practices

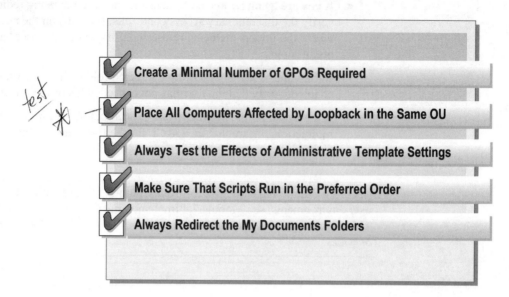

The following list provides best practices for managing user environments:

- Create a minimal number of GPOs containing administrative template settings. It can be difficult to manage user environments properly if you create too many GPOs containing these settings.

- Place all computers to which you want to apply the loopback processing mode in their own OU. There should not be any user accounts in that OU. Then you can create and link a GPO with configured settings that specifically set up the user environment on these computers.

- Always test the effects of administrative template settings. Create a test environment that is parallel to your production environment. Give selected users an additional user account that resides in a test OU and have them perform their normal tasks to ensure that there are no problems. If you are going to lock down user desktops, ensure that you have the correct settings configured so that you do not inadvertently disrupt users' work.

- Make sure that scripts run in the preferred order so that you get the proper results. Windows 2000 processes Group Policy settings in a particular order. This process determines the order in which scripts run and the effects they have on computers and users.

- Always redirect the My Documents folders so users can access their personal data from any computer. It reduces logon and logoff times for roaming users, because files in the My Documents folder are only copied between the client computer and the server when users gain access to files. Redirecting My Documents allows you to back up users' data centrally.

Review

- Introduction to Managing User Environments
- Introduction to Administrative Templates
- Using Administrative Templates in Group Policy
- Assigning Scripts with Group Policy
- Using Group Policy to Redirect Folders
- Using Group Policy to Secure the User Environment
- Troubleshooting User Environment Management
- Best Practices

1. You do not want users to be able to open Control Panel and gain access to Display or any of the other applications. What do you do?

   Config. an admin. template to disable control panel.

2. Your network no longer needs a user administrative template setting that you configured. What do you do to change the registry back to the way it was before you configured the settings?

   Delete the template.

   In 2000, group policies will go in & out of registry easily.

3. The Research department employees need a shortcut on their desktops to a special third-party application that resides on a network server. There are no existing Group Policy settings that can provide this shortcut. There is a Research Department OU. What can you do?

4. Employees in the Production Department log on at different client computers. All users need to have their work data available to them at all times. What do you need to do?

Redirect my documents to a shared folder on a server.

5. You need to configure identical security settings for six domain servers that are in the same OU. What is the simplest method for doing this?

Create a template.

Have all in same OU, import template into Group Policy for the OU.

Microsoft®
Training &
     Certification

Module 9: Using Group Policy to Manage Software

Contents

Microsoft®

Overview

- **Introduction to Managing Software Deployment**
- **Windows Installer**
- **Deploying Software**
- **Configuring Software Deployment**
- **Maintaining Deployed Software**
- **Removing Deployed Software**
- **Troubleshooting Software Deployment**
- **Best Practices**

Microsoft® Windows® 2000 includes a new feature called Software Installation and Maintenance that uses Active Directory® directory service, Group Policy, and Windows Installer to install, maintain, and remove software on computers in your organization. By using a policy-based method for managing software deployment, you can ensure that the applications that users need to perform their jobs are available whenever and wherever they are needed.

At the end of this module, you will be able to:

- Describe how to manage software deployment by using Group Policy.
- Describe how Windows Installer is used for software installation and maintenance.
- Use Group Policy to deploy software.
- Use Group Policy to configure software deployment.
- Use Group Policy to maintain software.
- Use Group Policy to remove software.
- Troubleshoot common problems with software deployment.
- Apply best practices for deploying software.

Introduction to Managing Software Deployment

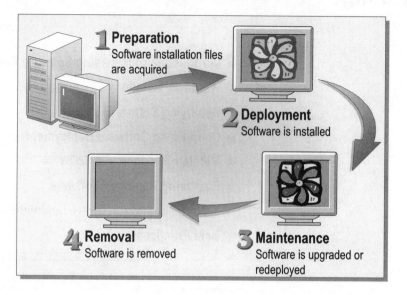

In Windows 2000, you can use Group Policy to manage the software deployment process centrally, or from one location. You can apply Group Policy settings to users or computers in a site, domain, or organizational unit (OU) to automatically install, upgrade, or remove software for the users and computers in the site, domain, or OU. By applying Group Policy settings to software, you can manage the various phases of software deployment without needing to visit each computer individually.

The following list describes each phase in the software installation and maintenance process:

1. *Preparation.* You prepare the files that enable an application to be deployed with Group Policy. To do this, copy the Windows Installer package files for an application to a software distribution point, which can be a shared folder on the server. You can acquire a Windows Installer package file from the application's vendor, or you can create a package file by using a third-party utility.

2. *Deployment.* An administrator creates a Group Policy object (GPO) that installs the software on the computer and links the GPO to an appropriate Active Directory container. The software actually installs either when the computer starts or when a user activates the application.

3. *Maintenance.* The deployed software is upgraded with the new version or redeployed with a service pack and patch. The software is automatically upgraded or redeployed either when the computer starts or when a user activates the application.

4. *Removal.* To eliminate software that is no longer required, remove the software package setting from the GPO that originally deployed the software. The software is automatically removed either when the computer starts or when a user logs on.

Windows Installer

[handwritten margin note: - MSI files = applications created specifically to work with WIN 2000 or above.]

Windows Installer Service	Windows Installer Package
■ Is a client-side service that fully automates the software installation and configuration process ■ Is used to modify or repair an existing application installation	■ Contains all of the information required by the Windows Installer service to install or uninstall an application ■ Consists of an .msi file and any external source files that are required to install the application ■ Contains summary information about both the application and the package ■ Contains a reference to an installation point where product files reside

Benefits of Employing Windows Installer
■ Resilient applications ■ Clean removal of files

To enable Group Policy to deploy and manage software, Windows 2000 uses Windows Installer, which contains the following two components:

- *Windows Installer service.* The Windows Installer service is a client-side service that fully automates the software installation and configuration process. The Windows Installer service can also modify or repair an existing installed application. The Windows Installer service installs an application either directly from the CD-ROM or through Group Policy.

- *Windows Installer package.* The Windows Installer package contains all of the information that the Windows Installer service requires to install or uninstall software. A package consists of a Windows Installer, or .msi file, and any external source files required to install or uninstall the software. An .msi package file also contains standard summary information about both the software and the package itself. It also contains the product files or a reference to an installation point where the product files reside.

The benefits of employing the Windows Installer technology include:

- *Resilient applications.* If a critical file is deleted or becomes corrupt, the application will automatically return to the installation source and acquire a new copy of the file, without requiring user intervention.

- *Clean removal.* Applications are uninstalled without leaving orphaned files or inadvertently breaking another application; for example, by deleting a shared file required by another application. Also, all application-related registry settings are removed.

Note   For more information about Windows Installer, see *The Windows Installer Service* under **Additional Reading** on the Web page on the Student Materials compact disc.

◆ Deploying Software

- Software Deployment

- Creating a Software Distribution Point

- Assigning Software

- Publishing Software

- Using Group Policy to Deploy Software Packages

- Setting Software Installation Defaults

You can use Software Installation, a component of Group Policy, to deploy software to users and computers. Deploying software ensures that required applications are available from any computer to which a user logs on. From the user's point of view, software is always available and functional. Administrators can either install software for users in advance, or give users the option to install the software that they require, as it is needed.

Software Deployment

has ".msi" extension

this is simply a shared folder

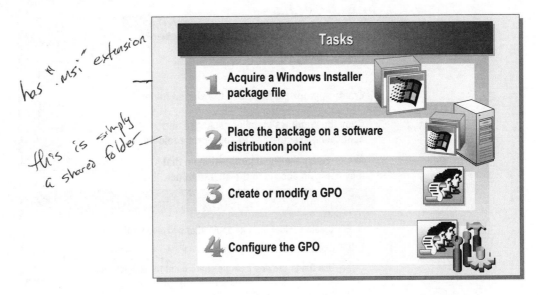

Tasks

1 Acquire a Windows Installer package file

2 Place the package on a software distribution point

3 Create or modify a GPO

4 Configure the GPO

When you deploy software, you are specifying how applications are installed and maintained within your organization. To use Group Policy to deploy new software, perform the following tasks:

1. Acquire a Windows Installer package file. You must have a package file for an application before that application can be deployed. A package contains an .msi file and necessary related installation files. The related installation files are the application files that are installed on the local hard disk.

2. Place the package file and any related installation files on a software distribution point. A software distribution point is a shared folder on your server.

3. Create or modify a GPO. You need to create or make necessary changes to a GPO for the container in which you want to deploy the application.

4. Configure the GPO to deploy the application. You can configure the GPO to deploy software for a user account or a computer account. This task also includes selecting the type of deployment that you need. Deployment types, and the differences between deploying an application to users and computers, will be discussed later in this module.

Creating a Software Distribution Point

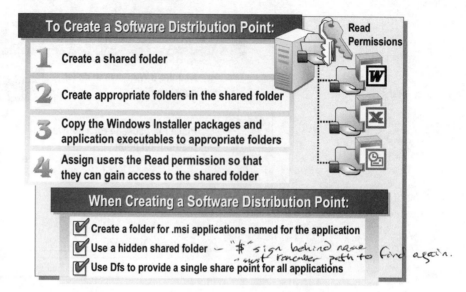

A software distribution point is a shared folder that contains the package files for deploying software. Installer packages and software files must be available on a software distribution point, so that when software is installed on a local computer, files are copied from this point to the computer. Keeping the files for each application together simplifies administration.

To create a software distribution point, perform the following tasks:

1. Create a shared folder.

2. Create the appropriate application folders in the shared folder.

3. Copy the Windows Installer packages and application executables to the appropriate folders.

4. Set the appropriate permission for the shared folder. Assign users the Read permission so that they can gain access to the software installation files on the software distribution point.

When creating a software distribution point, use the following guidelines:

- Create a folder named for the application for .msi packages, and place the .msi package file, and all required installation files, in that folder. To simplify administration, store .msi package files in the same location.

- Use a hidden shared folder (for example, *packages$*), to prevent users from browsing the contents of the shared folder on the software distribution point.

- Use Distributed file system (Dfs) to provide a single share point for all published applications, so you can take advantage of Dfs redundancy and load-balancing features.

Assigning Software

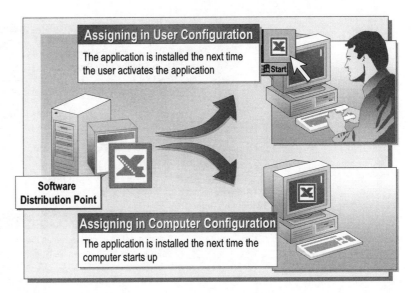

You assign software to make sure that users have all of the applications they need installed on their computers. The next time that the user logs on, the newly installed software is *advertised* on their desktops. When software is advertised, **Start** menu shortcuts and desktop icons for the application appear.

By assigning software packages, you ensure that:

- The software is always available to the user. Users will be able to access the software they need from any computer to which they log on. If the user starts a file that uses Microsoft Excel on a computer that does not have Excel, Excel will be installed on that computer when the user activates the file.

- The software is resilient. If for any reason the user deletes the software, it will be reinstalled the next time the user logs on and activates the application.

You can assign software to either users or computers:

- During user configuration. When you assign software to a user, the software is advertised on the user's desktop. Although the application is advertised when the user logs on, installation does not begin until the user double-clicks either the application's icon or a file type associated with the application, which is a method called document activation. If the user does not activate the application by using one of these methods, the software will not be installed, thus saving hard disk space and time.

- During computer configuration. When you assign software to a computer, no advertising takes place. Instead, when the computer starts up, the software is installed automatically. By assigning software to a computer, you can ensure that certain applications are always available on that computer, regardless of who is using it. However, assigning software to a computer does not work if the computer is a domain controller.

Publishing Software

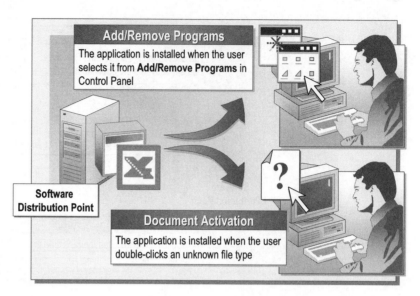

When you publish software, it becomes available for users to install on their computers, even though no shortcuts are added to the user's desktop or **Start** menu, and no local registry entries are made. Because users must install the published software, you can publish software only to users, not to computers. Users can install published software in one of two ways:

- Using Add/Remove Programs. A user can open Control Panel and double-click **Add/Remove Programs** to display the set of applications available. The user can then select the desired application and click **Install**.

- Using document activation. When an application is published in Active Directory, the file name extensions for the documents that it supports are registered in Active Directory. If a user double-clicks an unknown file type, the computer sends a query to Active Directory to determine whether there are any applications associated with the file name extension. If Active Directory contains such an application, the computer installs it.

Using Group Policy to Deploy Software Packages

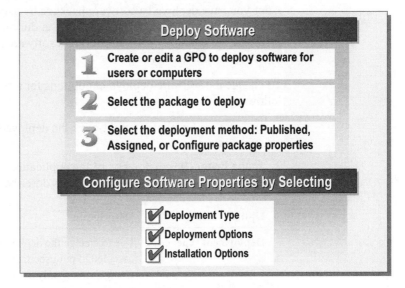

To install applications for users, or to make applications available for users to install when needed, you need to create a GPO that deploys those applications. Then link this GPO to the Active Directory container that contains the users or computers to which you want to deploy software.

Using a GPO to Deploy Software Packages

To use a GPO to deploy software, perform the following steps:

1. Create or edit a GPO in either **User Configuration** or **Computer Configuration**, depending on whether the software is to be assigned to users or computers, or published to users.

2. Expand **Software Settings**, right-click **Software Installation**, point to **New**, and then click **Package**. When the **File Open** dialog box appears, select the package file, and then click **Open**.

3. In the **Deploy Software** dialog box, select a deployment method, and then click **OK**.

Changing Options for Deployed Software Packages

After you have deployed a software package by using Group Policy, you can change the deployment options that were set during the initial deployment of software. For example, you can prevent a software package from being installed by using document activation.

To change the software deployment options for a software package, perform the following steps:

1. In Software Installation, right-click the deployed package, and then click **Properties**.

2. In the **Properties** dialog box of the application, click the **Deployment** tab, and set any combination of the options described in the following table.

Option	Description
Deployment type	Use to change the deployment type for software from assigned to published, or published to assigned. This change affects only new installations of the software, not software that has already been installed.
Deployment options	Use the Auto-Install this application by file extension activation option to install published software by using document activation. You may turn off this option for published software if you do not want the software to be automatically installed.
	Use the Uninstall this application when this GPO no longer applies to users or computers option to remove software when the software GPO no longer applies to a particular user, group of users, or computer. If a user or computer is moved to an organizational unit (OU) or domain where this GPO no longer applies, the deployed software will be uninstalled.
	Use the Do not display this package in Add/Remove Programs option to prevent the application from being displayed in Add/Remove Programs in Control Panel. This option restricts the ability of users to install software. Users can still install software by document activation or by gaining access to an advertised shortcut.
Installation user interface options	Windows Installer packages often come with two different setup interfaces. The basic interface installs the software by using default values. The maximum interface prompts the user to enter values. You can choose which interface to display to users during setup.

Setting Software Installation Defaults

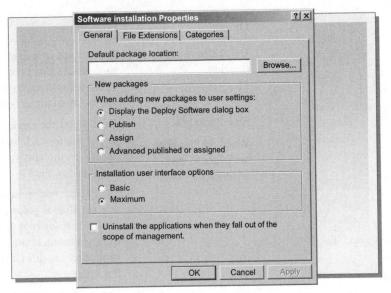

You set software installation default options for the current GPO by using the **General** tab on the **Software installation Properties** dialog box. These defaults are most useful when you will add several applications to a GPO at one time.

To set software installation default options, perform the following steps:

1. Create or edit a GPO in either **User Configuration** or **Computer Configuration**, depending on whether the software is to be assigned to users or computers, or published.

2. Expand **Software Settings**, right-click **Software Installation**, and then click **Properties**.

3. In the **Software installation Properties** dialog box, click the **General** tab, and set any combination of the options described in the following table.

Option	Description
Default package location.	The location of the software distribution point that contains the .msi package files. You can specify any location that contains the software package, but make sure that the distribution point is not on a local drive.
New Packages. **When adding new packages to user settings.**	The Display the Deploy Dialog box option displays a dialog box for each package file added to the GPO. This dialog box prompts you to either publish or assign the new package file.
	The Publish option automatically publishes by default a new installation package file under User Configuration (this option does not appear under Computer Configuration). If you are going to add several applications to this GPO that need to be published, use this option.
	Use the **Assign** option to automatically assign by default a new package file. If you are going to add several applications to this GPO that need to be assigned, use this option.
	Use the **Advanced published or assigned** option for finer control on a per-package basis. For example: using transforms.
Installation user interface options.	Windows Installer packages often come with two different setup interfaces. The basic interface installs the software by using default values. The maximum interface prompts the user to enter values. You can choose which interface to display to users during setup.
Uninstall the application when they fall out of the scope of management.	If a GPO no longer applies to a user, because the settings are on a new GPO, or the GPO has been deleted, the application and all related files will automatically be removed from the user's computer.

Note For more information about software installation, see *Software Installation and Maintenance* under **Additional Reading** on the Web page on the Student Materials compact disc.

◆ Configuring Software Deployment

- **Using Software Modifications**
- **Creating Software Categories**
- **Associating File Name Extensions with Applications**

Software Installation is an extension in Group Policy that includes options for configuring deployed software. By using Software Installation, you can deploy several different configurations of one application and control how that application is assigned or published whenever a user's duties change. You can also simplify the task of deploying software by categorizing programs listed in Add/Remove Programs and associating file name extensions with applications.

Using Software Modifications

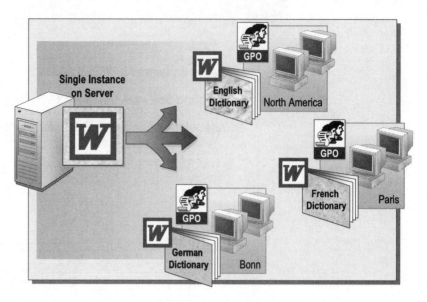

Deploying several different configurations of one application enables different groups in your organization to use a software package in different ways. You can use software modifications, or *.mst files*, to deploy several different configurations of one application. An .mst file is a custom software package that modifies how Windows Installer installs a packaged application.

For example, an international organization would like to deploy Microsoft Word 2000, but there are large segments of the organization that require localized dictionaries. Rather than manually configuring users' computers with the local dictionaries, you could use different GPOs and .mst files for each language to deploy several configurations of one application.

Important   You can add and remove modifications only during deployment of a software package, not after the deployment has occurred.

To add modifications for a software package, perform the following steps:

1. While you are adding a new package to a GPO or before the package has been deployed, open the **Properties** dialog box for the application package, and then click the **Modifications** tab.

2. On the **Modifications** tab, click **Add**.

3. In the **Open** dialog box, select the path and file name of the modification (.mst) file, click **Open**, and then click **OK**.

Note   You can also add multiple modifications. The modifications are applied according to the order that you specify in the **Modifications** list. To arrange the list, click a modification in the list, and click **Move Up** or **Move Down**.

Creating Software Categories

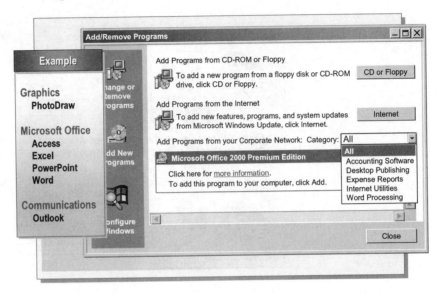

You can create software categories to logically group different applications under a specific heading. You can categorize the software deployed in an organization to allow users to choose from categories in Add/Remove Programs such as "Graphics," "Microsoft Office," or "Accounting," rather than from a long and arbitrary list of applications. Categorizing applications requires you to first create a category, and then assign the application to a category.

Creating Categories

Software categories function across domains. Any changes that you make are reflected throughout the domain. You can gain access to the **Categories** tab from within any OU. However, any changes that you make are reflected throughout the domain. The categories that you create are available for all software policies in that domain.

To create a category, perform the following steps:

1. Create or edit a GPO in either User Configuration or Computer Configuration, depending on whether the software is to be assigned to users or computers, or published.

2. Expand **Software Settings**. Right-click **Software Installation**, click **Properties**, and then click the **Categories** tab.

3. Click **Add**, **Modify**, or **Remove** to create and edit category names.

Assigning a Software Package to a Category

You can assign a software package to a category either when you deploy the application, or any time thereafter. You can also list Packages under more than one category, and assign a package to a category by using the **Categories** tab in the **Properties** dialog box for the package.

Associating File Name Extensions with Applications

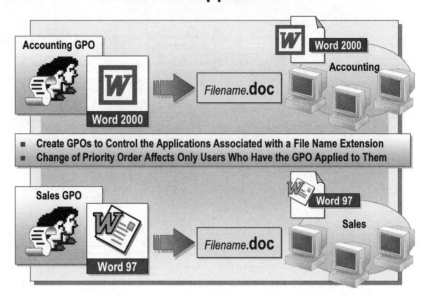

Active Directory maintains a list of file name extensions and published applications associated with these extensions. This is the list used by Windows Installer to install an application when a user double-clicks an unknown file type. Administrators cannot dictate the contents of this list, but they can determine the priority for installing or starting applications upon document activation.

For example, your organization might require the use of both Microsoft Word 97 and Word 2000. Each word processor may be preferred in a different department, but both of these applications use the .doc file name extension. You need to adjust the file name extension priorities for each department so that the preferred word processor is installed when the user activates a document.

To modify file name extension priorities, perform the following steps:

1. Open the GPO used to deploy the application.

2. Expand **User Configuration**, and then open the **Properties** dialog box for Software Installation.

3. In the **Software installation Properties** dialog box for Software Installation, click the **File Extensions** tab and then click **Up** or **Down** to set the priority order.

   The first application listed in Windows Installer will be the first application installed.

Application associations are managed on a per-GPO basis. Changing the priority order in a GPO affects only those users who have that GPO applied to them. If you set Word 2000 as the default application, it will be the default application for only the users affected by that GPO.

Note You may associate document types only with applications that have been deployed by using Group Policy. For example, you cannot associate the .doc file name extension with Word 97 unless you create a package file for deploying Word 97.

Lab A: Assigning and Publishing Software

Objectives

After completing this lab, you will be able to:

- Assign software to users in an OU by using Group Policy.
- Publish software to users in an OU by using Group Policy.

Prerequisites

Before working on this lab, you must have the knowledge and skills to create Group Policy objects.

Lab Setup

To complete this lab, you need the following:

- A computer running Windows 2000 Advanced Server that is configured as a domain controller.
- An OU structure. To create the required OUs and users, run the Software.vbs script file from C:\Moc\Win2154A\Labfiles.

Important   The lab does not reflect the real-world environment. It is recommended that you always use complex passwords for any administrator accounts, and never create accounts without a password.

Important   Outside of the classroom environment, it is strongly advised that you use the most recent software updates that are necessary. Because this is a classroom environment, we may use software that does not include the latest updates.

Estimated time to complete this lab: 30 minutes

Exercise 1
Assigning Software

Scenario

Northwind Traders has decided to centrally manage the deployment of applications to users. You want to ensure that Windows 2000 Support Tools are available to all users in the Information Services department.

Goal

In this exercise, you will use Group Policy to assign the Windows 2000 Support Tools to users in the Information Services OU.

Tasks	Detailed Steps
1. Create a GPO named Application Assignment Policy in the Information Services OU.	a. Log on as Administrator with a password of **password**. b. Open Active Directory Users and Computers from the **Administrative Tools** menu. c. Expand *domain*.**nwtraders.msft** (where *domain* is your assigned domain name), if necessary. d. Right-click **Information Services**, and then click **Properties**. e. On the **Group Policy** tab, click **New**. f. Type **Application Assignment Policy** and then press ENTER. g. Leave the Information Services Properties dialog box open.
2. Modify the Application Assignment GPO to assign the Veritas WinInstall LE package: • Assigned File Name: *computer*\Labfiles\ Packages\Swiadmle.msi (where *computer* is your assigned computer name).	a. In the **Information Services Properties** dialog box, select the **Application Assignment Policy** GPO, if necessary, and then click **Edit**. b. Under **User Configuration**, expand **Software Settings**, and then click **Software Installation**. c. Right-click **Software Installation**, point to **New**, and then click **Package**. d. In the **File name** box, type *computer***labfiles****packages** (where *computer* is your assigned computer name) and then click **Open**. e. Click **Swiadmle**, and then click **Open**. f. In the **Deploy Software** dialog box, click **Assigned**, and then click **OK**. *WinINSTALL LE appears in the list of deployed applications.* g. Close Group Policy, and then click **Close** to close the **Information Services Properties** dialog box. h. Close all open windows, and then log off.

Exercise 2
Testing Software Assignment

Scenario

After making changes to the Group Policy settings, you want to test that the software is assigned correctly.

Goal

In this exercise, you will test the software assignment from the previous exercise.

Task	Detailed Steps
1. Log on as Hduser to confirm that the Veritas WinInstall LE package is being assigned.	a. Log on as Hduser with a password of **password**.
❓ Does **VERITAS Software** appear on the **Programs** menu? Why or why not? *Yes, it's been deployed & assigned in the Grp. Policy.*	
1. *(continued)*	b. Open the VERITAS Software Console from the **VERITAS** menu.
❓ What happens? *Opens window/Console for Veritas.*	
1. *(continued)*	c. Close the VERITAS Software Console, and then log off.

Exercise 3
Publishing Applications

Scenario

The Information Services department uses the Cosmo application. You want to make it available to all users, but Cosmo is not an essential application. Users should be able to install Cosmo from Add/Remove Programs, but Cosmo should not automatically install.

Goal

In this exercise, you will use Group Policy to publish Cosmo to the Information Services OU.

Tasks	Detailed Steps
1. Create a GPO named Application Publishing Policy and linked to the Information Services OU. *linked to an OU*	a. Log on as Administrator with a password of **password**. b. Open Active Directory Users and Computers from the **Administrative Tools** menu. c. Expand *domain*.**nwtraders.msft**, if necessary. d. Open the **Properties** dialog box for the Information Services OU. e. On the **Group Policy** tab, click **New**. f. Type **Application Publishing Policy** and then press ENTER. g. Leave the Information Services Properties dialog box open.
2. Modify the Application Publishing GPO to publish Cosmo: • Assigned File Name: \\London\Labfiles\ Packages\Cosmo1\ Cosmo1.msi.	a. In the **Information Services Properties** dialog box, select the **Application Publishing Policy** GPO if necessary, and then click **Edit**. b. Under **User Configuration**, expand **Software Settings**, and then click **Software installation**. c. Right-click **Software installation**, point to **New**, and then click **Package**. d. Double-click **cosmo1**, click **cosmo1.msi**, and then click **Open**. e. In the **Deploy Software** dialog box, verify that **Published** is selected, and then click **OK**. f. Close all open windows and dialog boxes, and the log off.

Exercise 4
Installing a Published Application

Scenario

After making changes to the Group Policy settings to enable them to publish applications, you want to test those settings to verify that the published applications are installed correctly.

Goal

In this exercise, you will install a published application by using Add/Remove Programs and by opening a document.

Tasks	Detailed Steps

1. Log on as Hduser and then install the published application by using Add/Remove Programs.	a. Log on as Hduser with a password of **password**.
	
	b. In Control Panel, click **Add/Remove Programs**, and then click **Add New Programs**.
	
	    Cosmo 1 appears in the list of programs available from the network.
	
	c. Click **Add**.
	
	    Windows Installer installs Cosmo 1.
	
	d. In the **Cosmo 1** dialog box, click **OK**.
	
	e. Close Add/Remove Programs, and then close Control Panel.
	
	f. Verify that Cosmo 1 is installed, and then log off.

2. Log on as Csuser and determine whether Cosmo 1 is installed.	▪ Log on as Csuser with a password of **password**.
❓ Is Cosmo 1 installed? Why or why not? *No. Not installed by this user.* *App. is publishd, but user must install it.*	

Tasks	Detailed Steps
3. Install a published application through document invocation. • Open the following file: *computer*\Labfiles\ Packages\Cosmo.cs00 (where *computer* is your assigned computer name)	a. In the **Run** box, type *computer***labfiles****packages** in the **Open** box, and then click **OK**.
❷ Is the file Cosmo.cs00 associated with any application? No, 	
3. *(continued)*	b. Double-click **Cosmo.cs00**.
❷ What happens? Why? It opens. ? Then the app's icon appears in the Packages dialog box.	
3. *(continued)*	c. Close all open windows, and then log off.

◆ Maintaining Deployed Software

- **Upgrading Deployed Software**
- **Redeploying Software**

After software has been deployed, you may be required to modify it. You must be able to maintain or upgrade users' software to ensure that they have the most current version. The options available in Windows 2000 for maintaining software are upgrading software versions and redeploying software.

Upgrading Deployed Software

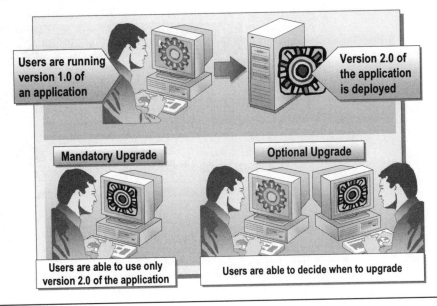

Because the tasks in an organization are dynamic and varied, you can use Group Policy to deploy and manage software by using upgrades that match the needs of the departments in your organization. The two types of upgrades are:

- *Mandatory upgrades.* Mandatory upgrades automatically replace an old version of software with an upgraded version. For example, if users are currently using software version 1.0, this version is removed, and software version 2.0 is installed the next time that the computer starts or the user logs on.

- *Optional upgrades.* Optional upgrades allow users to decide when to upgrade to the new version. For example, an optional upgrade allows users to determine if they want to upgrade to version 2.0 of the software or continue using version 1.0.

To deploy an upgrade, perform the following steps:

1. Deploy software version 2.0.

2. Open Software Installation, right-click the version 2.0, and then click **Properties**. In the **Properties** dialog box for package file, click the **Upgrades** tab.

3. In the **Packages that this package will upgrade** section, click **Add**, and then select version 1.0 of the application. If both versions 1.0 and 2.0 are native Windows Installer packages, this step will be done automatically.

4. Select the type of upgrade:

   - To perform a mandatory upgrade, select the **Required upgrade for existing packages** check box, and then click **OK**.

   - To perform an optional upgrade, clear the **Required upgrade for existing packages** check box, and then click **OK**.

Redeploying Software

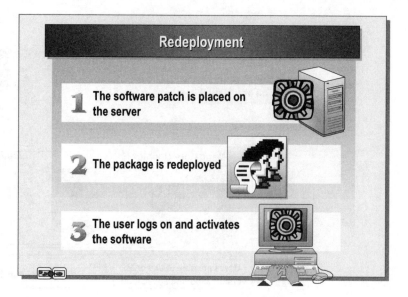

Redeployment is applying service packs and software patches to deployed software. When you mark a package file for redeployment, the software is advertised to everyone who has been granted access to the application, either through assigning or publishing. Then, depending on how the original package was deployed, one of three scenarios occurs:

- If the software was assigned to a user, the **Start** menu, desktop shortcuts, and registry settings relevant to that software will be updated the next time that the user logs on. The next time that the user starts the software, the service pack or software patch is automatically applied.

- If the software was assigned to a computer, the service pack or software patch will automatically be applied the next time that the computer starts up.

- If the software was published and installed, the **Start** menu, desktop shortcuts, and registry settings relevant to that software will be updated the next time that the user logs on. The next time that the user starts the software, the service pack or software patch is automatically applied.

To redeploy a software package, perform the following tasks:

1. Obtain the service pack or software patch from the application vendor and place the files in the appropriate installation folders.

   The service pack must include a new Windows Installer package file (.msi file). If it does not, you cannot redeploy the software, because only the original package file contains instructions for deploying the new files added by the service pack or software patch.

2. Open the GPO that originally deployed the software.

3. Open Software Installation, right-click the package file name, point to **All Tasks**, and then click **Redeploy Application**. In the **Redeployment** dialog box, click **Yes**.

   When the user logs on to the computer, the application will apply the service pack or software patch.

Removing Deployed Software

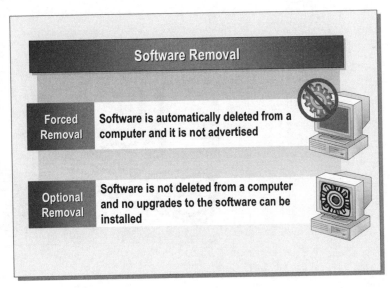

When you use Group Policy to deploy software, you can configure a GPO for removing software that is outdated or is no longer required by your organization. You can also remove old software by configuring the GPO to allow users to optionally upgrade to a new software package.

To remove the deployed software, perform the following steps:

1. Open the GPO that was originally used to deploy the software.

2. In Software Installation, right-click the name of the package, point to **All Tasks**, and then clicks **Remove**.

3. In the **Remove Software** dialog box, select one of the options described in the following table, and then click **OK**.

Option	Comments
Immediately uninstall software from users and computers (Forced removal)	Software is automatically deleted from a computer, either the next time that the computer is turned on or the next time that a user logs on (which is what occurs in the case of a user Group Policy setting). Removal takes place before the desktop appears.
Allow users to continue to use the software but prevent new installations (Optional removal)	Software is not actually removed from computers. The software will no longer be listed in Add/Remove Programs, but the users who had this software will still be able use it. If users manually delete the software, they will not be able to reinstall it.

Lab B: Upgrading and Removing Software

Objectives

After completing this lab, you will be able to:

- Use Group Policy to deploy mandatory upgrades of software.
- Use Group Policy to deploy optional upgrades of software.
- Use Group Policy to remove software previously deployed by using Group Policy.

Prerequisites

Before working on this lab, you must have the knowledge and skills necessary to create Group Policy objects.

Lab Setup

To complete this lab, you need the following:

- A computer running Windows 2000 Advanced Server that is configured as a domain controller.

Estimated time to complete this lab: 30 minutes

Exercise 1
Deploying Application Upgrades

Scenario

At Northwind Traders, all of your users are currently using the Cosmo1 application. Now you want to perform an optional upgrade to Cosmo2 for most of the organization. However, you want to force the users in the Customer Support OU to perform a mandatory upgrade. You do not want to visit every computer to manually install the software, so you will use Group Policy to perform the upgrades.

Goal

In this exercise, you will deploy both an optional and a mandatory upgrade to previously deployed applications.

Tasks	Detailed Steps
1. Deploy an optional upgrade from Cosmo1 to Cosmo2 for the Information Services OU. • GPO: Application Publishing Policy. • Application: Cosmo2 upgrades Cosmo1.	a. Log on as Administrator with a password of **password**. b. Open Active Directory Users and Computers from the **Administrative Tools** menu. c. Open the **Properties** dialog box for Information Services. d. On the **Group Policy** tab, click **Application Publishing Policy**, and then click **Edit**. e. Under **User Configuration**, expand **Software Settings**, and then click **Software installation**. f. Right-click **Software installation**, point to **New**, and then click **Package**. g. In the **Look in** box, click **packages**, double-click **Cosmo2**, click **Cosmo2**, and then click **Open**. h. In the **Deploy Software** dialog box, click **Advanced published or assigned**, and then click **OK**. i. On the **Upgrades** tab, click **Add**. j. Under **Package to upgrade**, select **Cosmo1**, click **OK**, and then click **OK** to close the **Cosmo 2 Properties** dialog box. *Cosmo 2 appears in the list of deployed software. Notice that the upgrade type is set to Optional.* k. Close Group Policy, and then click **OK** to close the **Information Services Properties** dialog box. l. Leave Active Directory Users and Computers open.
2. Create a new GPO linked to the Customer Support OU. Name the GPO Mandatory Upgrade Policy.	a. Open the **Properties** dialog box for the Customer Support OU. b. On the **Group Policy** tab, click **New**. c. Type **Mandatory Upgrade Policy** and then press ENTER. d. Leave the Customer Support OU Properties dialog box open.

Tasks	Detailed Steps
3. Deploy a mandatory upgrade from Cosmo1 to Cosmo2 for the Customer Support OU. • GPO: Mandatory Upgrade Policy. • Application: Cosmo2 upgrades Cosmo1.	a. In the **Customer Support Properties** dialog box, on the **Group Policy** tab, click **Mandatory Upgrade Policy**, and then click **Edit**. b. Under **User Configuration**, expand **Software Settings**, and then click **Software Installation**. c. Right-click **Software Installation**, point to **New**, and then click **Package**. d. Click **Cosmo2**, and then click **Open**. e. Click **Advanced published or assigned**, and then click **OK**. f. On the **Upgrades** tab, click **Add**. g. In the **Add Upgrade Package** dialog box, click **A specific GPO**, and then click **Browse**. h. In the **Domains, OUs and linked Group Policy Objects** list, double-click **Information Services.***domain*.**nwtraders.msft**, click **Application Publishing Policy**, and then click **OK**. i. In the **Add Upgrade Package** dialog box, ensure that **Cosmo 1 (Application Publishing Policy)** is selected, and then click **OK**. j. In the **Cosmo 2 Properties** dialog box, click **Required upgrade for existing packages**, and then click **OK**. *Cosmo 2 appears in the list of deployed software. Notice that the upgrade type is set to Required.* k. Close all open windows and dialog boxes, and then log off.

Exercise 2
Testing Application Upgrades

Scenario

After making changes to the Group Policy settings for the mandatory upgrade and the optional upgrade, you want to test those settings, to verify that the software is upgraded and that all of the components work correctly.

Goal

In this exercise, you will test the results of mandatory and optional upgrades.

Tasks	Detailed Steps
1. Log on as Hduser to test the optional upgrade.	a. Log on as Hduser with a password of **password**.
❓	Which version of Cosmo appears on the **Start** menu? Why? _1.0 → Not mandatory deploy;_
❓	How would this user upgrade to Cosmo 2? _Must install_ _Because it was published, must install through the_ _Add/Remove programs._
1. *(continued)*	b. Upgrade to Cosmo 2, and then log off.

Tasks	Detailed Steps
2. Log on as Csuser to test the mandatory upgrade.	a. Log on as Csuser with a password of **password**.
❓ Which version of Cosmo appears on the Start menu? Why? _V. 2.0._ _Because was assigned_	
2. *(continued)*	b. Open Cosmo 2 from the **Start** menu.
❓ What happens when you open Cosmo 2? _Installs_	
2. *(continued)*	c. Close all open windows, and then log off.

Exercise 3
Removing Deployed Software

Scenario

Your trial period for Cosmo 2 has expired, and you have decided to upgrade to the new package. You have been told that to get the best results from the Cosmo program, you should remove Cosmo 2, which is a limited trial version, before deploying the full version. You also will be phasing out the Veritas WinINSTALL LE application, which means that you want users to be able to continue using Veritas WinINSTALL LE, but you do not want users to be able to install it. You want to remove the software without visiting each computer. You can use Group Policy settings to perform this function for you.

Goal

In this exercise, you will remove an application that was deployed in a previous exercise, by using both forced removal and optional removal.

Tasks	Detailed Steps
1. Implement a forced removal of Cosmo 2, which was previously deployed in the Application Publishing Policy GPO.	a. Log on as Administrator with a password of **password**. b. Open Active Directory Users and Computers from the **Administrative Tools** menu. c. Open the **Properties** dialog box for Information Services. d. On the **Group Policy** tab, click **Application Publishing Policy**, and then click **Edit**. e. Under **User Configuration**, expand **Software Settings**, and then click **Software installation**. f. Right-click **Cosmo 2**, point to **All Tasks**, and then click **Remove**. g. In the **Remove Software** dialog box, ensure that **Immediately uninstall software from users and computers** is selected, and then click **OK**. h. Close Group Policy. i. Leave the Information Services Properties dialog box open.
2. Implement an optional removal of Veritas WinINSTALL LE, which was previously deployed in the Application Assignment Policy GPO.	a. On the **Group Policy** tab, click **Application Assignment Policy**, and then click **Edit**. b. Under **User Configuration**, expand **Software Settings**, and then click **Software installation**. c. Right-click **WinINSTALL LE**, point to **All Tasks**, and then click **Remove**. d. In the **Remove Software** dialog box, click **Allow users to continue to use the software, but prevent new installations**, and then click **OK**. e. Close all open windows and dialog boxes, and then log off.

Exercise 4
Testing the Removal of Deployed Applications

Scenario

Now that you have made the changes necessary to remove the deployed software, you need to test the results.

Goal

In this exercise, you will test the results of forced and optional removal of deployed applications.

Tasks	Detailed Steps
1. Log on as Hduser to test the removal of the applications.	a. Log on as Hduser with a password of **password**.

❓ Is Cosmo 2 still installed? Why or why not?

No — it was uninstalled at login

❓ Is Veritas WinINSTALL LE still installed? Why or why not?

Yes. It was optional.

Tasks	Detailed Steps
1. *(continued)*	b. Log off.
2. Log on as Administrator and then run the Rmous.vbs script file in the C:\Moc\Win2154A\Labfiles folder. This script removes all OUs created in the labs in this module.	a. Log on as Administrator with a password of **password**. b. Open the C:\Moc\Win2154A\Labfiles folder. c. Double-click **Rmous.vbs**, which removes all of the OUs created during the labs in this module. d. Restart your computer.

Troubleshooting Software Deployment

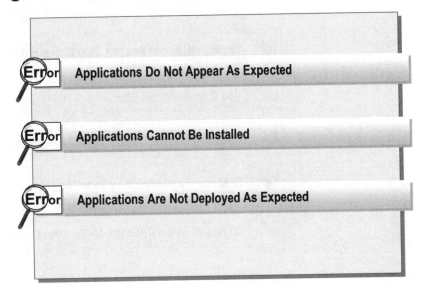

The following are some of the more common problems that you may encounter when using Group Policy to deploy software, and suggested strategies for resolving them:

- *Applications do not appear as expected.* This is most likely caused by a problem in the way that the applications were deployed. To determine whether an application has been assigned or published to a user, log on as that user and open Add/Remove Programs in Control Panel.

  - If the application appears in Add/Remove Programs, but there is no **Start** menu shortcut, this means that the application has been published rather than assigned.

  - If the application does not appear in Add/Remove Programs, the application was never deployed, it was deployed in the wrong OU, or the user is a member of a security group that is being filtered out from the effects of this GPO.

- *Application cannot be installed.* This is probably because a user cannot gain access to the software distribution point; for example, the server hosting that network may be unavailable. Verify that users have at least the Read an NTFS file system permission for the software distribution point.

- *Applications are not deployed as expected.* This is probably caused by Group Policy conflicts. It is possible to assign a user an application at one level of Active Directory (for example, at the domain level), and then deny them access to that application at a lower level (for example, at the OU level). Another probable cause is that applications can also be assigned to computers, and computer policy in most cases overrides user policy. If a user has been assigned Word, but Word has been marked for mandatory removal from a computer, that user will not receive Word when logging on to that computer.

Best Practices

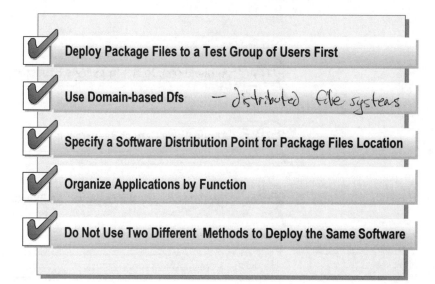

Consider the following best practices for using Group Policy to deploy and manage applications:

- Deploy package files gradually or to a test group of users first, before you make them available to all users. Gradual deployment and testing can help you to identify and resolve package problems before you deploy the application to the entire organization.

- Use domain-based Dfs for the software distribution points. Clients then attempt to install deployed software from a Dfs replica in their own site, thus reducing network traffic across slow wide area network (WAN) links.

- Specify a default software distribution point where package files are located if you will be publishing or assigning multiple applications in a GPO.

- Organize applications by function to make it easier to locate them when creating software policies. For example, create a folder named Graphic Tools in the software distribution shared folder, and then under the Graphic Tools folder, create a folder for each graphics application that you are deploying. Try to use folder names that are consistent with the software categories for the applications.

- Do not use two different methods to deploy the same software. Deploy software by assigning it either to users or to computers, but never to both users and computers.

Review

- **Introduction to Managing Software Deployment**
- **Windows Installer Technology**
- **Deploying Software**
- **Configuring Software Deployment**
- **Maintaining Deployed Software**
- **Removing Deployed Software**
- **Troubleshooting Software Deployment**
- **Best Practices**

1. Because Word 2000 is used on a daily basis by all of the users in your organization, you want to make sure that it is available, even if users delete the application by mistake. Which deployment method should you use to install this application if the application needs to be always installable?

   Assign it.
   (Group Policy would automatically re-install it if deleted).

2. You need to deploy an accounting application used only by users in the Payroll OU and the users must have access to that application. What deployment method should you use to install this application?

   Assign to Users instead of computers,

3. For organizations that have many published applications, how can you make it easy for users to locate applications that they need in Add/Remove Programs?

   create Categories. in Add/Remove,

4. Your company assigns a virus protection application, which is frequently updated, to all of the computers in your organization. You need to ensure that the latest version of the application is installed on all computers in the organization. What should you do when you receive the latest version of the application from the vendor?

Deploy as a mandatory upgrade.

Microsoft®
Training &
Certification

Module 10: Creating and Managing Trees and Forests

Contents

Overview

- ■ **Introduction to Trees and Forests**
- ■ **Creating Trees and Forests**
- ■ **Trust Relationships in Trees and Forests**
- ■ **The Global Catalog**
- ■ **Strategies for Using Groups in Trees and Forests**
- ■ **Troubleshooting Creating and Managing Trees and Forests**
- ■ **Best Practices**

Creating a single domain in Active Directory® directory service is the one of the most efficient and easy ways to administer the Active Directory infrastructure. However, when implementing the Active Directory infrastructure, you may want to consider additional domains if your organization requires additional functionalities. Some examples of these additional functionalities are security settings, such as account and password Group Policy settings, which must be applied at the domain level so that distinct security settings apply to the users in each domain. Multiple domains also allow you to decentralize administration to retain complete administrative control of the domain controllers in their domain. Another benefit of multiple domains is that they enable you to reduce replication traffic so that the only data replicated between domains are the changes to the global catalog server, configuration information, and schema.

Depending on your requirements, you can create additional domains, called *child domains*, in the same domain tree. Alternatively, you can create a *forest*. A forest consists of multiple domain trees. All domains that have a common root domain are said to form a *contiguous namespace*. The domain trees in a forest do not form a contiguous namespace.

At the end of this module, you will be able to:

- ■ Identify the purpose of trees and forests in Microsoft® Windows® 2000.

- ■ Create and manage trees and forests in Windows 2000.

- ■ Use trust relationships in trees and forests.

- ■ Use the global catalog to log on to a Windows 2000 network.

- ■ Implement the most effective group strategies to gain access to resources across trees and forests.

- ■ Troubleshoot common problems that can occur when creating and managing trees and forests in Windows 2000.

- ■ Apply best practices to creating and managing trees and forests in Active Directory.

◆ Introduction to Trees and Forests

- **What Is a Tree?**
- **What Is a Forest?**
- **What Is the Forest Root Domain?**
- **Characteristics of Multiple Domains**

By using both domain trees and forests, you can use both contiguous and noncontiguous naming conventions. Trees and forests are useful for organizations with independent divisions that must each maintain its own Domain Name System (DNS) names.

What Is a Tree?

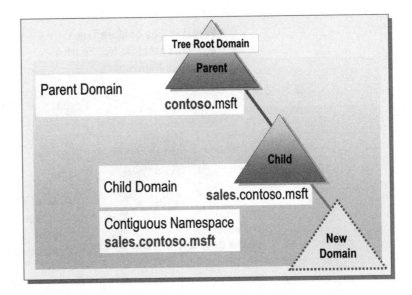

A *tree* is a hierarchical arrangement of Windows 2000 domains that share a *contiguous namespace*. A tree consists of one or more domains. A domain must exist in a tree.

When you add a new domain to a tree, the new domain is called a *child* domain. The name of the domain above the child domain is called a *parent* domain. The name of the child domain is a combination of the child domain name and the parent domain name separated by a period, to form its *DNS name*. This DNS name forms a contiguous namespace hierarchy. The top-level domain in a domain tree is sometimes called the *tree root domain*.

For example, a child domain named sales that has a parent domain named contoso.msft would form a fully qualified DNS domain name of sales.contoso.msft. Any new domain added to sales.contoso.msft becomes its child domain.

What Is a Forest?

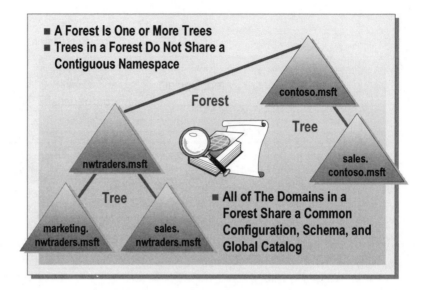

A *forest* is a collection of one or more trees. Trees in a forest do not share a contiguous namespace. The domains in a forest share a common configuration, schema, and global catalog.

For example, Contoso, Ltd. creates a separate organization called Northwind Traders. Contoso, Ltd. decides to create a new Active Directory domain name for Northwind Traders, called nwtraders.msft. As shown in the slide, the two organizations do not share a common namespace; however, by adding the new Active Directory domain as a new tree in an existing forest, the two organizations are able to share resources and administrative functions.

What Is the Forest Root Domain?

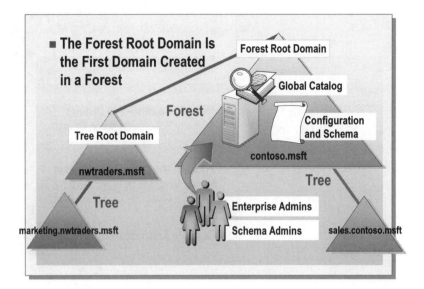

The *forest root domain* is the first domain created in a forest. The name of the forest root domain is used to refer to a given forest. The top-level domain of each tree, which is the tree root domain, has a trust relationship to the forest root domain. Therefore, the name of the forest root domain must not change.

The first domain controller in the forest root domain is configured to store the global catalog information. The forest root domain also contains the configuration and schema information for the forest.

The forest root domain contains two predefined forest-wide groups, Enterprise Admins and Schema Admins. These groups exist only in the forest root domain of an Active Directory forest. You add users who perform administrative tasks for the entire forest to these groups. When a domain is switched to native mode from mixed mode, these two predefined global groups automatically change to universal groups. The roles of these groups are the same in mixed mode and native mode, only the group scope changes.

The following table describes these groups and the predefined roles they are given when the forest root domain is created.

Predefined group name	Description
Enterprise Admins	It is a universal group if the domain is in native mode, a global group if the domain is in mixed mode. The group is authorized to make changes to the entire forest in Active Directory, such as by adding child domains. By default, the only member of the group is the Administrator account for the forest root domain.
Schema Admins	It is a universal group if the domain is in native mode, a global group if the domain is in mixed mode. The group is authorized to make schema changes in Active Directory. By default, the only member of the group is the Administrator account for the forest root domain.

Note The members of the Domain Admins group in the forest root domain can modify the membership of the Enterprise Admins and Schema Admins groups.

Characteristics of Multiple Domains

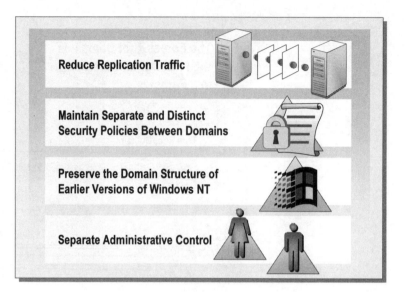

Consider having multiple domains in your organization because you can use multiple domains in Windows 2000 to:

- Reduce replication traffic. Implementing multiple domains, instead of one large single domain, allows you to optimize replication traffic. In multiple domains, only the changes to the global catalog server, configuration information, and schema, are replicated. Not all objects and attributes to all domain controllers in the domain are replicated. For example, if the network uses a slow wide area network (WAN) link, the replication of all objects in the forest uses up unnecessary bandwidth because objects are being replicated to locations where they are rarely used. Creating a separate domain for different locations reduces replication traffic and maintains network performance because replication occurs only in the locations that need the objects.

- Maintain separate and distinct security settings for different domains. To be able to apply different domain-level security settings to group of users, you must have multiple domains. For example, you can use a separate domain for administrators and other users if you want to have a more strict password Group Policy, such as a shorter interval of password changes for administrators.

- Preserve the domain structure of earlier versions of Microsoft Windows NT®. To avoid or postpone restructuring your existing Windows NT domains, you can upgrade each domain to Windows 2000 while preserving the existing domain structure.

- Separate administrative control. The members of the domain administrators group in a domain have complete control over all objects in that domain. If you have a subdivision in your organization that does not allow administrators outside the subdivision control over their objects, place those objects in a separate domain. For example, for legal reasons, it might not be prudent for a subdivision of an organization that works on highly sensitive projects to accept domain supervision from a higher-level Information Technology (IT) group.

◆ Creating Trees and Forests

- **Creating a New Child Domain**
- **Creating a New Tree**
- **Creating a New Forest**

After you have installed Active Directory and created a single domain, you can use the Active Directory Installation wizard, Dcpromo.exe, to guide you through the process of adding additional domains by creating trees and forests. The information that you must provide when you install Active Directory depends on whether you are creating a child domain in an existing forest or creating a new tree in an existing forest.

Creating a New Child Domain

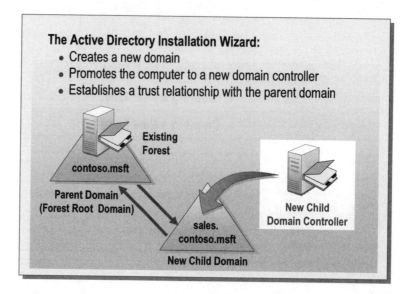

The Active Directory Installation Wizard:
- Creates a new domain
- Promotes the computer to a new domain controller
- Establishes a trust relationship with the parent domain

Existing Forest

contoso.msft

Parent Domain
(Forest Root Domain)

New Child
Domain Controller

sales.
contoso.msft

New Child Domain

After you establish the root domain, you can create additional domains within the tree if your network plan requires multiple domains. You must be a member of the Enterprise Admins group to create a child domain.

Each new domain within the tree will be a child domain of the root domain, or a child domain of another child domain.

For example, you create a domain named sales.contoso.msft, which is a child domain of the root domain, contoso.msft. The next domain that you create within that tree can be a child of constoso.msft or a child of sales.contoso.msft.

To create a child domain, perform the following steps:

1. In the **Run** box, type **dcpromo.exe** and then press ENTER.

2. In the Active Directory Installation wizard, complete the installation by using the information in the following table.

On this wizard page	Do this
Domain Controller Type	Click **Domain controller for a new domain**.
Create Tree or Child Domain	Click **Create a new child domain in an existing domain tree**.
Network Credentials	Specify the user name, password, and domain name of a user account in the Enterprise Admins group, which exists in the root domain of the forest.
Child Domain Installation	Specify the DNS name of the parent domain and the name of the new child domain.
Domain NetBIOS Name	Specify the NetBIOS name for the new domain.
Database and Log Locations	Specify locations for the Active Directory database and log files.

(continued)

On this wizard page	Do this
Shared System Volume	Specify the location for the shared system volume.
Permissions	Specify whether to set the default permissions on user and group objects to be compatible with computers running earlier versions of Windows, or only with Windows 2000–based servers. Enabling pre-Windows 2000 compatible permissions adds the Everyone group to the Pre-Windows 2000 Compatible Access group. This group has Read access to user and group object attributes that existed in Windows NT 4.0. You should select this option only after considering the impact that weaker permissions have on Active Directory security.
Directory Services Restore Mode Administrator Password	Specify a password to use when starting the computer in Directory Services Restore Mode.

After you specify the installation information, the Active Directory Installation wizard performs the following tasks:

- Creates a new domain.

- Promotes the computer in the new child domain to a domain controller.

- Establishes trust relationships between the child domain and the parent domain.

Creating a New Tree

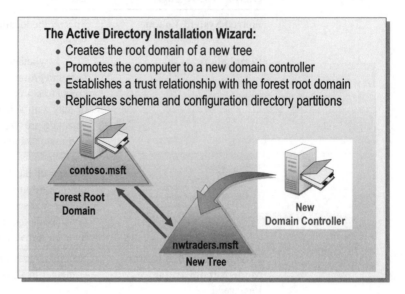

After you establish the root domain, you can add a new tree to the existing forest if your network plan requires multiple trees.

To create a new tree in an existing forest, perform the following steps:

1. In the **Run** box, type **dcpromo.exe** and then press ENTER.

2. In the Active Directory Installation wizard, complete the installation by using the information in the following table.

On this wizard page	Do this
Domain Controller Type	Click **Domain controller for a new domain**.
Create Tree or Child Domain	Click **Create a new domain tree**.
Create or Join Forest	Click **Place this new domain tree in an existing forest**.
Network Credentials	Specify the user name, password, and domain name of a user account in the Enterprise Admins group, which exists in the root domain of the forest.
New Domain Tree	Specify the DNS name for the new tree.

The remaining options in the Active Directory Installation wizard are identical to the options used for creating the new child domain. After you finish specifying the installation information, the Active Directory Installation wizard performs the following steps:

- Creates the root domain of a new tree.

- Promotes the computer in the new tree to a domain controller.

- Establishes trust relationships to the forest root domain.

- Replicates schema and configuration directory partitions.

Creating a New Forest

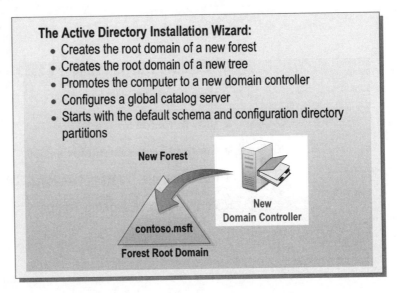

The Active Directory Installation Wizard:
- Creates the root domain of a new forest
- Creates the root domain of a new tree
- Promotes the computer to a new domain controller
- Configures a global catalog server
- Starts with the default schema and configuration directory partitions

New Forest

New Domain Controller

contoso.msft

Forest Root Domain

When you create a new forest, the root domains of all domain trees in the forest establish transitive trust relationships with the forest root domain. You must be a member of the local administrators group to create a new forest.

To create a new forest, perform the following steps:

1. In the **Run** box, type **dcpromo.exe** and then press ENTER.

2. In the Active Directory Installation wizard, complete the installation by using the information in the following table.

On this wizard page	Do this
Domain Controller Type	Click **Domain controller for a new domain**.
Create Tree or **Child Domain**	Click **Create a new domain tree**.
Create or **Join Forest**	Click **Create a new forest of domain trees**.

The remaining options in the Active Directory Installation wizard are identical to the options used for creating a new tree.

After you finish specifying the installation information, the Active Directory Installation wizard performs the following steps:

- Creates the root of a new forest.
- Creates the root of a new tree.
- Promotes the computer in the new forest to a domain controller.
- Configures a global catalog server.
- Starts with the default schema and configuration directory partition information.

◆ Trust Relationships in Trees and Forests

- **Transitive Trusts in Windows 2000**
- **How Trusts Work**
- **How Kerberos V5 Works**
- **Shortcut Trusts in Windows 2000**
- **Nontransitive Trusts in Windows 2000**
- **Verifying and Revoking Trusts**

Active Directory provides security across multiple domains through domain trust relationships based on the Kerberos version 5 protocol. A *domain trust* is a relationship established between domains that enables a domain controller in one domain to authenticate users in the other domain. The authentication requests follow a *trust path*.

A series of trust relationships for passing authentication requests between two domains defines a trust path. Trust paths are created automatically when you add domains to a Windows 2000 network. You can also manually create trusts when you want to share resources across domains that are not trusted or when you want to shorten the trust path.

Transitive Trusts in Windows 2000

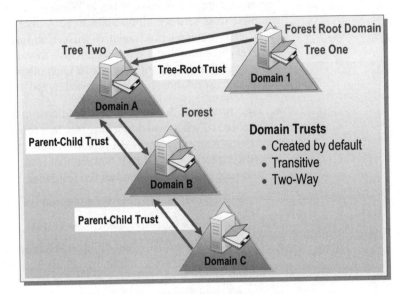

Each time you create a new domain tree in a forest, a trust path is automatically created between the forest root domain and the new domain tree. The trust path allows trust relationships to flow through all domains in the forest. Authentication requests follow these trust paths, so accounts from any domain in the forest can be authenticated by any other domain in the forest. These trusts are sometimes called *default domain trusts*.

Types of Domain Trusts

The following are the two types of domain trusts in Windows 2000:

- *Transitive trust.* A transitive trust means that the trust relationship extended to one domain is automatically extended to all other domains that trust that domain. For example, domain A directly trusts domain B. Domain B directly trusts domain C. Because both trusts are transitive, domain A indirectly trusts domain C.

- *Two-way trust.* A two-way trust means that there are two trust paths going in both directions between two domains. For example, domain A trusts domain B in one direction, and domain B trusts domain A in the other direction.

Types of Transitive Trusts

The advantage of transitive trusts in Windows 2000 domains is that there is complete trust between all domains in an Active Directory forest. Because every child domain has a transitive trust relationship with its parent domain, and every tree root domain has a transitive trust relationship with the forest root domain, all domains in the forest trust each other. The following types of transitive trust relationships can be established with Windows 2000 domains:

- *Tree-root trust.* A tree-root trust relationship is the trust relationship that is established when you add a new tree to a forest. Installing Active Directory automatically creates a trust relationship between the domain that you are creating and the forest root domain that is also the new tree root domain. A tree-root trust relationship has the following restrictions:

  - It can be set up only between the roots of two trees in the same forest.

  - It must be a transitive and two-way trust.

- *Parent-child trust.* A parent-child trust relationship is established when you create a new domain in a tree. Installing Active Directory automatically creates within the namespace hierarchy a trust relationship between the new domain, which is the child domain, and the domain that immediately precedes it, which is the parent domain. The parent-child trust relationship has the following characteristics:

  - It can exist only between two domains in the same tree and namespace.

  - The child domain trusts the parent domain.

  - The parent domain trusts the child domain.

  - The trusts between parent and child domains are transitive.

How Trusts Work

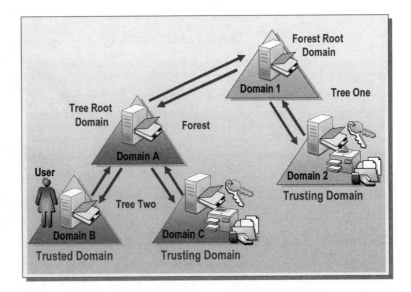

When a user attempts to gain access to a resource in another domain, the Kerberos V5 protocol must determine whether the *trusting* domain, which is the domain containing the resource to which the user is trying to gain access, has a trust relationship with the *trusted* domain, which is the domain to which the user is logging on. To determine this relationship, the Kerberos V5 security protocol travels the trust path between the domain controller in the trusting domain to the domain controller in the trusted domain.

When a user in the trusted domain attempts to gain access to a resource in another domain, the user's computer first contacts the domain controller in its domain to get authentication to the resource. If the resource is not in the user's domain, the domain controller uses the trust relationship with its parent and refers the user's computer to a domain controller in its parent domain. This attempt for locating a resource continues up the trust hierarchy, possibly to the forest root domain, and down the trust hierarchy until contacting a domain controller in the domain where the resource is located. The path that is taken from domain to domain is the trust path. The path that is taken is the shortest path following the trust hierarchy.

How Kerberos V5 Works

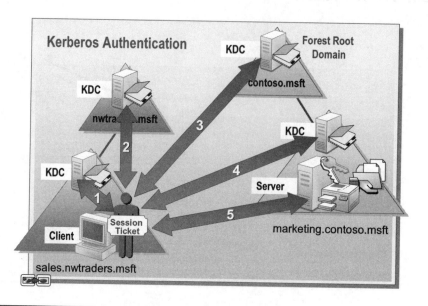

The Kerberos V5 protocol is the primary authentication protocol in Windows 2000; it verifies both the identity of the user and the integrity of the network services. The main components of the Kerberos V5 protocol are a client, a server, and a trusted third party to mediate between them. The trusted intermediary in the protocol is known as the *Key Distribution Center* (KDC). In Windows 2000, the domain controller functions as the KDC. The KDC runs on each domain controller as part of Active Directory, which stores all client passwords and other account information.

The Kerberos V5 services are installed on each domain controller, and a Kerberos V5 client is installed on each Windows 2000 workstation and server. A user's initial Kerberos authentication provides the user with a single logon to enterprise resources.

The Kerberos V5 authentication mechanism issues session tickets for accessing network services. These tickets contain encrypted data, including an encrypted key, which confirms the user's identity to the requested service.

When accessing resources across a forest, the client follows the Kerberos V5 protocol trust path. As an example to illustrate the authentication path, consider a tree, contoso.msft, in a forest and its child domain, sales.contoso.msft. The other tree, nwtraders.msft, in the forest consists of the child domain marketing.nwtraders.msft.

If a user in sales.nwtraders.msft needs to gain access to resources in marketing.contoso.msft. This process assumes that the user has previously authenticated with the network and has a Ticket Granting Ticket (TGT) for the sales.nwtraders.msft domain populated with the user's global and universal group memberships. The following Kerberos V5 authentication process occurs:

1. The user asks for a session ticket for the server in marketing.contoso.msft. The KDC in the sales.nwtraders.msft domain issues a TGT for the nwtraders.msft domain known as a referral ticket.

2. The user presents the KDC in the nwtraders.msft the TGT for that domain and is issued a TGT for the contoso.msft domain.

3. The user presents the KDC in the contoso.msft the TGT for that domain and is issued a TGT for the marketing.contoso.msft domain.

4. The user presents the KDC in the marketing.contoso.msft the TGT for that domain and is issued a ST for the contoso.msft domain. This ST is populated with the domain local group memberships from the marketing.contoso.msft domain.

5. The user presents the server session ticket to the server to gain access to resources on the server in marketing.contoso.msft. The server compares the SIDs include in the session ticket to the ACEs on the requested resource to determine if the user is authorized to access the resource.

Important   For more detailed information about the steps in the Kerberos V5 authentication process, see *Windows 2000 Kerberos Authentication* under **Additional Reading** on the Web page on the Student Materials compact disc.

Shortcut Trusts in Windows 2000

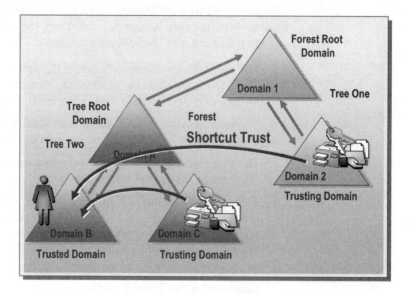

Shortcut trusts are one-way transitive trusts that you can use to optimize performance by shortening the trust path for authentication purposes. You manually create one-way shortcut trusts between Windows 2000 domains from the trusting domain to the trusted domain in the same forest. Even though shortcut trusts are one-way, you can also create a two-way relationship by manually creating two one-way trusts in each direction.

Shortcut trusts reduce the trust path by allowing a more direct connection between two domains that otherwise would require the path to travel up the hierarchy, possibly to the forest root domain, before it travels down to the other domain. The most effective use of shortcut trusts is when there is a number of users frequently accessing resources in another domain in the forest and the number of domains in the trust path that the client needs to connect to is numerous.

To illustrate an example of a shortcut trust in the same tree, assume users in domain B often need to gain access to resources in domain C. You can create a direct link from the trusting domain C to the trusted domain B by using a shortcut trust relationship so that domain A can be bypassed in the trust path.

To illustrate an example of a shortcut trust between two trees, assume users in domain B often need to gain access to resources in domain 2. You can create a direct link from the trusting domain 2 to the trusted domain B through a shortcut trust relationship so that data does not have to travel up through the forest root from one domain tree through the other.

Note For more information about how to create and manage shortcut trusts by using Active Directory Domains and Trusts, see the Windows 2000 Help.

Nontransitive Trusts in Windows 2000

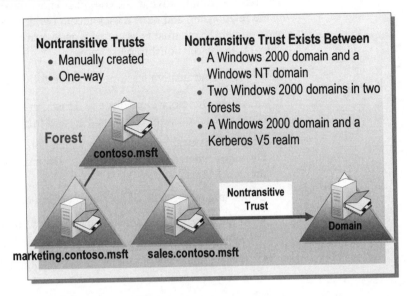

A *nontransitive trust relationship* can be created between Windows 2000 domains if a transitive trust relationship is not automatically provided.

What Is a Nontransitive Trust?

You must explicitly create a nontransitive trust. A nontransitive trust is one-way. To create a two-way nontransitive trust, you can manually create two one-way trusts in each direction.

Nontransitive trusts are the trust relationships that are possible between only the following:

- A Windows 2000 domain and a Windows NT domain. If one of these domains is an account domain and the other is a resource domain, the trust relationship is usually created as a one-way trust relationship.

- A Windows 2000 domain in one forest and a Windows 2000 domain in another forest. The relationship between these two domains is often called an *external trust*.

- A Windows 2000 domain and an Kerberos V5 protocol security realm.

Note A Kerberos V5 realm is a security boundary similar to a Windows 2000 domain.

Creating a Nontransitive Trust

To create a nontransitive trust, you must know the domain names to be included in the relationship and have a user account with permission to create trusts in each domain. Each trust is assigned a password that the administrators of both domains in the relationship must know.

To create a nontransitive trust, perform the following steps:

1. In Active Directory Domains and Trusts, in the console tree, right-click the domain that you want to administer, and then click **Properties**.

2. On the **Trusts** tab, depending on which domain you are on, click **either Domains trusted by this domain** or **Domains that trust this domain**, and then click **Add**.

3. Depending on the type of domain, perform one of the following tasks:

   • If the domain to be added is a Windows 2000 domain, type the full DNS name of the domain.

   • If the domain is running an earlier version of Windows, type the domain name.

4. Type the password for this trust, and then confirm the password.

5. Repeat steps 1 through 4 on the domain that forms the other part of the nontransitive trust relationship.

Verifying and Revoking Trusts

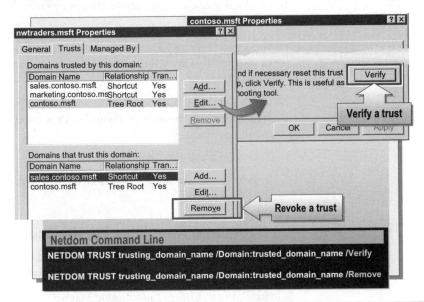

If you create nontransitive trusts, you will sometimes need to verify and delete, or revoke, the trust paths you created. You verify a trust to make sure it is working correctly and can validate authentication requests from other domains. You revoke a trust to prevent that authentication path from being used during authentication. You can use Active Directory Domains and Trusts or the **netdom** command to verify and revoke trust paths.

Verifying Trusts

To verify a trust by using Active Directory Domains and Trusts, perform the following steps:

1. In Active Directory Domains and Trusts, in the console tree, right-click one of the domains involved in the trust that you want to verify, and then click **Properties**.

2. On the **Trusts** tab, depending on which domain you are in, you use **Domains trusted by this domain** or **Domains that trust this domain** to select the trust to be verified.

3. Click the trust, and then click **Edit**.

4. Click **Verify/Reset**.

5. Repeat steps 1 through 4 to verify the trust for the other domain involved in the relationship.

Revoking Trusts

To revoke a trust by using Active Directory Domains and Trusts, perform the following steps:

1. In Active Directory Domains and Trusts, in the console tree, right-click one of the domains involved in the trust that you want to revoke, and then click **Properties**.

2. On the **Trusts** tab, depending on which domain you are in, use **Domains trusted by this domain** or **Domains that trust this domain** to select the trust to be revoked.

3. Select the trust, and then click **Remove**.

4. Repeat steps 1 through 3 to revoke the trust for the other domain involved in the relationship.

Verifying and Revoking Trusts Using Netdom

Netdom is a command-line utility that you can use to manage Windows 2000 domains and trust relationships from a command prompt window.

Use **netdom** to perform the following tasks:

- View all trust relationships.

- Enumerate direct trust relationships.

- Enumerate all (direct and indirect) trust relationships.

To verify a trust by using **netdom**, perform the following steps:

1. Open a command prompt window.

2. Type
   NETDOM TRUST trusting_domain_name /Domain:trusted_domain_name /Verify and press ENTER.

To revoke a trust using **netdom**, perform the following steps:

1. Open a command prompt window.

2. Type
   NETDOM TRUST trusting_domain_name /Domain:trusted_domain_name /Remove and press ENTER.

Lab A: Creating Domain Trees and Establishing Trusts

Objectives

After completing this lab, you will be able to:

- Create child domains in an existing forest.
- Remove an existing forest.
- Examine and verify trusts between domains.

Prerequisites

Before working on this lab, you must have knowledge and experience installing and removing Active Directory.

Lab Setup

To complete this lab, you need the Windows 2000 Advanced Server compact disc for the installation of the support tools during the lab.

Important   The lab does not reflect the real-world environment. It is recommended that you always use complex passwords for any administrator accounts, and never create accounts without a password.

Important   Outside of the classroom environment, it is strongly advised that you use the most recent software updates that are necessary. Because this is a classroom environment, we may use software that does not include the latest updates.

Student Computer IP Address, Domain, and FQDN Information

During this lab, you will be asked for your Internet Protocol (IP) address, domain, and fully qualified domain name (FQDN). Use this information from the following table to determine what to enter for these values. Your instructor will assign you a student number and provide the number to use in place of the *x* in the IP address.

Student number	IP address	Domain (*domain*)	FQDN
1	192.168.*x*.1	namerica1	vancouver.namerica1.nwtraders.msft
2	192.168.*x*.2	namerica1	denver.namerica1.nwtraders.msft
3	192.168.*x*.3	spacific1	perth.spacific1.nwtraders.msft
4	192.168.*x*.4	spacific1	brisbane.spacific1.nwtraders.msft
5	192.168.*x*.5	europe1	lisbon.europe1.nwtraders.msft
6	192.168.*x*.6	europe1	bonn.europe1.nwtraders.msft
7	192.168.*x*.7	samerica1	lima.samerica1.nwtraders.msft
8	192.168.*x*.8	samerica1	santiago.samerica1.nwtraders.msft
9	192.168.*x*.9	asia1	bangalore.asia1.nwtraders.msft
10	192.168.*x*.10	asia1	singapore.asia1.nwtraders.msft
11	192.168.*x*.11	africa1	casablanca.africa1.nwtraders.msft
12	192.168.*x*.12	africa1	tunis.africa1.nwtraders.msft
13	192.168.*x*.13	namerica2	acapulco.namerica2.nwtraders.msft
14	192.168.*x*.14	namerica2	miami.namerica2.nwtraders.msft
15	192.168.*x*.15	spacific2	auckland.spacific2.nwtraders.msft
16	192.168.*x*.16	spacific2	suva.spacific2.nwtraders.msft
17	192.168.*x*.17	europe2	stockholm.europe2.nwtraders.msft
18	192.168.*x*.18	europe2	moscow.europe2.nwtraders.msft
19	192.168.*x*.19	samerica2	caracas.samerica2.nwtraders.msft
20	192.168.*x*.20	samerica2	montevideo.samerica2.nwtraders.msft
21	192.168.*x*.21	asia2	manila.asia2.nwtraders.msft
22	192.168.*x*.22	asia2	tokyo.asia2.nwtraders.msft
23	192.168.*x*.23	africa2	khartoum.africa2.nwtraders.msft
24	192.168.*x*.24	africa2	nairobi.africa2.nwtraders.msft

Estimated time to complete this lab: 60 minutes

Exercise 1
Removing an Existing Forest

Scenario

After testing the features in Active Directory and the computer hardware, you will create the Northwind Traders forest. Before creating a new domain, you must remove the existing test forest environment and prepare your network settings for the new domain.

Goal

In this exercise, you will use the Active Directory Installation wizard to remove your existing domain and forest so that you can become a domain controller for a child domain. You will configure your network settings in preparation for the new domain.

Tasks	Detailed Steps
1. Remove your existing domain and forest. When prompted, restart your computer.	a. Log on as Administrator in your domain with a password of **password**.
	b. Run **dcpromo** to start the Active Directory Installation wizard.
	c. On the **Welcome to the Active Directory Installation Wizard** page, click **Next** to continue, and then click **OK** to close the message indicating that this domain controller is also a global catalog server.
	d. On the **Remove Active Directory** page, select the **This server is the last domain controller in the domain** check box, and then click **Next**.
	e. On the **Network Credentials** page, in the **User name** box, type **Administrator**
	f. In the **Password** box, type **password** and then click **Next**.
	g. On the **Administrator Password** page, in the **Password** and **Confirm password** boxes, type **password** and then click **Next**.
	h. On the **Summary** page, review the summary information, and then click **Next**. *The wizard takes several minutes to complete the removal of Active Directory from this computer.*
	i. On the **Completing the Active Directory Installation Wizard** page, click **Finish**, and then click **Restart Now** to restart your computer.
2. Remove the DNS subcomponent of Networking Services.	a. Log on as Administrator with a password of **password**.
	b. On the desktop, right-click **My Network Places**, and then click **Properties**.
	c. In the Network and Dial-up Connections window, on the **Advanced** menu, click **Optional Networking Components**.
	d. On the **Windows Components** page, under **Components**, clear the **Networking Services** check box, and then click **Next** to complete the removal of the DNS service. *The wizard finishes removing the DNS service.*

Tasks	Detailed Steps
3. Configure the Internet Protocol (TCP/IP) properties of your Local Area Connection to use the instructor computer, London 192.168.*x*.200 (where *x* is your assigned classroom network ID), for your preferred DNS server.	a. In the Network and Dial-up Connections window, right-click **Local Area Connection**, and then click **Properties**. b. Click **Internet Protocol (TCP/IP)**, and then click **Properties**. c. In the **Preferred DNS Server** box, type the IP address of London, which is **192.168.*x*.200** (where *x* is your assigned classroom network ID) and then click **OK**. d. In the **Local Area Connections Properties** dialog box, click **OK**, and then close the Network and Dial-up Connections window.
4. Configure the DNS suffix for your computer. When prompted, restart your computer. The primary DNS suffix is *domain*.nwtraders.msft (where *domain* is your assigned domain name).	a. On the desktop, right-click **My Computer**, and then click **Properties**. b. In the **System Properties** dialog box, on the **Network Identification** tab, click **Properties**. c. In the **Identification Changes** dialog box, click **More**. d. In the **DNS Suffix and NetBIOS Computer Name** dialog box, in the **Primary DNS suffix of this computer** box, type *domain*.**nwtraders.msft** (where *domain* is your assigned domain name) and then click **OK**. e. In the **Identification Changes** dialog box, click **OK**, and then click **OK** again to restart the computer for the changes to take effect. f. In the **System Properties** dialog box, click **OK**, and then click **Yes** to restart your computer.
5. Verify the proper configuration of Host Name, Primary DNS Suffix, and DNS servers according to the configuration table located in the Lab Setup section of this lab.	a. Log on as Administrator with a password of **password**. b. Open a command prompt window. c. At the command prompt, type **ipconfig /all** and then press ENTER to view your computer's TCP/IP configuration. d. Verify that the value of **Host Name** is your host name. Ensure that this value matches the first label of your FQDN entry, which is listed in the table in the Lab Setup section of this lab. e. Verify that the value of **Primary DNS Suffix** is the full domain name of your computer. Ensure that this value matches the last three labels of your FQDN entry listed, which is in the table in the Lab Setup section of this lab. f. Verify that the value of **DNS Servers** matches London's IP address: **192.168.*x*.200** g. Close all open windows.

Exercise 2
Creating a Child Domain

Scenario

Northwind Traders has designed their forest structure, which consists of a single domain tree with the root DNS name of nwtraders.msft. The corporate office is overseeing the rollout of the domain tree, and has already created the forest root domain nwtraders.msft. You must create the child domain for your region.

Goal

In this exercise, you will run the Active Directory Installation wizard to create the child domain for your region.

Tasks	Detailed Steps
Important: Perform this entire exercise only on the computer with the lower student number of the pair that is in the same child domain.	
1. Start the Active Directory Installation wizard to create: • A new domain controller for a new domain. • An existing domain tree. • For network credentials, use Administrator, password, and nwtraders.msft.	a. Run **dcpromo** to start the Active Directory Installation wizard. b. On the **Welcome to the Active Directory Installation Wizard** page, click **Next** to continue. c. On the **Domain Controller Type** page, ensure that **Domain controller for a new domain** is selected, and then click **Next**. d. On the **Create Tree or Child Domain** page, click **Create a new child domain in an existing domain tree**, and then click **Next**. e. On the **Network Credentials** page, type **Administrator** in the **User name** box, type **password** in the **Password** box, type **nwtraders.msft** in the **Domain** box, and then click **Next**.

Tasks	Detailed Steps
2. Complete the Active Directory installation process, providing the following information: • Full DNS name of domain.nwtraders.msft. • NetBIOS domain name of domain in uppercase characters. • Default locations for the database, log files, and shared system volume. • Permission compatible only with servers running Windows 2000. • A password of password for the Directory Services Restore Mode Administrator password. • Restart your computer when prompted.	a. On the Child Domain Installation page, click Browse. b. In the **Browse for Domain** dialog box, click **nwtraders.msft**, and then click **OK**. c. On the **Child Domain Installation** page, in the **Child domain** box, type *domain* and then click **Next**. d. On the **NetBIOS Domain Name** page, in the **Domain NetBIOS name** box, ensure that the value is the domain name, and then click **Next**. e. On the **Database and Log Locations** page, click **Next** to accept the default folder locations for both database files and log files. f. On the **Shared System Volume** page, click **Next** to accept the default folder location. g. On the **Permissions** page, click **Permissions compatible only with Windows 2000 servers**, and then click **Next**. h. On the **Directory Services Restore Mode Administrator Password** page, in the **Password** and **Confirm password** boxes, type **password** and then click **Next**. i. On the **Summary** page, review the summary information, and then click **Next**. *The wizard takes several minutes to complete the installation of Active Directory on this computer.* j. On the Completing the Active Directory Installation Wizard page, click Finish, and then click Restart Now to restart your computer.
3. Log on as Administrator in your domain after the domain controller restarts.	▪ Log on as Administrator in your domain with a password of **password**.

Exercise 3
Creating a Replica in a Child Domain

Scenario

Northwind Traders has designed their forest structure, which consists of a single domain tree with the root DNS name of nwtraders.msft. The corporate office is overseeing the rollout of the domain tree, and has already created all of the domains in the forest. Now the corporate office is strictly enforcing the guidelines that all domains should have at least two domain controllers to provide fault tolerance in case of a failure.

Goal

In this exercise, you will run the Active Directory Installation wizard to create a replica for the child domain of your region.

Tasks	Detailed Steps
⚠ **Important:** Perform this entire exercise only on the computer with the higher student number of the pair that is in the same child domain, and only after exercise 2 is complete.	
1. Start the Active Directory Installation wizard to create: • An additional domain controller for an existing domain. • For network credentials, use Administrator, **password**, and *domain*.**nwtraders.msft**.	a. Run **dcpromo** to start the Active Directory Installation wizard. b. On the **Welcome to the Active Directory Installation Wizard** page, click **Next** to continue. c. On the **Domain Controller Type** page, click **Additional domain controller for an existing domain**, and then click **Next**. d. On the **Network Credentials** page, type **Administrator** in the **User name** box, type **password** in the **Password** box, type *domain*.**nwtraders.msft** in the **Domain** box, and then click **Next**.
2. Complete the Active Directory installation process, providing the following information: • Full DNS name of *domain*.nwtraders.msft. • Default locations for the database, log files, and shared system volume. • A password of **password** for the Directory Services Restore Mode Administrator password. • Restart your computer when prompted.	a. On the Additional Domain Controller page, click Browse. b. In the **Browse for Domain** dialog box, expand **nwtraders.msft**, click *domain*.**nwtraders.msft**, and then click **OK**. c. On the **Additional Domain Controller** page, click **Next**. d. On the **Database and Log Locations** page, click **Next** to accept the default folder locations for both database files and log files. e. On the **Shared System Volume** page, click **Next** to accept the default folder location. f. On the **Directory Services Restore Mode Administrator Password** page, in the **Password** and **Confirm password** boxes, type **password** and then click **Next**. g. On the **Summary** page, review the summary information, and then click **Next**. 💻 *The wizard takes several minutes to complete the installation of Active Directory on this computer.* h. On the **Completing the Active Directory Installation Wizard** page, click **Finish**, and then click **Restart Now** to close the message asking to reboot your computer now.
3. Log on as Administrator in your child domain after the domain controller restarts.	▪ Log on as Administrator in your child domain with a password of **password**.

Exercise 4
Examining Trusts in a Forest

Scenario

Northwind Traders corporate administrators want to ensure that each region's domain in the nwtraders.msft domain tree is working correctly before moving forward with the second phase of their deployment plan. You must verify that the parent-child trusts between your region's domain and nwtraders.msft are working correctly.

Goal

In this exercise, you will verify the operation of the trusts between your region's domain and nwtraders.msft. This verification is necessary for the corporate office to determine that the nwtraders.msft domain tree that has just been created is functional and stable. You will also use the Netdom.exe support tool to verify the parent-child trust relationship.

Tasks	Detailed Steps
1. Test the trust between your child domain and nwtraders.msft, by using the Active Directory Domains and Trusts console.	a. Open Active Directory Domains and Trusts from the **Administrative Tools** menu, expand **nwtraders.msft**, and then click *domain*.**nwtraders.msft**. b. Right-click *domain*.**nwtraders.msft**, and then click **Properties**. c. In the *domain*.**nwtraders.msft Properties** dialog box, click the **Trusts** tab.
❓ How many parent-child trust relationships does your child domain have? *One — transitive, 2-way w/ nwtraders.msft.*	
1. *(continued)*	d. In the **Domains trusted by this domain** list, click **nwtraders.msft**, and then click **Edit** to view the properties of this trust link. e. In the **nwtraders.msft Properties** dialog box, click **Verify**. f. In the **Active Directory** dialog box, in the **User name** box, type **Administrator** In the **Password** box, type **password** g. Click **OK**, and then click **OK** again to close the message indicating that the trust has been verified.

Tasks	Detailed Steps
1. *(continued)*	h. If necessary, click **OK** to close the message indicating that a secure channel could not be established because there are currently are no logon servers available.
	i. Click **OK** to close the **nwtraders.msft Properties** dialog box, click **OK** to close the *domain*.**nwtraders.msft Properties** dialog box, and then close Active Directory Domains and Trusts.
2. Install the Windows 2000 Support Tools, if they are not already installed, by using all of the default options.	a. On your Windows 2000 Advanced Server compact disc, in the Support/Tools folder, run **Setup** to start the Windows 2000 Support Tools Setup wizard.
	b. On the **Welcome to the Windows 2000 Support Tools Setup Wizard** page, click **Next** to continue.
	c. On the **User Information** page, type your name in the **Name** box, type your organization in the **Organization** box, and then click **Next**.
	d. On the **Select An Installation Type** page, ensure that **Typical** is selected, and then click **Next**.
	e. On the **Begin Installation** page, click **Next** to begin the installation of the Windows 2000 Support Tools.
	The wizard takes a short time to complete the installation.
	f. On the **Completing the Windows 2000 Support Tools Setup Wizard** page, click **Finish**.
3. Verify the trust relationship between your child domain and nwtraders.msft by using the Netdom.exe tool, and then log off.	a. Open a command prompt window.
	b. At the command prompt, type **netdom help trust** and then press ENTER to view the available options.
	c. At the command prompt, type **netdom trust** *domain* **/Domain:nwtraders /UserD:Administrator /PasswordD:password /UserO:Administrator /PasswordO:password /verify** and then press ENTER to determine the state of the trust relationship.
	d. Close all open windows, and then log off.

◆ The Global Catalog

- **The Global Catalog and the Logon Process**
- **Creating a Global Catalog Server**

The *global catalog* contains the information that is necessary to determine the location of any object in Active Directory. The global catalog enables a user to log on to the network by providing universal group membership information and user principal name domain mapping information to a domain controller. Also, the global catalog server enables a user to find Active Directory information in the entire forest, regardless of the location of the information.

The first domain controller that you create in Active Directory is a global catalog server. You can configure additional domain controllers to be global catalog servers to balance the traffic from logon authentication and queries.

The Global Catalog and the Logon Process

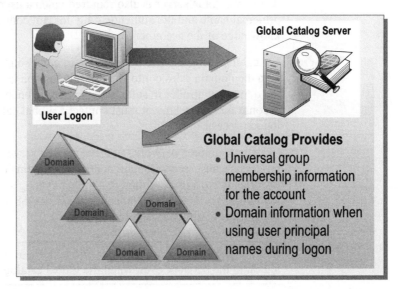

When you log on to a domain in native mode, the global catalog server provides universal group membership information for your account to the domain controller that processes the user logon information, and authenticates the user principal name.

Global Catalog and Universal Group Membership

When a user logs on to a domain in native mode, the global catalog server provides universal group membership information for the account to the domain controller that processes the user logon information. If a global catalog server is not available when a user initiates the network logon process and the user has logged on to the domain previously, Windows 2000 uses cached credentials to log on the user. If the user has not logged on to the domain previously, the user is able to log on to only the local computer.

During the logon process, an access token, which contains the groups to which the user belongs, is associated with the user. Because universal group membership is centrally stored in the global catalog, global catalog servers are used to identify the universal groups of which a user is a member.

Global Catalog and Authentication

A global catalog server is also required when a user logs on with a user principal name and the authenticating domain controller does not have direct knowledge of the account.

For example, Suzan Fine's account is in contoso.msft. She uses a computer that is in the domain sales.contoso.msft. She logs on as suzanf@contoso.msft. When the domain controller in sales.contoso.msft is unable to authenticate the user account for Suzan Fine, it must contact a global catalog server to complete the logon process.

In a single domain network, a global catalog server is not required for the logon process because every domain controller contains the information that is needed to authenticate a user. Although a global catalog server is not queried during the logon process in a single domain network, a global catalog server is required for other types of directory service queries.

Note When the user is a member of the Domain Admins group, the user can log on to the network even when the global catalog server is not available.

Creating a Global Catalog Server

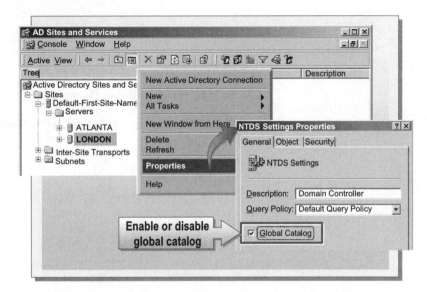

The first domain controller in a forest is automatically designated as a global catalog server. You can authorize any domain controller to be a global catalog server; however, one global catalog server is typically useful in each site.

To enable or disable a global catalog server, perform the following steps:

1. In Active Directory Sites and Services, in the console tree, expand the domain controller that will host or is hosting the global catalog.

2. Right-click **NTDS Settings**, and then click **Properties**.

3. Select or clear the **Global Catalog** check box.

◆ Strategies for Using Groups in Trees and Forests

- **Universal Groups and Replication**

- **Nesting Strategy Using Universal Groups**

- **Class Discussion: Using Groups in Trees and Forests**

Windows 2000 allows you to organize users and other domain objects into security groups to assign the same security permissions. Assigning security permissions to a group instead of to individual users ensures consistent security permissions across all members of a group. By using security groups to assign permissions, you can ensure that the discretionary access control lists (DACLs) on resources do not change often and are easy to manage and audit.

You can add or remove users from the appropriate security groups as needed. When you create a new user, you can add the user to an existing security group to completely define the user's permissions and access limits. You can add groups to other groups. Changing permissions for the group affects all users and groups within the group.

Universal Groups and Replication

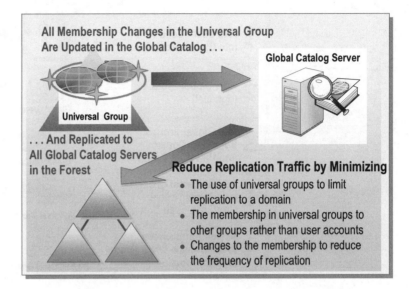

A list of universal group memberships is maintained in the global catalog. Global and domain local groups are listed in the global catalog, but their membership is not. Changes to the data stored in the global catalog are replicated to every global catalog in a forest. Whenever one member of a group with universal scope changes, the entire group membership must be replicated to all global catalogs in the domain tree or forest.

By minimizing the use of universal groups, you can limit the replication traffic to a single domain.

Consider minimizing the membership in universal groups to global groups, instead of to user accounts. This allows you to adjust the user accounts that are members of the universal group by adjusting the membership of the groups that are members of the universal group. Because adjusting the membership of the groups does not directly affect the membership of the universal group, no replication traffic is generated.

Reduce the amount of changes made to the membership of a universal group. This reduces the number of times the membership data is replicated to all the global catalog servers. If any change is made to the membership, the entire membership list is replicated.

Note An access token can contain up to 1,024 groups. Groups can have up to 5,000 members. The user's primary group membership, such as Domain Users, is not stored in the group membership list.

Nesting Strategy Using Universal Groups

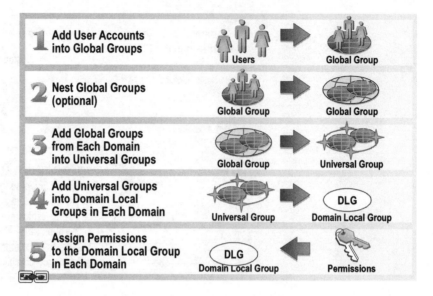

Use universal groups to consolidate groups that span multiple domains.

To consolidate groups that span multiple domains, perform the following steps:

1. In each domain, add user accounts for users with the same job function to global groups.

2. Nest global groups into a single global group to consolidate users. This step is optional, but is very useful if you need to manage large groups of users.

3. Nest the global group or multiple global groups from each domain into one universal group.

4. Add the universal groups to the domain local groups that are created for each resource.

5. Assign to the domain local groups the appropriate permissions for users in the group to gain access to resources.

By using this strategy, any membership changes in the global groups do not affect the membership in the universal groups.

The strategy described on this page uses A-G-G-U-DL-P and applies to the following circumstances:

- File and print permission.

- Active Directory Permissions in the domain name controller.

You can use A-G-U-P strategy for assigning permissions to:

- Configure naming conventions in Active Directory.

- Attribute permissions for attributes published to the global catalog.

Class Discussion: Using Groups in Trees and Forests

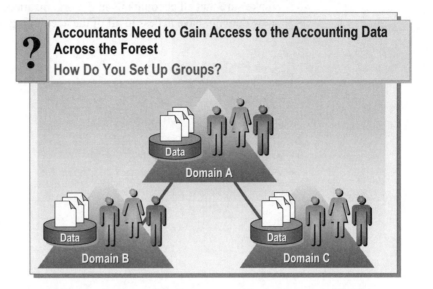

In this example, Contoso, Ltd. wants to react more quickly to market demands. It has been determined that the accounting data spanning multiple domains in the enterprise needs to be available to all of the accounting staff, which is also located in multiple domains. Contoso, Ltd. wants to create the entire group structure for the Accounting division, which includes the Accounts Payable and Accounts Receivable departments.

1. What would you do to ensure that the managers have the required access and that there is a minimum of administration?

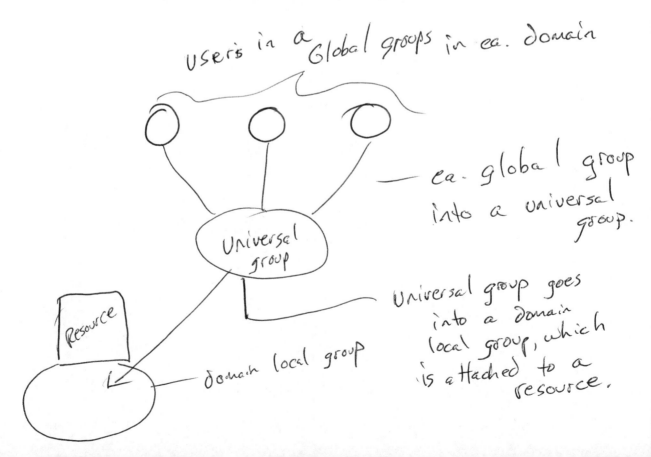

2. Contoso, Ltd. has experienced growth in their business and you must create a new domain. What changes would you make to your group structure to make sure that all accountants in the organization, including those in the new domain, have access to all of the accounting data?

Lab B: Using Groups in a Forest

Objectives

After completing this lab, you will be able to:

- Create and nest domain local, global, and universal security groups.

- Add global groups from other domains into universal groups.

- Switch the domain mode from mixed mode to native mode.

- Verify access to resources by using a group strategy that includes global, universal, and domain local groups.

- View the logged on user's access token, and observe the effects of group nesting.

Prerequisites

Before working on this lab, you must have:

- Knowledge about mixed and native domain modes.

- Knowledge and skills using domain local, global, and universal groups.

- Knowledge about replication latency, and how to manually initiate replication.

- Knowledge about access tokens and how group membership affects them.

Lab Setup

To complete this lab, you need to do the following:

- Run the batch file C:\Moc\Win2154a\Labfiles\Lrights.bat to set the log on locally user right for the users group.

Student Computer Information

During this lab, you will be asked for your student number, host name, and domain. Use the information from the following table to determine what to enter for these values. Your instructor will assign you a student number.

Student number (*n*)	Host name (*servername*)	Domain (*domain*)	FQDN
1	vancouver	namerica1	vancouver.namerica1.nwtraders.msft
2	denver	namerica1	denver.namerica1.nwtraders.msft
3	perth	spacific1	perth.spacific1.nwtraders.msft
4	brisbane	spacific1	brisbane.spacific1.nwtraders.msft
5	lisbon	europe1	lisbon.europe1.nwtraders.msft
6	bonn	europe1	bonn.europe1.nwtraders.msft
7	lima	samerica1	lima.samerica1.nwtraders.msft
8	santiago	samerica1	santiago.samerica1.nwtraders.msft
9	bangalore	asia1	bangalore.asia1.nwtraders.msft
10	singapore	asia1	singapore.asia1.nwtraders.msft
11	casablanca	africa1	casablanca.africa1.nwtraders.msft
12	tunis	africa1	tunis.africa1.nwtraders.msft
13	acapulco	namerica2	acapulco.namerica2.nwtraders.msft
14	miami	namerica2	miami.namerica2.nwtraders.msft
15	auckland	spacific2	auckland.spacific2.nwtraders.msft
16	suva	spacific2	suva.spacific2.nwtraders.msft
17	stockholm	europe2	stockholm.europe2.nwtraders.msft
18	moscow	europe2	moscow.europe2.nwtraders.msft
19	caracas	samerica2	caracas.samerica2.nwtraders.msft
20	montevideo	samerica2	montevideo.samerica2.nwtraders.msft
21	manila	asia2	manila.asia2.nwtraders.msft
22	tokyo	asia2	tokyo.asia2.nwtraders.msft
23	khartoum	africa2	khartoum.africa2.nwtraders.msft
24	nairobi	africa2	nairobi.africa2.nwtraders.msft

Estimated time to complete this lab: 30 minutes

Exercise 1
Implementing Groups Strategy

Scenario

Northwind Traders wants to react more quickly to market demands. It has been determined that the accounting data is located in various folders throughout the domains and needs to be available to the entire accounting staff which is located in multiple domains. Northwind Traders wants to create the entire group structure for the Accounting division, which includes the Accounts Payable and Accounts Receivable departments.

Goal

In this exercise, you will create three global groups: Accounting, Accounts Payable, and Accounts Receivable. You will add Accounts Payable and Accounts Receivable as members of Accounting. You will create the universal group, All Accounting, and then add the Accounting groups from all domains into this group. This will consolidate all of the accounting employees in the forest into the single universal group. You will create the domain local group, Local Data, and add the universal group as a member. You will assign Read permissions of the accounting data to the Local Data domain local group. To test the group structure, you will create a test user account and add this user account to the Accounts Payable group.

Tasks	Detailed Steps
Important: Perform task 1 only on the computer with the lower student number of the pair that is in the same child domain.	
1. Switch *domain*.nwtraders.msft (where *domain* is your assigned domain name) to native mode to allow extended group nesting and universal security groups.	a. Log on as Administrator in your domain with a password of **password**. b. Open Active Directory Users and Computers from the **Administrative Tools** menu. c. In the console tree, right-click *domain*.**nwtraders.msft** (where *domain* is your assigned domain name), and then click **Properties**. d. Click **Change Mode**, click **Yes** to close the confirmation dialog box, click **OK**, and then click **OK** again to close the message indicating that it may take 15 minutes or more for this information to replicate to all domain controllers.
Important: Perform task 2 only on the computer with the higher student number of the pair that is in the same child domain. Wait until task 1 is completed before starting task 2.	

Tasks	Detailed Steps
2. Manually initiate replication from your partner's domain controller to your domain controller to quickly replicate the domain mode change.	**a.** Open Active Directory Sites and Services from the **Administrative Tools** menu, expand **Sites**, expand **Default-First-Site-Name**, expand **Servers**, expand *servername* (where *servername* is the host name of your computer), and then click **NTDS Settings**.
	b. In the details pane, right-click the connection object that is from *partnerserver* (where *partnerserver* is the host name of your partner's computer), and then click **Replicate Now** to initiate the copying of changes from your partner's domain controller to your domain controller.
	c. Click **OK** to close the message indicating that replication has been initiated, and then close Active Directory Sites and Services.
	💻 *If an error message indicating the RPC service is unavailable, simply wait a moment and then repeat the Replicate Now operation.*
⚠️ **Important:** Perform the remaining tasks on both computers.	
3. Within *domain*.nwtraders.msft, create the following OU: *n*_Accounting (where *n* is your assigned student number).	**a.** Open, or switch to, Active Directory Users and Computers, and then in the console tree, expand *domain*.**nwtraders.msft**.
	b. Right-click *domain*.**nwtraders.msft**, point to **New**, and then click **Organizational Unit**.
	c. In the **New Object – Organizational Unit** dialog box, in the **Name** box, type *n*_**Accounting** (where *n* is your assigned student number), and then click **OK**.
4. Within the *n*_Accounting OU, create the following global security groups: *n*_Accounts Payable *n*_Accounts Receivable.	**a.** Right-click the *n*_**Accounting** OU, point to **New**, and then click **Group**.
	b. In the **New Object – Group** dialog box, in the **Group name** box, type *n*_**Accounts Payable**
	c. Ensure that **Group scope** is **Global** and **Group type** is **Security**, and then click **OK**.
	d. Repeat steps a and b, changing step b as required, to create the *n*_**Accounts Receivable** global security group.
5. Within the *n*_Accounting OU, create the *n*_Domain Accountants global group, and then add the department global groups, *n*_Accounts Payable and *n*_Accounts Receivable, as members.	**a.** Right-click the *n*_**Accounting** OU, point to **New**, and then click **Group**.
	b. In the **New Object – Group** dialog box, in the **Group name** box, type *n*_**Domain Accountants**
	c. Ensure that **Group scope** is **Global** and **Group type** is **Security**, and then click **OK**.
	d. Click the *n*_**Accounting** OU, in the details pane, right-click the *n*_**Domain Accountants** global group, and then click **Properties**.
	e. In the *n*_**Domain Accountants Properties** dialog box, click the **Members** tab, and then click **Add**.

Tasks	Detailed Steps
5. *(continued)*	f. In the **Select Users, Contacts, Computers, or Groups** dialog box, in the **Name** box, scroll to the bottom of the list and click *n*_**Accounts Payable**, click **Add**, click *n*_**Accounts Receivable**, click **Add**, and then click **OK**.
	g. In the *n*_**Domain Accountants Properties** dialog box, on the **Members** tab, ensure that *n*_Accounts Payable and *n*_Accounts Receivable are listed, and then click **OK**.
6. Within the *n*_Accounting OU, create the *n*_All Accountants universal security group and then add *n*_Domain Accountants as a member.	a. Right-click the *n*_**Accounting** OU, point to **New**, and then click **Group**.
	b. In the **New Object – Group** dialog box, in the **Group name** box, type *n*_**All Accountants**
	c. Under **Group scope**, click **Universal**, ensure **Group type** is set to **Security**, and then click **OK**.
	d. Click the *n*_**Accounting** OU, and in the details pane, right-click the *n*_**All Accountants** universal group, and then click **Properties**.
	e. In the *n*_**All Accountants Properties** dialog box, click the **Members** tab, and then click **Add**.
	f. In the **Select Users, Contacts, Computers, or Groups** dialog box, in the **Name** box, scroll to the bottom of the list and click *n*_**Domain Accountants**, click **Add**, and then click **OK**.
	Note: Typically a universal group contains members from multiple domains. Adding groups from other domains can be performed by selecting the domain in the Look in box, and selecting a group from the list.
	g. In the *n*_**All Accountants Properties** dialog box, on the **Members** tab, ensure that *n*_Domain Accountants is listed, and then click **OK**.
7. Create the *n*_Local Data domain local security group, and then add *n*_All Accountants as a member.	a. Right-click *n*_**Accounting**, point to **New**, and then click **Group**.
	b. In the **New Object – Group** dialog box, in the **Group name** box, type *n*_**Local Data**
	c. Ensure that **Group scope** is set to **Domain Local** and **Group type** is set to **Security**, and then click **OK**.
	d. Click the *n*_**Accounting** OU, in the details pane, right-click the *n*_**Local Data** domain local group, and then click **Properties**.
	e. In the *n*_**Local Data Properties** dialog box, on the **Members** tab, click **Add**.
	f. In the **Select Users, Contacts, Computers, or Groups** dialog box, in the **Name** box, scroll to the bottom of the list and click *n*_**All Accountants**, click **Add**, and then click **OK**.
	g. In the *n*_**Local Data Properties** dialog box, on the **Members** tab, ensure that *n*_All Accountants is listed as members of the *n*_**Local Data** domain local group, and then click **OK**.

Tasks	Detailed Steps
8. Create an empty text document C:\Report.txt and give Full Control permissions to only the *n*_Local Data domain local group.	a. In the **Run** box, type **C:** and then click **OK** to open the C:\ window. b. In the C:\ window, right-click an area of blank space, point to **New**, and then click **Text Document**. c. Rename the text document to **Report.txt**. d. Right-click **Report.txt**, and then click **Properties**. e. In the **Report Properties** dialog box, on the **Security** tab, and click **Add**. f. In the **Select Objects** dialog box, in the **Name** box, scroll to the bottom of the list and click *n*_**Local Data**, click **Add**, and then click **OK**. g. In the **Report Properties** dialog box, in the **Permissions** box, select the **Full Control Allow** check box. h. Clear the **Allow inheritable permissions from parent to propagate to this object** check box, and then click **Remove** to close the message asking whether to copy or remove the inherited permissions. i. Ensure that *n*_**Local Data** is the only entry and that it has Full Control permissions, and then click **OK**. j. Close the C:\ window.
9. Within the *n*_Accounting OU, create a user account with the following properties to test the group structure: • Full name: *n*_TestAccount • User logon name: *n*_TestAccount@nwtraders.msft • Add this user account to the *n*_Accounts Payable global group.	a. In Active Directory Users and Computers, click the *n*_**Accounting** OU. b. Right-click *n*_**Accounting**, point to **New**, and then click **User**. c. On the **New Object – User** page, in the **Full name** box, type *n*_**TestAccount** In the **User logon name** box, type *n*_**TestAccount** and then click **Next**. d. Click **Next**, and then click **Finish** to complete the wizard by using the defaults. e. Click the *n*_**Accounting** OU, and in the details pane, right-click the user *n*_**TestAccount**, and then click **Properties**. f. In the *n*_**TestAccount Properties** dialog box, on the **Member Of** tab, click **Add**. g. In the **Select Groups** dialog box, under the **Name** column, click *n*_**Accounts Payable**, click **Add**, and then click **OK**. h. In the *n*_**TestAccount Properties** dialog box, ensure the *n*_Accounts Payable global group is listed, and then click **OK**. i. Close Active Directory Users and Computers.
10. Log off from the domain controller, and then log on as *n*_TestAccount. Verify that you can gain access to the resource C:\Report.txt, and then delete the document.	a. Log off, and then log on as *n*_TestAccount in your domain without typing a password. b. Open the file, C:\Report.txt, and then type **Some Modifications** c. In this document, save and close the document. d. Delete the document C:\Report.txt.

Tasks	Detailed Steps
❓ Were you able to access the resource C:\Report.txt? *Yes.*	
11. Run C:\MOC\Win2154A\ Labfiles\Mytoken.exe to determine which groups *n*_TestAccount has in its access token.	**a.** Open a command prompt window. **b.** At the command prompt, type **C:\MOC\Win2154A\Labfiles\Mytoken.exe** and then press ENTER. 🖥️ *The access token information appears. First, the information displays the user information and other general information about the access token. Second, it displays the group information one security identifier (SID) entry per line. Finally, privileges of the user are displayed.*
❓ Does the access token for *n*_TestAccount contain the appropriate nested global groups, the universal group, and the domain local group following the membership path? Can you determine from the output of Mytoken which groups are nested? *Yes.* *?*	
11. *(continued)*	**c.** Close the command prompt window.
12. Log off and log on as Administrator, delete the *n*_Accounting OU, and then log off.	**a.** Log off, and then log on as Administrator in your domain with a password of **password**. **b.** Open Active Directory Users and Computers from the **Administrative Tools** menu, and then expand *domain*.**nwtraders.msft**. **c.** Right-click the *n*_**Accounting** OU, click **Delete**, click **Yes** to close the confirmation dialog box, and then click **Yes** to close the dialog box indicating that all of the objects contained in this object will also be deleted. **d.** Close Active Directory Users and Computers, close all open windows, and then log off.

Troubleshooting Creating and Managing Trees and Forests

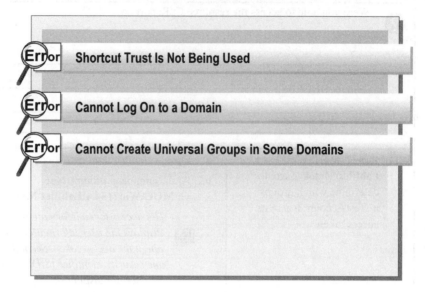

You may encounter problems when creating and managing trees and forests in Windows 2000. Here are some of the common problems that you may encounter and some strategies for resolving them:

- Shortcut trust is not being used. The possible cause could be that the trust was created in the wrong direction. Verify that the trusting and trusted domains are correct. If they are not, then delete both halves of the existing shortcut trust and recreate the shortcut trust in the other direction. Verify that the trust is functioning by using the **Verify** button in Active Directory Domains and Trusts or the Netdom.exe utility.

- Cannot log on to a domain. The possible cause could be that a global catalog server could not be located. The global catalog is needed to access universal group information and map user principal names to domains. Ensure that a global catalog server is running and available. Ensure that the network is functioning correctly from the authenticating domain controller and a global catalog server. Ensure that the DNS service is functioning. Also, verify the entries for global catalog servers in DNS to make sure that they are correct. The Global Catalog SRV record exists in the forest root domain only.

- Cannot create universal groups in some domains. The possible cause could be that the domains where you cannot create universal groups may not be in native mode. Verify the domain mode, and if required, change the domain mode from mixed mode to native mode, and then create universal groups.

Handwritten notes in margin:
- go into "domains & trusts" & check on it.
- Can't get to global catalog.

must be in Native mode.

Best Practices

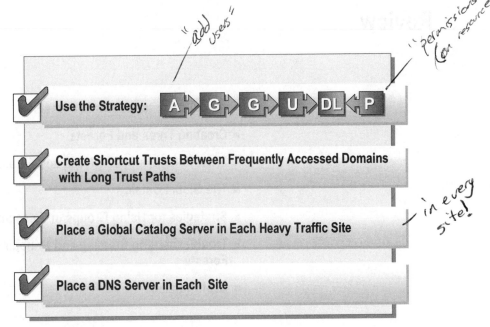

"add Users"

"permissions" (on resource)

Use the Strategy: A ▸ G ▸ G ▸ U ▸ DL ◂ P

Create Shortcut Trusts Between Frequently Accessed Domains with Long Trust Paths

Place a Global Catalog Server in Each Heavy Traffic Site

in every site!

Place a DNS Server in Each Site

Consider the following best practices for creating and managing Windows 2000 trees and forests:

- Use the A→G→G→U→DL←P group strategy. Keep membership in universal groups small, and use memberships that do not change often to reduce network replication traffic. This solution is recommended for file and print permissions and Active Directory permissions in the domain naming context. It is recommended that you use the A→G→U←P group strategy for Configuration naming context in Active Directory and attribute permissions for attributes published to the global catalog.

- Create shortcut trusts when many users from one domain frequently access resources in a domain with long trust paths. Shortcut trusts reduce the latency and network traffic needed to authenticate a user for the resource.

- Place a global catalog server in each site that has many users logging on to reduce network traffic and allow users to log on if the WAN link fails.

- Place a DNS server at each site. A DNS server must exist at each site so that local domain controllers and global catalog servers can be found if a WAN link fails. The DNS server must contain a replica of the forest root domain zone to enable users to find global catalog resource records.

Review

- Introduction to Trees and Forests
- Creating Trees and Forests
- Trust Relationships in Trees and Forests
- The Global Catalog
- Strategies for Using Groups in Trees and Forests
- Troubleshooting Creating and Managing Trees and Forests
- Best Practices

1. What role does the forest root domain play when new trees are created in the forest?

   You get an automatic 2-way trust between root & new tree.

2. Why would you create shortcut trusts?

   Speed up things; save bandwidth.
   by pass

3. What role does the global catalog play during the logon process?

   Universal group membership.
   (these exist on global catalog)

   * *(would find site fm. DNS server's SRV. records!)*

4. What is the benefit of small and relatively static membership for a universal group?

If put user in UG, and delete them, it sets off alot of replication.

5. The three domains in your network correspond to different branches of your organization in North America, Asia, and Europe respectively. Accountants in the three domains need to gain access to documents in all three domains. How do you set up the accountants' access to documents in all domains?

Users - Global - UG - DL - Resource.

Microsoft®
Training &
Certification

Module 11: Managing Active Directory Replication

Contents

Overview

- ■ **Introduction to Active Directory Replication**
- ■ **Replication Components and Processes**
- ■ **Replication Topology**
- ■ **Using Sites to Optimize Active Directory Replication**
- ■ **Implementing Sites to Manage Active Directory Replication**
- ■ **Monitoring Replication Traffic**
- ■ **Adjusting Replication**
- ■ **Troubleshooting Active Directory Replication**
- ■ **Best Practices**

Microsoft® Windows® 2000 Active Directory® directory service replication involves transferring and maintaining Active Directory data between domain controllers in a network. Active Directory uses a *multi-master replication model*. Multi-master means that there are multiple domain controllers, otherwise called masters, which have the authority to modify or control the same information. So the replication model must copy or replicate the data changed on one domain controller to another. The multi-master model must address the fact that changes can be made by more than one domain controller. By understanding how Active Directory replication is managed, you can control replication network traffic and ensure the consistency of Active Directory data across your network.

At the end of this module, you will be able to:

- ■ Identify the importance of replication in a Windows 2000 network.
- ■ Describe the components of replication and the replication process.
- ■ Describe how replication topology enables and optimizes replication throughout a network.
- ■ Describe how sites enable you to optimize Active Directory replication.
- ■ Use sites to manage Active Directory replication.
- ■ Monitor replication traffic.
- ■ Adjust the replication behavior to improve replication performance.
- ■ Troubleshoot common problems with Active Directory replication.
- ■ Apply best practices for managing Active Directory replication.

Introduction to Active Directory Replication

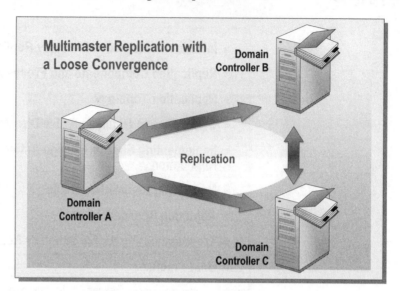

Replication is the process of updating information in Active Directory from one domain controller to the other domain controllers in a network. Replication synchronizes the copying of data on each domain controller. Synchronization ensures that all information in Active Directory is available to all domain controllers and client computers across the entire network.

When a user or administrator performs an action that initiates an update to Active Directory, an appropriate domain controller is automatically chosen to perform the update. This change is made transparently at one of the domain controllers.

Active Directory provides multi-master replication with loose convergence. Multi-master replication provides two advantages for Active Directory:

- With few exceptions, there is no single domain controller that, if unavailable, must be replaced before updates to Active Directory can resume.

- Domain controllers can be distributed across the network and located in multiple physical sites. Locating domain controllers at multiple physical sites enables fault tolerance.

Active Directory uses sites to identify well-connected computers within an organization to optimize network bandwidth. *Replication within sites* occurs between domain controllers in the same site, and is designed to work with fast, reliable connections. *Replication between sites* occurs between the domain controllers located on different sites, and is designed under the assumption that the network links between sites have limited bandwidth and availability.

◆ Replication Components and Processes

■ How Replication Works

■ Replication Latency

■ Resolving Replication Conflicts

■ Optimizing Replication

Replication of updates is initiated when one or more objects on a domain controller are added, modified, deleted, or moved. When one of these updates occurs, the replication process occurs between domain controllers through the interaction of components of replication. Replication in Active Directory propagates changes and tracks the changes among domain controllers. Each domain controller in a forest stores a copy of specific parts of the Active Directory structure. Although replication has the effect of synchronizing information in Active Directory for an entire forest of domain controllers, the actual process of replication occurs between only two domain controllers at a time. Because the domain controllers are both masters for the data and each has its own updatable copy, delay in replication across domain controllers may sometimes result in replication conflicts between domain controllers. Active Directory automatically resolves these conflicts.

Important   It is recommended that you secure the channels that Active Directory uses for replication. For more information on Securing Communication channels see Module 7, Securing Communication Channels, in Course 2150, *Designing a Secure Microsoft Windows 2000 Network*.

Or see the Technet article on Active Directory Replication over Firewalls at http://www.microsoft.com/technet/treeview/default.asp?url=/TechNet/ittasks/tasks/adrepfir.asp.

How Replication Works

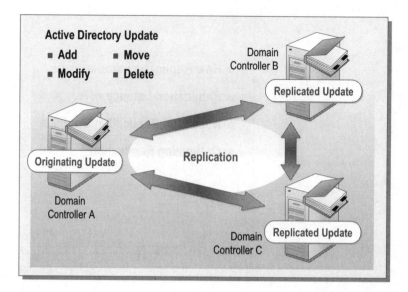

Replication of information in all domain controllers occurs because of changes made to Active Directory. Active Directory can be updated in one of the following ways:

- Adding an object to Active Directory, such as creating a new user account.

- Modifying an object's attribute values, such as changing the phone number for an existing user account.

- Modifying the name or parent of an object, and if necessary, moving the object into the new parent's domain. For example, you move the object from the sales domain to the service domain.

- Deleting an object from the directory, such as deleting user accounts for employees that no longer work for the organization.

Each update to Active Directory generates a request that can either commit or not commit to the database. A committed request is an *originating update*. After an originating update, the data must be replicated to all other replicas throughout the network.

An update performed at a domain controller that did not originate the update is called a *replicated update*. A replicated update is a committed update performed on one replica as a result of an originating or replicated update performed at another replica.

For example, when users change their passwords at Domain Controller A and Domain Controller A writes the password to the directory, this is considered an originating update. When Domain Controller A replicates the change to Domain Controller B and Domain Controller B updates its own copy of the directory, there is a replicated update at Domain Controller B.

Replication Latency

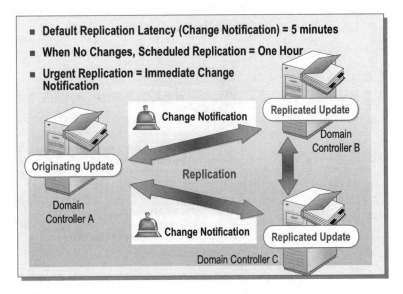

- Default Replication Latency (Change Notification) = 5 minutes
- When No Changes, Scheduled Replication = One Hour
- Urgent Replication = Immediate Change Notification

Change Notification

Replicated Update

Domain Controller B

Originating Update

Replication

Domain Controller A

Change Notification

Replicated Update

Domain Controller C

Replication latency is the time needed for a change made on one domain controller to be received by another domain controller. When an update is applied to a given replica, the replication engine is triggered.

Change Notification

Replication within a site occurs through a *change notification* process. When an update occurs on a domain controller, the replication engine waits for a configurable interval, which is five minutes by default, and then sends a notification message to the first replication partner, informing it of the change. Each additional direct partner is notified after a configurable delay, which is 30 seconds by default. Thus, the maximum propagation delay for a single change, assuming the default configuration and the three hop limit (*hops* means moving data from one domain controller to another domain controller), should be 15 minutes, which may include the 30 second configurable delay. When the replication partners receive the change notification, they copy the changes from the originating domain controller.

If no changes occur during a configurable period, which is one hour by default, a domain controller initiates replication with its replication partners to ensure that no changes from the originating domain controller were missed.

Urgent Replication

Attribute changes in Active Directory that are considered security-sensitive are immediately replicated by partners being immediately notified. This immediate notification is called *urgent replication*. Urgent replication sends notification immediately in response to urgent events instead of waiting the default period of five minutes. For example, urgent replication between domain controllers is prompted is when an administrator assigns an account lockout. *Account lockout* is a security feature that sets a limit on the number of failed authentication attempts that are allowed before the account is locked out from a further attempt to log on, and a time limit for how long the lockout is in effect.

Resolving Replication Conflicts

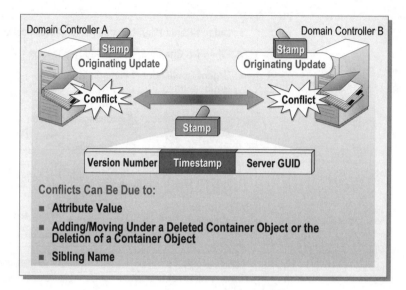

Conflicts Can Be Due to:

- **Attribute Value**
- **Adding/Moving Under a Deleted Container Object or the Deletion of a Container Object**
- **Sibling Name**

Because replication in Active Directory is based on a multi-master model, all computers that provide multi-master updates must handle potential conflicts that may arise when concurrent updates originating on two separate master replicas are inconsistent. When the updates are replicated, these concurrent updates cause a conflict. Active Directory both minimizes and resolves conflicts.

Types of Conflicts

There are three conflict types:

- Attribute value. This conflict occurs when an object's attribute is set concurrently to one value at one replica, and another value at a second replica.

- Add/move under a deleted container object or the deletion of a container object. This conflict occurs when one replica records the deletion of a container object, while another replica records the placement of any object that is subordinate to the deleted container object.

- Sibling name. This conflict occurs when one replica attempts to move an object into a container in which another replica has concurrently moved another object with the same relative distinguished name.

Minimizing Conflicts

To help minimize conflicts, domain controllers record and replicate changes to objects at the attribute level rather than the object level. Therefore, changes to two different attributes of an object, such as the user's password and postal code, do not cause a conflict even if they are changed at the same time.

Globally Unique Stamps

To aid in conflict resolution, Active Directory maintains a *stamp* that contains the version number, timestamp and server globally unique identifier (GUID) created during an originating update. This stamp travels with the update as it replicates.

The stamp has the following three components in order from most to least significant:

- *Version Number.* The version number starts at one and increases by one for each originating update. When performing an originating update, the version of the updated attribute is one number higher than the version of the attribute that is being overwritten.

- *Timestamp.* The timestamp is the originating time and date of the update according to the system clock of the domain controller that performed the originating update.

- *Server GUID.* The server GUID is the originating Directory System Agent (DSA) that identifies the domain controller that performed the originating update.

Resolving Conflicts

Conflicts are resolved by assigning a globally unique stamp to all originating update operations, such as add, modify, move, or delete. If there is a conflict, the ordering of stamps allows a consistent resolution in the following ways:

- Attribute value. The update operation that has the higher stamp value replaces the attribute value of the update operation with the lower stamp value.

- Add/move under a deleted container object or the deletion of a container object. After resolution occurs at all replicas, the container object is deleted, and the leaf object is made a child of the folder's special LostAndFound container. Stamps are not involved in this resolution.

- Sibling name. The object with the larger stamp keeps the relative distinguished name. The sibling object is assigned a unique relative distinguished name by the domain controller. The name assignment is the relative distinguished name + "CNF:" + a reserved character (the asterisk) + the object's GUID. This name assignment ensures that the generated name does not conflict with the name of any other object.

Optimizing Replication

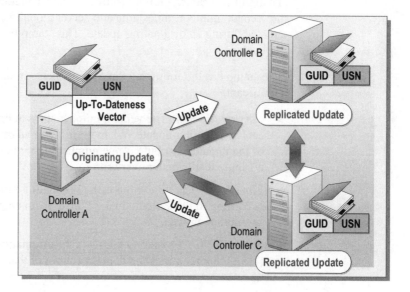

During replication, domain controllers use multiple paths for sending and receiving updates. Although using multiple paths provides both fault tolerance and improved performance, it can result in updates being replicated to the same domain controller more than once along different replication paths. To prevent these repeated replications, Active Directory replication uses *propagation dampening*. Propagation dampening is the process of reducing the amount of unnecessary data from traveling from one domain controller to another domain controller.

Update Sequence Numbers

To govern which data needs to be replicated, each domain controller maintains an array of vectors that makes replication more efficient. A *vector* is made up of a pair of data combining a GUID that is unique to each domain controller. This data is called an Invocation ID and a corresponding *update sequence number* (USN). When an object is updated, the domain controller assigns the changed USN. There is a USN on each attribute and a USN on each object. USNs are used to determine what needs to be updated in a replica. Each domain controller maintains its own distinct USN table for both originating and replicating updates.

Up-To-Dateness Vector

One of the vectors that is used by Active Directory replication is called the *up-to-dateness vector*. The up-to-dateness vector consists of database-USN pairs that are held by each domain controller, and represents the highest originating update received from each domain controller.

◆ Replication Topology

- Directory Partitions

- What Is Replication Topology?

- Global Catalog and Replication of Partitions

- Automatic Replication Topology Generation

- Using Connection Objects

The actual process of replication occurs between two domain controllers at a time, and in turn, replication synchronizes information in Active Directory for the entire forest of domain controllers. Creation of replication topology involves the determination of which domain controller replicates with other specific domain controllers. When this determination is made for all domain controllers, the result is the replication topology for replication.

Directory Partitions

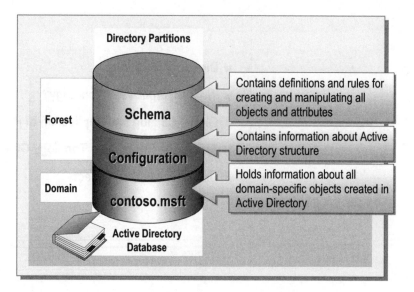

The Active Directory database is logically separated into directory partitions, a schema partition, a configuration partition, and domain partitions. The schema and configuration partitions are stored on all of the domain controllers of a forest. The domain partitions are stored on all of the domain controllers of the given domain. Because each partition is a unit of replication, each partition has its own replication topology. Replication is performed between directory partition replicas. Two domain controllers in the same forest often have several directory partitions in common. They always have at least two directory partitions in common, which are the schema and configuration partitions.

Schema Partition

The schema partition contains definitions of all objects and attributes that can be created in the directory, and the rules for creating and manipulating them. Schema information is replicated to all domain controllers in the forest, so regardless of the computer on which an object is created or modified, the schema partition must follow these rules. There can be only one schema per forest.

Configuration Partition

The configuration partition contains information about Active Directory structure, including what domains and sites exist, which domain controllers exist in each, and which services are available. Configuration information is replicated to all domain controllers in the forest. There can be only one configuration partition per forest.

Domain Partition

A domain partition holds information about all domain-specific objects created in Active Directory, including users, groups, computers, and organizational units. The domain partition is replicated to all domain controllers within its domain. There can be many domain partitions per forest.

What Is Replication Topology?

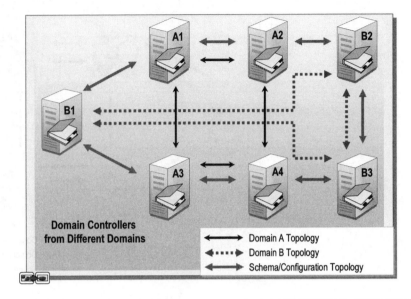

Replication topology is the pathway by which replication travels throughout a network. A single domain controller may have different replication partners for different partitions. Replication topology is created on the basis of information stored in Active Directory, and can differ depending on whether you are considering schema, configuration, or domain replication. The links connecting replication partners are called *connection objects*. A connection object represents a one-way replication path between two server objects and points to the replication source.

Domain controllers that are linked by a connection object are replication partners. Replication partners can be direct or transitive. *Direct replication partners* are domain controllers that are a direct source for Active Directory replication data. A domain controller also receives replication data through *transitive replication partners*. Transitive replication partners are domain controllers whose data is obtained indirectly through a direct replication partner. You can view transitive replication partners by using the Active Directory Replication Monitor utility.

Global Catalog and Replication of Partitions

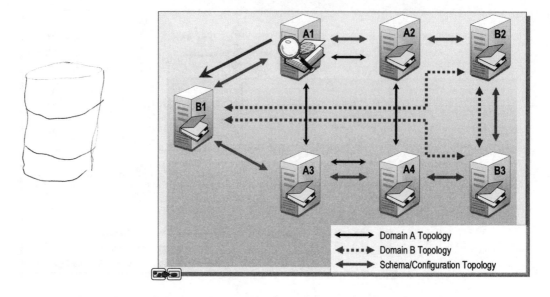

A *global catalog server* is a domain controller that stores the updatable directory partitions and a partial directory partition replica that contains a read-only copy of part of the information stored on that partition. Global catalog servers maintain a partial directory partition replica for all other domain partitions in the forest. These partial replicas contain a read-only subset, including all objects with only selected attributes, of the information in each domain partition. A full directory partition replica contains an updatable copy of all of the information stored on that partition.

When a new domain is added to the forest, the information about the new domain is stored in the configuration directory partition, which reaches the global catalog server and all domain controllers through replication of forest-wide information. Then each global catalog server becomes a partial replica of the new domain. When a new global catalog server is designated, this information is also stored in the configuration directory partition and replicated to all domain controllers in the forest, making all domain controllers aware of all of the global catalog servers in the forest.

Automatic Replication Topology Generation

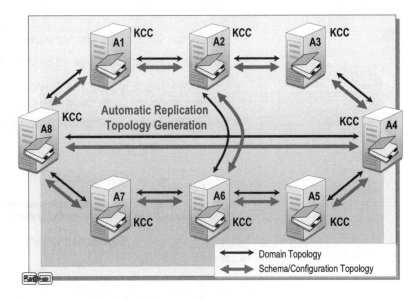

When you add domain controllers to a site, there must be a method for establishing a replication path between them. Active Directory accomplishes this with replication components and a process called the *Knowledge Consistency Checker* (KCC). The KCC is a built-in process that runs on each domain controller and generates the replication topology for the forest. The KCC runs at specified intervals and designates the replication routes between domain controllers on the basis of the most favorable connections that are available at the time.

To automatically generate a replication topology, KCC uses the information on sites and subnets that belong to sites (a *subnet* is the portion of a network that shares a common address component), the cost of sending data between these sites, and the network transports that can be used between the sites. The KCC calculates the best connections between each domain controller. Additionally, if replication within a site becomes impossible or has a single point of failure, the KCC automatically establishes new connection objects as necessary to resume Active Directory replication.

The default replication topology in a site is a bidirectional ring, which is made up of two complementary unidirectional connection objects. The ring is constructed with sufficient connections so that the average maximum number of hops that are required to replicate an originating update to all replicas of the given partition does not exceed three.

Using Connection Objects

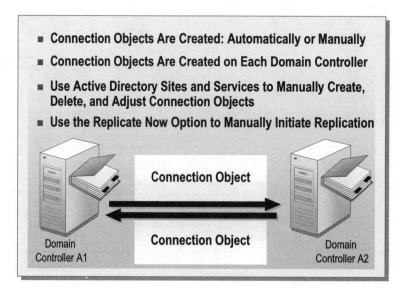

Connection objects are created in two ways, automatically and manually. Connection objects are created automatically by running KCC on the destination domain controller. An administrator can also create connection objects manually.

Connection objects are created on each domain controller and point to another domain controller for a source of information. KCC automatically creates connection objects in pairs, making two domain controllers sources for each other. Replication from any partition uses a single connection object. For example, to fully replicate directory information between domain controller A and domain controller B, two connection objects are required. One connection object enables replication *from* domain controller A *to* domain controller B, and this connection object exists in the NTDS Settings object of domain controller B. A second connection object enables replication *from* domain controller B *to* domain controller A, and this connection object exists in the NTDS Settings object of domain controller A.

You can manually create, delete, and adjust connection objects by using Active Directory Sites and Services. You can also manually initiate replication by right-clicking a connection object in Active Directory Sites and Services and then clicking **Replicate Now**.

To manually create, delete, or adjust connection objects, or to initiate replication between domain controllers, perform the following steps:

1. Open Active Directory Sites and Services, expand **Sites**, expand **Default-First-Site-Name**, and then expand **Servers**.

2. Select the domain controller to which you want a change replicated, and then click **NTDS Settings**.

3. Right-click the connection object for the replicating partner where the change was made, click **Replicate Now**, and then click **OK**.

Lab A: Tracking Active Directory Replication

Objectives

After completing this lab, you will be able to:

- Identify the results of the different types of replication conflicts: attribute, sibling name, and add/move under deleted container.

- Initiate replication of updates by using the connection objects for direct replication partners.

Prerequisites

Before working on this lab, you must have the knowledge and skills to create user accounts and organizational units.

Student Computer Information

During this lab, you will be asked for your student number, host name, and domain. Use this information from the following table to determine what to enter for these values. Your instructor will assign you a student number.

Student number (n)	Host name (servername)	Domain (domain)	FQDN
1	vancouver	namerica1	vancouver.namerica1.nwtraders.msft
2	denver	namerica1	denver.namerica1.nwtraders.msft
3	perth	spacific1	perth.spacific1.nwtraders.msft
4	brisbane	spacific1	brisbane.spacific1.nwtraders.msft
5	lisbon	europe1	lisbon.europe1.nwtraders.msft
6	bonn	europe1	bonn.europe1.nwtraders.msft
7	lima	samerica1	lima.samerica1.nwtraders.msft
8	santiago	samerica1	santiago.samerica1.nwtraders.msft
9	bangalore	asia1	bangalore.asia1.nwtraders.msft
10	singapore	asia1	singapore.asia1.nwtraders.msft
11	casablanca	africa1	casablanca.africa1.nwtraders.msft
12	tunis	africa1	tunis.africa1.nwtraders.msft
13	acapulco	namerica2	acapulco.namerica2.nwtraders.msft
14	miami	namerica2	miami.namerica2.nwtraders.msft
15	auckland	spacific2	auckland.spacific2.nwtraders.msft
16	suva	spacific2	suva.spacific2.nwtraders.msft
17	stockholm	europe2	stockholm.europe2.nwtraders.msft
18	moscow	europe2	moscow.europe2.nwtraders.msft
19	caracas	samerica2	caracas.samerica2.nwtraders.msft
20	montevideo	samerica2	montevideo.samerica2.nwtraders.msft
21	manila	asia2	manila.asia2.nwtraders.msft
22	tokyo	asia2	tokyo.asia2.nwtraders.msft
23	khartoum	africa2	khartoum.africa2.nwtraders.msft
24	nairobi	africa2	nairobi.africa2.nwtraders.msft

Important   The lab does not reflect the real-world environment. It is recommended that you always use complex passwords for any administrator accounts, and never create accounts without a password.

Important   Outside of the classroom environment, it is strongly advised that you use the most recent software updates that are necessary. Because this is a classroom environment, we may use software that does not include the latest updates.

Estimated time to complete this lab: 15 minutes

Exercise 1
Examining Data Conflicts with Multi-Master Replication

Scenario

Northwind Traders is developing an application that uses Active Directory to store its information. The program manager is concerned that replication conflicts may have caused the application data to become corrupt.

Goal

In this exercise, you will demonstrate how replication conflicts are handled by creating the three possible conflict types, which are attribute, add/move under deleted container, and sibling name.

Note: Students will work in pairs grouped by domain to complete this exercise.

Tasks	Detailed Steps
⚠ **Important:** Perform tasks 1 – 4 in this section on both *lowerserver* (where *lowerserver* is the computer with the lower student number of the pair) and *higherserver* (where *higherserver* is the computer with the higher student number of the pair) simultaneously. Read the steps for tasks 1– 4 before proceeding. Wait until both partners are ready before proceeding. Tasks 1 – 3 need to be completed by both partners within five minutes after starting, because the normal replication time is five minutes. Any update to Active Directory starts the five-minute replication timer.	
1. Within *domain*.nwtraders.msft (where *domain* is your assigned domain name), in the Users container, create a user account with the following properties: • Full name: Duplicate_User • User logon name: Duplicate_User@nwtraders.msft	a. Log on as Administrator in your domain with a password of **password**. b. Open Active Directory Users and Computers from the **Administrative Tools** menu. c. In the console tree, expand *domain*.**nwtraders.msft** (where *domain* is your assigned domain name), and then click **Users**. d. Right-click **Users**, point to **New**, and then click **User**. e. On the **New Object – User** page, in both the **Full name** and the **User logon name** boxes, type **Duplicate_User** and then click **Next**. **Note**: If possible, click **Finish** simultaneously with your partner on the next step. f. Click **Next**, and then click **Finish**.
2. Create the following organizational unit (OU): • *n*_ReplOU (where *n* is your assigned student number)	a. Right-click *domain*.**nwtraders.msft**, point to **New**, and then click **Organizational Unit**. b. In the **New Object – Organizational Unit** dialog box, in the **Name** box, type *n*_**ReplOU** (where *n* is your assigned student number) and then click **OK**.
3. In the *n*_ReplOU OU, create a user account with the following properties: • Full name: *n*_ReplUser • User logon name: *n*_ReplUser@nwtraders.msft	a. Right-click *n*_**ReplOU**, point to **New**, and then click **User**. b. On the **New Object – User** page, in both the **Full name** and the **User logon name** boxes, type *n*_**ReplUser** and then click **Next**. c. Click **Next**, and then click **Finish**.

Tasks	Detailed Steps
4. Verify that the replication occurred by refreshing the display in Active Directory Users and Computers.	a. Click *domain*.**nwtraders.msft**, and then press F5 to refresh the display. Continue to refresh the display periodically, until the *n*_**ReplOU** and *partnern*_**ReplOU** (where *partnern* is the student number of your partner's computer) organizational units are displayed, which may take five minutes to occur. b. Click **Users** after the two organizational units are displayed.

? What happened to the two Duplicate_User user accounts? Can you tell there was a replication conflict?

Attached a GUID # to one. - this tells that replication happened.

⚠ **Important:** Perform tasks 5 – 6 on *lowerserver* only. Wait until your partner is ready to perform tasks 7 – 9 immediately after you finish task 6. Tasks 5 – 9 need to be completed within five minutes after starting. This is a result of the normal replication time of five minutes.

5. Change the following properties of Duplicate_User: • Telephone number: 555-1212 • Office: 5/1093	a. Right-click **Duplicate_User** and then click **Properties**. b. On the **General** tab, in the **Telephone** number box, type **555-1212** c. In the **Office** box, type **5/1093** and then click **OK**.
6. Delete the *n*_ReplOU OU.	▪ Click *n*_**ReplOU**, press DELETE, click **Yes** to close the dialog box confirming the object deletion, and then click **Yes** again to close the dialog box confirming the deletion of all of the objects it contains.

⚠ **Important:** Perform tasks 7 – 9 on *higherserver* immediately after the completion of task 6.

7. Change the following properties of Duplicate_User: • Telephone number: 123-4567 • Description: Replication Test	a. Right-click **Duplicate_User**, and then click **Properties**. b. On the **General** tab, in the **Telephone** number box, type **123-4567** in the **Description** box, type **Replication Test** and then click **OK**.
8. Move *n*_ReplUser from *n*_ReplOU to *partnern*_ReplOU (where *partnern* is the student number of your partner's computer).	a. Click *n*_**ReplOU**, right-click *n*_**ReplUser**, and then click **Move**. b. In the **Move** dialog box, click *partnern*_**ReplOU**, and then click **OK**.

Tasks	Detailed Steps
9. Delete the *n_ReplOU* OU.	▪ Click *n_***ReplOU**, press DELETE, and then click **Yes** to close the dialog box confirming the object deletion.

⚠ **Important:** Perform task 10 on both *lowerserver* and *higherserver* upon the completion of task 9.

10. Verify that replication occurred by refreshing the display in Active Directory Users and Computers.	a. Click domain.**nwtraders.msft**, and then press F5 to refresh the display. Continue to refresh the display periodically, until both *n_***ReplOU** and *partnern_***ReplOU** are no longer displayed, which may take five minutes to occur. b. Click **Users** after the two OUs are not displayed.

❓ How did replication resolve the values of Telephone number, Office, and Description for Duplicate_User?

Accepted last telephone # entered; kept office & description same (no conflict w/ these)

❓ What happened to the deleted organizational unit and the moved user account under it?

Placed in "Lost & Found".

Exercise 2
Manually Initiating Replication

Scenario

The corporate testing group for Northwind Traders performs many verification tests in Active Directory. Often an update needs to replicate to another domain controller before testing continues. Manually initiating replication reduces the overall testing time.

Goal

In this exercise, you will initiate replication without having to wait for the normal replication period.

Note: Students will work in pairs grouped by domain to complete this exercise.

Tasks	Detailed Steps
⚠ **Important:** Perform task 1 on *lowerserver*. Task 2 can be performed on *higherserver* simultaneously.	
1. In the LostAndFound container, delete *n*_ReplUser.	a. In Active Directory Users and Computers, click **View**, and then, if necessary, click **Advanced Features** to display advanced features. b. Click **LostAndFound**, in the details pane, click *n*_**ReplUser**, press DELETE, and then click **Yes** to close the dialog box confirming the object deletion.
⚠ **Important:** Perform task 2 on *higherserver*. Task 1 does not need to be completed before starting task 2.	
2. Delete Duplicate_User, and Duplicate_User□CNF:*object GUID*.	a. In Active Directory Users and Computers, click **Users**, in the details pane, click **Duplicate_User**, hold down the CTRL key and then click **Duplicate_User□CNF:***objectGUID*. b. Ensuring that only the two duplicate users are selected, press DELETE, and then click **Yes** to close the dialog box confirming the two object deletions.
⚠ **Important:** Perform task 3 on both *lowerserver* and *higherserver* upon the completion of both task 1 and task 2.	

force replication

Tasks	Detailed Steps
3. Manually initiate replication from your partner's domain controller to yours.	a. Open Active Directory Sites and Services from the **Administrative Tools** menu, expand **Sites**, expand **Default**-First-Site-Name, expand **Servers**, expand *servername* (where *servername* is the host name of your computer), and then click **NTDS Settings**.
	b. In the details pane, right-click the connection object that is from *partnerserver* (where *partnerserver* is the host name of your partner's computer), and then click **Replicate Now** to initiate the copying of changes from *partnerserver* to *servername*.
	c. Click **OK** to close the message indicating that replication has been initiated, and then close Active Directory Sites and Services.
	If an error message indicating the RPC service is unavailable occurs, simply wait a moment and then repeat the Replicate Now operation.
4. Verify that replication occurred by refreshing the display in Active Directory Users and Computers and then log off.	a. In Active Directory Users and Computers, click *domain*.**nwtraders.msft**, and then press F5 to refresh the display.
	b. Click **Users** to verify the two duplicate users are no longer displayed, and then close Active Directory Users and Computers.
	c. Log off.

Was replication performed immediately upon completion of task 3? What difference would it have made if only your partner performed task 3 and you did not?

Yes.

None.

◆ Using Sites to Optimize Active Directory Replication

- ■ **What Are Sites?**
- ■ **Replication Within Sites**
- ■ **Replication Between Sites**
- ■ **Replication Protocols**

Replication ensures that all information in Active Directory is current on all domain controllers and client computers across your entire network. Many networks consist of a number of smaller networks, and the network links between these networks may operate at varying speeds. Sites in Active Directory enable you to control replication traffic and other types of traffic related to Active Directory across these various network links.

What Are Sites?

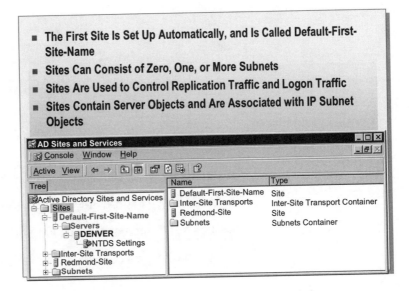

Sites help to define the physical structure of a network. A site is defined by a set of Transmission Control Protocol/Internet Protocol (TCP/IP) subnet address ranges. The first site is set up automatically when you install Windows 2000 Advanced Server on the first domain controller in a forest. The resulting first site is called *Default-First-Site-Name*. This site can be renamed.

A site can consist of no subnets or of one or more subnets. For example, in a network with three subnets in Redmond and two in Paris, the administrator can create a site in Redmond, a site in Paris, and then add the subnets to the respective sites.

A site may contain domain controllers from any domain in the forest. Sites consist of server objects. The server objects are created for a computer when it is promoted to a domain controller, and contain connection objects that enable replication.

You can use sites to control:

- *Replication traffic.* When a change occurs in Active Directory, sites can be used to control how and when the change is replicated to domain controllers in another site.

- *Logon traffic.* When a user logs on, Windows 2000 attempts to find a domain controller in the same site as the workstation.

- *Requests to Global Catalog.* When a request to a Global Catalog is required, a user computer or a Domain Controller finds a Global Catalog in the local site.

Replication Within Sites

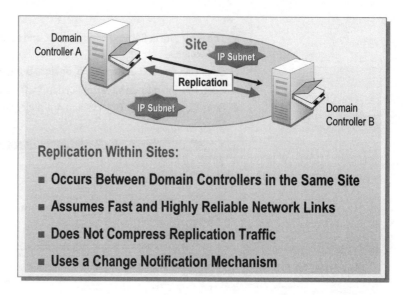

Replication within sites occurs between domain controllers in the same site. Because a site assumes fast, highly reliable network links, replication traffic within a site is *uncompressed*. Uncompressed replication traffic helps reduce the processing load on the domain controllers. However, this uncompressed traffic can increase the network bandwidth that is required for replication messages. The network connection is assumed to be both reliable and have available bandwidth. Replication by default occurs within a site through a change notification process.

Replication Between Sites

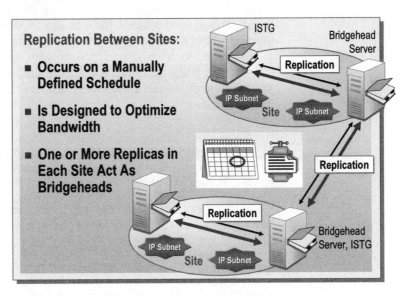

Replication between sites is designed under the assumption that the network links between sites have limited available bandwidth and may not be reliable.

Replication Scheduling

Replication between sites happens automatically after you define configurable values, such as a schedule and a replication interval. You can schedule replication for inexpensive or off-peak hours. By default, changes are replicated between sites according to a manually defined schedule and not according to when changes occur. Configurable values, such as a schedule or an interval, define when and how often replication occurs between sites. The schedule determines at which times replication is allowed to occur, and the interval specifies how often domain controllers check for changes during the time that replication is allowed to occur.

Compressed Traffic

Replication traffic between sites is designed to optimize bandwidth by compressing all replication traffic between sites. Replication traffic is compressed to 10 to 15 percent of its original size before it is transmitted. Although compression optimizes network bandwidth, it imposes an additional processing load on domain controllers.

Bridgehead Servers

When replication occurs between sites, one or more replicas in each site act as bridgeheads to another site in the topology. A server is automatically designated as a bridgehead server by using the Intersite Topology Generator (ISTG) in each site to perform replication between sites. After replication between sites is completed by using the bridgehead server, the bridgehead servers communicate all updates to all domain controllers within their sites by using the normal replication process.

If you want to restrict the domain controllers in which the ISTG can create connections between sites, select one or more domain controllers in the site that you want the ISTG to always consider as *preferred bridgehead servers*. These servers are used to replicate the changes from the site.

If the bridgehead server becomes unavailable, another bridgehead server is automatically chosen from the list of preferred bridgehead servers.

To verify which domain controller has the role of ISTG, perform the following steps:

1. In Active Directory Sites and Services, select a site in the Sites folder.

2. In the details pane, right-click the **NTDS Site Settings** object, and then click **Properties**.

Replication Protocols

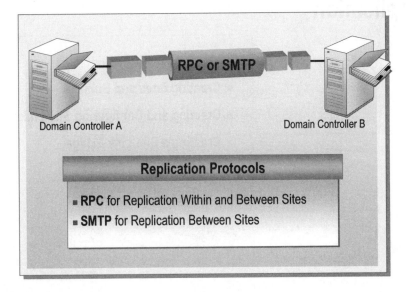

To ensure that computers in a network are able to communicate for sending and receiving updates during replication, they must share a common language known as a *replication protocol*. Within a single site, there is only one protocol used for replication. In a multiple-site structure, you must select one of the following replication protocols for replication between sites.

- *Remote procedure call (RPC)*. Active Directory replication uses RPC over IP for replication within a site. RPC is an industry standard protocol for client/server communications that is compatible with most types of networks. For replication within a site, RPC provides uniform, high-speed connectivity. When you configure replication between sites, you must choose between replication protocols, RPC over IP, or the Simple Mail Transfer Protocol (SMTP). However, the domain controllers must be in different domains and in different sites for you to use SMTP. In most cases, choose RPC over IP for replication between sites.

- *Simple mail transfer protocol (SMTP)*. SMTP supports schema configuration and global catalog replication but cannot be used to replicate the domain partition to domain controllers of the same domain. This is because some domain operations, for example Group Policy, require the support of the File Replication service (FRS), which does not yet support an asynchronous transport for replication. You need to use RPC for replicating the domain partition. A feature of SMTP replication is that a connection does not need to be established directly between the two replicating domain controllers. Instead, the information can be stored and forwarded to many mail servers until it reaches the destination domain controller at a later time.

Note Active Directory Sites and Services labels the protocol for connections within a site as RPC and the protocol for connections between sites as IP. Both labels, however, mean that the connection uses RPC over IP.

◆ Implementing Sites to Manage Active Directory Replication

- **Creating Sites and Subnets**
- **Creating and Configuring Site Links**
- **Creating a Site Link Bridge**

You can use subnets, site links, and site link bridges to help control the replication topology when configuring replication between sites. An efficient, reliable replication topology depends on the configuration of site links and site link bridges. You use Active Directory Sites and Services to create sites, subnets, site links, and site link bridges.

Creating Sites and Subnets

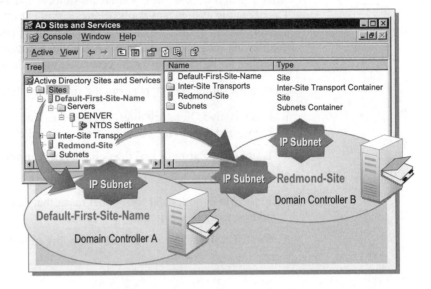

Computers on TCP/IP networks are assigned to sites based on the TCP/IP to which they have been configured. Because subnets group well-connected computers together, subnets are useful for identifying sites. To use sites for managing replication within or between sites, you create additional sites and subnets.

Creating a Site

To create a site, you must provide a name for the new site and associate the site with a site link. You must log on as a member of the Enterprise Admins group to create sites, or use the Secondary Logon service to start Active Directory Sites and Services in the security context of a member of the Enterprise Admins group.

To create a site, perform the following steps:

1. Open Active Directory Sites and Services from the **Administrative Tools** menu, in the console tree, right-click **Sites**, and then click **New Site**.

2. In the **Name** box, type the name of the new site.

3. Click a site link object, and then click **OK**.

Note   Select the default site link if it is the only link available.

Creating a Subnet Object

After you define your sites, you create subnets and associate them with sites. The operating system and applications use subnet information to reduce network traffic by finding the closest server to the client. Subnet information is used during the process of domain controller location to find a domain controller in the same site as the computer that is logging on.

To create a subnet object, perform the following steps:

1. Open Active Directory Sites and Services from the **Administrative Tools** menu, and then in the console tree, double-click **Sites**.

2. Right-click **Subnets**, and then click **New Subnet**.

3. In the **Address** box, enter the subnet address.

4. In the **Mask** box, enter the subnet mask that describes the range of addresses included in this site's subnet.

5. Choose a site with which to associate this subnet, and then click **OK**.

Creating and Configuring Site Links

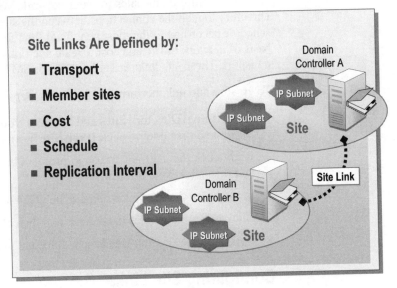

A *site link* is an object used to manage replication between sites. You can create site links that allow domain controllers from one site to replicate with the other site. Site links are defined by the following components:

- *Transport*. The networking technology that is used to transfer the data that is replicated.

- *Member sites*. Two or more sites that will be connected through the site link.

- *Cost*. Site link cost is a number that represents the priority an organization assigns to replication traffic between the sites. Cost reflects the speed and reliability of the underlying network. If there are multiple site links between two sites, replication will use the link with the lowest cost that is available. The cost ranges between one and 32767.

- *Schedule*. The times when replication will occur. Schedule defines a time range when replication is allowed over the link. The schedule range is one hour for a seven-day week.

- *Replication interval*. Replication interval defines how often replication occurs in a given schedule window. Replication intervals can range from 15 to 10,080 minutes.

Creating Site Links

After you configure the sites for your network, you create site links in Active Directory to map the connections between the sites. You can define the schedule according to the most beneficial time for replication to occur on the basis of network traffic and cost. Create site links that use a specific inter-site transport. These site links are either RPC or SMTP.

To create a site link, perform the following steps:

1. Open Active Directory Sites and Services from the **Administrative Tools** menu, and then double-click **Inter-Site Transport**.

2. Right-click the inter-site transport protocol that you want the site link to use, and then click **New Site Link**.

3. In the **Name** box, type the name to be given to the link.

4. Click two or more sites to connect, and then click **Add**.

5. Configure the site link's cost, schedule, and replication interval.

Configuring Site Links

Cost, replication interval, and schedule are properties of the site link. When you create the site link, these properties are set to the default values. The default value of cost is 100 and of replication interval is three hours, and the schedule available for replication is all periods of time.

To configure site links, perform the following steps:

1. Open Active Directory Sites and Services from the **Administrative Tools** menu, expand **Sites**, and then double-click **Inter-Site Transports**.

2. Click **IP** or **SMTP**, depending on which protocol the site link is configured to use.

3. Right-click the site link, and then click **Properties**.

4. On the **General** tab of the **Properties** dialog box, change the values for cost, replication interval, and schedule as needed, and then click **OK**.

Creating a Site Link Bridge

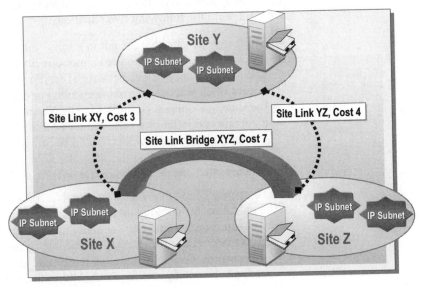

<table>
<tr><td>Multiple site link bridges work independently of one another.</td></tr>
</table>

A *site link bridge* consists of two or more site links. Site link bridges are used to connect two or more sites together and model the routing behavior of a network. The site link bridge enables transitivity between site links. By default, all site links are transitive; you do not need to create any site link bridges. You can turn off the Bridge all site links feature and manually create site link bridges that you require.

How to Create a Site Link Bridge

A site link bridge object for a specific transport between sites is created by specifying two or more site links. For example:

- Site link XY connects sites X and Y through an IP with a cost of 3.

- Site link YZ connects sites Y and Z through an IP with a cost of 4.

- Site link bridge XYZ connects XY and YZ.

The site link bridge XYZ implies that an IP message can be sent from site X to site Z directly with a cost of 3 plus 4, or 7. TCP/IP routing dictates the actual path that the message travels. Each site link in a bridge needs to have a site in common with another site link in the bridge. If not, the bridge cannot compute the cost from sites in the link to the sites in other links of the bridge.

To create a site link bridge, perform the following steps:

1. Open Active Directory Sites and Services from the **Administrative Tools** menu, expand **Sites**, and then in the console tree, right-click the inter-site transport folder for which you want to create a new site link bridge.

2. Right-click either **IP** or **SMTP**, depending on the protocol for which you want to create a site link bridge, and then click **New Site Link Bridge**.

3. In the **Name** box, type a name for the site link bridge.

4. Click two or more site links to be bridged, click **Add**, and then click **OK**.

When to Create a Site Link Bridge

You usually turn off the Bridge all site links feature and manually define site link bridges in the following two situations:

- There may be sites that are not in a fully-routed IP network. This means that domain controllers in one site cannot directly communicate with domain controllers in another site because of an IP routing constraint. This situation occurs when you use internal firewalls. For example, in the illustration on the slide, if a domain controller in site X cannot communicate directly with a domain controller in site Z, you turn off the Bridge all site links feature. If you have more site links that should be bridged, add more site link bridges to all site links excluding the site links XY and YZ, which contain the IP networks that cannot communicate directly with each other.

- There may be too many sites for the KCC on the ISTG domain controllers to calculate the topology on a schedule. If there are many topology connection paths, which are actually not required because better connection paths exist, reduce the number of possible connection paths to improve performance. To do this, turn off the Bridge all site links feature. Then add more site link bridges if required. Alternatively, you can turn off the KCC for topology generation between sites. However, turning off the KCC will not recalculate the topology if a site becomes unavailable and you will need to manually reconfigure the topology.

Lab B: Using Sites to Manage Active Directory Replication

Objectives

After completing this lab, you will be able to:

- Create a site, subnet, site link, and site link bridge.
- Configure the properties of a site link.

Prerequisites

Before working on this lab, you must have an understanding of TCP/IP subnets.

Student Computer Information

During this lab, you will be asked for your student number, host name, and IP address. Use this information from the following table to determine what to enter for these values. Your instructor will assign you a student number and the classroom network ID x.

Student number (n)	Host name (*servername*)	Domain (*domain*)	FQDN
1	vancouver	namerica1	vancouver.namerica1.nwtraders.msft
2	denver	namerica1	denver.namerica1.nwtraders.msft
3	perth	spacific1	perth.spacific1.nwtraders.msft
4	brisbane	spacific1	brisbane.spacific1.nwtraders.msft
5	lisbon	europe1	lisbon.europe1.nwtraders.msft
6	bonn	europe1	bonn.europe1.nwtraders.msft
7	lima	samerica1	lima.samerica1.nwtraders.msft
8	santiago	samerica1	santiago.samerica1.nwtraders.msft
9	bangalore	asia1	bangalore.asia1.nwtraders.msft
10	singapore	asia1	singapore.asia1.nwtraders.msft
11	casablanca	africa1	casablanca.africa1.nwtraders.msft
12	tunis	africa1	tunis.africa1.nwtraders.msft
13	acapulco	namerica2	acapulco.namerica2.nwtraders.msft
14	miami	namerica2	miami.namerica2.nwtraders.msft
15	auckland	spacific2	auckland.spacific2.nwtraders.msft
16	suva	spacific2	suva.spacific2.nwtraders.msft
17	stockholm	europe2	stockholm.europe2.nwtraders.msft
18	moscow	europe2	moscow.europe2.nwtraders.msft
19	caracas	samerica2	caracas.samerica2.nwtraders.msft
20	montevideo	samerica2	montevideo.samerica2.nwtraders.msft
21	manila	asia2	manila.asia2.nwtraders.msft
22	tokyo	asia2	tokyo.asia2.nwtraders.msft
23	khartoum	africa2	khartoum.africa2.nwtraders.msft
24	nairobi	africa2	nairobi.africa2.nwtraders.msft

Estimated time to complete this lab: 30 minutes

Exercise 1
Creating IP Subnet and Site Objects

Scenario

Northwind Traders is geographically distributed with many wide area network (WAN) links that connect these regions. Network bandwidth on these WAN links is scarce. Active Directory must be aware of which connections are local area network (LAN) and which are WAN to optimize replication and minimize the use of the network across WAN links. You will create IP subnet and site objects and associate subnets to sites.

Goal

In this exercise, you will create IP subnet and site objects in Active Directory. You will associate subnets with sites. This association informs Active Directory which IP subnets have high network bandwidth such as a LAN.

Note: Because of the limitations of the classroom setup, you will be creating subnet objects that do not match the classroom network. Therefore, the normal configuration step of moving the server objects into the new sites will not be performed in this lab.

Tasks	Detailed Steps
1. Create a new site with the name *servername*Site (where *servername* is the host name of your computer) and link it to DEFAULTSITELINK.	a. Log on as Administrator in your domain with a password of **password**. b. Click **Start**, point to **Programs**, point to **Administrative Tools**, hold down the SHIFT key and right-click **Active Directory Sites and Services**, and then click **Run as**. c. In the **Run As Other User** dialog box, type **Administrator** in the **User name** box, type **password** in the **Password** box, type **nwtraders.msft** in the **Domain** box, and then click **OK**. d. In the AD Sites and Services window, in the console tree, verify that **Active Directory Sites and Services [london.nwtraders.msft]** appears. e. In the console tree, right-click **Sites**, and then click **New Site**. f. In the **New Object – Site** dialog box, in the **Name** box, type *servername*Site (where *servername* is the host name of your computer). g. Under **Link Name**, click **DEFAULTIPSITELINK**, click **OK**, and then click **OK** again to close the message indicating that further configuration may need to be performed.
2. Create a new subnet object with the network ID of **10.10.*n*.0** (where *n* is your assigned student number), and a subnet mask of **255.255.255.0**. Associate this subnet object with your site *servername*Site.	a. In Active Directory Sites and Services, expand **Sites**, right-click **Subnets**, and then click **New Subnet**. b. In the **New Object – Subnet** dialog box, in the **Address** box, type **10.10.*n*.0** (where *n* is your assigned student number). c. In the **Mask** box, type **255.255.255.0** d. Under **Site Name**, click *servername*Site, and then click **OK**. e. Leave Active Directory Sites and Services open.

Exercise 2
Creating Site Links and Site Link Bridges

Scenario

The physical network of Northwind Traders has been used to create the Active Directory IP subnet and site objects. The sites on the corporate network backbone have already been configured. The site links and site link bridges need to be established to connect the remote sites to the corporate backbone sites. The Bridge all site links feature will be turned off by the corporate administrators after the site links and site link bridges for all remote sites have been configured and verified. You must create and configure the site link and site link bridge from your remote site to connect to the corporate backbone.

Goal

In this exercise, you will create IP site links between your site and Default-First-Site-Name. You will configure the replication time window and frequency and the cost of the links. You will create a site link bridge that connects your site link to DEFAULTIPSITELINK.

The DEFAULTIPSITELINK will represent the site link used to connect all of the corporate backbone sites. The Default-First-Site-Name will represent the main corporate site. The reason for creating site link bridges is to reduce processing requirements on the inter-site topology generator servers. Another reason is that a more deterministic replication path will result because all of the remote sites will only use the corporate backbone as the central hub for replication.

Tasks	Detailed Steps
1. Create a new IP site link called *servername*Site-CorpHQ and add the sites Default-First-Site-Name and *servername*Site.	a. In Active Directory Sites and Services, expand **Sites**, expand **Inter-Site Transports**, and then click **IP**. b. Right-click **IP**, and then click **New Site Link**. c. In the **New Object – Site Link** dialog box, in the **Name** box, type *servername***Site-CorpHQ** d. In the **Sites not in this site link** box, click **Default-First-Site-Name**, click **Add**, click *servername***Site**, click **Add**, and then click **OK**.
2. Configure the *servername*Site-CorpHQ site link with a cost of 500, a frequency of 90 minutes, and a daily schedule of 11 P.M. to 6 A.M.	a. Click **IP**, and in the details pane, right-click *servername***Site-CorpHQ**, and then click **Properties**. b. In the *servername***Site-CorpHQ Properties** dialog box, in the **Cost** box, type **500** c. In the **Replicate every minutes** box, type **90** d. Click **Change Schedule**. e. In the **Schedule for** *servername***Site-CorpHQ** dialog box, select **Sunday** through **Saturday**, **6 AM to 10 PM**, click **Replication not Available**, click **OK**, and then click **OK** again to close the *servername***Site-CorpHQ Properties** dialog box.

Tasks	Detailed Steps
3. Create a new site link bridge called *servername*Site-CorpHQ-Bridge between *servername*Site-CorpHQ and DEFAULTIPSITELINK.	a. Right-click **IP**, and then click **New Site Link Bridge**. b. In the **New Object – Site Link Bridge** dialog box, in the **Name** box, type *servername***Site-CorpHQ-Bridge** c. Ensure that *servername***Site-CorpHQ**, and **DEFAULTIPSITELINK** are listed in the Site links in this site link bridge box. If there are no site links listed, in the Site links not in this site link bridge box, click *servername***Site-CorpHQ**, click **Add**, click **DEFAULTIPSITELINK**, click **Add**, and then click **OK**.
4. Remove *servername*Site from DEFAULTIPSITELINK, and then log off.	a. Click **IP**, and in the details pane, right-click **DEFAULTIPSITELINK**, and then click **Properties**. b. In the **DEFAULTIPSITELINK Properties** dialog box, in the **Sites in this Site link** box, click *servername***Site**, click **Remove**, and then click **OK**. c. Close Active Directory Sites and Services, close all open windows, and then log off.

◆ Monitoring Replication Traffic

- **What Is Replication Monitor?**
- **Using Replication Monitor to Monitor Replication Traffic**
- **Using Repadmin to Monitor Replication Traffic**

You can adjust your replication topology based on replication traffic patterns. To help adjust replication traffic patterns, you need to be able to view the replication traffic throughout your network. You can view replication traffic by using Replication Monitor and the **repadmin** command-line utility.

What Is Replication Monitor?

> ## With Replication Monitor You Can:
>
> - Display the Replicating Partner
> - Display Each USN Value, the Number of Failed Attempts, Reason, and Flags
> - Poll the Server at an Administrator-Defined Interval
> - Monitor the Count of Failed Replication Attempts
> - Show Which Objects Have Not Yet Replicated
> - Synchronize Between Just Two Domain Controllers
> - Trigger the KCC into Recalculating the Replication Topology

Replication Monitor displays in graphical format the replication topology of connections between servers on the same site. It enables administrators to view low-level status and performance of replication between Active Directory domain controllers. It also includes functions that are wrapped application programming interfaces (APIs) to make it easy to write a replication script with just a few lines of code.

With Replication Monitor, you can:

- See which computers are replicating information both directly and transitively.

- Display each USN value, the number of failed replication attempts, the reason for failed attempts, and the flags used for direct replication partners. If the failure meets or exceeds an administrator-defined value, it can write to an event log and send mail.

- Poll the server at an administrator-defined interval to get current statistics and replication state, and to save a log file history.

- Allow administrators to show which objects have not yet replicated from a particular computer.

- Allow administrators to synchronize between two domain controllers.

- Allow administrators to use the KCC to recalculate the replication topology.

You can run the Replication Monitor utility on any domain controller, member server, or stand-alone computer that runs Windows 2000 Advanced Server.

Note For more information about Replication monitoring in Active Directory, see the Windows 2000 Help.

Using Replication Monitor to Monitor Replication Traffic

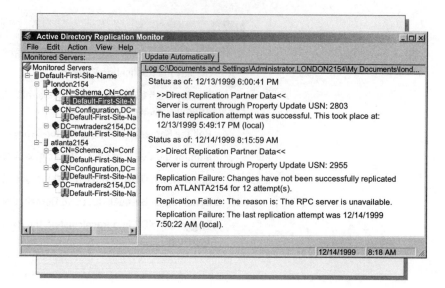

Use Replication Monitor to view replication between domain controllers in a domain. To start and configure Replication Monitor, perform the following steps:

1. On the **Start** menu, point to **Programs**, point to **Windows 2000 Support Tool**s, click **Tools**, and then click **Active Directory Replication Monitor**.

2. On the **View** menu, click **Options**.

3. On the **Active Directory Replication Monitor Options** page, click the **Status Logging** tab, click **Display Changed Attributes when Replication Occurs**, and then click **OK**.

4. Right-click **Monitored servers**, and then click **Add Monitored Server**.

5. In the Add Server to Monitor wizard, click **Add the server explicitly by name**, and then click **Next**.

6. In the **Enter the name of the server to monitory explicitly** box, type the server name, and then click **Finish**.

Using Repadmin to Monitor Replication Traffic

Administrators use the **repadmin** command to view the replication topology from the perspective of each domain controller. You can also use the **repadmin** command to manually create the replication topology, force replication events between domain controllers, and view both the replication metadata, which is information about the data, and up-to-dateness vectors.

To run the **repadmin** command, perform the following step:

- At the command prompt, type
  repadmin *command arguments* [/**u**:[*domain*]*user* /**pw**:{*password*|***}]

The following examples use some of available command arguments for the **repadmin** command:

- To display the replication partners for domain controller named domaincontroller1, use the syntax

  repadmin /showreps domaincontroller1.contoso.msft

- To display the highest Update Sequence Number on the domain controller named domaincontroller2, use the syntax

  repadmin /showvector dc=contoso,dc=msft domain controller2.contoso.msft

- To display the connection objects for the domain controller named domaincontroller1, use the syntax

  repadmin /showconn server2.microsoft.com

Note For more information about the arguments that can be used with the **repadmin** command, you can read the usage statement, which is obtained by running **repadmin /?** at the command prompt.

Adjusting Replication

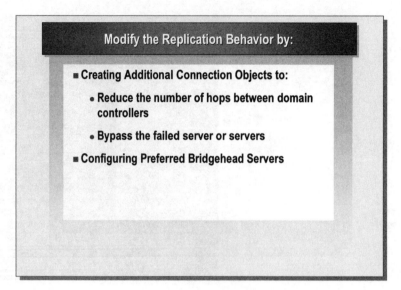

Active Directory replication occurs automatically and reliably with no administrative intervention, other than that required to configure sites and site links. An administrator can use Active Directory Sites and Services to modify a replication topology by adding or removing connection objects, and limit ISTG's choices of bridgeheads.

Creating Additional Connection Objects

Generally, you manually create connection objects only if the connections that KCC creates do not connect domain controllers that an administrator wants connected. The following situations may require additional connections between domain controllers within a site or between sites:

- When you want to reduce the number of hops from the default of three to one or two hops between domain controllers within a site.

- When failures occur between domain controllers in different sites. If failures occur, KCC detects the failures and automatically reroutes connections to bypass the failed server or servers.

Note   Before you create additional connections, it is important to consider the cost of the additional connections compared with the cost of the default configuration.

When you modify the connection objects, the following rules apply:

- The KCC will not automatically delete a connection object that has been manually created.

- If you create a connection to the same server that the KCC would normally create, the KCC will not create an additional connection.

- At any time, if a domain controller can not get updates from its current replication partners, it will use the KCC to establish as many new connection objects as necessary to other domain controllers to resume Active Directory replication.

Configuring Preferred Bridgehead Servers

You can limit the choice of servers that ISTG can designate as bridgeheads by selecting one or more domain controllers in the site that you contains the servers that you want ISTG to always consider as preferred bridgehead servers.

To limit ISTG's choices of bridgeheads, perform the following steps:

1. Open Active Directory Sites and Services, expand **Sites**, expand the site that contains the servers that you want to configure as preferred bridgehead servers, and then expand **Servers**.

2. Open the **Properties** dialog box for the server object that you want to become a preferred bridgehead server.

3. Select the IP or SMTP transport and then click **Add**.

Note   For more information about the registry entries and configuration entries in Active Directory that are needed to adjust replication, see appendix A "Adjusting Replication" on the Student Materials compact disc.

Lab C: Monitoring Replication

Objectives

After completing this lab, you will be able to:

- Monitor replication by using Replication Monitor.
- Monitor replication by using the **repadmin** utility.

Lab Setup

To complete this lab, you need the Windows 2000 Advanced Server compact disc to install the Windows 2000 Support Tools.

Estimated time to complete this lab: 15 minutes

Exercise 1
Using Support Tools to Monitor Replication

Scenario

You have just finished the installation and configuration of a replica domain controller for a child domain of the Northwind Traders forest root domain. The domain controller's replication configuration needs to be verified to ensure replication is working properly.

Goal

In this exercise, you will use Replication Monitor to determine the replication directory partitions for your domain controller. You will also view your replication topology and server properties. You will then use the **repadmin** utility to view detailed information about your replication partners.

Tasks	Detailed Steps
1. Install (if not already installed) the Windows 2000 Support Tools with all of the default options.	a. Log on as Administrator in your domain with a password of **password**.
	b. If the Windows 2000 Support Tools have not already been installed, from your Windows 2000 Advanced Server compact disc, under the Support/Tools folder, run Setup to start the Windows 2000 Support Tools Setup wizard.
	c. On the **Welcome to the Windows 2000 Support Tools Setup Wizard** page, click **Next** to continue.
	d. On the **User Information** page, type your name in the **Name** box, type your organization in the **Organization** box, and then click **Next**.
	e. On the **Select An Installation Type** page, ensure that **Typical** is selected and then click **Next**.
	f. On the **Begin Installation** page, click **Next** to begin the installation of the Windows 2000 Support Tools.
	📺 *The wizard takes a short time to complete the installation.*
	g. On the **Completing the Windows 2000 Support Tools Setup Wizard** page, click **Finish**.
2. Identify the replication directory partitions for your domain controller by using Active Directory Replication Monitor.	a. Click **Start**, point to **Programs**, point to **Windows 2000 Support Tools**, point to **Tools**, and then click **Active Directory Replication Monitor**.
	b. On the **Edit** menu, click **Add Monitored Server**.
	c. In the **Add Server to Monitor** dialog box, click **Add the server explicitly by name**, and then click **Next**.
	d. In the **Enter the name of the server to monitor explicitly** box, type *servername* (where *servername* is the host name of your computer) and then click **Finish**.

Tasks	Detailed Steps
❓	Using the information from Active Directory Replication Monitor, list the directory partitions that are replicated to your domain controller.

DC = specific, DC = nwtraders, DC = msft
CN = Schema, CN = configuration, DC = nwtraders, DC = msft
CN = Configuration, DC = Nwtraders, DC = msft

Tasks	Detailed Steps
2. *(continued)*	e. Expand each replication directory partition, and then examine the replication partners for each partition. **Note**: An icon with two connected computers indicates a direct partner. An icon with a single computer indicates a transitive partner.
3. View your replication topology by using Active Directory Replication Monitor.	a. In Active Directory Replication Monitor, right-click *servername*, and then click **Show Replication Topologies**. b. In the View Replication Topology window, on the **View** menu, click **Connections Objects Only**. c. Right-click the *servername* icon, and then click **Show Intra-Site Connections**. 🖥️ *The lines drawn to your domain controller represent your inbound connections.* d. Close the View Replication Topology window.
4. View the configuration of your domain controller by using Active Directory Replication Monitor.	a. In Replication Monitor, right-click *servername*, and then click **Properties**. b. In the **Server Properties** dialog box, click the **Server Flags** tab. 🖥️ *The properties with a check indicate the feature is enabled. An 'X' instead of a check indicates the domain controller does not have that feature enabled.* c. In the **Server Properties** dialog box, click the **FSMO Roles** tab. 🖥️ *The listing displayed is the operations master role holders as known by this domain controller.* d. In the **Server Properties** dialog box, click the **Inbound Replication Connections** tab. Scroll through the description of why the connection objects were established. Click **OK** to close the **Server Properties** dialog box. e. Close Active Directory Replication Monitor.

Tasks	Detailed Steps
5. View the detailed configuration of your replication partners using **repadmin**, and then log off.	**a.** Open a command prompt window. **b.** At the command prompt, type **repadmin /?** to display its usage, and then review the usage for the /showreps option. **c.** At the command prompt, type **repadmin /showreps** and then press ENTER to display details for inbound neighbors and outbound neighbors for change notification.
❓ Use the information from **repadmin** to determine when the last schema directory partition replication was made and why it was made. _____ _____ _____ _____	
5. *(continued)*	**d.** Close the command prompt window, close all other open windows, and then log off.

Troubleshooting Active Directory Replication

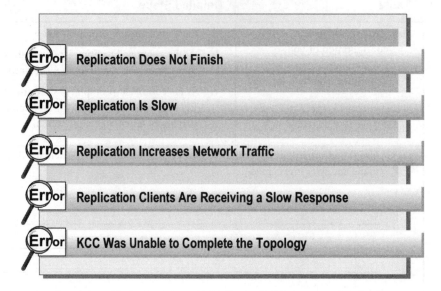

Ineffective replication can result in Active Directory not functioning properly, such as new user accounts not being recognized, outdated directory information, or unavailable domain controllers. You may encounter problems related to replication in Active Directory. Most problems can be remedied with Active Directory Sites and Services. Some of the common problems are:

- Replication does not finish. The possible cause could be that the sites containing the client computers and domain controllers are not connected by site links to domain controllers in other sites in the network. This results in a failure to exchange directory information between sites. To overcome this problem, create a site link from the current site to a site that is connected to the rest of the sites in the network.

- Replication is slow. The possible cause is that the topology and schedule of the site links cause the replication of information to go through many sites serially before all sites are updated. For example, site A can communicate with site B on Monday, site B can communicate with site C on Saturday. A change originating in Site A on Tuesday will not be given to Site C until a week from Saturday.

- Replication increases network traffic. The possible problem could be that the current network resources are insufficient to handle the amount of replication traffic. This problem can also affect services unrelated to Active Directory, because the exchange of information in Active Directory is consuming an inordinate amount of network resources. To solve this problem, you can use sites and schedule the replication to occur during off-peak hours when there is more network bandwidth available for replication.

- Replication clients are receiving a slow response for authentication, directory information, or other services. The possible cause could be that the client computers must request authentication, information, and services from a domain controller through a low-bandwidth connection. If there is a site that serves a client computer's subnet well, associate that subnet with the site. If a client computer that is experiencing slow response for services is isolated from domain controllers, and you plan to create another site that includes the client computer, create a new site with its own domain controller. You can also install a connection with more bandwidth.

- KCC was unable to complete the topology for the distinguished name of the site. If this message appears in the Directory Service log in Event Viewer, it indicates that there is an exception in the KCC. To log more information, increase the value of the **9 Internal Processing** registry entry and **1 Knowledge Consistency Checker** registry entry to three and wait 15 minutes. The registry entries are at the location: **HKEY_LOCAL_MACHINE\SYSTEM\CurrentControlSet\Services\ NTDS\Diagnostics.** Alternatively, you can also run **repadmin /kcc**, and reset the value of the registry entry to 0. By default, only the most important events are logged in KCC. You can increase the level of detail by modifying the value in the **Replication Events** entry in an event log.

Best Practices

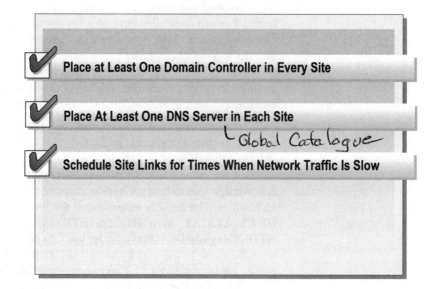

The following list provides best practices for administering Active Directory:

- Place at least one domain controller in every site, and create a global catalog on at least one domain controller in each site. Sites that do not have their own domain controllers and at least one global catalog are dependent on other sites for directory information, making the usage of network bandwidth between sites less efficient. Also, placing a domain controller in every site and a global catalog on the domain controller in each site can make the site less susceptible to WAN failures.

- Place at least one Domain Name System (DNS) server in each site. Sites that do not have their own DNS server are dependent on other sites for name resolution information, making the usage of network bandwidth between sites less efficient. Also, placing a DNS server in every site can make the site less susceptible to WAN failures.

- Schedule site links for times when network traffic is slow. This type of scheduling reduces the replication traffic on the network.

Review

- **Introduction to Active Directory Replication**
- **Replication Components and Processes**
- **Replication Topology**
- **Using Sites to Optimize Active Directory Replication**
- **Implementing Sites to Manage Active Directory Replication**
- **Monitoring Replication Traffic**
- **Adjusting Replication**
- **Troubleshooting Active Directory Replication**
- **Best Practices**

1. All domain controllers in replication are connected in a loop. Therefore, during replication, updates can be replicated to domain controllers more than once. How does Active Directory prevent this from happening?

   Uses Up-to-dateness "etc. Vector

2. An administrator changes the telephone number on a user object in Active Directory on one domain controller. A short time later, the user changes his pager number on another domain controller. What happens to the two changes when they are replicated to domain controllers throughout the domain?

   No conflict, since these are two different attributes

3. When you observe your Active Directory replication topology on your network, you notice that one of your most capable servers is not the bridgehead server. What can you do to make this server a bridgehead?

   make it a bridgehead server.

4. You want to limit the replication traffic between two domain controllers connected by a WAN link. You also want this link to be used only for replication traffic at night. What should you do?

    Make them sites & config. site links so can control replication.

5. To reduce congestion on your network, the Network Services group in your organization has created a new high-speed backbone on a separate IP subnet for servers in your location. What should you do before you move your domain controllers to the new backbone?

    Backbone should have it's own subnet & be associated w/ a site.

6. Which utility allows you to view the status of replication on domain controllers in the domain?

    Repadmin or Monitor.

Microsoft®
Training &
Certification

Module 12: Managing Operations Masters

Contents

Overview

- **Introduction to Operations Masters**
- **Operations Master Roles**
- **Managing Operations Master Roles**
- **Managing Operations Master Failures**
- **Best Practices**

An *operations master* is a domain controller that performs a specific role in Microsoft® Windows® 2000 Active Directory® directory service and may control a specific set of directory changes. For each role, only the domain controller holding that role can make the associated directory changes. There are ways to move these roles from one domain controller to another, even if an operations master fails. Knowing the specific operations master roles that each domain controller holds in an Active Directory network can help you take advantage of data replication and network bandwidth.

At the end of this module, you will be able to:

- Define an operations master, and describe its importance in an Active Directory network.

- Describe the functions of each of the five operations master roles in a forest.

- Determine, transfer, and seize an operations master role.

- Describe the effects of, and how to respond to, an operations master failure.

- Apply best practices for managing an operations master.

Introduction to Operations Masters

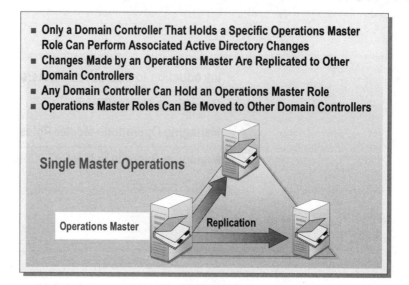

- Only a Domain Controller That Holds a Specific Operations Master Role Can Perform Associated Active Directory Changes
- Changes Made by an Operations Master Are Replicated to Other Domain Controllers
- Any Domain Controller Can Hold an Operations Master Role
- Operations Master Roles Can Be Moved to Other Domain Controllers

Single Master Operations

Operations Master   Replication

Active Directory supports multi-master replication of directory changes among all domain controllers in a forest. During multi-master replication, a replication conflict can potentially occur if concurrent originating updates are performed on the same data on two different domain controllers.

To avoid these conflicts, some operations are performed in *single master* (not permitted to occur at different places in the network at the same time) fashion by making a single domain controller responsible for the operation. These operations are grouped together into specific roles within the forest or within a domain. These roles are called *operations master roles.* For each operations master role, only the domain controller holding that role can make the associated directory changes. The domain controller responsible for a particular role is called an *operations master* for that role.

Active Directory stores information about which domain controller holds a specific role. Clients that can query Active Directory use this information to contact an operations master when necessary. Any domain controller can potentially be configured as an operations master. It is possible to move an operations master role to other domain controllers, even when the current operations master role holder is unavailable.

◆ Operations Master Roles

- **Operations Master Default Locations**
- **Schema Master**
- **Domain Naming Master**
- **PDC Emulator**
- **RID Master**
- **Infrastructure Master**

Active Directory defines five operations master roles, each one of which has a default location. The five operations master roles are:

- Schema master

- Domain naming master

- Primary domain controller (PDC) emulator

- Relative identifier (RID) master

- Infrastructure master

The schema master and domain naming master are per-forest roles, meaning that there is only one schema master and one domain naming master in the entire forest. The other operations master roles are per-domain roles, meaning that each domain in the forest has its own PDC emulator, RID master, and infrastructure master. So, in a forest with only one domain, there are five operations master roles. In a forest with more than one domain, there are more than five roles because the per-domain roles need to exist in each domain.

Operations Master Default Locations

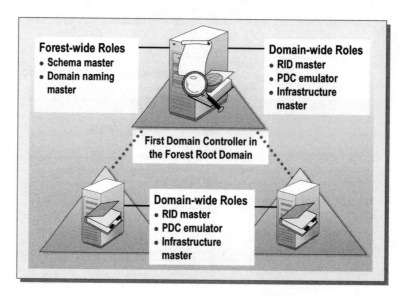

Operations master roles are either forest wide or domain wide.

- Forest-wide roles are unique for a forest. The schema master and the domain naming master are forest-wide roles. This means that there is only one schema master and one domain naming master in the entire forest.

- Domain-wide roles are unique for each domain in a forest. The PDC emulator, the RID master, and the infrastructure master are domain-wide roles. This means that each domain in a forest has its own PDC emulator, RID master, and infrastructure master.

By default, the first domain controller of a new forest holds all five operations master roles. The first domain controller for each new domain joining an existing forest holds the three domain-wide operations master roles for the new domain.

As the network expands, the operations master placement would be as follows:

- In a forest with only one domain, there are five operations master roles.

- In a forest with more than one domain, there are two per-forest operations master roles. The three per-domain operations master roles are duplicated for each domain.

Schema Master

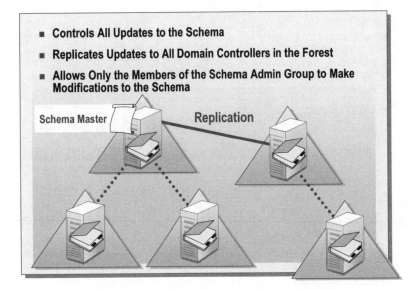

- **Controls All Updates to the Schema**
- **Replicates Updates to All Domain Controllers in the Forest**
- **Allows Only the Members of the Schema Admin Group to Make Modifications to the Schema**

Schema Master   Replication

The *schema master* controls all originating updates to the schema. The schema contains the master list of object classes and attributes that are used to create all Active Directory objects, such as computers, users, and printers. The domain controller that holds the schema master role is the only domain controller that can perform write operations to the directory schema. These schema updates are replicated from the schema operations master to all other domain controllers in the forest. Having only one schema master per forest prevents any conflicts that would result if two or more domain controllers attempt to concurrently update the schema. Only the Schema Admins group can make modifications to the schema.

Domain Naming Master

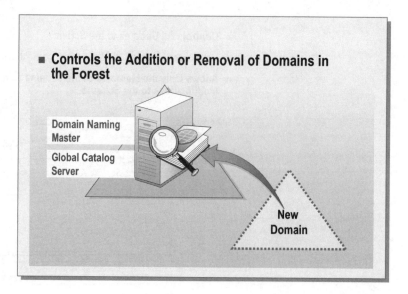

The *domain naming master* controls the addition or removal of domains in the forest. There is only one domain naming master per forest.

When you add a new domain to the forest, only the domain controller holding the domain naming master role has the right to add the new domain. The domain naming master manages this process, preventing multiple domains from joining the forest with the same domain name. When you use the Active Directory Installation wizard to create a child domain, it contacts the domain naming master and requests the addition or deletion. The domain naming master is responsible for ensuring that the domain names are unique. Note that if the domain naming master is unavailable, you cannot add or remove domains.

The domain controller holding the domain naming master role must also be a global catalog server. When the domain naming master creates an object that represents a new domain, it verifies by querying the global catalog server that no other object, including domain objects, is using the same name as the new object. Because the domain naming master verifies the name of a new object by querying the global catalog server, the global catalog must run on the same domain controller as the one holding the domain naming master role. The domain naming master also manages the naming of sites to ensure that a duplicate site is not created.

PDC Emulator

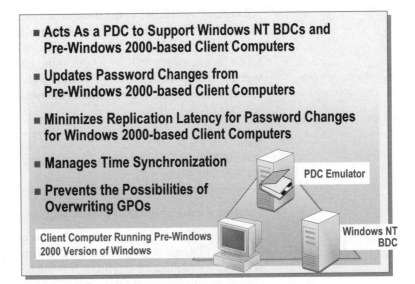

- Acts As a PDC to Support Windows NT BDCs and Pre-Windows 2000-based Client Computers
- Updates Password Changes from Pre-Windows 2000-based Client Computers
- Minimizes Replication Latency for Password Changes for Windows 2000-based Client Computers
- Manages Time Synchronization
- Prevents the Possibilities of Overwriting GPOs

PDC Emulator

Client Computer Running Pre-Windows 2000 Version of Windows

Windows NT BDC

The *PDC emulator* acts as a Microsoft Windows NT® PDC to support any backup domain controllers (BDCs) running Windows NT within a mixed-mode domain. The PDC emulator is the first domain controller that is created in a new domain.

The PDC emulator performs the following roles:

- Acts as the PDC for any existing BDCs.

   If a domain contains any BDCs or client computers that are running pre-Windows 2000 versions of Windows, the PDC emulator functions as a Windows NT PDC. The PDC emulator services client computers and replicates directory changes to any BDCs running Windows NT.

- Manages password changes from computers running Windows NT, Windows 95, or Windows 98, which need to be written to the directory.

- Minimizes replication latency for password changes.

   Replication latency is the time needed for a change made on one domain controller to be received by another domain controller. When the password of a client computer running Windows 2000 is changed on a domain controller, that domain controller immediately forwards the change to the PDC emulator. If a password was recently changed, that change takes time to replicate to every domain controller in the domain. If a logon authentication fails at another domain controller because of a bad password, that domain controller will forward the authentication request to the PDC emulator before rejecting the logon attempt.

- Synchronizes the time on all domain controllers throughout the domain to its time.

  All domain controllers in the domain get their time synchronized to the clock of the PDC emulator of that domain. The PDC emulator of the domain gets its clock set to the PDC emulator's clock in the forest root domain. The forest root domain's PDC emulator should be configured to synchronize with an external time source. The end result is that the time kept by the clocks of all Windows 2000-based computers in the entire forest is within seconds of each other.

  Note Only when the domain is in mixed mode does the domain controller that holds the PDC emulator role synchronize with BDCs running Windows NT versions 4.0 or 3.51.

- Prevents the possibilities of overwriting Group Policy objects (GPOs).

  The Group Policy snap-in, by default, runs on the domain controller that holds the PDC emulator role for that domain. This is done to reduce the potential for replication conflicts. It is not a requirement, however that a Group Policy object (GPO) be updated on this domain controller.

RID Master

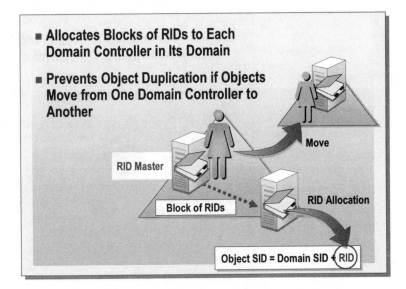

- **Allocates Blocks of RIDs to Each Domain Controller in Its Domain**
- **Prevents Object Duplication if Objects Move from One Domain Controller to Another**

RID Master
Move
Block of RIDs
RID Allocation
Object SID = Domain SID + RID

The *relative identifier (RID) master* allocates blocks of RIDs to each domain controller in the domain. Whenever a domain controller creates a new security principal, such as a user, group, or computer object, it assigns the object a unique security identifier (SID). This SID consists of a domain SID, which is the same for all security principals created in the domain, and a RID, which is unique for each security principal created in the domain.

The RID master supports creating and moving objects as follows:

- *Creating objects.* To allow a multi-master operation to create objects on any domain, the RID master allocates a block of RIDs to a domain controller. When a domain controller needs an additional block of RIDs, it initiates communication with the RID master. The RID master allocates a new block of RIDs to the domain controller, which the domain controller assigns to the new objects.

  The process of creating the objects and communicating to the RID master for additional blocks of RIDs can be repeated as many times as necessary. If a domain controller's RID pool is empty, and the RID master is unavailable, new security principals cannot be created on that domain controller. You can view the RID pool allocation by using the **dcdiag** utility.

- *Moving objects.* When you move an object between domains, you must initiate the move on the RID master that currently contains the object. This prevents the possible duplication of objects. If an object were moved, but there were no single master that kept this information, then it would be possible to move the object to multiple domains without realizing that a previous move had already taken place.

  The RID master deletes the object from the domain when the object is moved from that domain to another domain.

Infrastructure Master

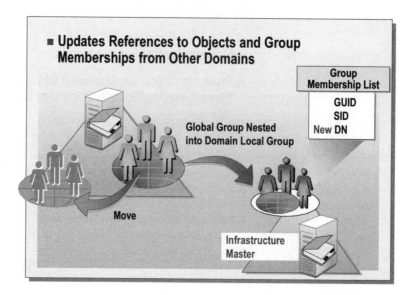

The *infrastructure master* is used to update object references in its domain that point to the object in another domain. The object reference contains the object's globally unique identifier (GUID), distinguished name and possibly a SID. The distinguished name and SID on the object reference are periodically updated to reflect changes made to the actual object. These changes include moves within and between domains as well as the deletion of the object.

Group Membership Identification

If SID or distinguished name modifications to user accounts and groups are made in other domains, the group membership for a group on your domain that references the changed user or group needs to be updated. The infrastructure master for the domain in which the group (or reference) resides is responsible for this update; it distributes the update through normal replication throughout its domain.

The infrastructure master updates object identification, by the following rules:

- If the object moves at all, its distinguished name will change because the distinguished name represents its exact location in the directory.

- If the object is moved within the domain, its SID remains the same.

- If the object is moved to another domain, the SID changes to incorporate the new domain SID.

- The GUID does not change regardless of location (the GUID is unique across domains).

Note   In a single domain forest, the infrastructure master does not need to function because there are no external object references for it to update.

Infrastructure Master and the Global Catalog

The infrastructure operations master should not be the same domain controller that hosts the global catalog. If the infrastructure master and the global catalog are the same computer, the infrastructure master will not function because it does not contain any references to objects that it does not hold. In this case, the domain replica data and the global catalog server data cannot exist on the same domain controller.

The infrastructure master for a domain periodically examines the references, within its replica of the directory data, to objects not held on that domain controller. It queries a global catalog server for current information about the distinguished name and SID of each referenced object. If this information has changed, the infrastructure master makes the change in its local replica. These changes are replicated using normal replication to the other domain controllers within the domain.

should not be on same machine (domain controller) as the Global Catalogue!

◆ Managing Operations Master Roles

- **Determining the Holder of an Operations Master Role**
- **Transferring an Operations Master Role**
- **Seizing an Operations Master Role**

When you create a Windows 2000 domain, Windows 2000 automatically configures all of the operations master roles. However, it may be necessary to reassign an operations master role to another domain controller in the forest or in the domain. To reassign an operations master role to another domain controller:

- Determine the holder of the operations master role.
- Transfer the operations master role.
- Seize the operations master role.

Determining the Holder of an Operations Master Role

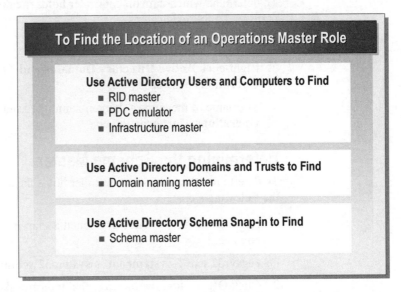

To Find the Location of an Operations Master Role

Use Active Directory Users and Computers to Find
- RID master
- PDC emulator
- Infrastructure master

Use Active Directory Domains and Trusts to Find
- Domain naming master

Use Active Directory Schema Snap-in to Find
- Schema master

Before you consider moving an operations master role, you may need to determine which domain controller holds a specific operations master role. Authenticated Users have the permission to determine where the operations master roles are located. Depending on the operations master role to be determined, you use one of the following Active Directory consoles:

- Active Directory Users and Computers
- Active Directory Domains and Trusts
- Active Directory Schema

Determining the RID Master, the PDC Emulator, and the Infrastructure Master

To determine which domain controller holds the RID master, PDC emulator, or infrastructure master roles, perform the following steps.

1. Open Active Directory Users and Computers.

2. In the console tree, right-click **Active Directory Users and Computers**, and then click **Operations Masters**.

3. Click the **RID**, **PDC**, or **Infrastructure** tab.

   The name of the current operations master appears under **Operations master**.

Determining the Domain Naming Master

To determine which domain controller holds the domain naming master role, perform the following steps:

1. Open Active Directory Domains and Trusts.

2. Right-click **Active Directory Domains and Trusts**, and then click **Operations Master**.

   The name of the current domain naming master appears in the **Change Operations Master** dialog box.

Determining the Schema Master

To determine which domain controller holds the schema master role, perform the following steps:

1. Register the Active Directory Schema snap-in by running the following command:

   type → **regsvr32.exe %systemroot%\system32\schmmgmt.dll**

2. Click **OK** to close the message that indicates the registration succeeded.

3. Create a custom Microsoft Management Console (MMC) console.

4. Add the Active Directory Schema snap-in to the console.

5. In the console tree, right-click **Active Directory Schema**, and then click **Operations Master**.

   The name of the current schema master appears in the **Change Schema Master** dialog box.

Note   To identify an operations master in a different domain, connect to the domain before clicking **Operations Masters**. To identify the operations master in a different forest, connect to the domain by typing the domain name of the forest before clicking **Operations Masters**.

Transferring an Operations Master Role

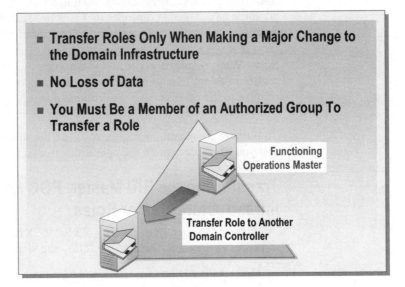

- **Transfer Roles Only When Making a Major Change to the Domain Infrastructure**

- **No Loss of Data**

- **You Must Be a Member of an Authorized Group To Transfer a Role**

Functioning Operations Master

Transfer Role to Another Domain Controller

In most cases, the placement of operations master roles in a forest does not require changes as the forest grows, which means that role placements do not require revisions. However, when you plan to decommission a domain controller, reduce the connectivity of your network, or change the global catalog server status of a domain controller, you need to review your plan and transfer operations master roles as necessary. Transferring an operations master role means moving it from one functioning domain controller to another. To transfer roles, both domain controllers must be up and running and connected to the network.

There is no loss of data during a role transfer. The process of role transfer involves replicating the current operations master directory to the new domain controller, which ensures that the new operations master has the most current information available. This transfer of the role object uses the normal directory replication mechanism.

To transfer an operations master role, you must have the appropriate permissions to do so. The following table lists the groups of which you must be a member to have permissions to change an operations master role.

Operations master	Authorized group
Schema master	The Change Schema Master permission is granted by default to the Schema Admins group.
Domain naming master	The Change Domain Master permission is granted by default to the Enterprise Admins group.
PDC emulator	The Change PDC permission is granted by default to the Domain Admins group.
RID master	The Change Rid Master permission is granted by default to the Domain Admins group.
Infrastructure master	The Change Infrastructure Master permission is granted by default to the Domain Admins group.

> **Important**   Transfer roles only when making a major change to the domain infrastructure, such as decommissioning a domain controller that holds a role or adding a new domain controller that is better suited to hold a specific role.

> **Note**   When a domain controller is demoted to a member server, all operations master roles are relinquished to other domain controllers. To control the transfer of roles to the other domain controllers, transfer the roles prior to demotion.

To transfer an operations master role, use the same Active Directory snap-in that you use to determine the operations master role.

Transferring the RID Master, PDC Emulator, and Infrastructure Master Roles

To transfer the operations master role for the RID master, PDC emulator, or infrastructure master, perform the following steps:

1. Open Active Directory Users and Computers.

2. In the console tree, right-click **Active Directory Users and Computers**, and then click **Connect to Domain Controller**.

3. In the list of available domain controllers, click the domain controller that will become the new operations master, and then click **OK**.

4. In the console tree, right-click the icon of the domain controller that will become the new operations master, and then click **Operations Masters**.

5. Click the tab for the operations master role you want to transfer, such as PDC, and then click **Change**.

> **Caution**   Ensure that you do not transfer the infrastructure master role to a domain controller that hosts the global catalog.

Transferring the Domain Naming Master Role

To transfer the domain naming master role to another global catalog server, perform the following steps:

1. Open Active Directory Domains and Trusts.

2. In the console tree, right-click **Active Directory Domains and Trusts**, and then click **Connect to Domain Controller**.

3. In the list of available domain controllers, click the domain controller that will become the new domain naming master, and then click **OK**.

4. In the console tree, right-click **Active Directory Domains and Trusts**, and then click **Operations Master**.

5. The name of the domain controller you selected appears.

6. Click **Change**.

> **Note**   Ensure that the domain controller that holds the domain naming master role also hosts the global catalog.

Transferring the Schema Master Role

To transfer the schema operations master role, perform the following steps:

1. Open Active Directory Schema.

2. In the console tree, right-click **Active Directory Schema**, and then click **Change Domain Controller**.

3. Click **Specify Name**, type the name of the domain controller to which you want to transfer the schema master role, and then click **OK**.

4. In the console tree, right-click **Active Directory Schema**, and then click **Operations Master**.

5. The name of the domain controller you selected appears.

6. Click **Change**.

Note　You need to register the schema admin snap-in, Schmgmt.dll, before opening the Active Directory schema.

Seizing an Operations Master Role

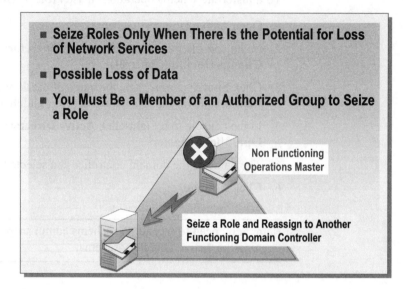

- **Seize Roles Only When There Is the Potential for Loss of Network Services**
- **Possible Loss of Data**
- **You Must Be a Member of an Authorized Group to Seize a Role**

Non Functioning Operations Master

Seize a Role and Reassign to Another Functioning Domain Controller

---

Seizing an operations master role means forcing a transfer of an operations master role from a domain controller that has failed to a functioning domain controller.

Seizing an operations master role is a drastic step that you should consider only if the current operations master will never be available again. If the cause of the failure is a networking problem or a software or hardware failure that you can resolve in a timely manner, wait for the operations master role holder to become available again. You should seize a role only if it cannot be transferred. Unlike role seizure, a role transfer ensures that only one domain controller holds the role, and that the role holder has an updated role object set.

Important   Before proceeding with the role seizure, you must permanently disconnect from the network the domain controller that currently holds the operations master role.

Before you seize an operations master role, you should determine which domain controller holds the operations master role. After you determine the current role holder, seize the operations master role by using either the Active Directory console you used for determining or transferring a role, or the **ntdsutil** command. Finally, verify that the functioning domain controller has accepted its new operations master role.

Seizing the PDC Emulator and Infrastructure Master Roles

To seize an operations master role for the PDC emulator or infrastructure master, perform the following steps:

1. Open Active Directory Users and Computers.

2. In the console tree, right-click **Active Directory Users and Computers**, and then click **Operations Masters**.

Note It may take some time for the data to display because it is waiting for a response from the current holder of the operations master role. Because the current role holder has failed and cannot respond, the last updated information appears.

---

3. In the **Operations Master** dialog box, click the tab of the operations master role you want to seize.

4. Click **Change**, and when the message appears indicating a transfer is not possible, click **Yes** in the confirmation dialog box.

5. Click **OK** on the warning page, and then click **OK** to perform a forceful transfer.

6. Click **OK** to close the **Operations Master** dialog box.

7. Verify the new holder of the operations master role that you seized.

Seizing Other Operations Master Roles

Temporary loss of the schema master, domain naming master, or RID master is ordinarily not visible to end users, and does not usually inhibit your work as an administrator. Therefore, this is usually not a problem worth fixing. However, if you anticipate an extremely long outage of the domain controller holding one of these roles, you can seize that role to the standby operations master domain controller. But seizing any of these roles is a step that you would take only when the outage is permanent, as in the case when a domain controller is physically destroyed and cannot be restored from backup media.

An operations master that has its role seized should not become operational because of the possibility of having multiple operations masters online for the same role. Before seizing the role, you must ensure that the outage of this domain controller is permanent by physically disconnecting the domain controller from the network.

Using Ntdsutil to Seize a Role

To use the **ntdsutil** command to seize an operations master role, perform the following steps:

1. In the **Run** box, type **cmd** and then press ENTER.

2. At the command prompt, type **ntdsutil**

3. At the **ntdsutil** prompt, type **roles**

4. At the **fsmo maintenance** prompt, type **connections**

5. At the **server connections** prompt, type **connect to server** followed by the fully qualified domain name (FQDN) of the domain controller that will be the new role holder.

6. At the **server connections** prompt, type **quit**

7. At the **fsmo maintenance** prompt, type one of the following commands to seize the appropriate operations master:

   - **Seize RID master**

   - **Seize PDC**

   - **Seize infrastructure master**

   - **Seize domain naming master**

   - **Seize schema master**

8. At the **fsmo maintenance** prompt, type **quit**

9. At the **ntdsutil** prompt, type **quit**

10. Verify the new holder of the operations master role that you seized.

◆ Managing Operations Master Failures

- **Failure of the PDC Emulator or the Infrastructure Master**
- **Failure of Other Operations Masters**

The effects of a failure of an operations master on the network depend on the role of the operations master. Some of the operations master roles are crucial to the operation of the network, whereas others can be unavailable for quite some time before their absence becomes a problem. You will notice that an operations master is unavailable when you try to perform some function controlled by the particular operations master.

If the cause is a networking problem or a server failure, and the problem will be resolved soon, wait for the operations master to become available again. If the domain controller that currently holds the operations master role has failed, you must determine if it can be recovered and brought back online.

Generally, you want to seize the role of the failed operations master to prevent long-term network failure. For the PDC emulator and infrastructure operations master roles, it is safer to perform a seizure than for the other operations master roles.

Failure of the PDC Emulator or the Infrastructure Master

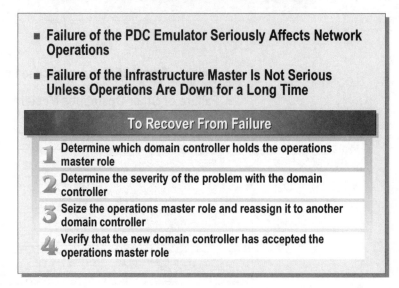

The failure of the PDC emulator may more seriously affect network users than the failure of other operations master roles because the PDC emulator is a role holder for more common network operations.

PDC Emulator Failure

Failure of the PDC emulator causes:

- Loss of support of client computers running pre–Windows 2000 versions of Windows for password changes.
- Loss of latency reduction for password updates.
- Possible loss of time synchronization among domain controllers.

Infrastructure Master Failure

Temporary failure of the infrastructure operations master is not as serious as failure of the PDC emulator. End users may not notice that it is not functioning. Its role has minimal impact unless you move a large number of objects.

If the infrastructure master will be unavailable for a long time, seize the role and give it to a domain controller that is not a global catalog server. When the original domain controller returns to service, you may or may not transfer the infrastructure role back to the original domain controller.

Managing PDC Emulator or Infrastructure Master Failure

To recover from a failure of the PDC emulator and infrastructure master, perform the following steps:

1. Determine which domain controller holds the operations role.
2. Determine the severity of the problem with the domain controller.
3. Seize the operations master role and give it to another domain controller. In the case of the infrastructure master, make sure that the receiving domain controller it is not a global catalog server.
4. Verify that the new domain controller has accepted the operations master role.

Failure of Other Operations Masters

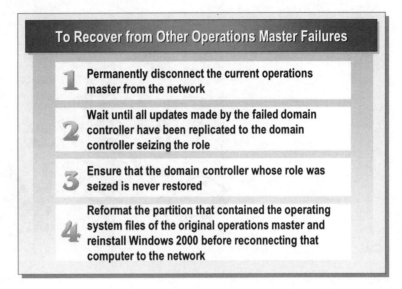

To Recover from Other Operations Master Failures

1 Permanently disconnect the current operations master from the network

2 Wait until all updates made by the failed domain controller have been replicated to the domain controller seizing the role

3 Ensure that the domain controller whose role was seized is never restored

4 Reformat the partition that contained the operating system files of the original operations master and reinstall Windows 2000 before reconnecting that computer to the network

Temporary unavailability of the schema master, RID master, and domain naming master roles is not immediately visible to network users. When possible, it is best to transfer or restore these operations master roles from backup instead of seizing the role because there is always a possibility of replication errors in the data. Consider seizing the role of these operations masters only when all other options are exhausted.

If you must recover from an RID master, schema master, or domain naming master failure, use the following guidelines:

1. Disconnect the current operations master from the network before proceeding with the role seizure. To perform the seizure, use the **ntdsutil** command.

2. Wait until any and all updates made by the failed domain controller have been replicated to the domain controller seizing the role. This ensures that the changes that were made just prior to the failure of the original domain controller are not lost.

3. Ensure that the domain controller whose role was seized is never restored. It may have updates that it made but never replicated to the other domain controllers. The computer on which the role was seized must be removed from the domain.

4. Reformat the partition that contained the operating system files of the original operations master and reinstall Windows 2000 before reconnecting that computer to the network.

Lab A: Managing Operations Masters

Objectives

After completing this lab, you will be able to:

- Determine the operations master for each of the five roles.
- Transfer an operations master role to another domain controller.
- Seize an operations master role from a failed domain controller.
- Use Ntdsutil.exe to manage operations masters.

Prerequisites

Before working on this lab, you must have an understanding of the latency in Active Directory replication and how to initiate replication manually.

Important The lab does not reflect the real-world environment. It is recommended that you always use complex passwords for any administrator accounts, and never create accounts without a password.

Important Outside of the classroom environment, it is strongly advised that you use the most recent software updates that are necessary. Because this is a classroom environment, we may use software that does not include the latest updates.

Estimated time to complete this lab: 45 minutes

Exercise 1
Determining Operations Masters

Scenario

Northwind Traders is developing a disaster recovery plan. One important consideration is the distribution of the operations master roles. There will not be more than one operations master role on a domain controller. The operations master roles will be distributed across multiple domain controllers to minimize the impact of a failure at any one location.

Goal

In this exercise, you will determine which domain controller holds each of the two forest operations master roles, which are schema master and domain naming master. You will also determine which domain controller holds each of the three operations master roles in your domain, which are relative identifier (RID), primary domain controller (PDC) emulator, and infrastructure master. The three tasks will provide you with the necessary information for you to write your results in the following table. No role transfers or seizes are made in this exercise.

Operations Master	Domain Controller's FQDN
1. Schema	london-nwtraders. msft
2. Domain naming	london. msft nnwtraders. msft
3. RID	denver. spacific1. nwtraders. msft
4. PDC emulator	"
5. Infrastructure	perth. spacific1. nwtraders. msft denver.

Tasks	Detailed Steps
1. Determine the current schema master by using the Active Directory Schema console.	a. Log on as Administrator in your domain with a password of **password**.
	b. In the **Run** box, type **regsvr32.exe %systemroot%\system32\schmmgmt.dll** and then click **OK** to register the Active Directory Schema snap-in. Click **OK** to close the message that indicates the registration succeeded.
	c. In the **Run** box, type **mmc** click **OK** to open a new console, and then add the snap-in, **Active Directory Schema**.
	d. In the console tree, expand **Active Directory Schema**.
	e. In the console tree, right-click **Active Directory Schema**, and then click **Operations Master**.
	If the role holder status displays 'ERROR', the connection was not attempted. You must click, or expand, the Active Directory Schema node (step d) before right-clicking it (step e).

Tasks	Detailed Steps
❓	What additional step must you perform to transfer this role to your domain controller? *Change domain controller.*
1. *(continued)*	**f.** Using the information in the **Change Schema Master** dialog box, fill in line 1 of the table above with the name for the schema master. **Note**: The computer with the current focus, by default, is the schema master. **g.** Click **Cancel** to close the **Change Schema Master** dialog box, and then close the Active Directory Schema console without saving the settings.
2. Determine the current domain naming master by using the Active Directory Domains and Trusts console.	**a.** Open Active Directory Domains and Trusts from the **Administrative Tools** menu. **b.** Right-click Active Directory Domains and Trusts, and then click Operations Master. **c.** Using the information in the **Change Operations Master** dialog box, fill in line 2 of the table at the beginning of this lab with the FQDN for the domain naming master. **d.** Click **Close** to close the **Change Operations Master** dialog box, and then close Active Directory Domains and Trusts.
3. Determine the current role holder for the RID, PDC emulator, and infrastructure master by using the Active Directory Users and Computers console.	**a.** Open Active Directory Users and Computers from the **Administrative Tools** menu. **b.** In the console tree, right-click Active Directory Users and Computers, and then click Operations Masters. **c.** In the **Operations Master** dialog box, by using the information on each tab, fill in lines 3 through 5 of the table at the beginning of this lab with the FQDN for the RID, PDC emulator, and infrastructure master. **d.** Click **Cancel** to close the **Operations Master** dialog box, and leave Active Directory Users and Computers open.

Exercise 2
Transferring the Infrastructure Master Role

Scenario

After monitoring global catalog queries, Northwind Traders developed a plan to redistribute the global catalog server role among the domain controllers. Because the infrastructure master will not perform correctly on a global catalog, the plan also includes placement of this role on particular domain controllers.

Goal

In this exercise, you will transfer the infrastructure master role to the specified domain controller. It is recommended that the domain controller should be in the same site as a global catalog server, but it should not be on a global catalog server. This is because the infrastructure master frequently contacts a global catalog server.

Note: Students will work in pairs grouped by domain to complete this exercise.

Tasks	Detailed Steps
⚠ **Important:** Perform the following task on both *infraserver* (where *infraserver* is the name of the infrastructure master) and *otherserver* (where *otherserver* is the name of the other domain controller in this domain).	
1. Verify the current holder of the infrastructure master role.	a. In Active Directory Users and Computers, in the console tree, right-click **Active Directory Users and Computers**, and then click **Operations Masters**. b. In the **Operations Master** dialog box, click the **Infrastructure** tab. *Notice that the current role holder is infraserver.*
⚠ **Important:** Perform the following task on *otherserver* only.	
2. Transfer the infrastructure master role from *infraserver* to *otherserver*.	a. In the **Operations Master** dialog box, click **Change**, and then click **Yes** to close the message confirming the transfer. b. Click **OK** to close the message indicating that the operations master role was successfully transferred, click **OK** again to close the **Operations Master** dialog, and then close Active Directory Users and Computers.
⚠ **Important:** Perform the following task on *infraserver* after the previous task is completed.	

Tasks	Detailed Steps
3. Verify that *infraserver* has been updated with the information that the transfer of the infrastructure master role took place.	a. To refresh the information displayed in the **Operations Master** dialog box, click **Cancel** to close the **Operations Master** dialog box in Active Directory Users and Computers.
	b. In the console tree, right-click Active Directory Users and Computers, and then click Operations Masters.
	c. In the **Operations Master** dialog box, click the **Infrastructure** tab. Notice that *otherserver* is now the infrastructure master role holder.
	d. Click **Cancel** to close the **Operations Master** dialog box, and then close Active Directory Users and Computers.

Exercise 3
Seizing the PDC Emulator Role

Scenario

The Northwind Traders Help Desk received an increasing number of complaints from users who run Windows NT version 4.0 on their computers stating that they are not able to change their passwords. The domain controller holding the PDC emulator role that performs this task has failed. The hardware part needed to repair the failed domain controller will take more than a week to acquire. Because this role performs critical operations, the Help Desk decided to seize the role from the domain controller. This was not a difficult decision because the domain was in native mode and there were no backup domain controllers (BDCs) that might have needed a full synchronization.

Goal

In this exercise, you will simulate a hardware failure on the domain controller by turning off the computer. Then you will seize the PDC emulator and give this role to another domain controller. You will then fix the simulated hardware failure and transfer the PDC emulator role back to the original domain controller.

Note: Students will work in pairs grouped by domain to complete this exercise.

Tasks	Detailed Steps
⚠	**Important:** Perform the following task on *PDCserver* (where *PDCserver* is the name of the PDC emulator) only.
1. Simulate a hardware failure by turning off *PDCserver*.	**a.** Close all open windows. **b.** Click **Start**, click **Shut Down**, click **Shut down**, and then click **OK**.
⚠	**Important:** Perform the following task on *otherserver* (where *otherserver* is the name of the other domain controller in this domain) after the previous task is complete.
2. Verify the current role holder of the PDC emulator by using Active Directory Users and Computers.	**a.** Open Active Directory Users and Computers from the **Administrative Tools** menu. **b.** In the console tree, right-click Active Directory Users and Computers, and then click Operations Masters. 🖥 *The **Operations Masters** dialog box may take a while to appear because it is waiting for a response from the RID master role holder. Expect a similar delay when clicking the other two operations master tabs.* **c.** In the **Operations Master** dialog box, click the **PDC** tab.

Tasks	Detailed Steps
❓ Is *otherserver* able to determine that the PDC emulator role holder is offline?	
Yes.	
3. Seize the PDC emulator role from *PDCserver* and give it to *otherserver* by using Active Directory Users and Computers.	**a.** Although a message indicates that the role cannot be transferred, click **Change**, and then click **Yes** to close the confirmation message.
	b. Click **OK** to close the warning message that states "Transferring the PDC role to this machine may cause a full sync on all NT4 BDCs."
	Note: This warning appears because the role transfer may cause a potentially large amount of network traffic when the BDCs are synchronized. This warning can be safely ignored because the domain is in native mode, meaning BDC synchronization cannot be performed.
❓ What was the operation that just failed?	
FSMO operation (see CD for answer) *"Flexible single master operation"*	
3. *(continued)*	**c.** Click **OK** to close the message indicating that a forced transfer was attempted.
	🖥 *The seize operation is being performed.*
	d. Click **OK** to close the message indicating that the operations master role was successfully transferred.
	e. Click **OK** to close the **Operations Master** dialog box, and then close Active Directory Users and Computers.
⚠ **Important:** Perform the following tasks on *PDCserver* after the previous task is complete.	
4. Start *PDCserver* and log on as Administrator.	▪ Start *PDCserver* and log on as Administrator.

"Back-up Domain Controller" in W2K to NT4
Primary Domain Controller in NT4

Tasks	Detailed Steps
5. Initiate replication with *otherserver* by using Active Directory Sites and Services.	a. Open Active Directory Sites and Services from the **Administrative Tools** menu. b. Expand **Sites**, expand **Default-First-Site-Name**, and then expand **Servers**. c. Expand *PDCserver*, and then click **NTDS Settings**. d. Right-click a connection that is from *otherserver*, click **Replicate Now**, and then click **OK** to close the **Replicate Now** message indicating that replication occurred. *If an error message appears stating that the RPC service is unavailable, wait a moment and try again. It may take some time for all of the necessary services to start after restarting the computer.* e. Close Active Directory Sites and Services.
6. Verify that *PDCserver* has been updated with the information that the seizure of the PDC emulator role took place by using Active Directory Users and Computers.	a. Open Active Directory Users and Computers from the **Administrative Tools** menu. b. Right-click **Active Directory Users and Computers**, and then click **Operations Masters**. c. In the **Operations Master** dialog box, click the **PDC** tab.
❓ How does *PDCserver* know that *otherserver* is now the PDC emulator? _It knows it because of the forced replication._	
7. Transfer the PDC emulator role from *otherserver* back to *PDCserver*.	a. In the **Operations Master** dialog box, click **Change** to transfer the role holder back to the original server, *PDCserver*. b. Click **Yes** to close the message confirming the transfer, click **OK** to close the message indicating the operations master role was successfully transferred, and then click **OK** to close the **Operations Master** dialog box. c. Close Active Directory Users and Computers.

Exercise 4
Using ntdsutil to Transfer Operations Master Roles

Scenario

A consultant hired by Northwind Traders recommended a remote management strategy that used only command-line utilities. An additional goal was to perform these tasks from a telnet session.

Goal

In this exercise, you will use the command-line utility Ntdsutil.exe to determine all current role holders and to transfer the RID master.

Note: Students will work in pairs grouped by domain to complete this exercise.

Tasks	Detailed Steps
⚠	**Important:** Perform the following tasks on both *RIDserver* (where *RIDserver* is the name of the RID master) and *otherserver* (where *otherserver* is the name of the other domain controller in this domain).
1. Determine the current operations masters by using the **ntdsutil** utility.	a. Open a command prompt window. b. At the command prompt, type ntdsutil and then press ENTER. c. At the ntdsutil prompt, type ? and then press ENTER to display the help information for this menu. **Note:** You can also view the help for any menu by typing **?** or **Help** and then pressing ENTER. d. At the **ntdsutil** prompt, type **domain management** and then press ENTER to display the domain management prompt. **Note:** You need to enter only enough letters of each keyword to distinguish it from each the others. For example, d m would be short for domain management. In addition, keywords are not case sensitive. e. At the **domain management** prompt, type **connections** and then press ENTER to display the server connections prompt. f. At the **server connections** prompt, type **connect to server** *servername* (where *servername* is the name of your computer), and then press ENTER. **Note:** If you want to connect to the server with different credentials from those of the locally logged on user, use **set creds %s %s %s**. View Help for more information. g. At the server connections prompt, type info and then press ENTER to display the current connection information. h. At the server connections prompt, type quit and then press ENTER to return to the domain management prompt. i. At the domain management prompt, type select operation target and then press ENTER to display the select operation target prompt. j. At the select operation target prompt, type list roles for connected server and then press ENTER to display all of the role holders this server knows about.

Tasks	Detailed Steps
1. *(continued)*	**k.** At the **select operation target** prompt, type **quit** and then press ENTER to return to the domain management prompt. **l.** At the **domain management** prompt, type **quit** and then press ENTER to return to the **ntdsutil** prompt.
2. View the maintenance options available in the **ntdsutil** utility.	**a.** At the **ntdsutil** prompt, type **roles** and then press ENTER to display the **fsmo maintenance** prompt. **Note:** fsmo (which stands for "flexible single master operation") is the previous name for an operations master. **b.** At the **fsmo maintenance** prompt, type **?** and then press ENTER to display all of the fsmo maintenance options. Notice that all seize and transfer operations are available.
⚠ **Important:** Perform the following task on *otherserver* after the previous task is complete.	
3. Transfer the RID master role from *RIDserver* to *otherserver* by using **ntdsutil**.	**a.** At the **fsmo maintenance** prompt, type **transfer RID master** and then press ENTER. **b.** Click **Yes** to close the message confirming the transfer. **Note:** You can suppress these confirmation dialog boxes for use in automation or a telnet session. This is performed at the **ntdsutil** prompt by typing **popups off**. **c.** At the **fsmo maintenance** prompt, type **quit** and then press ENTER to return to the **ntdsutil** prompt.
⚠ **Important:** Perform the following task on both *RIDserver* and *otherserver* after the previous task is complete.	
4. Close the **ntdsutil** utility and the command prompt window, and then log off.	**a.** At the **ntdsutil** prompt, type **quit** and then press ENTER to exit the utility. **b.** Close the command prompt window, close all other open windows, and then log off.

Best Practices

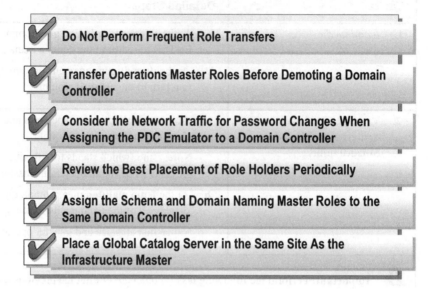

Consider the following best practices for using operations masters:

- Do not perform frequent role transfers. Perform role transfers only when making a major change to the domain infrastructure, such as when demoting a domain controller role holder, or when adding a new domain controller that is more suitable for some roles than the current holder.

- Transfer the operations master roles held by a domain controller before demoting the domain controller. This ensures that the transfer of a role is successful before you demote the domain controller. This also allows you to choose the new role holder and verify that the transfer is successful.

- Consider the network traffic associated with password changes when assigning the PDC emulator master role to a domain controller. Do this because there may be frequent network traffic from other domain controllers and pre–Windows 2000–based client computers because of user account password changes.

- Periodically review the best placement of the role holders in your network. The optimal placement of role holders may change because of network changes, usage patterns, or risk analysis.

- Assign the schema master and the domain naming master role to the same domain controller. It is easier to secure one domain controller than to secure two domain controllers, as would be necessary if the schema master and domain naming roles were on separate domain controllers. Also, the same group in an organization usually owns the domain controllers that hold the schema master and domain naming master roles.

- Place a global catalog server in the same site as the infrastructure master. This reduces network traffic when the infrastructure master enumerates its external references when updating them.

Review

■ Introduction to Operations Masters

■ Operations Master Roles

■ Managing Operations Master Roles

■ Managing Operations Master Failures

■ Best Practices

1. Which operations masters are domain wide and which are forest wide?

2. Which operations use the PDC emulator master role?

3. Is there a way to get an operations master role back online when the current domain controller holding the role has been damaged beyond repair?

4. If the domain naming master were unavailable, which operations could not be performed?

5. Why should you not seize the schema master role?

Course Evaluation

Your evaluation of this course will help Microsoft understand the quality of your learning experience.

At a convenient time between now and the end of the course, please complete a course evaluation, which is available at http://www.metricsthatmatter.com/survey.

Microsoft will keep your evaluation strictly confidential and will use your responses to improve your future learning experience.

Microsoft®
Training &
Certification

Module 13: Maintaining the Active Directory Database

Contents

Microsoft®

Overview

- **Introduction to Maintaining the Active Directory Database**
- **The Process of Modifying Data in Active Directory**
- **The Garbage Collection Process**
- **Backing Up Active Directory**
- **Restoring Active Directory**
- **Moving the Active Directory Database**
- **Defragmenting the Active Directory Database**
- **Best Practices**

Microsoft® Windows® 2000 Active Directory® directory service stores its information in a transactional database, therefore it is able to maintain the integrity of the data after a failure. The causes of a failure can range from hardware failure to a complete system loss, such as in the case of fire. The Active Directory database uses transaction log files to recover information regarding corrupted data. After recovering this information, Active Directory uses replication to recover data from other domain controllers in the domain. The interactions of Active Directory components provide the basis for how Active Directory backs up and retrieves data.

Backing up and restoring data is essential to maintaining the Active Directory database. You can back up and restore Active Directory by using the graphical user interface (GUI) and command-line tools provided in Microsoft Windows 2000 Advanced Server.

At the end of this module, you will be able to:

- Describe the importance of maintaining the Active Directory database.
- Describe the process of modifying data in Active Directory.
- Describe the garbage collection process in Active Directory.
- Back up the system state data by using the Backup utility.
- Restore Active Directory by restoring the system state data.
- Move the Active Directory database to a new location.
- Defragment the Active Directory database.
- Apply best practices for maintaining the Active Directory database.

Introduction to Maintaining the Active Directory Database

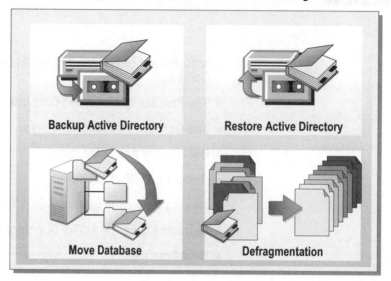

Maintaining the Active Directory database is an important administrative task that needs to be regularly scheduled to help recover lost or corrupted data and repair the Active Directory database. When domain controllers do not function because of hardware or software problems, users may not be able to gain access to needed resources or to log on to the network. Windows 2000 Advanced Server provides the following tasks, which you can use for maintaining the Active Directory database:

- Back up Active Directory. You can use the Backup utility in Microsoft Windows 2000 to back up information in Active Directory. The information in Active Directory is backed up as part of the system state data.

- Restore Active Directory. When Active Directory is corrupted or deleted, or objects in Active Directory are changed or deleted. You can also use the Backup utility to restore Active Directory because it is part of the system state data.

- Move the Active Directory database to a new location. You move a database to a new location when you defragment the database. Moving the database does not delete the original database, so you can use the original database in case the defragmented database does not work or becomes corrupted. Also, if you have limited disk space, you can add another hard disk drive and move the database to the new hard disk drive.

- Defragment the database. Frequent updates to the database lead to an inefficient use of space in the database. Defragmenting the database can reorder the data, and in certain situations, can reduce the file size.

The Process of Modifying Data in Active Directory

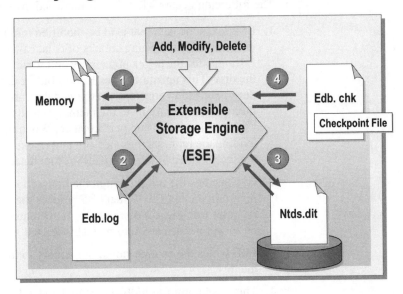

Each request to Active Directory to add, modify, or delete an object or attribute is treated as an individual *transaction*. A transaction is a set of changes, such as inserts, deletes, and updates, that act as an atomic unit.

Active Directory has its own database engine, called the Extensible Storage Engine (ESE), which stores all Active Directory objects. The ESE uses a concept of transactions and log files to ensure the integrity of the Active Directory database.

The Files in Active Directory

Active Directory includes the following files:

- Ntds.dit. This single file is the Active Directory database and stores all of the Active Directory objects on the domain controller. The .dit extension means directory information tree. The default location is the *systemroot*\NTDS folder. Each transaction in Active Directory is recorded in one or more transaction log files that are associated with the Ntds.dit file.

- Edb*.log. This is a transaction log file. The default transaction log file name is Edb.log. Each transaction log file is 10 megabytes (MB). When Edb.log is full, it is renamed to Edb*nnnnn*.log, where *nnnnn* is an increasing number starting from one.

- Edb.chk. This is a checkpoint file used by the database engine to track the data not yet written to the Active Directory database file. The checkpoint file is a pointer that maintains the status between memory and the database file on disk. The checkpoint file pointer indicates the starting point in the log file from which the information needs to be recovered if there has been a failure.

- Res1.log and Res2.log. These are the reserved transaction log files. The amount of disk space reserved on a drive or folder for the transaction logs is 20 MB. This reserved disk space provides the transaction log files sufficient room to shut down if all other disk space is being used.

The Database Modification Process

The following occurs when data is modified in Active Directory:

1. ESE loads the data that is to be modified into memory. ESE caches the disk in memory by swapping chunks of data, called pages, in and out of memory. ESE updates the pages in memory and writes new or updated pages back to the disk. This update enables ESE to buffer data in memory so that ESE does not need to constantly retrieve data from the hard disk. Making multiple modifications to the memory results in fewer writes to the disk. This caching speeds up performance. When users make requests, ESE starts loading the requests into memory and marks the pages. These marked pages are then written to the information store database on the disk.

2. ESE secures the transaction in the transaction log file, Edb.log, and creates a record in the log file. When ESE reaches the end of a transaction log file, it renames Edb.log to Edb*nnnnn*.log and creates a new log file. Old log files no longer needed are automatically deleted.

3. ESE writes the change stored in memory to the database file, Ntds.dit, on the disk.

4. The checkpoint file, Edb.chk, is updated, which indicates that the transaction in the log file has been committed to the database.

The Garbage Collection Process

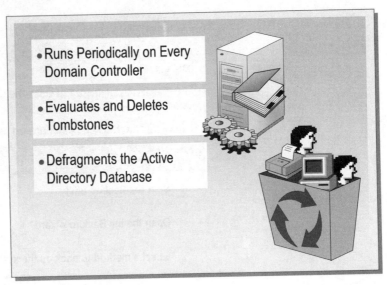

- Runs Periodically on Every Domain Controller

- Evaluates and Deletes Tombstones

- Defragments the Active Directory Database

Garbage collection is a process that runs on every domain controller after every 12 hours of continuous operation to delete objects that are expired, or tombstoned, and defragment the database. You can change the garbage collection interval. The garbage collection is used for the following tasks:

- Evaluate and delete tombstones. Tombstones are markers that indicate that an object has been deleted. Rather than immediately physically deleting a designated object, the database removes most of its attributes, moves it to the Deleted Objects folder, and then marks the object as being tombstoned. There is a delay between the time an object is marked with the originating delete and the time it is physically removed from the database. This delay period is called the *tombstone lifetime*. The delay exists to provide an interval during which the originating domain controller can replicate the deletion to other domain controllers in the forest. The database removes the tombstoned object at the completion of the tombstone lifetime. You can configure the tombstone lifetime interval or use the default of 60 days.

- Defragment the database. The defragmentation process rearranges how the data is written in the database, and in some cases compacts the database. Defragmentation can occur either automatically or manually. The garbage collection process always uses the online defragmentation process.

Note To configure the garbage collection interval and tombstone lifetime, use ADSI Edit to connect to the Configuration container of the domain controller. In the configuration partition, open the properties of Configuration/Services/ Windows NT/Directory Service. In the **Select a property to view** box, click the down arrow and scroll down to the garbageCollPeriod attribute and the tombstoneLifetime attribute and edit the values. The default value appears as <not set>.

Backing Up Active Directory

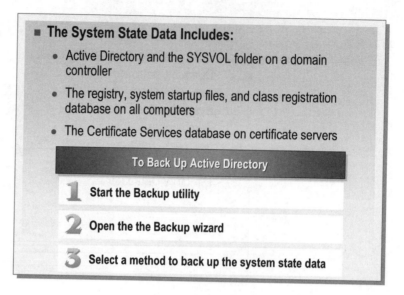

The System State Data Includes:

- Active Directory and the SYSVOL folder on a domain controller
- The registry, system startup files, and class registration database on all computers
- The Certificate Services database on certificate servers

To Back Up Active Directory

1 Start the Backup utility

2 Open the the Backup wizard

3 Select a method to back up the system state data

Backup in Windows 2000 Advanced Server has several features that make backing up Active Directory very easy. You can also integrate backing up Active Directory into your regular backup procedures without interrupting the network or the operation of the domain controller you are backing up.

The System State Data

Also, when you back up Active Directory, Backup automatically backs up all of the system components and distributed services upon which Active Directory is dependent. This dependent data is known collectively as the *system state data*.

The system state data on a domain controller includes the following:

- *Active Directory* (only on domain controllers).

- *The SYSVOL shared folder* (only on domain controllers). The SYSVOL folder is a shared folder that contains Group Policy templates and logon scripts.

- *The registry*. The registry is a database repository for information about the computer's configuration.

- *System startup files*. The system startup files are required during the initial startup phase of Windows 2000 Advanced Server.

- *Class registration database*. The class registration is a database of information about Component Services applications.

- *The Certificate Services database* (if the server is operating as a certificate server). The Certificate Services database contains certificates that Windows 2000 Advanced Server uses to authenticate users.

Backing Up the System State Data

To back up the system state data, perform the following steps:

1. On the **Start** menu, point to **Programs**, point to **Accessories**, point to **System Tools**, and then click **Backup**.

2. Click the **Backup Wizard** icon to open the Backup wizard.

3. You back up the system state data on a local computer in one of the following three ways:

   - In the Backup wizard, on the **What to Back Up** page, click **Only back up the System State data**.

   - In the Backup wizard, on the **Items to Back Up** page, expand **My Computer**, and then select the **System State** check box.

   - In the **Backup** dialog box, on the **Backup** tab, expand **My Computer**, and then select the **System State** check box.

You can use the advanced backup options in Backup to set or configure parameters, such as data verification, hardware compression, media labels, whether you want the backup job appended to a previous job, and whether you want to schedule the backup to run unattended at another time. Data verification enables Backup to check whether there are differences between the files it backed up from the domain controller and those copied to the backup media. The results of the verification are reported in Event Viewer.

Important For full disaster recovery, back up all hard disks and the system state data. To perform this backup, run Backup, and in the Backup wizard, on the **What to Back Up** page, select **Back up everything on my computer**.

Guidelines for Backing Up System State Data

Observe the following guidelines when backing up system state data:

- You must have the permission to back up files and folders. The members of the Administrators, Backup Operator, and Server Operator groups have the permission to back up files/folders by default.

- System state data does not contain Active Directory unless the server on which you are backing up the system state data is a domain controller.

- You can back up the system state data by itself, or you can back up the system state data as part of your regular backup procedures.

- You can back up the system state data while the domain controller is online.

Important Because Backup supports only local backups of Active Directory, you must perform a backup on every domain controller in the enterprise to entirely back up Active Directory. You cannot back up Active Directory on a remote computer without using third party tools, such as VERITAS.

◆ Restoring Active Directory

- ■ What Is a Nonauthoritative Restore?
- ■ Performing a Nonauthoritative Restore
- ■ What Is an Authoritative Restore?
- ■ Performing an Authoritative Restore

Windows 2000 provides you with the ability to restore the Active Directory database if it becomes corrupted or is destroyed due to hardware or software failures. There are two methods for restoring replicated data on a domain controller. You can reinstall the domain controller, and then let the normal replication process repopulate the new domain controller with data from its replicas, or you can use Backup to restore replicated data from backup media without reinstalling the operating system or reconfiguring the domain controller. There are two methods for restoring Active Directory from backup media, which are the *nonauthoritative* method and the *authoritative* method.

When you want to restore a recently deleted object to its previous undeleted state, perform an authoritative restore of that object. However, in cases in which you need to recover Active Directory from hardware failure, you need to perform only a nonauthoritative restore from the most recent backup. After the nonauthoritative restore, Active Directory replication automatically begins propagating any changes from other domain controllers that occurred after the time of the backup.

What Is a Nonauthoritative Restore?

- **A Nonauthoritative Restore Reinstates the Active Directory Data to the State Before the Backup**

- **Distributed Services Are Restored from Backup Media and the Restored Data Is Then Updated Through Replication**

- **Backup Performs Only a Nonauthoritative Restore of Active Directory**

- **After Restoring Active Directory, Windows 2000 Automatically:**
  - Performs a consistency check, and recalculates the indexes in the the database
  - Updates Active Directory and FRS

A nonauthoritative restore reinstates the Active Directory data to the state it was in before the backup. If any objects were updated or deleted before the backup, when replication occurs, the restored data will be updated to the current state of the objects.

During a nonauthoritative restore, the distributed services on a domain controller are restored from backup media and the restored data is then updated through normal replication. Each restored directory partition is updated with that of its replication partners. One example of a situation in which you use nonauthoritative restore is a hard disk failure that requires replacing the primary hard disk on a domain controller. You format the new disk, recreate the partitions as they were before the failure, reinstall Windows 2000 Advanced Server on the primary partition, restore all data files that you had on the computer, and then restore the distributed services, including the entire Active Directory.

Backup performs only a nonauthoritative restore of Active Directory. When the domain controller is brought online after a nonauthoritative restore, it detects that the restored data has not been updated since the backup was performed. Therefore, after you have restored Active Directory, Windows 2000 automatically:

- Performs a consistency check on and recalculates the indexes in the Active Directory database.

- Updates Active Directory and File Replication service (FRS) with data from their replication partners.

Performing a Nonauthoritative Restore

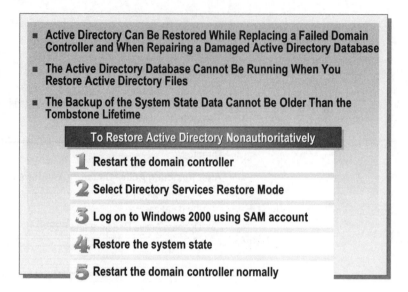

- **Active Directory Can Be Restored While Replacing a Failed Domain Controller and When Repairing a Damaged Active Directory Database**
- **The Active Directory Database Cannot Be Running When You Restore Active Directory Files**
- **The Backup of the System State Data Cannot Be Older Than the Tombstone Lifetime**

To Restore Active Directory Nonauthoritatively

1 Restart the domain controller

2 Select Directory Services Restore Mode

3 Log on to Windows 2000 using SAM account

4 Restore the system state

5 Restart the domain controller normally

You can restore Active Directory nonauthoritatively during the process of replacing a failed domain controller, and when repairing a damaged Active Directory database.

If the operating system on a domain controller is functioning normally, but the Active Directory database is damaged, you must restart the computer, select the **Directory Services Restore Mode** advanced startup option, and then use Backup to restore the latest system state data. Because Active Directory is part of the system state data on a domain controller, you must restore the system state data to restore Active Directory. Backup cannot replace Active Directory files while Active Directory is running. Therefore, you must start the operating system by using the **Directory Services Restore Mode** advanced startup option.

Important You cannot restore Active Directory from a backup that is more than the tombstone lifetime, which is 60 days by default. A domain controller keeps track of deleted objects for only this period.

If you have only one domain controller, any changes that you made since the last backup are lost. If you have multiple domain controllers, and the age of the backup is less than the tombstone lifetime, restore the backup that you have and then let the replication between domain controllers make Active Directory current.

To restore Active Directory nonauthoritatively, perform the following steps:

1. Restart the domain controller, and then press F8 to display the advanced startup options.

2. Select **Directory Services Restore Mode** to start Windows 2000; however, this selection does not automatically start Active Directory.

3. Log on to Windows 2000 by using the Administrator account that resides in the local user account database on the domain controller.

4. Use Backup to restore the latest system state data.

5. Restart the domain controller as you normally would.

   After the computer restarts, Windows 2000 Advanced Server performs consistency checks, initializes (re-indexes) the Active Directory database, and updates Active Directory information and FRS data from the computer's replication partners. If there are multiple domain controllers, after replication has occurred, the domain controller's Active Directory database is made current.

Warning   When you restore the system state data, Backup erases the system state data that is currently on your computer and replaces it with the system state data that you are restoring. Depending on how old the system state data is, you may lose configuration changes that you have recently made to the computer. To minimize the risk of losing your configuration changes, back up this data regularly.

What Is an Authoritative Restore?

- **An Authoritative Restore Allows You to Mark Specific Information in the Database**

- **Authoritative Restore Occurs After Nonauthoritative Restore Has Been Performed**

- **The Version Number of Each Object Marked As Authoritative Is Increased by 100,000 for Each Day**

- **The Domain Controller with the Higher Version Number for the Same Object Replicates over the Domain Controller with the Lower Version Number**

An authoritative restore is the method that you use to restore individual Active Directory objects in a domain with multiple domain controllers. By using an authoritative restore, you can mark specific information in the database as current, thus preventing replication from overwriting that information. When you restore container objects, all objects in the organizational unit (OU) are also restored.

An authoritative restore occurs after a nonauthoritative restore has been performed. An authoritative restore is typically used to restore Active Directory to a previously known state; for example, before Active Directory objects were erroneously deleted.

Note You cannot mark the schema directory partition as authoritative; therefore, schema changes cannot be undone using an authoritative restore.

When you mark an object as authoritative, it has the highest *version number* in Active Directory. The version is a number, starting at one, that is incremented for each originating update to the Active Directory database. By default, the version number of each object marked as authoritative is increased by 100,000 for each day between when the backup occurred and when the restore occurred. Increasing the version number ensures that when replication of that object occurs, the authoritatively restored value replaces any update that occurred since the backup. The assumption is that the object did not change 100,000 times every day since the backup. During replication, the version number is checked before the timestamp to avoid replication conflicts. The version number is stored as a 64-bit value. You can change the default increment number for the new version number.

When two domain controllers have different version numbers for the same object, the change with the highest number replicates over the other copy of the object. By assigning the highest version number to the objects, you ensure that updates to the object since the backup do not overwrite the authoritative value during replication. Only deletions or changes that occur to the authoritatively restored object take effect.

For information about on how version numbers are used to help resolve replication conflicts, see Module 11, "Managing Active Directory Replication," in Course 2154, *Implementing and Administering Microsoft Windows 2000 Directory Services*.

Note If you do not use an authoritative restore, the restored object has the version number that it had when it was backed up. Any change to the object after backup, such as an incorrect deletion, has a higher version number. The changed object version would replicate over the restored object version. If you have only one domain controller, this scenario does not apply.

Performing an Authoritative Restore

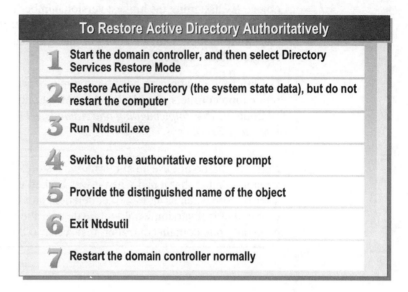

Ntdsutil.exe is a utility that allows you to mark Active Directory objects as authoritative so that they receive a higher version number, which prevents recently changed data on other domain controllers from overwriting that information during replication.

To implement an authoritative restore, perform the following steps:

1. Start the domain controller, press F8, and then on the **Advanced Startup Options** menu, click **Directory Services Restore Mode**. You select this mode because Active Directory cannot be running during this process. Log on using the Administrator account that resides in the local user account database on the domain controller.

2. Restore Active Directory to its original location. Also, restore Active Directory to an alternate location when you need to perform an authoritative restore on SYSVOL. Use Backup to restore the system state data, but *do not restart* the computer when prompted after the restore.

3. Open a command prompt window, and run Ntdsutil.exe.

4. Switch to the **authoritative restore** prompt. At the **ntdsutil** prompt, type **authoritative restore**

5. At the **authoritative restore** prompt, type

   restore subtree *distinguished_name_of_object*

   where *distinguished_name_of_object* is the distinguished name, or path, to the object. For example, if you want to restore an OU called Sales, which existed directly below the domain called contoso.msft, type

   restore subtree OU=Sales,DC=contoso,DC=msft

   For more information about distinguished user names, see appendix C, "LDAP Names," on the Student Materials compact disc.

6. Type **quit** and then press ENTER. Type **quit** again, and then press ENTER to exit **ntdsutil**.

7. Restart the domain controller as you normally would.

When you perform an authoritative restore of the Active Directory database, or a portion of the Active Directory database including Group Policy objects, you must perform an additional procedure involving the SYSVOL folder to ensure the proper elements are authoritatively restored.

After the SYSVOL folder is published by the File Replication service (FRS), copy the SYSVOL folder, and copy only Group Policy folders corresponding to the restored Group Policy objects from the alternate location to the existing locations. You can verify that the copy was successful by checking the contents of the SYSVOL\domain folder.

Lab A: Backing Up and Restoring Active Directory

Objectives

After completing this lab, you will be able to:

- Perform a backup of the Active Directory database.
- Perform a nonauthoritative restore of the Active Directory database.
- Perform an authoritative restore of the Active Directory database.

Prerequisites

Before working on this lab, you must have:

- Knowledge and experience initiating Active Directory replication.
- Experience creating objects in Active Directory.

Important   The lab does not reflect the real-world environment. It is recommended that you always use complex passwords for any administrator accounts, and never create accounts without a password.

Important   Outside of the classroom environment, it is strongly advised that you use the most recent software updates that are necessary. Because this is a classroom environment, we may use software that does not include the latest updates.

Scenario

You are verifying Northwind Traders disaster recovery procedures for Active Directory. These procedures document backing up the system state data on domain controllers and then restoring it. Of particular interest to the organization is the safe restoration of accidentally deleted organizational units.

Estimated time to complete this lab: 30 minutes

Exercise 1
Backing Up Active Directory

Scenario

Northwind Traders developed disaster recovery procedures. The backup procedures need to be tested to ensure they are adequate before they are implemented in the entire organization.

Goal

In this exercise, you will create a test organizational unit that will be deleted after a backup of the computer's system state data.

Note: You will work with a partner and be grouped by domain in this exercise.

Tasks	Detailed Steps
1. Within *domain*.nwtraders.msft (where *domain* is your assigned domain name), create the following OU: • Backup_*servername* (where *servername* is the host name of your computer).	**a.** Log on as Administrator in your domain with a password of **password**. **b.** Open Active Directory Users and Computers from the **Administrative Tools** menu. **c.** In the console tree, expand *domain*.**nwtraders.msft** (where *domain* is your assigned domain name), right-click *domain*.**nwtraders.msft**, point to **New**, and then click **Organizational Unit**. **d.** In the **New Object – Organizational Unit** dialog box, in the **Name** box, type **Backup_***servername* (where *servername* is the name of your computer), and then click **OK**.
⚠ **Important:** Wait until both you and your partner complete task 1 before starting task 2.	
2. Initiate replication with your partner's domain controller.	**a.** Open Active Directory Sites and Services from the **Administrative Tools** menu. **b.** Expand **Sites**, expand **Default-First-Site-Name**, expand **Servers**, expand *servername*, and then click **NTDS Settings**. **c.** Right-click the connection object from your partner's server, click **Replicate Now**, and then click **OK** to close the message indicating that replication was successful. **d.** In Active Directory Users and Computers, click *domain*.**nwtraders.msft** and press F5 to refresh the display. **e.** Verify that both organizational units **Backup_***servername* and **Backup_***partnerserver* (where *partnerserver* is the host name of your partner's computer) appear. **Note**: If your partner's organizational unit does not appear, perform steps c and d again. **f.** Close Active Directory Sites and Services.

Tasks	Detailed Steps
3. Start the backup of your domain controller's system state data to a file called C:\Backup.bkf by using detailed logging.	a. Click **Start**, point to **Programs**, point to **Accessories**, point to **System Tools**, and then click **Backup**. b. In the **Backup – [Untitled]** window, on the **Tools** menu, click **Options**. c. In the **Options** dialog box, on the **Backup Log** tab, click **Detailed** to enable detailed logging, and then click **OK**. d. In the **Backup –[Untitled]** window, click **Backup Wizard**. e. On the **Welcome to the Windows 2000 Backup and Recovery Tools** page, click **Next** to continue. f. On the **What to Back Up** page, click **Only back up the System State data**, and then click **Next**. g. On the **Where to Store the Backup** page, in the **Backup media or file name** box, type **C:\Backup.bkf** and then click **Next**. h. On the **Completing the Backup Wizard** page, click **Finish**. i. Proceed to task 4, allowing the backup process to continue in the background.
4. While allowing the backup process to complete in the background, determine the invocation ID for the domain controller that will perform the restore.	a. Open a command prompt window. b. At the command prompt, type **repadmin /showreps** *restoreserver* (where *restoreserver* is the host name of the computer with the lower student number of the pair), and then press ENTER.

> **?** What is the purpose of the invocation ID?
>
> Write down the invocation ID (or copy and paste it to a text file) of *restoreserver*. This information will be used for comparisons in a later exercise.
>
> Is this invocation ID different from the objectGUID?

Used to ID the server.

Yes, invocation ID is diff. fm. object GUID.
9b50168b – eaef – 422b – bd71 – 9928d39db5a8

5. While allowing the backup process to complete in the background, determine the version number of Backup_*restoreserver* (where *restoreserver* is the host name of the computer with the lower student number of the pair).	a. At the command prompt, type **repadmin /showmeta "ou=Backup_***restoreserver***,dc=***Domain***,dc=nwtraders,dc=msft"** and then press ENTER.

Tasks	Detailed Steps
❓ What is the version number for the **name** attribute of the Backup_*restoreserver* organizational unit? *64l6 — "1"*	
5. *(continued)*	**b.** Close the command prompt window.
6. After the backup process completes, view the report, and then close Backup.	**a.** In Backup, in the **Backup Progress** dialog box, click **Report**. **b.** Review the backup log to see the files that are part of the system state for a domain controller, and then close the log file. **c.** In the **Backup Progress** dialog box, click **Close**, and then close Backup.
7. Delete both test organizational units: Backup_*servername* and Backup_*partnerserver* (where *partnerserver* is the host name of your partner's computer).	**a.** In Active Directory Users and Computers, click **Backup_***servername*, press DELETE, and then click **Yes** to close the message confirming the deletion. **b.** Click **Backup_***partnerserver*, press DELETE, and then click **Yes** to close the message confirming the deletion. **c.** Close Active Directory Users and Computers.

Exercise 2
Restoring Active Directory

Scenario

Northwind Traders developed disaster recovery procedures. The restore procedures, including authoritative restore, need to be tested before they are implemented in the entire organization.

Goal

In this exercise, you will restore the most recent backup prior to the deletion of the test organizational units. For one of the test organizational units, you will perform an authoritative restore.

Note: Only the domain controller with the lower student number of the pair is used in this exercise. This domain controller is designated as the restore server.

Tasks	Detailed Steps
⚠️ **Important:** Perform this exercise only on the domain controller designated as the restore server.	
1. Restart your domain controller in Directory Services Restore Mode, and then log on as Administrator.	a. Close any open applications and restart your domain controller. b. When the **Boot Loader** menu appears or when the message "For troubleshooting and advanced startup options for Windows 2000, press F8" appears at the bottom of the screen, press F8. c. On the **Windows 2000 Advanced Options** menu, click **Directory Services Restore Mode**, and then press ENTER. d. Log on as Administrator in your domain with a password of **password**, and then click **OK** to close the message indicating that Windows is running in safe mode.
2. Restore your domain controller's system state from a file named C:\Backup.bkf.	a. Open Backup. b. In the **Backup –[Untitled]** window, on the **Welcome** tab, click **Restore Wizard** to start the Restore wizard. c. On the **Welcome to the Restore Wizard** page, click **Next** to continue. d. On the **What to Restore** page, expand **File**, expand **Media created**, select the **System State** check box, and then click **Next**. e. On the **Completing the Restore Wizard** page, click **Finish**. f. In the **Enter Backup File Name** dialog box, in the **Restore from backup file** box, type **C:\Backup.bkf** and then click **OK**. g. After the restore process completes, click **Close**, click **No** to close the message asking to restart you computer, and then close Backup.

Tasks	Detailed Steps
3. After the restore process is completed, mark the Backup_*restoreserver* OU to be restored authoritatively.	a. Open a command prompt window. b. At the command prompt, type **ntdsutil** and then press ENTER. c. At the **ntdsutil** prompt, type **authoritative restore** and then press ENTER. d. At the **authoritative restore** prompt, type **?** and then press ENTER. *Review the available options.* e. At the **authoritative restore** prompt, type **restore subtree "ou=Backup_***restoreserver***,dc=***domain***,dc=nwtraders,dc=msft"** press ENTER, and then click **Yes** to close the message confirming the authoritative restore. f. At the **authoritative restore** prompt, type **quit** and then press ENTER to change to the previous menu. g. At the **ntdsutil** prompt, type **quit** and then press ENTER to exit **ntdsutil**.
4. Restart the domain controller and log on as Administrator.	a. Close the command prompt window, and then restart the computer. b. Log on as Administrator in your domain with a password of **password**.

Exercise 3
Verifying a Restore of Active Directory

Scenario

Northwind Traders developed disaster recovery procedures. The verification procedures of an authoritative and nonauthoritative restore need to be tested before they are implemented in the entire organization.

Goal

In this exercise, you will verify that the restore operation was successful by examining both authoritative and nonauthoritative data.

Tasks	Detailed Steps
1. Initiate replication with your partner's domain controller.	a. Open Active Directory Sites and Services, expand **Sites**, expand **Default-First-Site-Link-Name**, expand **Servers**, expand *servername*, and then click **NTDS Settings**.
	b. Right-click the connection object from your partner's server, click **Replicate Now**, and then click **OK** to close the message indicating that replication was initiated.
	Note: If an error message appears stating the RPC service is unavailable, wait a moment and then repeat step c. It may take some time to get all of the necessary services running after restarting the computer.
	c. Close Active Directory Sites and Services.
	d. Open Active Directory Users and Computers, click *domain*.**nwtraders.msft**, and then press F5 to refresh the display.
❓ Which Backup_*servername* organizational units are still in Active Directory after replication with your partner's computer and why?	

Back-up denver because was restored authoritatively (?)
Perth was not because it was deleted thru process of replication (?)

Tasks	Detailed Steps
1. *(continued)*	e. Close Active Directory Users and Computers.
2. Determine any changes made to the invocation ID for the domain controller that performed the restore.	▪ At a command prompt, type **repadmin /showreps** *restoreserver* and then press ENTER.

Tasks	Detailed Steps
❓ Is the invocation ID for the *restoreserver* the same value as it was before the restore? Is this invocation ID different from the objectGUID?	
	No.
	Yes.
	26c6f708 - dbde - 4e6b - 9109 - f4a513e1f58b
3. Determine any changes made to the version number of Backup_*restoreserver*, and then log off.	a. At a command prompt, type **repadmin /showmeta "ou=Backup_***restoreserver***,dc=***domain***,dc=nwtraders,dc=msft"** and then press ENTER.
❓ What is the version number for the name attribute of the Backup_*restoreserver* organizational unit?	
	6965 *"100,001"*
	adds 100,000
3. *(continued)*	b. Close the command prompt window, close all other open windows, and then log off.

Moving the Active Directory Database

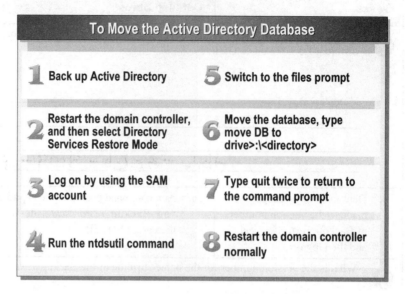

You use the **ntdsutil** command-line utility in Directory Services Restore mode to move the database from one location to another location on the disk. The **ntdsutil** command-line utility moves the database files to a new location and then updates the registry keys so that Active Directory restarts from the new location.

To move the Active Directory database, perform the following steps:

1. Back up Active Directory as a precautionary measure. You can back up Active Directory while online if in the Backup wizard, you have selected either the option to back up everything on the computer, or the option to back up the system state data.

2. Restart the domain controller, press F8 to display the **Windows 2000 Advanced Options** menu, click **Directory Services Restore Mode**, and then press ENTER.

3. Log on by using the Administrator account and the password defined for the Local Administrator account in the Security Accounts Manager (SAM).

4. At the command prompt, type **ntdsutil** and then press ENTER.

5. Type **files** and then press ENTER. This switches you to the **files** prompt, so that you can manage the Ntds.dit database file.

6. After you establish a location that has enough drive space for the database to be stored, type the following, and then press ENTER:

   move DB to *<drive>:\<directory>*

   where *<drive>* and *<directory>* is the path to the location where you want to place the database.

   Note You must specify a directory path. If the path contains any spaces, the entire path must be surrounded by quotation marks, for example, "C:\New folder"

   The database named Ntds.dit is moved to the location that you specified.

7. Type **quit** and then press ENTER. To return to the command prompt, type **quit** again.

8. Restart the domain controller as you normally would.

Note You can also move the transaction log files to another location. The **Move logs to** *<drive>:\<directory>* command moves the transaction log files to the new directory specified by *<drive>:\<directory>* and updates the registry keys so that the directory service restarts from the new location.

◆ Defragmenting the Active Directory Database

- **What Is Defragmentation?**
- **Defragmenting a Database**

Over a period of time, fragmentation occurs as records in the Active Directory database are deleted and new records are added. When the records are fragmented, the computer must search the Active Directory database each time the Active Directory database is opened to find all of the records, which slows down response time. Fragmentation also degrades the overall performance of Active Directory database operations. To overcome this problem of fragmentation, you *defragment* the Active Directory database. Defragmentation is the process of rewriting records in the Active Directory database to contiguous sectors to increase the speed of access and retrieval. When records are updated, these updates are saved on the largest contiguous space in the Active Directory database.

What Is Defragmentation?

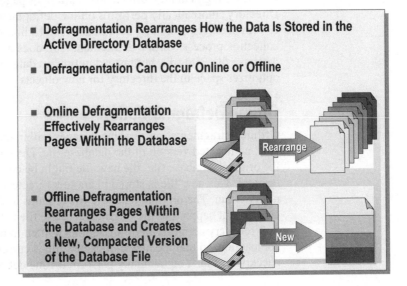

- **Defragmentation Rearranges How the Data Is Stored in the Active Directory Database**

- **Defragmentation Can Occur Online or Offline**

- **Online Defragmentation Effectively Rearranges Pages Within the Database**

  Rearrange

- **Offline Defragmentation Rearranges Pages Within the Database and Creates a New, Compacted Version of the Database File**

  New

Defragmentation rearranges and compacts data storage in the Active Directory database. To update the Active Directory database file, ESE quickly updates the database; however, it does not make the most efficient use of space in the database. Therefore, Active Directory rewrites parts of the database to contiguous sectors on a hard disk, thereby increasing the speed through which users can gain access to and retrieve data. For example, data is written to pages one through 100, and then at a later time, data is deleted, freeing pages 12, 55, and 87. The next time data is written, it may get written on pages 12, 55, and 87, which would slow the response time. However, if you defragment the Active Directory database, pages 12, 55, and 87 would be grouped together, so that all of the data would be placed on pages one through 97, and pages 98 through 100 would be free to contain the new data.

Therefore, database defragmentation is necessary to efficiently use the space allocated to the database. Defragmentation can take place online while the computer is functioning as a domain controller or offline while the computer is functioning as a stand-alone server.

Online Defragmentation

Online defragmentation effectively rearranges pages within the database. Active Directory automatically performs online defragmentation of the database at certain intervals, which by default is every 12 hours, as part of the garbage collection process. Online defragmentation does not reduce the size of the database file, Ntds.dit, but instead optimizes data storage in the database and optimizes space in the directory for new objects.

Offline Defragmentation

Offline defragmentation rearranges pages within the database, and creates a new, compacted version of the database file. Depending on the fragmentation of the original database file, the new file might be considerably smaller than the original. This new file is stored in another directory that is chosen when the utility is run. The original database file remains in the same location. The only change that happens to the original database file is that it is first soft recovered. Soft recovery commits any transactions written to the log files before the compaction, so that the new compacted file is current with the log files and the checkpoint file. You manually perform offline defragmentation of the database.

Defragmenting a Database

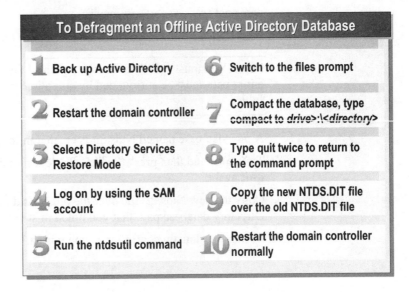

To Defragment an Offline Active Directory Database

1 Back up Active Directory

2 Restart the domain controller

3 Select Directory Services Restore Mode

4 Log on by using the SAM account

5 Run the ntdsutil command

6 Switch to the files prompt

7 Compact the database, type compact to *drive>:\<directory>*

8 Type quit twice to return to the command prompt

9 Copy the new NTDS.DIT file over the old NTDS.DIT file

10 Restart the domain controller normally

Online defragmentation occurs automatically during the garbage collection process. Offline defragmentation must be performed manually and is necessary only if you want to create a new, compacted version of the original database file.

To defragment an offline Active Directory database, perform the following steps:

1. Back up Active Directory as a precautionary measure.

2. Restart the domain controller, and then press F8 to display the **Windows 2000 Advanced Options** menu.

3. Select **Directory Services Restore Mode**, and then press ENTER.

4. Log on by using the Administrator account and the password defined for the Local Administrator account in the offline SAM.

5. At the command prompt, type **ntdsutil** and then press ENTER.

6. Type **files** and then press ENTER. This switches you to the **files** prompt so that you can manage the NTDS database file.

7. Establish a location that has enough drive space for the compacted database to be stored. Type the following, and then press ENTER:

   compact to *<drive>*:*<directory>*

   where *<drive>* and *<directory>* is the path to the location.

   Note   You must specify a directory path. If the path contains any spaces, the entire path must be surrounded by quotation marks; for example, "C:\New folder."

   A new database named Ntds.dit is created in the path that you specified.

8. Type **quit** and then press ENTER. To return to the command prompt, type **quit** again.

9. Copy the new Ntds.dit file over the old Ntds.dit file in the current Active Directory database path that you noted in step 6.

10. Restart the domain controller as you normally would.

Lab B: Maintaining the Active Directory Database

Objectives

After completing this lab, you will be able to:

- Perform an offline defragmentation of the Active Directory database.
- Run integrity and semantic database checks of the Active Directory database.
- Move the Active Directory database to another folder.
- Redirect Active Directory to use the database file located in a different folder.

Prerequisites

Before working on this lab, you must have knowledge and experience using advanced startup options in Windows 2000.

Estimated time to complete this lab: 30 minutes

Exercise 1
Performing an Offline Defragmentation

Scenario

Northwind Traders had not initially planned which domain controllers would be global catalog servers. The result was that too many domain controllers were designated as global catalog servers. As soon as Northwind Traders realized this problem, they established an appropriate number of global catalog servers. Therefore, a large number of domain controllers that had been used as global catalog servers were now being used as domain controllers again. A maintenance schedule was defined to take domain controllers offline and perform an offline defragmentation and other database maintenance checks on these domain controllers. The primary reason for these checks is to reclaim disk space by reducing the size of the Ntds.dit database file. The domain controller's system state data was already backed up in preparation for this task.

Goal

In this exercise, you will move the database on your domain controller to an alternate location and then perform an offline defragmentation. This will reclaim any disk space that was used by the global catalog information. You will perform a database integrity check and a semantic database analysis on the defragmented database. You will reconfigure Active Directory to use this database file without deleting the original files. After the new database is successfully online, you will delete the old database files.

Tasks	Detailed Steps
1. Restart your domain controller in Directory Services Restore Mode, and then log on as Administrator.	a. Log on as Administrator in your domain with a password of **password**.
	b. Restart your domain controller.
	c. When the message "For troubleshooting and advanced startup options for Windows 2000, press F8" is displayed at the bottom of the screen, press F8.
	d. On the **Windows 2000 Advanced Options** menu, click **Directory Services Restore Mode**, and then press ENTER.
	e. If prompted for the operating system, select **Microsoft Windows 2000 Advanced Server**, and then press ENTER.
	f. Log on as Administrator with a password of **password** and then click **OK** to close the message that indicates Windows is running in safe mode.
2. Determine the current file size of the database by using the **ntdsutil** utility.	a. Open a command prompt window.
	b. At the command prompt, type **ntdsutil** and then press ENTER.
	c. At the **ntdsutil** prompt, type **files** and then press ENTER to change to the **file maintenance** menu.
	d. At the **file maintenance** prompt, type **info** and then press ENTER to display the size of the database files.

Tasks	Detailed Steps
❓ What is the size of the Ntds.dit file? What are the locations of the Database, Backup directory, Working directory, and Logs directory? *10.1 Mb* *C:\WINNT\NTDS*	
3. Move the database and log files to C:\2154_original.	a. At the **file maintenance** prompt, type **move db to c:\2154_original** and then press ENTER to move the database files to this alternate location. b. At the **file maintenance** prompt, type **move logs to c:\2154_original** and then press ENTER to move the log files to this alternate location. c. At the **file maintenance** prompt, type **info** and then press ENTER to verify the paths were also updated.
4. Perform an offline defragmentation of the database to C:\Winnt\n=Ntds.	▪ At the **file maintenance** prompt, type **compact to c:\winnt\ntds** and then press ENTER to defragment the database.
5. Redirect the directory services path to: • Database – C:\Winnt\Ntds\Ntds.dit • Backup dir – C:\Winnt\Ntds\Dsadata. bak • Working dir – C:\Winnt\Ntds • Log dir – C:\Winnt\Ntds	a. At the file maintenance prompt, type set path db c:\winnt\ntds\ntds.dit and then press ENTER. b. At the **file maintenance** prompt, type **set path backup c:\winnt\ntds\dsadata.bak** and then press ENTER. c. At the **file maintenance** prompt, type **set path working dir c:\winnt\ntds** and then press ENTER. d. At the **file maintenance** prompt, type **set path logs c:\winnt\ntds** and then press ENTER. e. At the **file maintenance** prompt, type **info** and then press ENTER to verify the paths have been set correctly.
❓ What is the size of the defragmented Ntds.dit file? Is it smaller than the original Ntds.dit file? *6.1 Mb — yes*	

Tasks	Detailed Steps
6. Run an integrity check and semantic database analysis on the defragmented database file. Review the summary log created by the semantic database analysis.	a. At the **file maintenance** prompt, type **integrity** and then press ENTER to run the database integrity check. A message indicates that the operation completed successfully. b. At the **file maintenance** prompt, type **quit** and then press ENTER to return to the **ntdsutil** prompt. c. At the **ntdsutil** prompt, type **semantic database analysis** and then press ENTER to go to the **semantic checker** prompt. d. At the **semantic checker** prompt, type **go** and then press ENTER to run the semantic database analysis. *A message indicates the file storing the summary results. Note the file name for use in step g.* *dsdit. dmp. 0* e. At the **semantic checker** prompt, type **quit** and then press ENTER to return to the ntdsutil prompt. f. At the **ntdsutil** prompt, type **quit** and then press ENTER to return to the command prompt. g. At the command prompt, type **notepad** *dsdit_file* (where *dsdit_file* is the log file indicated by the semantic database analysis in step d), and then press ENTER. h. Review the summary, close Notepad, and then delete the log file.
7. Restart the domain controller, log on, verify Active Directory is working correctly, delete the original database files, and then log off.	a. Close the open command prompt window, and then restart the computer. b. Log on as Administrator in your domain with a password of **password**. c. Open Event Viewer, and then click **Directory Service**. d. Verify that no recent errors were logged since the restart, and then close Event Viewer. e. If there are no current Active Directory errors, delete the folder named C:\2154_original to free the disk space currently used by the original database files. f. Close all open windows, and then log off.

Best Practices

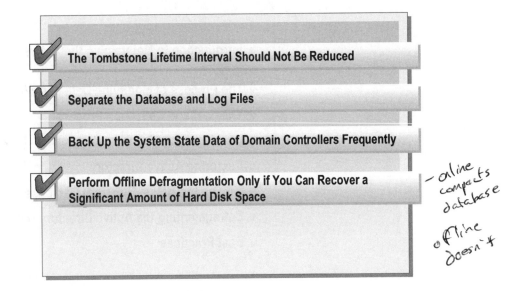

The following list provides best practices for implementing disaster recovery in Active Directory:

- The tombstone lifetime interval should not be reduced. When a domain controller is restored, backup compares the tombstone lifetime with the backup date and will not restore the system state data if the backup is older than the tombstone lifetime. The restored domain controller is not aware of deletions that have their tombstone removed, which can lead to inconsistencies between domain controllers. Therefore, it is recommended that tombstone lifetime be maintained at a value greater than either expected replication latency or backup interval, whichever is greater.

- Separate the database and log files. Move the database and log files to separate hard disks to prevent them from competing with the input output (I/O) of the operating system. Also, move the database and log files to separate hard disks to separate the I/O from each other.

- Back up the system state data of domain controllers frequently, so that you have the most current data to restore. Back up the system state data at least weekly, after you install new software, make configuration changes, or add new objects to Active Directory. Even if your domain has multiple domain controllers that can replicate Active Directory, multiple disasters can occur.

- Perform offline defragmentation only if you can recover a significant amount of disk space that you can use for other tasks. For example, if the domain controller was once a global catalog server for a multiple domain forest but was later removed, you can free a significant amount of disk space by using the offline defragmentation method.

Review

- **Introduction to Maintaining the Active Directory Database**
- **The Process of Modifying Data in Active Directory**
- **The Garbage Collection Process**
- **Backing Up Active Directory**
- **Restoring Active Directory**
- **Moving the Active Directory Database**
- **Defragmenting the Active Directory Database**
- **Best Practices**

1. What is the purpose of the garbage collection process?

   Picks up expired tombstones.

2. What is the purpose of the tombstone lifetime and how does this affect the restore operation?

   See p.5
   Gives us time to restore – delete OU – do an authoritative restore.

3. When you start one of the domain controllers in your domain, you receive an error message indicating that Active Directory cannot start because the Active Directory database is damaged. How do you restore the Active Directory database and make sure that it is current?

4. Someone incorrectly deleted an OU in Active Directory. What should you do?

   Restore system state data — mark OU as authoritative

5. You are planning to defragment the Active Directory database. What is the precaution you should take so that the original database is not deleted in case there is a problem during defragmentation?

   Make a copy

6. What type of defragmentation would you perform to create a new, compacted version of the database file?

   Offline would make an non-compact version.

Microsoft®
Training &
Certification

Module 14:
Implementing an Active Directory Infrastructure

Contents

Overview

- ■ **Business Scenario**
- ■ **Requirements for the Active Directory Infrastructure**
- ■ **Class Discussion: How to Implement the Active Directory Infrastructure**
- ■ **Lab A: Implementing the Active Directory Infrastructure**

This module will provide you the opportunity to apply the knowledge and skills that you learned in this course to implement and administer an Active Directory® directory service infrastructure. You will implement Active Directory based on the business requirements of a fictitious organization.

At the end of this module, you will be able to:

- ■ Describe the infrastructure of a fictitious organization.
- ■ Identify the business requirements for implementing the Active Directory infrastructure.
- ■ Describe how to implement the Active Directory infrastructure.
- ■ Perform the tasks necessary to implement the Active Directory infrastructure.

Business Scenario

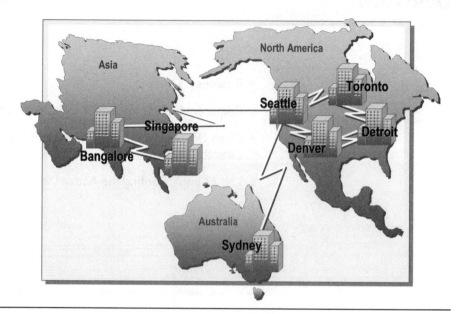

In this module, a fictitious organization named Contoso, Ltd. will be used to demonstrate how to implement an Active Directory infrastructure based on an organization's business requirements. Contoso, Ltd. is a worldwide organization with 50,000 employees.

The following are the business specifications of the different regions of Contoso, Ltd.

- The North American region has 25,000 employees:

    - 24,500 employees are located in the four primary locations, and the other employees are located in the 10 branch offices in other major North American cities.

    - Three of the four primary locations are separate business units and operate independently. The fourth primary location is corporate headquarters.

    - Each branch office has 50 or fewer employees. The employees need access to resources in all four primary locations. But the employees seldom need access to resources in other locations.

    - T1 lines connect the four primary locations. All branch offices are connected to the nearest primary location by 128 kilobits per second (Kbps) lines.

- The Asian region has 15,000 employees:

  - The employees are located in the two locations, Bangalore and Singapore. There are 8,000 employees at the Bangalore location and 7,000 employees at the Singapore location. These locations make up a single business unit.

  - The employees need occasional access to resources in the corporate location in North America, but seldom need access to resources in the Australian location.

  - The Bangalore and Singapore locations are connected to each other and to the North American location by T1 lines.

- The Australian region has 10,000 employees:

  - All employees are located in a single location, Sydney.

  - The employees need occasional access to resources in the corporate location in North America, but seldom need access to resources in the Asian location.

  - The Australian location is connected to the North American location by a 128 Kbps line.

- Contoso, Ltd.'s growth is expected to be minimal over the next three years.

- There are three main departments within Contoso, Ltd.: Accounting, Human Resources, and Information Services. Each of these departments is further divided into smaller departments and each location has employees from each of these departments.

Requirements for the Active Directory Infrastructure

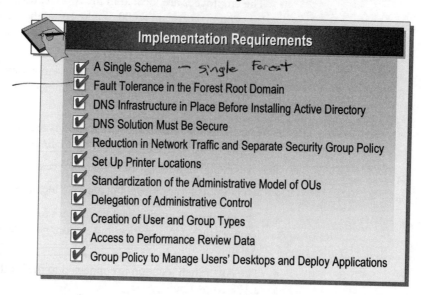

[handwritten: DNS & Active Dir.]

Implementation Requirements

- ☑ A Single Schema *[handwritten: → single forest]*
- ☑ Fault Tolerance in the Forest Root Domain
- ☑ DNS Infrastructure in Place Before Installing Active Directory
- ☑ DNS Solution Must Be Secure
- ☑ Reduction in Network Traffic and Separate Security Group Policy
- ☑ Set Up Printer Locations
- ☑ Standardization of the Administrative Model of OUs
- ☑ Delegation of Administrative Control
- ☑ Creation of User and Group Types
- ☑ Access to Performance Review Data
- ☑ Group Policy to Manage Users' Desktops and Deploy Applications

[handwritten left margin: Must have Act. Dir. integrated → Domain controller & DNS → 2 machines]

The implementation of the Active Directory infrastructure for Contoso, Ltd. should include the following requirements in the infrastructure:

- Use a single schema for the entire organization.

- Provide directory services and Domain Name System (DNS) fault tolerance in the forest root domain.

- Put the DNS infrastructure in place before installing Active Directory.

- Secure the DNS solution so that only authorized clients may register in DNS. *[handwritten: — DNS integrated into Active Dir.; then can choose secure updates]*

- Reduce network traffic between the North American, Asian, and Australian locations, and apply separate security Group Policy settings to the different locations.

- Set up printer locations so that users can easily locate the printers near them.

[handwritten left margin: Ea. will have Accounting, IT, Hum. Res.]

- Standardize the administrative model of organizational units (OUs) across all locations.

- Delegate administrative responsibility for OUs to appropriate employees.

- Create appropriate types of users and groups depending on their job requirements.

- Require each location to maintain performance review files of employees. All managers in the organization need access to this information.

- Implement Group Policy to manage users' desktops and deploy applications.

◆ Class Discussion: How to Implement the Active Directory Infrastructure

- ■ Installing and Configuring DNS

- ■ Installing Active Directory

- ■ Creating Sites and Site Links

- ■ Setting Up Printer Locations

- ■ Creating the OU Structure and Delegating Administrative Control

- ■ Creating Users and Groups

- ■ Implementing Group Policy

Based on the business scenario of Contoso, Ltd., you will implement a solution that uses Active Directory and Group Policy to satisfy the business requirements of the organization. In this section, you will discuss the plan for implementing DNS, Active Directory, sites and site links, printer locations, OU structure across domains, users and groups, and Group Policy.

Installing and Configuring DNS

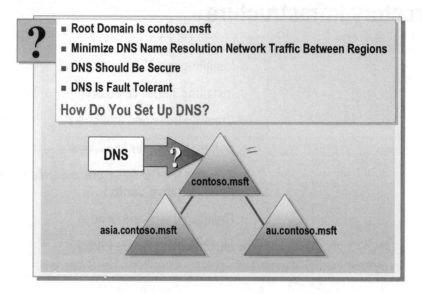

- **Root Domain Is contoso.msft**
- **Minimize DNS Name Resolution Network Traffic Between Regions**
- **DNS Should Be Secure**
- **DNS Is Fault Tolerant**

How Do You Set Up DNS?

Contoso, Ltd. wants to install a DNS structure before installing Active Directory. DNS will enable all client computers running Microsoft® Windows® 2000 to resolve domain and computer names, define namespaces, and locate the physical components of Active Directory The DNS domain name is contoso.msft.

1. How do you minimize DNS name resolution network traffic between the North American, Asian, and Australian regions?

   —DNS servers on ea. domain.
   Delegate author. So ea. domain is a zone
   child domains — secondary zone

2. How do you ensure that DNS is secure so that only authorized clients can register in DNS?

   Integrated w/ domain controller.
   Secure dynamic updates

3. How do you provide DNS fault tolerance in the forest root domain?

   Have 2 servers.

Installing Active Directory

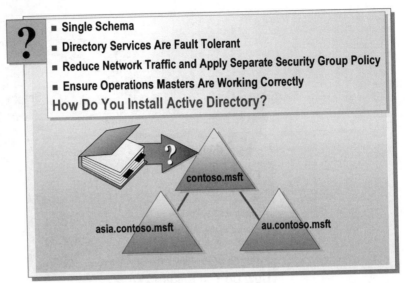

- Single Schema
- Directory Services Are Fault Tolerant
- Reduce Network Traffic and Apply Separate Security Group Policy
- Ensure Operations Masters Are Working Correctly

How Do You Install Active Directory?

contoso.msft

asia.contoso.msft

au.contoso.msft

Contoso, Ltd. wants to decentralize administration and centralize management of resources by installing Active Directory. The names of the Asian and Australian domains are asia.contoso.msft and au.contoso.msft, respectively.

1. How do you ensure that there is a single schema across the Contoso, Ltd. network?

   Single forest.

2. Contoso, Ltd. wants to reduce network traffic between domains. Each region also has separate security Group Policy requirements. How do you ensure that these requirements are fulfilled?

   Seperate domains in ea. region.

3. How do you ensure that directory services are fault tolerant in the forest root domain?

   2 domain controllers.

4. How do you ensure that all operations masters are working correctly?

   See CD —
   ✱ Know for test.

Creating Sites and Site Links

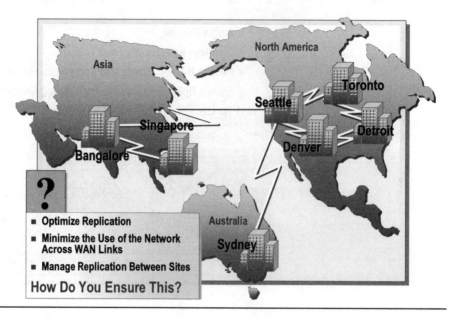

The North American region has four primary locations, Seattle, Toronto, Denver, and Detroit, as well as 10 branch offices. The employees in the Asian region are located in the Bangalore and Singapore locations. The employees of the Australian region are all located in Sydney.

1. What sites do you create to reduce replication traffic among the primary locations in the three main regions of Contoso, Ltd.?

2. Contoso, Ltd. is geographically distributed with many wide area network (WAN) links connecting the North American, Asian, and Australian regions. Network bandwidth on these WAN links is limited. Active Directory must be aware of which connections are local area networks (LANs) and which are WANs to optimize replication and minimize the use of the network across WAN links. What do you do to ensure this?

   IP subnets = diff. networks.

3. Contoso, Ltd. wants to define the schedule for replication between sites. The schedule is according to the most beneficial time for replication to occur on the basis of network traffic and cost. How do you manage replication between sites?

   Site link.

   test.

Setting Up Printer Locations

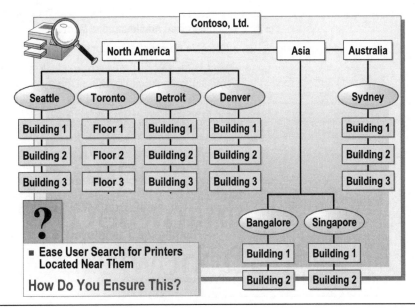

Contoso, Ltd. will have an Active Directory network configured with seven sites, and each site will correspond to IP subnet objects. Also, an IP addressing scheme will be present, and will correspond to the geographical and physical layout of the Contoso, Ltd. network. There are multiple office buildings at each location. The organization wants to implement printer locations to allow employees to locate and connect to print devices that are physically located near the employee.

1. Contoso, Ltd. has already met the requirements for implementing printer locations, and has devised a naming convention. What are the four main tasks that need to be performed to configure printer locations?

these must match names —
{ — line in properties of printer
— Properties of subnet — tab that says "location"
— tracking in group policy

2. How many subnet objects do you need to create to support the printer location feature at the building level?

Printer locations in Group Policy — so when user brings queries for printer, the response comes back only with printers on their floor.

Subnet must be tied into the printer name — 1 name.

Creating the OU Structure and Delegating Administrative Control

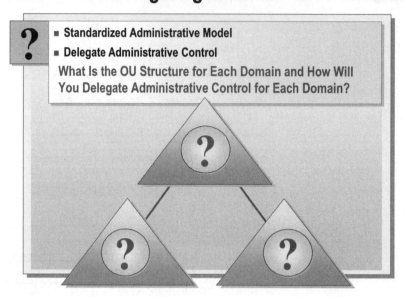

Contoso, Ltd. has three main departments: Information Services, Human Resources, and Accounting. The organization has decided upon a delegated administration model, and one administrator from each department will be responsible for managing the resources and users in that department. The following table lists the names of the subsidiary departments under the three main departments.

Main departments	Subsidiary departments
Information Services	Help Desk
	Applications
	Operating Systems
	Messaging
	Customer Support
Human Resources	Benefits
	Payroll
	Training
	Recruiting
Accounting	Accounts Payable
	Accounts Receivable

1. Each of the departments in Contoso, Ltd. is a separate OU. How do you ensure that the administrative model for OUs is standard across all domains in the network of your organization?

2. How do you ensure that one administrator from each department is responsible for managing the resources and users in that department?

Creating Users and Groups

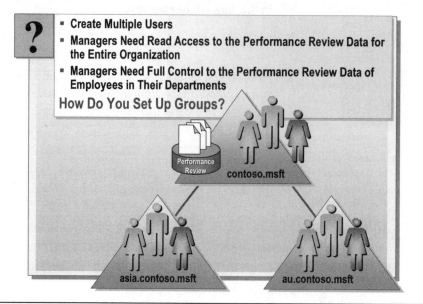

The managers of each department at Contoso, Ltd. are responsible for completing the performance reviews for their direct reports. Other managers, when considering an internal transfer of an employee from one department to another department, can reference the performance review data. Therefore, all managers require Read access to the performance review data. The managers for each department need Full Control access to the performance review data of the employees in their departments.

1. The Users.txt text file contains the information on all users who are to be added to each domain. How do you ensure that multiple users are created with minimal effort?

2. The performance review data is stored in a single file server for each domain. The data is grouped under folders by department name. Each domain has Information Services, Human Resources, and Accounting departments. What proposed group structure enables all managers to have only Read access to the performance review data for the entire organization?

3. What proposed group structure enables department managers to have Full Control access to the performance review data of the employees in their departments?

Implementing Group Policy

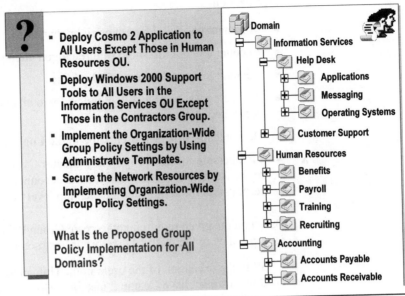

Contoso, Ltd. requires you to use administrative template settings to implement the following Group Policy settings across the entire organization:

- Disk quotas must be enabled on all computers.

- The disk quota limit must be enforced on all computers.

- The default quota limit for all users must be 100 megabytes (MB) and the warning level must be 75 MB.

- An event should be logged when the warning level and the quota limits are exceeded.

- Access to Windows Update must be denied.

- All users in all domains must not be able to run Freecell (Freecell.exe), Minesweeper (Winmine.exe), Pinball (Pinball.exe), and Solitaire (Sol.exe) applications.

- The users responsible for administering OUs must have access to only the following Microsoft Management Console (MMC) snap-ins: Active Directory Users and Computers, Group Policy, Group Policy tab for Active Directory Tools, Administrative Templates (Users), and Administrative Templates (Computers).

Contoso, Ltd. also requires you to secure the network resources by implementing the following Group Policy settings across the entire organization:

- Minimum password length of eight characters.
- Account lockout threshold of three logon attempts.
- Account lockout duration of 60 minutes.
- All users must be able to log on locally to all computers, including domain controllers.
- Do not display the last user name in the **Log On to Windows** dialog box.
- Membership in the Group Policy Creator Owners group must be restricted to the Administrator account and the accounts belonging to the users responsible for administering each top level OU.

Based on the given requirements, create Group Policy objects and implement Group Policy in the Active Directory infrastructure.

1. With the exception of the users in the Human Resources OU, all users in all domains must have Cosmo 2 installed. How do you deploy the Cosmo 2 application?

2. With the exception of Contractors who work in the Messaging department, all users in the Information Services OU, in all domains, must be able to install the Windows 2000 Support Tools if they choose to. How do you deploy the Windows 2000 Support Tools application?

3. The administrators responsible for each of the top level OUs (Information Services, Human Resources, and Accounting) must be able to link and unlink Group Policy objects (GPOs), create new GPOs, and edit only the GPOs they create. How do you delegate administrative control?

Lab A: Implementing the Active Directory Infrastructure

Objectives

After completing this lab, you will be able to:

- Set up the DNS services based on the business requirements of a fictitious organization.

- Install Active Directory based on the business requirements of a fictitious organization.

- Create and configure sites and site links based on the business requirements of a fictitious organization.

- Set up printer locations based on the business requirements of a fictitious organization.

- Implement the OU structure and delegate administrative control based on the business requirements of a fictitious organization.

- Set up users and groups based on the business requirements of the fictitious organization.

- Implement Group Policy across all domains based on the business requirements of the fictitious organization.

Prerequisites

Before working on this lab, you must have:

- An understanding of the components of Active Directory.

- An understanding of how Active Directory uses the DNS service.

- Knowledge of and skills transferring operations master roles.

- Knowledge of and skills working with Active Directory Users and Computers.

- Knowledge of and skills creating and configuring sites and site links.

- Knowledge of and skills defining printer location names and setting up printer locations.

- Knowledge of and skills creating domain user accounts and groups.

- Knowledge of and skills bulk importing data into Active Directory.

- An understanding of Active Directory permissions.

- Knowledge of and skills implementing Group Policy.

Lab Setup

To complete this lab, perform the following steps:

1. Log on as Administrator for nwtraders.msft.

2. Run the script C:\Moc\Win2154a\Labfiles\Rmad.vbs.

3. When the computer restarts, log on as Administrator.

   The computer will complete its tasks and then restart again.

Note This script removes all the server objects in the forest with the exception of London, runs Dcpromo.exe by using an answer file to demote the domain controller to a standalone server, removes the preferred DNS server, and removes the primary DNS suffix.

Important The lab does not reflect the real-world environment. It is recommended that you always use complex passwords for any administrator accounts, and never create accounts without a password.

Important Outside of the classroom environment, it is strongly advised that you use the most recent software updates that are necessary. Because this is a classroom environment, we may use software that does not include the latest updates.

Estimated time to complete this lab: 150 minutes

Exercise 1
Planning the Implementation of the Active Directory Infrastructure

Scenario

For Contoso, Ltd., before implementing an Active Directory infrastructure, a best practice is to plan and prepare for the implementation. The diagrams in this exercise will help you to prepare for the implementation by gathering the information for the implementation plan that was reviewed during the class discussion.

Note: You will be assigned a group number. Use this group number along with the names that you define for the domains. For example, if your group number is 1, then the domain name for the Asian location would be asia1.contoso1.msft.

Goal

In this exercise, you will complete the implementation planning worksheets for the required domains, DNS, sites and OUs for Contoso, Ltd.

DNS Domain Structure

In the following worksheet, provide the DNS domain names and the reverse lookup zone name for your DNS structure. Also, provide the IP address and the computer name for each of the four computers that you will configure as DNS servers. You will use this information when implementing the DNS infrastructure.

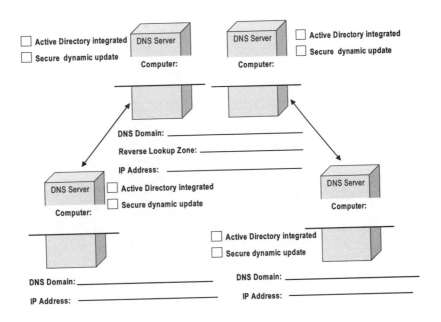

Active Directory Domain Structure

In the following worksheet, provide Active Directory domain names. Also, identify which computer will be configured as the domain controller for the forest root, the additional domain controller for the forest root, and the domain controller for the child domains. You will use this information when implementing Active Directory.

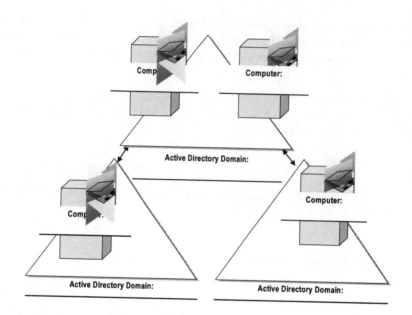

Site Structure

In the following worksheet, provide a name for each site and site link for Contoso, Ltd. You will use this information when configuring sites and site links.

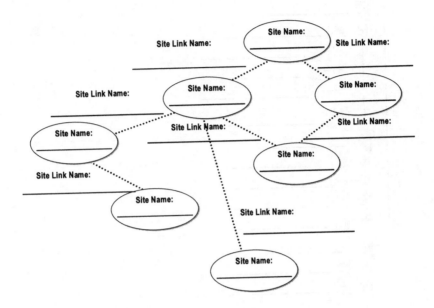

Organizational Unit Structure

In the following worksheet, provide the OU structure names. You will use this information when creating the common OU structure for each domain.

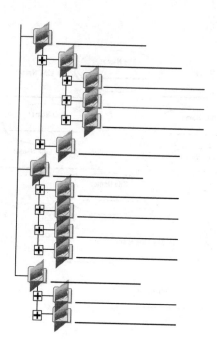

Exercise 2
Installing and Configuring DNS

Scenario

The functional specification requires a working DNS infrastructure to be in place before you install Active Directory. Each Active Directory domain will maintain its own DNS information.

Goal

In this exercise, you will install and configure DNS for each computer you identified as DNS server. You will configure a forward lookup zone for each of the Active Directory domains and a single reverse lookup zone for the forest. You will also configure all forward and reverse lookup zones to support dynamic update. It is a best practice to verify that DNS is installed and configured properly before you create the Active Directory domain structure. Use your planning worksheet to complete this exercise.

Tasks	Detailed Steps
1. Install and configure DNS on each computer.	a. Configure the DNS suffix for your computer. When prompted, restart the computer. b. Start the Windows Components wizard, and install the Domain Name System (DNS) subcomponent of Networking Services. Copy the required files from the Windows 2000 Advanced Server compact disc.
⚠ **Important:** Only perform the following tasks on the first DNS server in the contoso*x*.msft domain.	
2. Create forward and reverse lookup zones.	a. Add a standard primary forward lookup zone for contoso*x*.msft (where *x* is your assigned group number). b. Add a standard primary reverse lookup zone for your classroom network ID. c. Configure the Internet Protocol (TCP/IP) properties of your Local Area Connection to use your computer for DNS.
3. Configure DNS to support dynamic update.	a. Configure the forward lookup zone for contoso.msft to support dynamic update. b. Configure the reverse lookup zone for your subnet to support dynamic update. c. Use the **ipconfig** command to re-register your computer's DNS records. d. Refresh DNS to display the pointer resource record in the reverse lookup zone.
4. Use **nslookup** to test DNS.	a. Confirm that DNS can resolve a host name to an IP address. b. Confirm that DNS can resolve an IP address to a host name.
5. Delegate authority for each sub domain.	▪ Perform a new delegation in contoso*x*.msft to a DNS server in each sub domain.

Tasks	Detailed Steps
⚠ **Important:** Only perform the following tasks on the second DNS server in the contoso*x*.msft domain.	
6. Create secondary forward and reverse lookup zones of contoso*x*.msft.	**a.** Add a standard secondary forward lookup zone for contoso*x*.msft (where *x* is your assigned group number). **b.** Add a standard secondary reverse lookup zone for your classroom network ID. **c.** Configure the Internet Protocol (TCP/IP) properties of your Local Area Connection to use your computer for DNS. **d.** Confirm that DNS can resolve a host name to an IP address.
⚠ **Important:** Only perform the following tasks on the DNS servers in the sub domains.	
7. Create the primary forward lookup zone for your domain.	**a.** Use the **Configure the server** wizard to add a standard primary forward lookup zone for your domain. **b.** Configure the Internet Protocol (TCP/IP) properties of your Local Area Connection to use your computer for DNS.
8. Create a secondary reverse lookup zone for your domain.	▪ Add a standard secondary reverse lookup zone for your domain from the zone created in contoso*x*.msft.
9. Configure DNS to support dynamic update.	**a.** Configure the forward lookup zone for your domain to support dynamic update. **b.** Use the **ipconfig** command to re-register your computer's DNS records.
10. Use **nslookup** to test DNS.	**a.** Confirm that DNS can resolve a host name to an IP address. **b.** Confirm that DNS can resolve a host name in the forest root domain to an IP address. 🖥 *If you have a problem resolving a host name in the forest root domain, look in Root Hints to verify that the DNS server that is authoritative for contosox.msft is listed.*

Exercise 3
Installing Active Directory

Scenario

Now that the DNS infrastructure is in place and properly configured, you can create the Active Directory domain structure for Contoso, Ltd.

Goal

In this exercise, you will install Active Directory to create a single forest with two child domains. You will also configure the forest root domain for fault tolerance, implement Active Directory integrated zones, and transfer infrastructure master to a non-global catalog server. Use your planning worksheet to complete this exercise.

Tasks	Detailed Steps

1. Create the Active Directory domain structure.	■ Use the Active Directory Installation wizard to create:
	  ● The forest root domain.
	  ● Two child domains.

2. Configure the forest root domain for fault tolerance.	■ Create an additional domain controller for the forest root domain.
3. Implement Active Directory integrated zones in each domain.	a. Convert all of the forward lookup zones to Active Directory-integrated. b. Convert the primary reverse lookup zone to Active Directory-integrated. c. Enable secure updates for Active Directory integrated zones.
4. In the forest root domain, transfer infrastructure master to a non-global catalog server.	a. Determine which domain controller holds the infrastructure master role and which domain controller is a global catalog server. b. If necessary, transfer the infrastructure master to a domain controller that is not a global catalog server.

Exercise 4
Creating Sites and Site Links

Scenario

The North American region has four primary locations: Seattle, Detroit, Toronto, and Denver. The employees in the Asian region are located equally in two locations, Bangalore and Singapore. The employees of the Australian region are all located in Sydney.

Goal

In this exercise, you will create and configure sites and site links based on the information in the following table. Use your planning worksheet to complete this exercise.

IP Site Links	Cost	Frequency (minutes)	Schedule
Seattle – Toronto	100	90	Sun-Sat 7A.M.–1A.M. GMT
Seattle – Denver	100	120	Sun-Sat 12P.M.–1A.M. GMT
Seattle – Bangalore	200	90	Sun-Sat 12A.M.–1A.M. GMT
Seattle – Sydney	900	90	Sun-Sat 12A.M.–2A.M. GMT
Toronto – Detroit	100	180	Sun-Sat 4P.M.–1A.M. GMT
Detroit – Denver	100	200	Sun-Sat 3P.M.–1A.M. GMT
Bangalore – Singapore	100	60	Always available

Tasks	Detailed Steps
1. Create sites for each region.	▪ Use Active Directory Sites and Services to create sites for each region.
2. Create and configure all of the site links.	a. Create all of the site links. Refer to your planning worksheet for the site link names. b. Configure the cost, frequency, and schedule for each site link by using the information the table.

Exercise 5
Publishing Printers and Using Printer Locations

Scenario

To use printers more effectively, printers in each location will be published in Active Directory and the printer location feature will be configured to easily find a printer in the user's location.

Goal

In this exercise, you will create subnet objects, publish printers, and configure the printer location feature based on the scenario. For creating printer locations, use the subnet information in the following table.

Site	Location	Subnet
Denver	US/Denver/Building 1	10.10.1.0/24
Denver	US/Denver/Building 2	10.10.2.0/24
Denver	US/Denver/Building 3	10.10.3.0/24
Seattle	US/Seattle/Building 1	10.15.1.0/24
Seattle	US/Seattle/Building 2	10.15.2.0/24
Seattle	US/Seattle/Building 3	10.15.3.0/24
Toronto	CA/Toronto/Floor 1	10.20.1.0/24
Toronto	CA/Toronto/Floor 2	10.20.2.0/24
Toronto	CA/Toronto/Floor 3	10.20.3.0/24
Detroit	US/Detroit/Building 1	10.30.1.0/24
Detroit	US/Detroit/Building 2	10.30.2.0/24
Detroit	US/Detroit/Building 3	10.30.3.0/24
Bangalore	India/Bangalore/Building 1	10.40.1.0/24
Bangalore	India/Bangalore/Building 2	10.40.2.0/24
Singapore	Singapore/Building 1	10.50.1.0/24
Singapore	Singapore/Building 2	10.50.2.0/24
Sydney	Australia/Building 1	10.60.1.0/24
Sydney	Australia/Building 2	10.60.2.0/24
Sydney	Australia/Building 3	10.60.3.0/24

Tasks	Detailed Steps
1. Create and configure the subnet objects for each site.	a. Create the subnet objects and assign them to the appropriate site. b. Configure the location field for the subnet objects.
2. Enable the printer location feature.	▪ Use Group Policy to enable the printer location for each domain.
3. Create and publish a printer for each location.	▪ Create and publish a printer for each location and ensure the location information utilizes the location information from the subnet objects.

Exercise 6
Creating the OU Structure and Delegating Administrative Control

Scenario

There is a common OU structure in all of the domains in Contoso, Ltd. There are three main OUs: Information Services, Human Resources, and Accounting. The organization has decided upon a delegated administration model, and one administrator from each OU will be responsible for managing the resources and users in that OU.

Goal

In this exercise, you will create a common OU structure for each domain in the entire forest, and delegate administrative control of each of the three top level OUs to a different administrator. Use your planning worksheet to complete this exercise.

Note: Perform all of the following tasks in each domain.

Tasks	Detailed Steps
1. Create a common OU structure.	▪ Create OUs within each domain. Use the same names that you defined during the planning exercise.
⚠ **Note:** Perform the following task after completing Task 1 in Exercise 7.	
2. Delegate administrative control.	▪ Use the Delegation of Control wizard to assign Active Directory permissions for creating, deleting, and managing user accounts, groups, and printers in the Information Services OU, the Human Resources OU, and the Accounting OU to any one user in that OU.

Exercise 7
Creating Users and Groups

Scenario

The managers of each department at Contoso, Ltd are responsible for conducting the performance reviews for their direct reports. Other managers can use the performance review data when considering an internal transfer of employee from one department to another department. Therefore, all managers require the Read access to the performance review data. The managers for each department need Full Control access to the performance review data of the employees in their department.

Goal

In this exercise, you will create multiple users to populate the OUs through bulk import by using the common OU structure. You will create appropriate groups to enable all managers to have only Read access to the performance review data for the whole organization. You will also create appropriate groups to enable department managers to have Full Control access to the performance review data of the employees in their department.

Note: Perform all of the following tasks in each domain.

Tasks	Detailed Steps
1. Create multiple users accounts.	a. Prepare the Users.txt file for use with the **csvde** bulk import utility. b. Perform a bulk import of Users.txt. c. Verify that the bulk import was successful.
2. Create a global group called Contractors in the Messaging OU.	▪ Create a global group called Contractors in the Messaging OU.
3. Create folders and files for the performance review data.	a. Create and share the folder C:\Performance Data on one server in each domain. b. Create subfolders Information Services, Human Resources, and Accounting under the Performance Data folder. c. Create a blank text file in each of the subfolders.
4. Create groups for managers in the Accounting division who require Read access to the performance review data for the whole organization.	a. Create appropriate global groups in each department OU. b. Add the department global groups into a Domain Managers global group. c. Add the Domain Managers global group into a universal group. d. Add the Universal group into domain local groups for each domain. e. Assign Read permission to the domain local groups.
5. Create groups for managers who require Full Control access to the performance review data of the employees in their department.	a. Create appropriate global groups and add them into a department global group. b. Add department global groups into each domain local group. c. Assign Full Control permission to the domain local group for a department.

Exercise 8
Implementing Group Policy

Scenario

Contoso, Ltd. wants to deploy the Cosmo 2 application to all users except those in the Human Resources OU, and Windows 2000 Support Tools to all users in the Information Services OU except those in the Contractors group. They also want you to implement the organization-wide Group Policy settings by using Administrative Templates, and secure the network resources by implementing organization-wide Group Policy settings.

Goal

In this exercise, you will apply Block Inheritance, apply filtering by using DACLs, implement the Group Policy settings by using Administrative Templates, secure the network resources by implementing Group Policy settings, and delegate administrative control for implementing Group Policy.

Tasks	Detailed Steps
1. Deploy the Cosmo 2 application so that it is available to all users, except the users in the Human Resources OU.	▪ Apply Block Inheritance on the Human Resources OU.
2. Deploy the Windows 2000 Support Tools application so that it is available to all users in the Information Services OU, except the users who are members of the Contractors group in the Messaging OU.	a. Create and link a GPO to the Information Services OU that publishes the Windows 2000 Support Tools. b. Modify the DACL of this GPO so that the members of the Contractors group in the Messaging OU are denied Apply Group Policy permission.
3. Implement organization-wide Group Policy settings.	a. Create new GPOs linked to the appropriate OUs. b. Edit the administrative template settings for the new GPO to: • Enable disk quotas on all computers. • Enforce the disk quota limit on all computers. • Set the default quota limit for all users to 100 MB and the warning level to 75 MB. • Log an event when the warning level and the quota limits are exceeded. • Deny access to Windows Update. • Prevent users in all domains from running Freecell (Freecell.exe), Minesweeper (Winmine.exe), Pinball (Pinball.exe), and Solitaire (Sol.exe) applications. • Enable access to the MMC snap-ins: Active Directory Users and Computers, Group Policy, Group Policy tab for Active Directory Tools, Administrative Templates (Users), and Administrative Templates (Computers) to the users responsible for administering OUs.

Tasks	Detailed Steps
3. *(continued)*	**c.** Verify that the Group Policy settings contained in the Admin Template GPO are being properly applied.
4. Secure the network resources.	**a.** Create new GPOs as required to implement the following settings: • Minimum password length of eight characters. • Account lockout threshold of three logon attempts. • Account lockout duration of 60 minutes. • All users must be able to log on locally to all computers, including domain controllers. • Do not display the last user name in the **Log On to Windows** dialog box. • Membership in the Group Policy Creator Owners group must be restricted to the Administrator account and the accounts belonging to the users responsible for administering each top-level OU. **b.** Verify that the modifications to the Additional Security Settings Policy GPO are being applied correctly.

Exercise 9
Verifying the Implementation

Scenario

Now that you have implemented the Active Directory infrastructure for Contoso, Ltd., you need to verify the implementation.

Goal

In this exercise, you will verify that:

- You can correctly configure domains and ensure that the global catalog is working.
- The minimum password length is set correctly.
- The group structure has been correctly defined and proper access to resources is in place.
- The printer location feature is enabled and that all of the buildings are properly defined.
- The OU delegation and Group Policy has been implemented.
- Replication is working correctly on all domain controllers.

Tasks	Detailed Steps
1. Verify that the domains and global catalog are working correctly.	■ Log on using Sandra Martinez's user principal name from another domain.
2. Verify that managers have Full Control access over the performance review data in their department and Read permissions on the performance data in the other departments.	a. Test the Full Control access over the data in the Accounting department. b. Test the Read access over the data in the other departments.
3. Verify that the minimum password length of eight characters is in effect.	■ Attempt to change Sandra Martinez's password to a string of less than eight characters.
4. Verify that the printer location feature is functioning.	■ In the **Find Printers** dialog box, click **Browse** and verify that all building printer locations are displayed.
5. Verify that the OU delegation is correct.	a. Verify that the user delegated permission for the Information Services OU can create user accounts for all of the OUs under Information Services. b. Verify that the user delegated permission for the Information Services OU cannot create user accounts under the Human Resources OU.

Tasks	Detailed Steps
6. Verify that the Group Policy objects are configured correctly.	**a.** Log on as a user under the Human Resources OU and verify that the Cosmo 2 application is not available and the Windows 2000 Support Tools application is available.
	b. Create a user account in the Messaging OU that is a member of the Contractors group. Then log on as that user and ensure that the Windows 2000 Support Tools application is not available and the Cosmo 2 application is available.
7. Verify that replication is working correctly on all domain controllers.	**a.** Check the directory service event log.
	b. Use Replication monitor to verify that connection objects exist between domain controllers.

Course Evaluation

Your evaluation of this course will help Microsoft understand the quality of your learning experience.

To complete a course evaluation, go to http://www.metricsthatmatter.com/survey.

Microsoft will keep your evaluation strictly confidential and will use your responses to improve your future learning experience.

Microsoft®
Training &
Certification

Appendix A: Adjusting Replication

Microsoft®

Registry Entries

To make adjustments to replication, you can specify desired values for registry entries. To modify the thresholds for excluding nonresponding servers, use the following registry entries in **HKEY_LOCAL_MACHINE**\SYSTEM\CurrentControlSet\Services\NTDS\ Parameters, with the data type REG_DWORD:

The following table lists the values of registry entries for replication between sites.

Registry entries	Value
IntersiteFailuresAllowed	Number of failed attempts Default: 1
MaxFailureTimeForIntersiteLink (secs)	Time that must elapse before being considered stale, in seconds Default: 7200 (2 hours)

For optimizing connections within a site, use the following registry entries:

Registry entries	Value
NonCriticalLinkFailuresAllowed	Number of failed attempts Default: 1
MaxFailureTimeForNonCriticalLink	Time that must elapse before considered stale, in seconds Default: 43200 (12 hours)
Repl topology update delay (secs)	Time interval that the Knowledge Consistency Checker will wait before running its first replication topology check, in seconds Default: 300 (5 minutes)
Repl topology update period (secs)	Time interval at which the Knowledge Consistency Checker (KCC) performs a review of the topology, in seconds Default: 900 (15 minutes)

For immediate neighbor connections within a site, use the following registry entries:

Registry entries	Value
CriticalLinkFailuresAllowed	Number of failed attempts Default: 0
MaxFailureTimeForCriticalLink	Time that must elapse before considered stale, in seconds Default: 7200 (2 hours)
Replicator notify pause after modify (secs)	Delay between the change to the Active Directory and first replication partner notification, in seconds Default: 300 (5 minutes
Replicator notify pause between DSAs (secs)	Notification delay between domain controllers, in seconds Default: 30

Configuration Entries in Active Directory

An understanding of some replication events, such as enabling reciprocal replication and change notification is required for those administrators who need to modify the replication behavior beyond the default behavior.

Enabling Reciprocal Replication

Replication between sites exhibits *request-pull behavior* where the destination site, or the receiver, requests changes from the sending site, or source, according to a schedule. Replication within a site, on the other hand, exhibits *notify-pull behavior* where the receiver is notified of changes by the source, and the receiver then requests the changes from the source). *Reciprocal replication* allows one domain controller to initiate replication to and from another domain controller. Reciprocal replication is typically used when a domain controller is connected through a dial-up connection.

To enable reciprocal replication between two sites, perform the following steps:

1. In ADSI Edit, expand the Configuration container.

2. Move to the Inter-SiteTransports container, and then select **CN=IP**.

Note   You cannot enable reciprocal replication for SMTP links because a direct connection is not established between the domain controllers.

---

3. Right-click the site link object for the sites for which you want to enable reciprocal replication, and then click **Properties**.

4. In the **Select a property to view** box, select **options**.

5. In the **Edit Attribute** box, if the **Value(s)** box shows **<not set>**, type **2** in the **Edit Attribute** box, and then click **Set**.

   If the **Value(s)** box already contains a value, you must derive the new value by using a Boolean BITWISE-OR calculation on the old value. For example, if the value in the **Value(s)** box is 1, calculate 0001 OR 0010 to equal 0011. Type the integer value of the result in the **Edit Attribute** box; for this example, the value is 3.

Enabling Change Notification

Change notification is a mechanism by which a domain controller notifies a replication partner that it has changes. Replication within a site occurs as a response to changes; as changes occur on one domain controller, it notifies its replication partner, which prompts the partner to request the changes. When a domain controller performs an update to an attribute, it sends notification to its replication partner within a specified time following the change.

Enabling Change Notification Within a Site

For changes that occur within a site, there is a "holdback timer" that determines the interval between the time a change is made and the time that the source server notifies its replication partners. This interval serves to stagger network traffic caused by replication. When a domain controller makes an originating or replicated change to a directory partition, it starts the timer. When the timer expires, the domain controller notifies all of its replication partners (for that directory partition and within the site) that it has changes. If a partner is not engaged in requesting changes from another partner, it sends its change request to the notifying server.

The default value for the holdback timer is 300 seconds, or 5 minutes. To change the default registry setting, you can set a new value in the **Replicator notify pause after modify (secs)** entry in HKEY_LOCAL_MACHINE\SYSTEM\CurrentControlSet\Services\NTDS\Parameters.

Note   Very small values for this timer generate redundant notifications, which can decrease performance.

A domain controller does not notify all of its replication partners at one time. By delaying between notifications, the domain controller spreads out the load of responding to replication requests from its partners. The default delay between notifications is 30 seconds. To change the default delay, set a new value in the **Replicator notify pause between DSAs (secs)** entry in HKEY_LOCAL_MACHINE\SYSTEM\CurrentControlSet\Services\NTDS\Parameters.

Enabling Change Notification Between Sites

By default, changes are replicated between sites according to a schedule and not according to when changes occur. For this reason, the greatest replication latency across the forest is the sum of the greatest replication latencies along the single longest replication path of any directory partition.

For special circumstances, you can configure change notifications on connections between sites. By modifying the site link object, you can enable change notification between sites for all connections that occur over that link. Use ADSI Edit to enable change notification between sites.

To enable change notification between sites, perform the following steps:

1. In ADSI Edit, expand the **Configuration** container. Move to the Inter-Site Transports container, and then select **CN=IP**.

Note   You cannot enable change notification for SMTP links.

---

2. Right-click the site link object for the sites for which you want to enable change notification, and then click **Properties**.

3. In the **Select a property to view** box, select **options**.

4. In the **Edit Attribute** box, if the **Value(s)** box shows **<not set>**, type **1** in the **Edit Attribute** box, and then click **Set**.

    If the **Value(s)** box contains a value, you must derive the new value by using a Boolean BITWISE-OR calculation on the old value, as follows: old_value BITWISE-OR 1. For example, if the value in the **Value(s)** box is 2, calculate 0010 OR 0001 to equal 0011. Type the integer value of the result in the **Edit Attribute** box; for this example, the value is 3.

Enabling change notifications across site links propagates all change notifications. With change notification between sites set, changes propagate to the remote site with the same frequency that they are propagated within the source site, including changes that warrant urgent replication.

Appendix B:
Determining Slow
Network Connections

Algorithm Used by Group Policy to Detect Slow Network Links

Group Policy can detect a slow network connection by using an algorithm. The algorithm that Group Policy uses to determine whether a link should be considered slow is as follows:

1. The client computer that is attempting to process Group Policy sends a zero byte file to the authenticating domain controller, or server, which then returns the file to the client. The client measures the time it takes for the file to complete the round trip, and if it is less than ten milliseconds, the client assumes a fast link is present and sets the fast link flag.

2. If the round trip time in step 1 is more than 10 milliseconds, the client saves the round trip time. Name this value time_1.

3. Next, the client sends a compressed file that is two kilobytes (KB) in size to the server, which then returns the file to the client. The client again measures the time it takes the file to complete the round trip. Name this value time_2.

Note The file that is sent to the server in this step is actually a JPEG file. JPEG files are compressed by definition. A compressed file is used because of the fact that data sent through a modem is frequently compressed and compressing the file would make the link appear faster than it really is.

---

4. The client repeats step 3 two more times. Name these values time_3, and time_4.

5. Next, the client subtracts the value for time_1 from time_2, time_3 and time_4. This is done to remove the overhead caused by session setup. Name these values delta_1, delta_2 and delta_3.

6. The average of the values for delta_1, delta_2 and delta_3 is calculated. Name this value avg.

7. Finally, the connection speed is calculated as (the units are shown for clarity):

(Connection Speed kilobits/second) = 2*(2 KB)*(8 bits/byte)*(1,000 milliseconds/second)/(avg milliseconds)

Because 2 KB of data move through each modem, Ethernet card, or other device in the link once in each direction, there is a total of 4 KB, or 2 times the 2 KB, processed. This is why a leading factor of 2 is on the right side of the equation.

Note The connection speed calculated is the average of the upload and download speeds. In most cases, this average is the same as the download speed itself. However, in some cases the upload and download speeds are different enough that you should take this into account. An example of this is Asymmetric Digital Subscriber Line (ADSL). Using ADSL, you might have upload speeds of 128 kilobits per second (Kbps) and download speeds of 768 Kbps.

To specify the threshold value for slow link detection for computer configuration Group Policy settings, you use the Computer Configuration\Administrative Templates\System\Group Policy\Group Policy slow link detection setting. To set this value for user configuration Group Policy settings, you use the User Configuration\Administrative Templates\System\Group Policy\ Group Policy slow link detection setting. The allowed value range is 0 to 4,294,967,200 Kbps. A value of zero indicates that all links should be considered fast.

Microsoft®
Training &
Certification

Appendix C: LDAP
Names

Microsoft®

Understanding LDAP Names of Objects

Because Lightweight Directory Access Protocol (LDAP) is the protocol used for accessing Active Directory, some Active Directory operations require the use of LDAP naming paths. The protocol specification for LDAP specifies that an object is represented by a series of domain components, organizational units (OUs), and common names that form a path to the object within the directory. LDAP naming paths include the following:

- Distinguished names
- Relative distinguished names
- Uniform resource locators (URLs)

LDAP Distinguished Names

The full path to an object from the directory root is an LDAP distinguished name. It consists of a series of attributes with their values, which are separated by commas, beginning with the most specific reference. When a search context does not exist, it is always used to find an object.

Example

For example, the distinguished name for a user called Don Hall in the Sales department of Contoso, Ltd. is:

CN=Don Hall,OU=Sales,DC=contoso,DC=msft

Microsoft® Windows® 2000 uses the distinguished name attributes listed in the following table.

Key	Attribute	Description
DC	Domain Component	A component of the Domain Name System (DNS) name of the domain, such as com.
OU	Organizational Unit	An organizational unit that can be used to contain other objects.
CN	Common Name	Any object other than domain components and organizational units, such as user and computer objects.

Note LDAP allows for additional name attributes, but Windows 2000 uses only the attributes in the preceding table.

LDAP Relative Distinguished Names

The LDAP relative distinguished name is the portion of the LDAP distinguished name that uniquely identifies the object in its container. Its composition varies depending upon the extent of the existing search context established by the client.

Example

The following table provides examples of distinguished names, the search contexts established by the client, and relative distinguished names.

Distinguished name	Relative distinguished name
OU=Sales,DC=contoso,DC=msft	OU=Sales
CN=Don Hall,OU=Sales,DC=contoso, DC=msft	CN=Don Hall
CN=Judy Lew,OU=Shipping, DC=europe,DC=contoso,DC=msft	CN=Judy Lew

LDAP URLs

An *LDAP URL* is a concatenation of the domain controller's name and the LDAP distinguished name of the object being located. You can use LDAP URLs in Active Directory Service Interface (ADSI) scripts to gain access to Active Directory™ directory service objects. An LDAP URL contains the address of the server to which you want to connect and the distinguished name of the object you reference.

Example

In the following example:

```
LDAP://server1.contoso.msft/CN=Don
Hall/CN=Users/DC=contoso/DC=msft
```

The LDAP URL queries the domain controller server1.contoso.msft, for the object with the common name Don Hall in the Users container in the domain contoso.msft.

Viewing LDAP Object Names

Many utilities in Active Directory display an object's LDAP name. To view the LDAP name of an object in Active Directory Users and Computers:

1. On the **View** menu, click **Advanced**.
2. Click the object that you want to view, and then click **Properties**.
3. Click the **Object** tab.

   Active Directory Users and Computers displays the object's name in the **Object Pathname** box.

Appendix D: Common User Account Attributes

This appendix contains the attribute names for the attributes displayed on the main pages of the *user* **Properties** dialog box in Active Directory™ Users and Computers.

Object Attributes Not Displayed

Display name	Attribute name
DN	distinguishedName
Common name	cn
Object class	objectClass

General Page

Display name	Attribute name
First name	givenName
Last name	sn
Name	name
Description	description
Office	physicalDeliveryOfficeName
Telephone	telephoneNumber
E-mail	mail
Home page	wWWHomePage

Account Page

Display name	Attribute name
User logon name	userPrincipalName
User logon name (pre-Windows 2000)	sAMAccountName
Logon Hours	logonHours
Logon To	userWorkstations
Account options	userAccountControl
Account expires	accountExpires

Profile Page

Display name	Attribute name
Profile path	profilePath
Logon script	scriptPath
Home directory	homeDirectory
Shared documents folder	userSharedFolder

Address Page

Display name	Attribute name
Street	streetAddress
P.O. Box	postOfficeBox
City	l
State/Province	st
ZIP/Postal Code	postalCode
Country/Region	countryCode

Organization Page

Display name	Attribute name
Title	title
Department	department
Company	company
Manager	manager
Direct reports	directReports

Telephone/Notes Page

Display name	Attribute name
Home	homePhone
Pager	pager
Mobile	mobile
FAX	facsimileTelephoneNumber
IP Phone	ipPhone
Comments	info

Using Active Directory Schema to View Object Attributes

You can use the Active Directory Schema Microsoft® Management Console (MMC) snap-in to view the defined list of attributes for Active Directory directory service. To view this list, perform the following steps:

1. Register the Active Directory Schema snap-in by running the following command:

   regsvr32.exe %systemroot%\system32\schmmgmt.dll

2. Click **OK** to close the message that indicates the registration succeeded.

3. Create a custom MMC console.

4. Add the Active Directory Schema snap-in to the console.

5. In Active Directory Schema, in the console tree, expand **Active Directory Schema** and then click **Attributes**. The list of attributes appears in the details pane.

Using ADSI Edit to View Object Attributes

Active Directory Service Interfaces (ADSI) Edit is a support tool in Microsoft Windows® that you use to view and modify object attributes in Active Directory. ADSI Edit is the registry editor tool for Active Directory.

1. Install Windows Support Tools by running setup in the Support\Tools folder from the Windows 2000 CD.

2. On the **Start** menu, point to **Programs**, point to **Windows 2000 Support Tools**, click **Tools**, and then click **ADSI Edit**.

3. In the ADSI Edit window, in the console tree, expand the folders and then click a container.

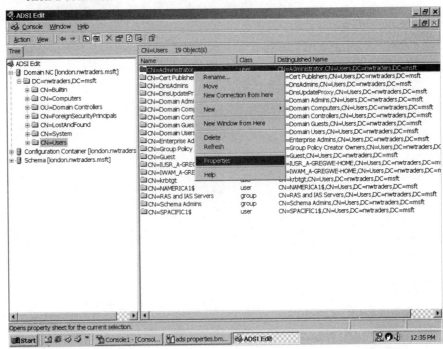

4. In the details pane, right-click an object and then click **Properties**.

5. In the **Properties** dialog box for the object, in the attributes list, click an attribute to display its value. The value of the selected attribute is displayed below with the option to modify the value.

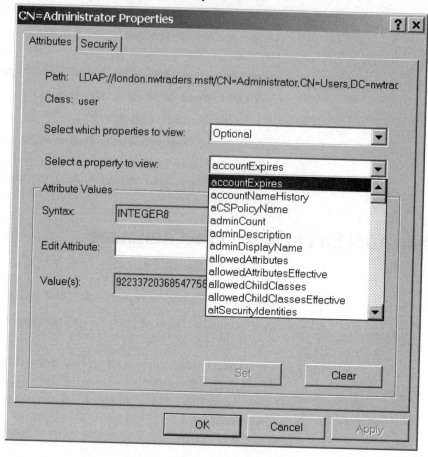

Appendix E: Using ADSI Programming to Automate Administrative Tasks

Objectives

After completing this lab, you will be able to:

- Create multiple Active Directory™ directory service objects.

- Modify multiple Active Directory objects.

- Delete multiple Active Directory objects.

Prerequisites

Before working on this lab, you must have:

- A basic understanding of the Active Directory directory service.

- A basic understanding of the Lightweight Directory Access Protocol (LDAP).

- Experience writing batch files.

Lab Setup

To complete this lab, you need the following:

- A computer running Microsoft® Windows® 2000 Server configured as a domain controller.

- Cr_user.vbs, Mod_user.vbs, Del_user.vbs, and Users.txt found in the appendix folder on the Student Materials compact disc.

For More Information

For more information about using Active Directory Service Interfaces (ADSI), see http://msdn.microsoft.com/developer/windows2000/adsi.

Lab Design

The lab is designed so that the student uses three ADSI scripts to create, modify, and delete multiple user objects. The first script retrieves data from a text file, which is modified by the student to use with the other two scripts. Each exercise builds on the work from the previous exercise.

Scenario

You are an enterprise administrator who must add, modify, and delete hundreds of users, groups, and organizational units (OUs) from the network every day. You want to automate most of these tasks by using the Windows Script Host and ADSI scripting.

Your objective is to:

- Create a Human Resources OU.
- Add several users and their job titles in the Human Resources OU.
- Modify several users' job titles.
- Delete several users.

Estimated time to complete this lab: 60 minutes

Background

ADSI is a set of generic interfaces that allow you to access and manipulate different directory services. This lab will focus on the Windows 2000 Active Directory directory service.

There are several different ways to access Active Directory. It is recommended that you use ADSI as the strategic application programming interface (API) to access Active Directory. ADSI uses the LDAP protocol to communicate with Active Directory.

When using a script to gain access to an object in Active Directory, you must provide the LDAP namespace, the programmatic identifier, which is ProgID, and the path to the object, which is ADsPath. Then you will bind to the domain to provide a reference point for creating and modifying Active Directory objects.

The Namespace

A *namespace* is simply a set of names in which all names are unique. For example, files stored on a disk drive reside in the *file system namespace*. The unique name of a file is based on where it is stored in the file system namespace, for example:

```
C:\public\documents\adsi\adsi_spec_v3.doc
```

Directory service namespaces also identify the objects they contain by unique names, which are usually based on the location in the directory where the object can be found. For example, in Active Directory, a given object might have a name like this:

```
CN=jsmith, OU=Sales, DC=nwtraders, DC=msft
```

The ProgID and ADsPath

ADSI defines a naming convention that can uniquely identify an ADSI object in a heterogeneous environment. These names are called *ADsPath strings*. ADsPath strings consist of a ProgID (for example LDAP:, WinNT:) and the provider's specific path.

The following table provides examples of ADsPath strings.

ADSI object	Path
Organizational unit in the nwtraders domain	`LDAP://OU=Sales, DC=nwtraders, DC=msft`
Exchange object on Exchange Server	`LDAP://exch01/O=Microsoft`
jsmith user in the Sales OU of the nwtraders domain	`LDAP://CN=jsmith, OU=Sales, DC=nwtraders, DC=msft`
comp1 in the Redmond domain	`WinNT://REDMOND/comp1, computer`
alice, a local user on the comp1 computer	`WinNT://REDMOND/comp1/alice`

Notice that each ProgID is synonymous with a unique namespace.

The Root DS Entry

The LDAP standard, which is defined in RFC 2251, requires that all LDAP directories maintain a special entry, called the *rootDSE object*. This entry provides a set of standard operational attributes that the user can read to find out fundamental characteristics of the directory and the server. The rootDSE can also provide any number of attributes specific to a vendor.

One of the standard operational attributes is *defaultNamingContext*. This attribute contains the distinguished name of the directory root. In Windows 2000, this is the distinguished name of the domain container at the root of the current tree. By reading the defaultNamingContext attribute from the rootDSE, you can determine the domain to which you are logged on at run time.

ADSI provides a special mechanism for binding to the rootDSE by using the ADSpath "LDAP:// rootDSE."

```
set Root = GetObject("LDAP://RootDSE")
```

Next, you retrieve the default naming context:

```
DomainPath = Root.Get("DefaultNamingContext")
```

Then you bind to the root of the domain:

```
Set Domain = GetObject("LDAP://"& DomainPath)
```

These three lines of code appear first in most of the ADSI scripts that you create. This code sets the reference point in your script so that you can create users, groups, and organizational units in the domain.

You should never use a specific server name. Additionally, under most circumstances, you should avoid binding to a single server. Active Directory supports serverless binding (as shown in the previous example), which means it is not necessary to specify a server if you are accessing Active Directory in the domain of the user who is logged on. When processing your bind call, ADSI finds the Windows 2000 domain controller in the domain of the user who is currently logged on.

Creating Organizational Units

You can now use the domain object to create other objects such as organizational units. You need to create the Human Resources OU. The sample code to create the OU object is as follows:

```
Set ou_HR = Domain.Create("organizationalUnit", "OU=Human
Resources")
ou_HR.Put "Description", "Human Resources"
ou_HR.SetInfo
```

The **Create** method accepts the class name and the name of the new object. At this point, the object is not committed to Active Directory. You will, however, have an ADSI/COM object reference on the client. This ADSI object enables you to set or modify attributes by using the **Put** method. The **Put** method accepts the attribute name and the value of the attribute. Still, no objects are committed to the directory; everything is cached on the client side.

When you call the **SetInfo** method, the changes (in this case, object creation and attribute modification) are committed to Active Directory. These changes are *transacted*, which means that you see either the new object with all of the attributes you have set, or no object at all. Open Active Directory Users and Computers to verify that the organizational unit objects appear.

Creating User Accounts

You now need to create users in the organizational unit. The sample code for creating a user is as follows:

```
Set usr = ou_HR.Create("user", "CN=James Smith")
usr.Put "samAccountName", "jasmith"
usr.Put "userPrincipalName", "jasmith" & "@" &
Domain.Get("name")
usr.AccountDisabled = False
usr.SetInfo
usr.SetPassword "password"
usr.SetInfo
```

Notice that you must specify the samAccountName. The samAccountName is a mandatory attribute for the user class. Before you can create an instance of an object, you must set all mandatory attributes. The user account's samAccountName is used to log on from computers running Microsoft Windows 95, Microsoft Windows 98, or Microsoft Windows NT®. Computers running Windows 2000 understand the samAccountName. However, when both the client and domain controller are running Windows 2000, you can log on by using the user principal name. In this example, James's user principal name is set to jasmith@*your_domain*. If James moves to a different domain in the forest, he can continue to use his user principal name.

You enable the user's account by setting the AccountDisabled property to FALSE. Administrators are also able to assign a password by using the **SetPassword** method. However, the **SetPassword** method works only if the object has been created in the directory. You need to call the **SetInfo** method before attempting to set the user's password.

Note   The sample code to create a new group is as follows:

```
Set Users = GetObject("LDAP://CN=USERS," & DomainPath)
Set grp = Users.Create("group", "CN=HR Admins")
grp.Put "samAccountName", "HRadmins"
grp.SetInfo
```

In the first line, the ADSI object is set to the Users container. The group, HR Admins, is then created in that container. The samAccountName is a mandatory attribute, which is added to provide backward compatibility. In this example, tools in Microsoft Windows NT version 4.0, such as User Manager, recognize HRadmins instead of HR Admins.

In this lab, rather than creating each object individually as shown in the previous examples of the sample code, the script retrieves the user names from a text file and creates several objects by using a loop construct.

Exercise 1 Creating Objects by Using ADSI

Goal

In this exercise, you will use a script to create the Human Resources OU and several user accounts in the OU. The user names and job titles will be copied into the script from a text file.

Tasks	Detailed Steps
1. Open the Users.txt file and create five additional users, following the convention illustrated by the three existing users.	a. Open Users.txt in the appendix folder on the Student Materials compact disc. b. Add five more users to the end of the text file by using the following format: `username:Project Lead:Full Name` c. Save the file, and then close Notepad.
2. Examine, test and verify the Cr_user.vbs script.	a. Right-click **Cr_user.vbs** in the appendix folder, and then click **Edit**. b. Examine the annotated code, particularly those sections that can be customized to meet your needs. c. Close Notepad. d. Double-click **Cr_user.vbs**, and then click **OK** in any Windows Script Host message boxes that appear. e. Open Active Directory Users and Computers, and then verify that all of the user accounts have been created in the Human Resources OU.

Exercise 2 Modifying Objects by Using ADSI

Goal

In this exercise, you will use a script to edit several user accounts in the OU. The user names and job titles will be copied into the script from a text file.

Tasks	Detailed Steps
1. Open the Users.txt file and change several of the job titles, and then save the file as Change.txt.	a. Open Users.txt in the appendix folder on the Student Materials compact disc. b. Change the Project Lead job titles to Project Manager, by using the following format: `username:Project Manager` c. Save the file as Change.txt, and then close Notepad.
2. Examine, test and verify the Mod_user.vbs script.	a. Right-click **Mod_user.vbs** in the appendix folder, and then click **Edit**. b. Examine the annotated code, particularly those sections that can be customized to meet your needs. c. Close Notepad. d. Double-click **Mod_user.vbs,** and then click **OK** in any Windows Script Host message boxes that appear. e. Open Active Directory Users and Computers, and then verify that the user accounts have been modified in the Human Resources OU.

Exercise 3 Deleting Objects by Using ADSI

Goal

In this exercise, you will use a script to delete several user accounts in the OU. The user names will be copied into the script from a text file.

Tasks	Detailed Steps
1. Open the Change.txt file, remove those user names that you do not want to delete, and then save the file as Remove.txt.	a. Open Change.txt in the appendix folder on the Student Materials compact disc. b. Change the file to include only those user names that you want to delete, by using the following format: `username` c. Save the file as remove.txt, and then close Notepad.
2. Examine, test and verify the Del_user.vbs script.	a. Right-click **Del_user.vbs** in the appendix folder, and then click **Edit**. b. Examine the annotated code, particularly those sections that can be customized to meet your needs. c. Close Notepad. d. Double-click **Del_user.vbs,** and then click **OK** in any Windows Script Host message boxes that appear. e. Open Active Directory Users and Computers, and then verify that the user accounts have been modified in the Human Resources OU.

Notes

Notes

Notes

Notes

Notes

Notes

Notes

Notes